Light Horse

The mounted soldier is one of the most evocative symbols in Australian military history. Now a celebrated part of Australia's army heritage, the role and very existence of mounted troops in modern warfare was being called into question at the time of its most crowning military moments. Light horse regiments, particularly those that served in South Africa, Palestine and the trenches of Gallipoli, played a vital role in Australia's early military campaigns.

Based on extensive research from both Australia and Britain, this book is a comprehensive history of the Australian Light Horse in war and peace.

Historian Jean Bou examines the place of the light horse in Australia's military history throughout its existence, from its antecedents in the middle of the nineteenth century, until the last regiment was disbanded in 1944.

Jean Bou is a historian at the Australian War Memorial and a Visiting Fellow with the Strategic and Defence Studies Centre, Australian National University.

OTHER TITLES IN THE AUSTRALIAN ARMY HISTORY SERIES

Series editor
David Horner

Phillip Bradley *The Battle for Wau: New Guinea's Frontline 1942–1943*
Mark Johnston *The Proud 6th: An Illustrated History of the 6th Australian Division 1939–1946*
Garth Pratten *Australian Battalion Commanders in the Second World War*

LIGHT HORSE

A HISTORY OF AUSTRALIA'S MOUNTED ARM

JEAN BOU

CAMBRIDGE UNIVERSITY PRESS
Cambridge, New York, Melbourne, Madrid, Cape Town, Singapore, São Paulo, Delhi

Cambridge University Press
477 Williamstown Road, Port Melbourne, VIC 3207, Australia
www.cambridge.org
Information on this title: www.cambridge.org/9780521197083

© Jean Bou 2010

First published 2010

Edited by Cathryn Game
Design by Rob Cowpe Design
Typeset by Aptara Corp.
Printed in China by Prinplus

National Library of Australia Cataloguing in Publication data
Bou, Jean.
Light Horse : a history of Australia's mounted arm / Jean Bou.
9780521197083 (hbk.)
Australian Army history series.
Includes index.
Bibliography.
Australia. Army. Australian Light Horse – History.
World War, 1914–1918 – Regimental histories – Australia.
World War, 1914–1918 – Campaigns – Palestine.
940.41294

ISBN 978-0-521-19708-3 hardback

Reproduction and Communication for educational purposes
The Australian *Copyright Act 1968* (the Act) allows a maximum of
one chapter or 10% of the pages of this publication, whichever is the greater,
to be reproduced and/or communicated by any educational institution
for its educational purposes provided that the educational institution
(or the body that administers it) has given a remuneration notice to
Copyright Agency Limited (CAL) under the Act.

For details of the CAL licence for educational institutions contact:

Copyright Agency Limited
Level 15, 233 Castlereagh Street
Sydney NSW 2000
Telephone: (02) 9394 7600
Facsimile: (02) 9394 7601
Email: info@copyright.com.au

Reproduction and Communication for other purposes
Except as permitted under the Act (for example a fair dealing for the
purposes of study, research, criticism or review) no part of this publication
may be reproduced, stored in a retrieval system, communicated or
transmitted in any form or by any means without prior written permission.
All inquiries should be made to the publisher at the address above.

Cambridge University Press has no responsibility for the persistence or
accuracy of URLs for external or third-party internet websites referred to in
this publication and does not guarantee that any content on such websites is,
or will remain, accurate or appropriate. Information regarding prices, travel
timetables and other factual information given in this work are correct at
the time of first printing but Cambridge University Press does not guarantee
the accuracy of such information thereafter.

Every effort has been made to trace copyright holders of papers held by the
Imperial War Museum, and the author and the Imperial War Museum would
be grateful for any information that might help to trace those whose
identities or addresses are not currently known.

Contents

List of maps	vi
Acknowledgements	vii
Author's note	ix
Abbreviations	xii
Introduction	1
1 Ancestors: Australia's colonial mounted troops, 1803–99	13
2 Tough lessons: South Africa, 1899–1902	38
3 The Hutton era: Founding the light horse, 1901–05	60
4 Unfulfilled promise: The militia light horse, 1905–20	87
5 The light-horsemen 1: Citizen mounted troops and Australian society	115
6 Mounted rifles: The light horse at war, 1914–17	140
7 Cavalry: The light horse at war, 1917–19	170
8 The light-horsemen 2: The light-horseman at war	204
9 The final years: The light horse at home, 1921–44	227
Conclusion	256
Epilogue	262
Appendix: The 'Beersheba charge photo'	264
Notes	280
Bibliography	331
Index	350

Maps

1	South Africa, 1899	40
2	Distribution of light horse regiments, 1903	71
3	Distribution of light horse regiments, 1913	100
4	The Sinai Desert and southern Palestine, 1916–17	155
5	Palestine and adjoining territory, 1917–18	174
6	Distribution of light horse regiments, late 1930s	245
7	The charge at Beersheba, 31 October 1917	271

Acknowledgements

This book began as a postgraduate thesis and, as a result, my first thanks are still directed to Professors Peter Dennis and Jeffrey Grey at the School of Humanities and Social Sciences at the Australian Defence Force Academy. Peter guided me through the first iteration of this work while Jeff stood in for Peter in his absence, provided considerable advice and suggested the topic to me too many years ago. More recently Professor David Horner, editor of the Australian Army History Series, has guided me through the process of making it into a book. Roger Lee of the Army History Unit has let me use the unit's resources in a variety of ways and, in supplying those resources, Andrew Richardson deserves particular thanks, but the contribution of others will not be forgotten. I also thank the Army History Unit for providing an Army History Research Grant, which enabled me to look at archival material in Britain.

Other historians have helped considerably during the production of this book, and I owe thanks, in no particular order, to Dr Peter Stanley, Dr Craig Wilcox, Lieutenant-Colonel Ian van der Waag, James Morrison, Dr Al Palazzo, Dr David Kenyon, Terry Kinloch, Dr Stephen Clarke and Dr John Connor. Dr Stephen Badsey was of particular help in developing my thinking about British mounted troops in the late nineteenth and early twentieth centuries. I also need to thank Steve Becker for allowing me to use his unpublished material on the Western Frontier Force.

Many librarians and archivists have helped me over the years. Christopher Dawkins at the Australian Defence Force Academy's library was of particular help in the early days, as was other staff there. The staff at the Australian War Memorial's Research Centre, the Imperial War Museum, the National Library of Australia, the British National Archives, the National Archives of Australia (in Canberra and Melbourne particularly, but also Adelaide), the State Records of New South Wales and the Queensland State Archives have provided the greatest assistance. Kay Dancey and Jenny Sheehan of the Australian National University did an admirable job with the maps for this book.

In researching the 'Beersheba charge photo' I incurred debts to Matthew Woodhead, Robert Nichols, Geoff Smith, Bill Woerlee, Pat Gallagher, Warwick Cary and Dick Adams; to Ian Affleck and Andrew Jack of the Australian War Memorial's photographs section, and to Bill Roberts and his astronomer colleagues at the Australian National University. Ian Jones and Neil McDonald kindly answered my telephone queries regarding the photograph. Several of these people helped through the Australian Light Horse Association discussion forum, from which others helped with various matters along the way. In this respect Jeff Pickerd should also be added to the list.

I would also like to thank the Trustees of the Imperial War Museum for allowing access to its collections and to the copyright holders of the papers of Field Marshal Lord Chetwode and Major-General Sir Henry Hodgson for allowing me to quote from these collections. Similarly I would like to thank the trustees of the Liddell Hart Centre for Military Archives, King's College, London, for allowing me access to their collections and permission to quote parts of them here. Richard Chauvel also kindly gave me permission to use the papers of Lieutenant-General Sir Harry Chauvel.

Thanks is also due to Bruce Vandervort, editor of the *Journal of Military History*, for allowing me to reproduce parts of my article 'Cavalry firepower and swords', which was published in the journal in January 2007.

The final and biggest thanks are for my family, Renae, Sébastien and Sophie, for their forbearance and support.

Author's note

Throughout its history there was no set way to write or abbreviate titles of the light horse, light horse regiments or light horse brigades. Different officers and men wrote in reference to themselves, their units or their formations, either of the Australian Light Horse or, more simply, the Light Horse. Similarly brigades or regiments described themselves by appending their structural titles to these two common choices. Abbreviations were presented in a plethora of variations. A regimental title could be abbreviated, for example, to ALH Regt, Aust. LH, ALHR or LHR, to list just a few. For ease of reading and a sense of uniformity I have throughout this book used only the terms Light Horse Regiment (abbreviated as LHR) and Light Horse Brigade (abbreviated as LH Bde).

Similarly, during the period the light horse existed it was common to describe any officer holding a command appointment, up to at least brigade command, as the officer commanding. At the risk of anachronism, but in order to maintain clarity, I have opted instead to use the modern conventions of the Australian Army in describing officers holding command appointments, these being:

Description	Appointment
Commander	Brigade or divisional command
Commanding Officer (CO)	Unit command (regiment)
Officer Commanding (OC)	Subunit (squadron)

This book also refers continually to three types of mounted troops that existed in the British and dominion military forces of the late nineteenth and early twentieth centuries. Unfortunately they were, and still are, subject to much confusion and ill-considered interchangeability. Although this book will further explain the differences between them, the following definitions of the terms within the British imperial context are included to ensure clarity.[1]

Cavalry: traditional horsed soldiers, usually, but not always, of a professional nature. They were capable of conducting reconnaissance, outpost duties, attack and defence either mounted or, by the First World War, dismounted. Their point of differentiation was their extensive training and skill with a bladed weapon in the form of the cavalry sword or lance. In the years just before the First World War a process of cavalry reform meant that dismounted action with the rifle (and machine-gun) was considered as important as mounted action with the sword and that either mode of fighting could be seamlessly taken up without prejudicing the other. By that time also mounted tactics emphasised fire and manoeuvre, and relatively dispersed formations.

Mounted infantry: soldiers who were trained to fight exclusively on foot and who were provided with animals only as a form of locomotion. Their origins were as small *ad hoc* units raised in Britain's colonial wars to provide mobile infantry and sometimes to take up some of the outpost and reconnaissance duties of cavalry if they were not available. By the First World War they had become strictly defined as mobile infantry to be used in the same tactical way as traditional infantry except *in extremis*.

Mounted rifles: horsed soldiers who were often, but not always, citizen soldiers and who were trained to undertake the same duties as cavalry, namely reconnaissance, outpost duties, attack and defence, with a firearm only. Organised along the same lines as cavalry (i.e. in squadrons and regiments rather than companies and battalions), they were intended as a replacement for cavalry when it was not available or as a cavalry auxiliary if they were. They existed because of the contemporary debates about horsemen and firepower, and because creating full cavalrymen from part-time citizen soldiers was thought to be too difficult. Mounted rifles generally used a simplified cavalry drill and doctrine, and are best conceived of as a sort of abbreviated cavalry. Although intended for dismounted use, they were not the same as mounted infantry in their tactical application. A mounted rifles unit or formation was, at best, about half the size of its infantry equivalent and hence could not develop the mass, depth or firepower of infantry in either attack or defence. Mounted rifles, like dismounted cavalry, tended to skirmishing, rapid fire and manoeuvre, surprise attack and putting every available rifle in the firing line in an attempt to quickly overwhelm the enemy. A long firefight was generally an anathema and was to be avoided. The differences between mounted rifles and cavalry were small, and during the First World War a number of pre-war mounted rifles organisations, including the Canadian Mounted

Rifles, the yeomanry and most of the light horse, were equipped with the sword and made the relatively small final step to becoming cavalry.

The difficulty in using these terms, particularly mounted infantry and mounted rifles, was and is their frequent misuse. Mounted rifles, despite their cavalry-like role, have often been misrepresented as mounted infantry. To confuse the two is to misunderstand their respective operational employment and underestimate the value that soldiers themselves place on their role in defining themselves. Others, such as Sir Harry Chauvel, referred to mounted rifles (much more accurately) as cavalry.[2] Compounding the confusion was that in colonial campaigns, most notably during the Boer War, the distinctions tended to break down. In Australia the demarcations between the three mounted branches were clearly set out just after Federation by the General Officer Commanding, Major-General Sir Edward Hutton. Unusually, and because of Hutton's keen interest in the area, this was somewhat ahead of practice in Great Britain. It was not until just a few years before the First World War that the British Army introduced similarly clear definitions. Although mounted infantry did not see service on the Western Front during the First World War, it was employed in the Sinai and Palestine in the form of the Imperial Camel Corps.

Abbreviations

1st AH	1st Australian Horse
AAG	Assistant Adjutant-General
AC	Armoured Car(s)
ADC	*aide de camp*
Adjt	Adjutant
ADMS	Assistant Director of Medical Services
AG	Adjutant-General
AHQ	Army Headquarters
AIC	Australian Instructional Corps
AIF	Australian Imperial Force
AIR	Australian Infantry Regiment
A&I Staff	Administrative and Instructional Staff
AMD	Australian Mounted Division
AMF	Australian Military Forces
ANZAC	Australian and New Zealand Army Corps
A&NZMD	Australian & New Zealand Mounted Division
AQMG	Assistant Quartermaster-General
AWM	Australian War Memorial (Record Series)
Bde	Brigade
BM	Brigade Major
Bn	Battalion
Brig-Gen	Brigadier-General
Bty	Battery
Capt	Captain
Cav. Div.	Cavalry Division
CGS	Chief of the General Staff
CMF	Citizen Military Forces
CO	Commanding Officer
Col	Colonel
Col. Off.	Colonial Office

Coy	Company
Cpl	Corporal
CSC	Colonial/Chief Secretary's Correspondence – NSW
CSO	Chief Staff Officer
DAG	Deputy Adjutant-General
DAQMG	Deputy Assistant Quartermaster-General
Div.	Division
DMC	Desert Mounted Corps
DMO	Director of Military Operations
DMT	Director of Military Training
DQMG	Deputy Quartermaster-General
EEF	Egyptian Expeditionary Force
FM	Field Marshal
Gen	General
GHQ	General Headquarters
GOC	General Officer Commanding
GOC-in-C	General Officer Commanding-in-Chief
HAC	Honourable Artillery Company
HQ	Headquarters
ICC	Imperial Camel Corps
IG	Inspector-General
IMD	Imperial Mounted Division
LH Bde	Light Horse Brigade
LHCMA	Liddell Hart Centre for Military Archives
LHR	Light Horse Regiment
Lt	Lieutenant
Lt-Col	Lieutenant-Colonel
Lt-Gen	Lieutenant-General
Maj	Major
Maj-Gen	Major-General
MD	Military District
NAA	National Archives of Australia
NCO/NCOs	Non-commissioned officer(s)
NLA	National Library of Australia
NSW	New South Wales
NSWL	New South Wales Lancers
NSWMR	New South Wales Mounted Rifles
NZ&A Div.	New Zealand and Australian Division
NZEF	New Zealand Expeditionary Force
NZMR	New Zealand Mounted Rifles

OC	Officer Commanding
ORs	Other ranks (i.e. all soldiers below the rank of lieutenant)
Pl	Platoon
PRO-AJCP	Public Record Office – Australian Joint Copying Project
PRO-WA	Public Record Office of Western Australia
QDF	Queensland Defence Force (pre-Federation)
Qld	Queensland
QM	Quartermaster
QMG	Quartermaster-General
QMI	Queensland Mounted Infantry
QSA	Queensland State Archives
Regt	Regiment
RHA	Royal Horse Artillery
RMC	Royal Military College, Duntroon
RO	Regimental/routine order(s)
SA	South Australia
SAMR	South Australian Mounted Rifles
SASR	South Australian State Records
Sen	Senator
Sgt	Sergeant
SRNSW	State Records of New South Wales
Sqn	Squadron
SSgt	Staff Sergeant
Tas	Tasmania
TMI	Tasmanian Mounted Infantry
TNA (UK)	The National Archives (United Kingdom)
Tp	Troop
Tpr	Trooper
Vic	Victoria
VMR	Victorian Mounted Rifles
WA	Western Australia
WAMI	Western Australian Mounted Infantry
WO	Warrant Officer
YMD	Yeomanry Mounted Division

Introduction

The mounted soldier is perhaps one of the most evocative symbols in Australian military history. Although by no means negligible, the military achievements of such men were restricted largely to the veld of South Africa, the trenches of Gallipoli and, more famously, the sands of the Sinai and the rocky hills of Palestine. In purely military terms the contribution of the Australian light horse to the general victory in the First World War seems relatively minor compared to the efforts of the Australian Imperial Force (AIF) fighting on the Western Front. There the Australian Corps took part in some of the largest battles of the war and played its part in the final battles that brought Germany to seek an armistice. By comparison the campaign in the Middle East was something of a strategic backwater, but it was a seemingly cleaner and less vicious war in which the front line moved, battles produced more than long casualty lists, and bravery and boldness might still, in the minds of many, as evidenced by Beersheba and other battles, sway the day. The men who fought on the Western Front have hardly been forgotten, but it was the actions of their mounted military compatriots in the Palestine theatre that, when combined with a continuing romantic ideal of mounted soldiers, has gone on to capture a remarkable place in the collective memory.

For many students of Australian military history the quintessential Australian soldier (in as much as such a person exists) of the First World War might be thought of as the 'digger', the infantryman who fought at Gallipoli or the Western Front. There is much to be said for this view, and it is certainly the case that the battles such men fought and the conditions they endured are among the most examined aspects of Australia's military heritage; the number of books about them grows each year. Yet an examination of popular representations of Australian soldiers of the First World War produces an intriguing result: that the memory of the light horse and the light-horseman has found a number of manifestations that no other arm of the Australian Army, including the infantrymen of Gallipoli and the Western Front, has come close to matching. Certainly the representations of infantrymen are common on the war memorials that are a fixture of the Australian landscape, but outside the cities and larger towns it is not uncommon to find that the ghostly figure atop a monument is instead a light-horseman. Beyond war memorials it is difficult to find depictions of the infantrymen, gunners or the dozens of other military employment categories of the men of the AIF.

Conversely the light horse seems to go from strength to strength. When the Reserve Bank of Australia chose to put the visage of the soldier and engineer John Monash on its $100 note, for example, it selected as its key design elements a field gun with crew, an image of Simpson and his donkey, and no fewer than three separate images of light-horsemen. During the First World War Monash commanded first an infantry brigade, then an infantry division and, as the commander of the Australian Corps, had no more than one light horse regiment under his hand. That a representation of him should then be surrounded by mounted men who mostly fought in a completely different theatre, and contain no images of the infantrymen he did in fact command, is incongruous to say the least, but it does suggest how pervasive is the romance and remembrance of the light horse. Similarly when an Australian Army recruiting advertisement called 'Army Rise' was aired in 2008 it sought to emphasise the army's heritage, not with pictures of Gallipoli or the Western Front (they are perhaps too grim for an advertisement anyway), but with film taken of light-horsemen marching past somewhere in Palestine. In cinema the charge of Beersheba has been recreated twice for major feature films, first in Charles Chauvel's 1940 production of *Forty Thousand Horsemen* and again in 1987 for *The Light Horsemen*. The battle of Beersheba, a one-day affair brought to a dramatic conclusion by a charge by two regiments of light horse, is undoubtedly well suited to a cinematic presentation, but it is interesting to compare this double telling of a mounted action in Palestine with the complete dearth of film representations of Australians fighting on the Western Front. The 1980s television mini-series *1915* and *Anzacs* are as close as anyone has come to doing something similar to treat the infantry and artillery actions of Gallipoli, France and Belgium. Even Peter

Weir's *Gallipoli* is constructed around the disastrous dismounted charge of light-horsemen at the Nek.

Perhaps the most remarkable example of the continuing popular appeal of the light horse is the habit of a growing group of people who spend their weekends taking part in the activities of light horse re-enactment groups. Undoubtedly tied into a sentiment of what might be best termed 'equine nostalgia', at present there are more than 30 such groups around the country whose members keep horses, dress in light horse uniforms and spend their spare time tent-pegging, taking part in parades and otherwise ensuring that the light horse is not forgotten.[1] In 2007, 50 of them travelled to Israel and re-enacted the charge at Beersheba on the ninetieth anniversary of the battle. These groups operate under the overarching guidance of the Australian Light Horse Association, which has as its aim to 'preserve the History and Tradition of the Australian Light Horse and its predecessors'.[2] To this end it maintains a web site with a discussion forum and produces a member magazine as well as its own manuals of riding and dress. Although there are other re-enactment groups, there seems to be nothing as organised or sizeable as that which is trying to preserve the traditions of the army's long-extinct mounted branch.

Given this popular interest it is remarkable that the historiography of the light horse and its predecessors is, if not thin, then remarkably incomplete. The literature is still dominated by Henry Gullett's volume of the Australian First World War official history, *The Australian Imperial Force in Sinai and Palestine*. Gullett's examination of the campaign is the starting point for anyone interested in the Australian aspects of the campaign but, like all volumes of the official history, it is perhaps 'more frequently referred... to than actually read';[3] the inevitable consequence of which is that, although pervasive, its influence has possibly now become more impressionistic than detailed. The commonly held, oft-repeated and (as will be seen) incorrect contention that the light horse were mounted infantry has a number of contributing historical threads, but the ubiquity of that idea can be traced to what appears to be an uncritical acceptance of Gullett's simplification of the light horse's military role for a lay audience.[4] Similarly the popular image of the light-horseman owes a great deal to Gullett's impressive, but somewhat polished, sketch of a uniformed extension of the bushman ideal. What is more, this sketch has evolved into what is largely a stereotype, a mounted extension of the Anzac legend in which such ideas as mateship, egalitarianism, the bush ethos and irreverence tend to be stressed.

Beyond Gullett there are certainly books that offer some insights into the Australian mounted branch. Alec Hill's excellent biography of Lieutenant-General Sir Harry Chauvel, *Chauvel of the Light Horse*, for example, is a valuable and readable insight into the life of the officer most commonly associated with the light horse. Ian Jones's volume of the Time-Life series *Australians at War: The Australian Light Horse*, and its subsequent revision as *A Thousand Miles of Battles*, is based on detailed research into the wartime light horse and is a good introductory book. However, such books have their limitations as they are targeted at juvenile readers and prone to heroic language. More generally there are a large number of unit histories that can be drawn on by those interested. Many of these were written after the war and are no longer generally available unless one has the wherewithal to buy first editions from rare-book sellers. Regimental histories do continue to be produced, typically for units that did not have histories published after the Great War or in the form of works that detail the history of their descendant units in the Royal Australian Armoured Corps. There are also periodic editions of books aimed at popular audiences that deal with some aspect of the light horse's involvement in the Palestine campaign. Some of these are admirable in themselves, but go over much the same ground as the books already mentioned, or aim to keep digger mythology alive.

Among all this work there is as yet no history that deals specifically with the light horse as a military institution through its entire existence. That which does exist is confined to the light horse at war or only goes beyond the war at the regimental level. There has thus far been no effort to delve into the long-term development of Australia's mounted military forces, to analyse how they evolved, to consider what place they had in defence thinking, to look at the development of their tactical thinking, or to examine the way they interacted with the society around them, particularly at home. This book is an effort to fill this gap and is an institutional history of the light horse, not just at war but also from the raising of its colonial antecedents in the mid-nineteenth century through Federation to the disbandment of the last regiment during the Second World War. It will also examine the resource that is essential to any military institution, the men who constituted its ranks.

The light horse came into existence and had its crowning military moments at a time when the role and very existence of mounted troops in modern warfare was increasingly being questioned. Too often the light horse is examined in isolation, typically being presented as something uniquely Australian. That it might have something in common with other mounted troops raised elsewhere is rarely considered, and in some cases a deliberate contrast is created between the supposedly innovative or modern light horse and the just as supposedly hidebound fools to be found elsewhere, often exemplified by pointing to British regular cavalrymen.[5] Related to this is a common view that by the beginning of the twentieth century military horsemen were an anachronism on modern battlefields: casualties in waiting who would ride to their death at the ill-considered order of some dull-minded general whose military imagination belonged in the nineteenth century. The origins of this latter idea are manifold, but have a great deal to do with scapegoating of senior generals after the First World War by various people, often politicians or theorists of mechanised warfare, who were selective or misleading in using history to deflect blame or advocate their vision of the future.[6] Both of these ideas require challenging. Australia's light horse and its colonial predecessors did not develop in isolation, and in many ways they reflected thinking and practice evident elsewhere in the British Empire. Similarly, as historians are beginning to realise, that thinking and practice was remarkably forward-thinking, and Britain's cavalry and mounted troops, and the multitudinous imperial extensions of them, underwent a remarkable process of reform between the 1880s and the First World War, which meant that in 1914 they were a thoroughly modernised force – contrary to common thought, the charge of the Light Brigade at Balaklava was not an everlasting tactical template.[7] In order to understand the light horse it is necessary briefly to consider its imperial backdrop.

Mounted troops in the British Empire, 1850–1918

By the end of the nineteenth century the position of cavalry on the European battlefield was by no means certain. The adoption of new, more accurate, longer-ranged and increasingly quick-firing weapon technology, which had commenced in the middle of the century and proceeded apace thereafter, cast a shadow over the role and place of horse-mounted soldiers. What should be done in response to such developments proved to be a hotly debated subject right up to the eve of the First World War.

Although the problem was already being appreciated by the middle years of the nineteenth century, it was the experiences of the American Civil War and later wars in Europe, particularly the Franco-Prussian War of 1870–71, that did much to stimulate thinking. In North America the defensive power of rifle-equipped infantry had been manifest. The fact that to many observers traditional cavalry did not seem to exist in America but had apparently been supplanted by horsemen who moved about on horses and fought with rifles or carbines was thought to be a remarkable development. It was not an entirely accurate assessment because mounted action had remained part of the American cavalrymen's skills. Some also noted the apparent use of cavalry columns made up of rifle-equipped horsemen accompanied by artillery, which had operated independently and mounted deep raids into enemy territory.[8] Similarly observers noted the apparent difficulties that had faced cavalry making traditional cavalry charges in pitched battle during the Franco-Prussian War, but also noted the effectiveness of the German cavalry in fulfilling the long-established cavalry roles of reconnaissance and screening its army from its opponents, a duty that required not just skill with bladed weapons, the sword or lance – known as the *arme blanche* (meaning literally 'white arm') in the parlance of the time – but also skill with firearms so as to overcome localised resistance or win information.[9]

Not surprisingly, military pundits began to analyse the events of these and other wars and theorise about what should be done to ensure that cavalry, which was still the most mobile element of any army, remained a useful arm. There was no shortage of theorists, and the considerable number of books published were reinforced by contributions to the service journals and other periodicals. One of this multitude was Lieutenant-Colonel George Denison, commander of the Governor-General's Body Guard in Canada, who wrote two books: *Modern Cavalry: Its Organisation, Armament and Employment in War* in 1868, and *A History of Cavalry from the Earliest Times: With Lessons for the Future* in 1877. In these books he argued strongly that cavalry must abandon its traditional tactical approach, in which the *arme blanche* was the main and sometimes only weapon, to embrace firepower. Indeed firepower should be embraced to such a point that most horse soldiers should become mounted riflemen prepared to dismount to use their weapons in fulfilling the traditional roles of cavalry, particularly in reconnaissance and outpost duties. He did not dismiss the possibility of the charge completely, but thought that training for it should be restricted to a limited number of specialised troops, and that the *arme blanche* should perhaps be replaced with a pistol.[10] Although ultimately just one voice among many, and by no means the only man to take a similar view, Denison's arguments should be particularly noted because among those who found his work interesting was a British officer, Edward Hutton, who would have a profound influence on the development of Australia's mounted troops.

Theorising was one thing, but what also had to be considered was the experiences in Britain's colonies where mounted troops performed different roles from those who stayed in Britain preparing for the next European war. In the colonies the British Army was faced with the dilemma of patrolling and controlling large tracts of territory, usually with a minimum of manpower at its disposal. Because cavalry regiments were expensive to maintain, this task, as often as not, fell to infantry regiments. Still, the necessity of having horse-mounted troops remained and, in order to cover the large expanses of the empire's frontiers, local commanders often used the expedient of mounting part or all of an infantry unit to accomplish the task.[11] In Australia, for example, a portion of the 3rd Regiment of Foot was mounted on horses as early as 1825 to combat bushrangers. A similar practice was often used in the Cape Colony, and it was here in 1827 that the first dedicated mounted rifle unit in the British Army was raised when the Cape Mounted Rifles was formed from the mounted elements of the Cape Regiment.[12]

Cavalry too were compelled to vary its methods when on colonial service. Sent to Canada in 1838, the 7th Hussars and the King's Dragoon Guards were issued with carbines, and the commanding officer of the latter regiment stressed the importance of skirmishing and outpost duties for cavalry.[13] Colonial garrisons mounted on horseback and equipped with a firearm could patrol more widely and more quickly than infantry. They were well suited to the type of skirmishing that usually took place with colonial malcontents and indigenes, and enabled a generally overstretched British Army to employ whatever troops were at hand. Later in the century, in an extension of the principle, mounted infantry proved to be valuable in the Zulu War of 1879, the First Boer War of 1881 and the Egyptian War of 1882. In these locations it had primarily been a case of, in the words of one officer, 'the legitimate cavalry [having yet] to be arranged for, and where any available means on the spot [having] necessarily to be utilised for that purpose'.[14]

From these colonial experiences and experiments there were efforts to apply a new nomenclature to the different forms of mounted soldier that were beginning to appear in the British Army and its colonial offshoots. 'Cavalry' was a term applied to the type of organisation it had for centuries; that is, mounted squadrons armed primarily with the *arme blanche*. Although in its various forms it could be made responsible for the wide variety of tasks that cavalry traditionally fulfilled, it trained with the mounted charge as its primary action. 'Mounted rifles' was a term used most often to describe troops who, although equipped primarily with a rifle, were designed to be used in the traditional roles of the light cavalry, such as skirmishing, scouting and screening. 'Mounted infantry' was traditionally just that: regular infantry mounted as an expedient for a particular duty or campaign. Organised on traditional infantry unit guidelines, for these troops the horse, or whatever other form of beast they were given, was simply a means of speedy locomotion from which they would alight to fight the battle as standard infantry. Unfortunately for all concerned, the terms 'mounted rifles' and 'mounted infantry' were subject to confusion, and were often used interchangeably. Subsequently they became the subject of much confusion and abuse by partisans in the ensuing debates about cavalry reform. That the roles of the two branches often overlapped in campaigns where no other mounted troops were available, and where mounted infantry had to fulfil the role of cavalry or mounted rifles, made it all the more difficult.

The early *ad hoc* arrangements for mounted infantry on campaign had been sufficient for some time but, with its colonial commitments, and with a cautious eye on the possible utility of mounted infantry in European warfare, the British Army became increasingly interested in formalising the mounted infantry organisations. Cost was a factor, and by adopting a part-time training scheme for regular infantrymen, the number of mounted men the army had at its disposal theoretically jumped to the tune of two battalions worth, but the cost was just £700 a year to maintain.[15] In 1888 the then Adjutant-General, Viscount Wolseley, established two schools of mounted infantry in Britain for the training of infantry detachments drawn from regular army battalions.[16] The detachments trained at the schools before returning to their battalions where they could be drawn upon should a campaign require it.

In the meantime there emerged from the late 1880s and early 1890s a reformist movement within the cavalry that embraced what has been called a cavalry hybrid; that is, horsemen who were trained with the *arme blanche* as their primary weapon and for which the charge remained a key tactic, but who were also equipped and trained to undertake dismounted duties with a firearm when circumstances dictated. One young cavalry officer who became prominent as a reformer wrote in 1890: 'Every cavalry soldier must thoroughly understand that his proper place is on horseback, his proper mode of action the charge. Only in cases where cavalry cannot obtain its object by executing a charge, should men be dismounted in order to use the carbine [but] unless a cavalry force is by instruction and practice ready to fight on foot its usefulness will be curtailed and it cannot be considered efficient.'[17]

This officer was a young Douglas Haig. He and another officer, John French, were both cavalrymen who also happened to be key voices in the cavalry reform movement that existed before the First World War. Both would go on to command the British Expeditionary Force on the Western Front during the Great War and be soundly criticised for their commands, which would have more than a little to do with the post-war condemnations of the so-called cavalry general mentality that is supposed to have been evident during the war.[18]

By the 1890s the idea that cavalry should act either mounted or dismounted depending on the situation had become commonplace, if not universally adopted – inevitably there were conservatives who opposed the changes. Many regiments took their shooting seriously and spent more time practising their skirmishing tactics. Charge tactics were changing, too, and there was less of the traditional knee-to-knee variety and more focus on open formations.[19]

With the cavalry undergoing a process of reform and the mounted infantry having been given a formalised start, not surprisingly, an argument began among various army officers about the respective roles, duties and methods of tactical employment that should be employed. Should mounted infantry merely act as supplement to cavalry on campaign, or should it be developed to replace it? Should cavalry be further reformed towards fire action and maybe do away with the *arme blanche* altogether or, indeed, should it be restricted to just the *arme blanche* as its only weapon and have mounted riflemen attached to provide fire? These questions and a great many others were vigorously argued in service forums throughout the 1880s and 1890s and beyond.

The experiences of mounted troops in the Boer War (1899–1902) will be examined later in this book, but because the nature of the war in South Africa provided anyone with a partisan view on the future of mounted troops with enough examples to support their particular view, there soon erupted another debate about the future direction of mounted troops. Regular mounted infantry proved to have its limitations, but once these units gained enough experience they, and the irregular colonial mounted rifle units raised in vast numbers for service in South Africa (and which included the Australian contingents), often performed as well as cavalry on campaign, so there emerged a view that cavalry proper might be done away with altogether or reformed to more closely approximate the mounted rifle model. The new Commander-in-Chief of the British Army, Field Marshal Lord Roberts, who had commanded the British Army in South Africa in 1900, in March 1903 abolished the lance as a weapon of war and stated 'that although the cavalry are armed with the carbine (or rifle) and sword, the carbine (or rifle) will henceforth be considered as the Cavalry soldier's principal weapon'.[20]

Roberts, who had spent most of his career in India, had not properly realised the extant work of reformist cavalry officers, who were loosely aligned and in contact with each other (but by no means homogeneous in their views), and who had been advocating a similar course for more than a decade. What made their views different from the sort of reform advocated by some of the other proponents of mounted firepower, was their belief that cavalry could be reformed to accommodate both mounted and dismounted action and did not have to make an absolute choice between one course or the other. They generally believed that firepower had to be embraced and that by using rifles and machine-guns as fire support (in an extension of the long-established idea of horse artillery), the possibilities of mounted action might be again opened to them.[21]

Roberts wanted cavalry reform, but he differed from the cavalry reformers in believing that the rifle had supplanted the *arme blanche*. Reformist cavalrymen like John French and Douglas Haig, by contrast, believed that the sword and lance were central and that the rifle, although vital, was a supplement to the bladed weapons This distinction was felt to guard against the erosion of 'cavalry spirit', a general term that meant something to cavalrymen but seemed vague to outsiders, but which encapsulated the cavalry's view of itself as the mobile arm *par excellence*. The gap between the two views was, in reality, quite small, but personalities and military cliques clashed, and the matter of the abolition of the lance, although of little real consequence, became a symbol around which cavalry officers rallied in their objection to what they thought was Roberts's high-handedness and meddling. The differences would come to appear huge as the debate about the future of mounted troops erupted out of the officers' mess, the service journals and the War Office into the public sphere of books and letters to *The Times*. In truth the heat cooled quickly as Roberts lost his appointment as Commander-in-Chief with the abolition of the post and its replacement with a committee. Nevertheless there would be continuing rounds of the argument right up to the eve of the Great War, with Roberts weighing in from retirement, sometimes assisted by the historian-cum-polemicist Erskine Childers, who wrote several books on the subject.[22]

Regardless, the key reformist cavalrymen had gone on to change their branch of the service, a process helped by the occupation of key appointments by persons with an interest. In 1905 consideration was given to converting the *ad hoc* regular mounted infantry into a permanent standing force, but the idea was not taken up. With the cavalry having been equipped with the rifle as the infantry and their tactics modified to encompass dismounted work, there seemed to be an ever-diminishing reason to continue with mounted infantry. In 1908 and 1909 the Mounted Infantry Schools in Egypt and India were closed, and the remaining two in Ireland and England met a similar fate on the eve of the First World War.[23] Because the mounted infantry no longer had high-ranking patrons, no particular efforts were made to save the force. In September 1913 the Army Council decided that mounted infantry would not be used in a European war, and the two existing mounted brigades, a mix of cavalry and mounted infantry, were broken up.[24]

This was not to say that horsemen armed only with rifle did not have a place. Drawing on colonial experience and the long-understood difficulty of producing fully trained cavalrymen, the part-time citizen horse soldiers around the empire had been mostly converted to mounted riflemen; that is, they were horsemen organised along the lines of cavalry who undertook cavalry roles, but their training was limited to using the rifle and not shock action. It was in this mould that the light horse was created.

In Britain, cavalry modernisation continued – fire and manoeuvre tactics were improved and machine-guns were introduced so that every cavalry regiment had two in its organisation, doing much to boost firepower. The army's senior cavalryman, Sir John French, also moved at various times to censure cavalry officers when pro-mounted attitudes sometimes got out of hand, or when insufficient emphasis was given to dismounted work.[25]

In 1912 a new edition of the training manual *Cavalry Training* appeared.[26] Previous editions had been used to push the various points of view that had been argued over in the previous decade, but this edition, produced without the backdrop of those tensions, was without the ideological baggage of its predecessors. It told its readers that the principal characteristic of cavalry was its 'power to move with rapidity, to fight when moving, to seize fleeting opportunities, and to cover long distances in a short time'.[27] Whether that should be done by sword or rifle seemed now a discretionary matter. The balance between fire and shock action that had been in the previous editions but had been obscured by rhetoric came to the fore. Regimental and formation training emphasised reconnaissance and protection duties and, building on the trends of the last ten or more years, work on the range took up much time; some units had better shooting results than some infantry battalions.[28] The upshot of this was that in 1914 British cavalry were most willing to dismount and use fire when it was called for. There would be numerous mounted actions by British and dominion cavalry during the First World War, and many cavalrymen would continue to see mounted action as the defining role of cavalry, but their ability to act effectively dismounted gave them valuable flexibility.

British Empire cavalry would face significant challenges during the First World War, but in those periods or campaigns where mobile operations were undertaken, the reforms would come to prove their worth, and in this book the events in Palestine provide a prime example. The most heated debates about the future of mounted troops had taken place in Britain, but as with most things in an empire the results were not confined to there. Across the empire the consequences of the new thinking would flow and have their own effects, although the results were not necessarily the same. The book is concerned with the mounted troops of one of Britain's dominions, and how the mounted soldiers of Australia reflected and responded to ideas about modern mounted warfare will be reflected in the chapters to follow.

CHAPTER 1

ANCESTORS
Australia's colonial mounted troops, 1803–99

In March 1899 a detachment of 106 soldiers from the New South Wales Lancers lined Sydney's Circular Quay before they embarked in SS *Nineveh* and steamed to England, where they would become the first formed body of troops from Australia to train with the British Army regulars in Britain. Although something of a military milestone in itself, the trip was only a consolation prize to some in the regiment; they had instead been hoping to get a contingent away for active service against Britain's enemies on India's North-West Frontier, but had been foiled largely by an uncooperative colonial government – military adventurism was not to everyone's taste. It was no accident that one of Australia's colonial mounted regiments was enthusiastic, organised and, perhaps, competent enough to consider such an endeavour. By 1899 the Australian colonies maintained a substantial number of men in cavalry, mounted rifle and mounted infantry units, which within a few years, and after a war in South Africa, would be organised into the Australian Light Horse. These units, often called corps in the parlance of the period, had largely been raised since 1885, but most of them could point to a series of colonial predecessors, imperial exemplars and other influences as part of their past. The light horse was not created from nothing, and in order to understand the mounted arm that was established after Australia's Federation it is necessary to examine its predecessors.

The first body of mounted troops raised in any Australian colony was the Governor's Body Guard. Created in Sydney in 1803 by Governor Ralph Darling, made up initially of well-behaved convicts (with just 14 members in 1810) and dressed in dragoon uniform, the guard's chief value lay in getting messages and information around the colony. One of its members, Thomas Andlesack, played a key role in apprehending the leaders of the Irish convict uprising at Castle Hill in 1804, but otherwise its history was militarily uneventful, being made part of the Mounted Police in 1840, then disbanded in 1860.

The mobility that horses could give colonial soldiers meant that other corps were not long in coming. To combat the growing menace of horse-mounted bushrangers in the Sydney, Newcastle and Bathurst regions, Governor Thomas Brisbane mounted part of the colonial garrison, the 3rd Regiment of Foot (the Buffs), on cart horses in 1825. This experiment led in turn to the foundation of the Mounted Police, a force that proved particularly valuable in early Australia thanks to its abilities in catching escaped convicts and pursuing bushrangers.[1] Less lauded but perhaps militarily more significant was its influence on the frontier where the mobility conferred by horses made the hitherto difficult task of quelling troublesome Aborigines much easier. Horses gave mounted policemen and soldiers the ability to outpace and out-endure the fleet-footed and elusive Aborigines and, perhaps more so than any other single development, revolutionised military action on the frontiers.[2] So useful were mounted troops thought to be in policing the colony that when bushranging became a serious problem again in the late 1830s there was strong rumour in the colony that a cavalry regiment would be sent out to quash the threat. This did not happen, but when the infantry of the 40th Regiment arrived in Melbourne in 1852 to police the new Victorian goldfields, one of its companies was promptly mounted to escort the colony's gold and combat its bushrangers.[3]

The first mounted military force raised in an Australian colony from its citizens for the purpose of defence rather than policing was the South Australian Volunteer Cavalry, raised in 1840. Created as part of the South Australian Volunteer Militia Brigade, it was not much of a start, and a poor colonial economy and other disturbances meant that whatever training was undertaken had ceased by the middle of its first year, although a return from 1842 shows that it managed some organisational presence for a few years more. The unit does not seem to have survived for long enough to help the next mounted unit raised in that colony, the Adelaide Mounted Rifle Corps, which superseded it in 1855.[4]

This corps was but one of a number of colonial units established around Australia in response to the Crimean War and the widespread colonial concern that a Russian naval raider or landing party might be

TOURNAMENT OF THE VICTORIAN VOLUNTEER LIGHT HORSE, CASTLEMAINE.—See page 190.

Photo 1 Victorian mounted troops display their skills at a military tournament in 1870. Victoria's mounted corps were relatively successful during these early years, a contrast to those of most colonies where units folded within a few years of their establishment. (State Library of Victoria IAN07/11/70/192)

despatched to attack the relatively unprotected Australian colonies. Sharing similar anxieties, a group of Sydneysiders had gathered in George Street in September 1854 to form the Yeomanry Cavalry Corps.[5] Their southern counterparts contributed to the cause by raising the Victorian Yeomanry Corps in the second half of 1855.[6] War scares proved the greatest impetus to the creation of new mounted corps during this period in Australia's colonies, and in 1860 the fear that Napoleon III was about to attempt an invasion of Britain brought about another wave of volunteering.

Throughout the 1860s and '70s a significant number of mounted units were raised throughout the Australian colonies. Several units that had been created in Victoria, for example, were amalgamated into the Royal Victorian Cavalry Regiment in 1862. Tasmanians made an effort with the First Light Cavalry Corps around Launceston in 1860 and, after the early failure of this corps, again in 1879 with the Tasmanian Volunteer Light Horse in the same district. In Western Australia the Pinjarrah

Mounted Volunteers was raised in 1862, followed by the Union Troop of Western Australian Mounted Volunteers, which converted to a horse artillery troop in 1872.[7] South Australia raised the Reedbeds Cavalry, the Regiment of South Australian Volunteer Cavalry, and then the Duke of Edinburgh's Light Dragoons. The Queensland Mounted Rifles was established in 1862 and, after part of it was disbanded, was retitled the Queensland Light Horse.

Apart from Victoria, where the mounted corps remained relatively vigorous throughout the 1870s, most of these early colonial military corps proved to be fleeting, often burning brightly for a few years before running out of spark and fuel. With their origins in the numerous war scares that periodically swept the colonies and the empire during the nineteenth century, volunteer corps and their military or civilian superiors found that men were often very willing, initially at least, to join their local unit out of a desire to defend their homes and homeland. As the threat of war receded, however, this basic motivation soon tended to recede also. Thus left with little likelihood of an actual conflict to motivate the men, volunteer units had to trust that the training they conducted, and the public events they attended, were enough to maintain the interest of officers and the other ranks. Often, however, the corps, with minimal official backing and scanty organisation, were not up to the task. Queensland's volunteers of 1860 were, for example, discovering by 1862 that the only interesting activities were range practices and the occasional ceremonial parade.[8] Not surprisingly, enlistments and enthusiasm soon fell off, a situation that tended to be general through the whole military volunteer system and by no means restricted to the mounted corps.[9]

The lack of pay was a particular problem, and the men were often burdened with considerable personal financial expenses in order to be a volunteer, although the degree of government support varied from time to time and colony to colony. Victoria's early mounted volunteers, for example, had been offered arms, uniforms and basic accoutrements, but Queensland had offered only arms and ammunition to its 1860 volunteers.[10] All the military items required of the volunteer and not paid for by the government had to be paid for out of the soldier's pocket or, if he were lucky, by funds otherwise raised by the committees that managed many volunteer corps. A mounted soldier could easily be faced with the high cost of providing his own uniform, often his equipment or part thereof, and always his own saddlery and horse. To this was often added the regular cost of transporting himself to the place where he was to drill each week. It is not surprising, therefore, that in the early 1860s the Sandhurst Troop of the Victorian forces was beginning to complain of the 'irksome' expenses attached to their chosen pastime.[11]

There were other problems, too, and most mounted units were raised and maintained in rural areas with relatively small populations. New corps could usually draw on the enthusiasm of the local men, but once these initial enlistments grew tired of their commitment there remained in the district an ever-diminishing pool of men who had not been part of the unit and who were willing to try soldiering.[12] As a result most corps tended to shrink quickly after the initial spurt of enthusiasm had spent itself. One of the ways to ameliorate or exacerbate such a problem was the quality of the men appointed to lead in these corps, but, although commissions were confirmed by the government, in most cases positions of rank in volunteer corps were filled by a ballot of the members and, not surprisingly, those who filled key positions were not always those most suitable. Although enthusiasm, some study and a degree of natural authority could go some way to making the military experience more definite and rewarding for the citizen soldiers under command, the lack of proper training, inexperience or the indifference of a key officer could severely affect a corps.[13]

Broader social trends also had their influence, and a British regular officer told a Queensland parliamentary committee in 1866 that the local volunteer system had failed due to the apathetic attitude of the colonists, 'the migratory nature of the population, and to the want of interest shown in the movement by persons of position'.[14] Popular opinion in general, and that of the press in particular, could be scathing. When the newly raised and only partially uniformed Sandhurst Troop made its first public appearance, one Victorian newspaper noted their irregular dress and poor horses before concluding that 'if they did not recall to collection a famous troop which a great Shakespearian captain flatly refused to march through Coventry with, certainly merited the suggestion of a bystander that they ought to be sent there'.[15] *The Moreton Bay Courier*, no supporter of citizen soldiering, was even harsher on their Queensland counterparts, deriding them as 'very bad riders on very questionable cattle arranged ... in a row on the cricket ground ... [trying] to look like the hope of the country'.[16]

Perhaps just as fundamental was the far from definite role mounted corps would play in the colony's defence should they be required to do so. Given their reliance on the fervour of their citizens, governments seemed prepared to accept whatever was on offer provided the strain on the exchequer was not too great. The units themselves tended to take on whatever military shape their members fancied and, not surprisingly, many of these colonial soldiers were quite keen to ape their cousins in Britain in both form and function. The Pinjarrah Mounted Volunteers, for example, in one of the more blatant displays of imitation, chose to adopt the uniform of the 6th Dragoon Guards while their short-lived compatriots, the Union Troop of Western Australian Mounted Volunteers, adopted a hussar uniform.[17] Purported military roles could be just as haphazard as the sartorial choices, even within individual colonies. The Kyneton Corps had offered their services to the Victorian government as mounted riflemen, but their colleagues at Sandhurst were apparently keener on being traditional cavalry.[18]

Despite their colonial setting, units that took the title of mounted rifles were often also imitating the trends of the home country, where various mounted rifle volunteers corps had been established after 1860, themselves often in imitation of the Cape Mounted Rifles, a successful unit raised in the Cape Colony earlier in the century. This frequently unruly grassroots approach was compounded by an often unclear view about the place of mounted troops in the minds of governments and their military administrators. Official opinion on the role and place of mounted troops in the colonial military forces varied considerably. In 1858 one South Australian parliamentarian had expressed his view that there was little value in using coastal fortresses to defend the coast against the most likely form of attack, a landing party from a frigate or privateer, and that a body of irregular horsemen 'might be readily brought to the coast in case of an emergency'.[19] There, he told the house: 'If they were not in a position to fight, they could run away – (a laugh) – and even in the last extremity if they became invisible to the enemy, it would clearly show them that they had not been exterminated... [With] fifty men such as he had described, they would be able to stop a force of 200 invaders.'[20]

For some even such a basic mounted scheme was too much. In 1865 John Hart, chairman of a South Australian commission into the colonial defences, and P. Egerton-Warburton, a major in the volunteers and the Commissioner of Police, wrote of their staunch opposition to any expenditure on mounted troops in a dissenting opinion in the commission's final report, believing that a slight augmentation to the mounted police would suffice in the event of an armed incursion.[21] It was a view that, as a colonel, Egerton-Warburton would repeat in a similar 1876 report after he had become commandant of South Australia's volunteer forces.[22] An 1881 New South Wales royal commission took a similar view when its report expressed interest in a suggestion from the Inspector-General of

Police that 300 mounted policemen could be used for vedette and outpost duty if required.[23]

Given these military and social circumstances, it is hardly surprising that the mounted corps that had been born in the long series of war scares from the mid-1850s and the late 1870s were in complete decline by the early 1880s. Most corps lasted only a few years before they were overtaken on the colonial establishments by others in different districts. Often colonial governments simply gave up on mounted units and, upon the disbandment of the remaining units in Western Australia and Tasmania in 1883, only South Australia and Victoria maintained any mounted troops as part of their colonial forces.

The depleted colonial ranks were again replenished from 1885 when a new war scare, this time stemming from Anglo-Russian tension on the Afghan frontier, brought a new wave of military enthusiasm. Fed also by the war Britain was fighting in the Sudan and the despatch of a New South Wales contingent to that conflict during the same year, there followed a new wave of mounted units across almost all the colonies. The large and popular Victorian Mounted Rifles joined the lone remnant troop of the Victorian Cavalry that year. In New South Wales the government found itself faced with applications from all over the colony to raise and equip troops of volunteer cavalry, including one offer from a cattle station-owning family in the colony's north, the Chauvels, to raise a cavalry force for actual service on the North-West Frontier of India, the seat of the Anglo-Russian tensions. Their offer was declined, but they were invited to raise a corps for the colonial defence forces, an invitation they then took up.[24] This corps proved to be the founding military experience for one of Charles Chauvel's sons, Harry, who would go on to a long and illustrious career inextricably entwined with Australia's mounted troops. Five mounted infantry corps were also raised in Queensland in 1885, although three had folded within the year.[25] South Australia's existing Adelaide Mounted Rifles converted to lancers in 1886 and were joined in the same year by the South Australian Volunteer Mounted Rifles. Only in Tasmania and Western Australia did no new mounted units come into existence between 1885 and the end of the decade.

What is significant about the mounted corps raised in the eastern colonies and South Australia during this period is that these bodies were, in contrast to earlier efforts, broadly successful and managed to survive as viable organisations. Although they were by no means free of the problems that had beset earlier corps, in these bodies it is possible to recognise the beginnings of the units that eventually became the light horse after

Photo 2 Corporal Walter Vernon of the Sydney Light Horse Volunteers (or sometimes the Sydney Lancers) in his uniform, which had just arrived from England in 1886. Colonial units frequently aped British regular and yeomanry units in form and fashion, and this uniform was based on that of the 5th (Royal Irish) Lancers. (AWM P01208.018)

Federation. The relative success of these units of the 1880s and 1890s owed much to changing views towards colonial defence in general, and mounted troops in particular, which began in the second half of the 1880s and would last until the end of the century. Of considerable importance also was the basis on which these new corps were raised and organised.

The Victorian Mounted Rifles, raised in 1885 by the Victorian-born but Indian Army-trained Colonel Tom Price, was established on a large, although unpaid, scale. Its establishment of a thousand members was organised into 45 detachments in nine companies spread throughout Victoria and linked by the public rail network.[26] Central to the success of this unit was the permanent staff, with the commanding officer, adjutant and 18 sergeant-majors being paid by the government to commit their full time and energy to its efficient operation.[27]

New South Wales's effort was led by the Sydney Light Horse Volunteers, which made their first public appearance in March 1885 when they were part of the parade to mark the departure of the New South Wales contingent to the Sudan. Towards the end of that year the colonial commandant converted them to lancers after his return from the Sudan, so that some 'pomp and circumstance' might be added to the troop that had started regularly acting as the Governor's escort. By the end of 1886 this troop had been joined by another seven of cavalry around the colony. Collectively they were known as the New South Wales Cavalry Brigade Reserves, under the command of Captain Malcolm Macdonald, one of the founders of the Sydney Light Horse and a veteran of Indian frontier fighting where he had been the one-time commander of the Poona Horse.[28] The organisation was a loose one with each troop wearing different uniforms and carrying varying types of arms. It was added to in 1888 when a number of companies of partially paid mounted infantry were raised throughout the colony, which were then organised as the Mounted Infantry Regiment under Major H. Lassetter, an ex-regular imperial infantry officer, during 1889. A brief addition to this regiment was the Corps of Permanent Mounted Infantry, which was raised in 1888 as a training school for officers; but it was removed from the establishment in July 1889 to save costs.[29] The cavalry, after being made to abandon their colourful old-style uniforms for more a serviceable brown one in 1889, were taken on to the partially paid establishment in January 1890, which did much to assure their future.[30]

In Queensland the two mounted infantry corps still surviving at the end of 1885, and some additional corps that were raised soon after, began to find some stability from 1887 by converting from unpaid volunteers to part-paid militia.[31] The Darling Downs Mounted Infantry was added to the existing corps around Brisbane, Bundaberg, Gympie, Mackay and Charters Towers in 1890, and a further reorganisation rearranged the colony's mounted units into the Queensland Mounted Infantry in 1897.[32] South Australia kept its mounted corps on a largely volunteer basis but was still able to maintain the small corps of lancers and mounted rifles throughout the late 1880s and into the 1890s when the two were amalgamated into the South Australian Mounted Rifles in 1895.[33] Tasmania was unable or unwilling to find the personnel or money for any mounted troops and would not have any again until after the first Tasmanian troops had sailed for South Africa and the Boer War in 1899. Western Australia, similarly short of cash, laboured on with its volunteer force, and its mounted arm was made up of small, relatively token, corps through the 1890s.[34] Those mounted formations in the mainland eastern colonies that had been established on a relatively stable basis were, however, now in a position to capitalise on a significant shift in defence thinking in Australia in the decade to come.

Colonial defence concerns of the nineteenth century stemmed from the development of steam-powered warships in the middle of the century. Steam warships, not being reliant on traditional wind and trade routes, could potentially avoid the Royal Navy and operate close to Australian shores where they might be in a position to raid the main coastal cities or hold them to ransom. For this reason military minds had focused mostly on the construction, maintenance and manning of coastal fortresses from the 1860s until the late 1880s.[35] Although mobile land forces had been viewed as having an important role in supporting forts and stopping any enemy that might try to land away from the fixed defences, it was not until the late 1880s that the idea of the mobile units perhaps being an asset in their own right was gaining momentum.

This was partly because by the early 1890s the range of modern naval guns was becoming such that ships could bombard key colonial cities from deep water instead of having to run the gauntlet of fixed defences as they would once have had to do, thus diminishing their importance.[36] Of equal significance was a growing view that a form of citizen soldiery could be an effective method of defending the colonies, a concept that had already been a significant factor in the outbursts of volunteer enthusiasm in the preceding decades but which received renewed impetus in the 1880s, given the outcome of the First Anglo-Boer War of 1880–81. During that brief war, the citizen-based Boer army had twice beaten the British Army in the field, first at Laing's Nek, then more famously at Majuba Hill, and in doing so the fledgling Boer Republic had maintained its independence from Britain. The example of Boer farmers, who had little training apart from their life of shooting and riding on the veld, defeating the famed, disciplined regulars of the British Army was one that led many Australian citizen soldiers and their supporters to feel more strongly that a force of citizen soldiery was the perfect model to emulate. It was not a view necessarily confined to the Australian colonies, and it fed into the empire-wide thinking and excitement that lay behind the citizen soldiering movement.

Mounted troops could take particular comfort from the fighting in South Africa as the Boers had fought the war essentially as mounted riflemen. Equipped with a rifle and made mobile by their small and hardy veld-raised horses, the Boer commandos could obviously be compared with the growing number of mounted rifle and mounted infantry bodies being raised throughout the Australian colonies. These too, being mostly based in rural areas, could see themselves as farmer-soldiers ready to grab their rifle and horse in order to spring to the defence of their homeland with the everyday skills they had acquired in the bush. This combined with a view, which had a growing number of local and British adherents, that mounted infantry and mounted rifles were an increasingly important arm of the British Army, particularly in colonial situations. Observations on the American Civil War also played their part, and the writings of the cavalry theorist, George Denison, were certainly known to Australians with an interest. One parliamentarian, again a South Australian, told the house that, as Denison had argued, 'mounted infantry [was] the most important force of the future [and what the colony] wanted was 200 or 300 mounted riflemen in the neighbourhood of Adelaide'.[37]

Drawing, perhaps a little selectively, from these overseas experiences colonial mounted rifle and infantry corps increasingly began to practise what was called, at the time, 'skirmishing tactics'; that is, 'being proficient in marksmanship in the field, highly mobile, and capable of taking advantage of natural cover'.[38] These were the sort of tactics and skills that had long been the lot of the light cavalry (and light infantry), which units like the Cape Mounted Rifles had been practising since the 1820s in a colonial context, and which were gaining increased currency at this time among the established armies of Europe in light of the experiences of the Franco-Prussian War.[39] One historian has contended that Tom Price was given command of the Victorian Mounted Rifles because his experience in India had taught him the skills and value of the irregular tactics employed there by mounted rifle-style units.[40] This developing attitude towards the citizen soldier in general, and mounted rifle and mounted infantry units in particular, was to become all the more important from the late 1880s after the visit of a high-ranking British officer to conduct a review of the defence of the Australian colonies.

Major-General J. Bevan Edwards visited all the Australasian colonies in 1889 in order to review the forces and advise the respective governments as 'to the uniform organisation of their local forces with a view to enabling them to co-operate effectively in the event of joint action becoming necessary'.[41] He recommended a variety of reforms to each of the colonies, including the major one of establishing a broadly common structure of forces throughout the colonies, which could be brought together in time of emergency so that '30 000 or 40 000 men could be rapidly concentrated to oppose an attack upon any of the chief cities'.[42] This combined force would have the dual purpose of creating a greater deterrent for any prospective attacker and creating a greater sense of security in these distant colonies, thereby hopefully reducing the number of 'unseemly scares which take place whenever the relations of the mother country with a foreign power are somewhat strained'.[43]

The focus on a combined colonial defence effort acted as a counter to the traditional favour towards the local defence of colonial capitals and other key points with fortifications. Edwards recommended that defence of the Australian colonies should now be based on mobile forces brigaded in such a way that, upon hostilities breaking out, they could be formed into divisions without regard to the colony from where the brigade originated. These mobile brigades were to be balanced forces made up of all arms in which mounted troops would play an important, but by no means dominant, role.

Of significance was Edwards's evident preference for the colonial mounted rifle and mounted infantry corps over the local cavalry corps. The cavalry of New South Wales, already 420 strong, represented a force of reasonable size that could perhaps be utilised, but Victoria and South Australia's small corps received no particular encouragement. In the same report he recommended that the cavalry corps of New Zealand would 'be of greater use if they were drilled and equipped to act as mounted infantry'. His proposed organisation for the mobile brigades contained no provision for any traditional cavalry, but he reported to Victoria that no 'part of your force will be of greater use in war than the Mounted Rifles, and it is the arm most suited to the defence of Australian Colonies'. South Australia was encouraged to make their mounted rifles partially paid and reorganise them into a regiment 'as it would take the place of cavalry in time of war'. Queensland was urged to give 'every encouragement... to this important branch of your forces', and to New South Wales he recommended that the establishment of the mounted infantry should be dramatically increased from its 297 personnel to more than a thousand, organised into three regiments with permanent staff as administrators and instructors.[44]

These proposals were never carried out to their full extent. The establishment of a field force of 30 000 to 40 000 soldiers was still beyond the organisational, technical and financial resources of the colonial military forces and, as yet, also beyond Australian political development. London had also taken a dim view of some aspects of his report. There the Colonial Defence Committee, although generally agreeing with its contents, believed that Edwards had grossly overplayed the likely threat to Australia, declaring, quite realistically, that 'there is no British territory so little liable to aggression as that of Australasia'.[45] Still, the spirit of his report endured and large, all-arms field forces remained part of Australian defence thinking, if not implementation, until well after Federation. Furthermore, the focus he placed on mobility gave mounted troops an increasingly significant place in the military organisations of the late pre-Federation period.

The growing value of mounted troops in general, and of mounted rifles and mounted infantry in particular, was reflected during the late 1880s and into the 1890s by the apparent development of Australian soldiers and interested bystanders beginning to *think* about their colonial mounted corps. This development is best reflected in the perhaps arcane, but nonetheless important, facet of military endeavour, the writing of training manuals.

Most branches of the colonial forces, including cavalry units, seem to have been generally content to make use of the many relevant manuals produced in Great Britain for their training.[46] By contrast mounted rifle and mounted infantry corps were increasingly interested in making local modifications to what was on offer from London. The move was gradual and uneven, and often reflected the confusion, by no means isolated to Australia, surrounding the military roles of mounted rifles and mounted infantry, but which was nevertheless real. South Australia, for example, made moves during the 1880s to produce a number of mounted manuals for the instruction of its own troops. In 1888 it published a mounted rifle manual that outlined the mounted rifleman as fulfilling a similar role to the cavalryman, and it was followed the next year by the *Regulations and Field Service Manual for Mounted Infantry*.[47] Given that at this time South Australia only had some lancers and was in the process of raising some mounted rifles, the publication of a manual ostensibly aimed at the creation of mounted infantry is somewhat incongruous, but it is possible that they had in mind an imperial model and were contemplating mounting some infantry as an expedient should the situation demand it. Any doctrinal confusion was perhaps cleared up in 1891 when a new *Manual of Drill and Field Service for Mounted Rifles* was produced.

These manuals were first small steps and were essentially reproductions of the relevant imperial texts, there being little or no modification for what might have been seen as local conditions. Queensland, however, soon produced a manual for its mounted infantry in 1892 that, although it drew heavily on British examples for the basic drill, had noteworthy local content. Most significantly, Queensland's Staff Officer for Mounted Infantry, Major Percy Ricardo, added to it an introduction that clearly stated a conception of what mounted infantry were and how they were to be of service to that colony if required:

The following should be kept constantly in view by officers and men of Mounted Infantry:
1. That as there is no cavalry in the Queensland Defence Force, Mounted Infantry may sometimes be called upon to perform work which would other wise fall to the lot of cavalry, but it must be impressed on the men that *they are in no sense cavalry*, their horses being provided merely as a means of locomotion [italics in original].
2. That it must be clearly understood that, whereas in the Imperial Service recruits for Mounted Infantry are picked Infantry Soldiers, in the Queensland Defence Force, on the contrary, Mounted Infantry are chiefly composed of horse owners who can ride, but who have little or no knowledge of infantry drill.[48]

The Queensland authorities seemed adamant that their mounted troops would, despite being recruited and trained as horsemen, remain strictly in the role of mounted infantry. The fear that the mounted infantry might take on cavalry airs became a recurrent local theme, and a few years later one Queensland official expressed particular concern that there was 'great danger of Mounted Infantry forgetting their real function – of Infantry provided with horse to carry them – and [becoming] a kind of Cavalry'.[49]

New South Wales also underwent a period in which it decided what its mounted troops should look like and do, but in this case it was driven by an imperial officer with an established and clear vision for mounted troops who would make the mounted forces of New South Wales the most complete and well organised in the Australian colonies.

Edward Hutton, a colonel in the British Army but with the local rank of major-general, arrived in New South Wales to take up the command of the colony's forces in late May 1893.[50] With considerable colonial war experience in various parts of Africa, Hutton was also, importantly, one of the British Army's foremost protagonists in the debates about the future of mounted troops and a particular proponent of mounted infantry. From an infantry rather than cavalry background, he had commanded the mounted infantry made up from the King's Royal Rifles in the Egyptian War of 1882, and been involved with the raising and running of the instructional Mounted Infantry School, established at Aldershot in 1888 under the auspices of Lord Wolseley.[51] A long-established advocate of this branch of the British Army, he had spoken on it at the Royal United Service Institution in London as early as 1886.[52] More broadly, he was an officer firmly convinced of the value of rifle-equipped mounted soldiers.[53]

Like many officers of his generation and doctrinal inclination, he had been influenced by interpretations of the American Civil War and the First Anglo-Boer War, the latter experienced at first hand. Although he never acknowledged him directly, Hutton's thinking and the examples he often drew on bore a remarkable resemblance to those of George Denison, and it seems likely that he was a key influence. More broadly, Hutton's views on mounted troops also dovetailed well with an enthusiasm for imperial defence cooperation, and during this stay in Australia he developed the (perhaps somewhat self-congratulatory) belief that the mounted troops of the Australian colonies were their greatest military resource. After he returned to England later in the decade he told an audience at the Military Society at Aldershot that in regard to Australian colonies 'the arm of the country is undoubtedly the Mounted branch' and that, from an imperial perspective, a contingent drawn from them 'would be worth their weight in Westralian gold upon any campaign in which British troops may be engaged'.[54]

Upon his arrival in Sydney Hutton found two mounted elements under his command. The New South Wales Cavalry, partially paid since 1890, was still relatively loosely organised with different detachments sometimes carrying different types of weapons, although the lance was quickly becoming the preferred weapon, and they now had a single, relatively drab uniform. The mounted infantry were more homogeneous, but the two bodies were of about the same size with 420 cavalrymen and 418 mounted infantrymen in the colony in 1892.[55] Together this total body of mounted troops, called the Mounted Regiment, could contain up to 900 personnel, depending on how the various detachments around the colony were maintaining their numbers.

Hutton was dissatisfied, however, and outlined a proposal for a reorganisation to the New South Wales government in June 1893. Much of it dealt with organisational matters, particularly as he believed that the existing regiment of 900 men under one commander was 'beyond the capability of any one Commanding Officer ... and [was] inconsistent with all precedent'.[56] Accordingly the Mounted Regiment was renamed the Mounted Brigade and placed under the unpaid command of the now lieutenant-colonel, but ageing, Malcolm Macdonald, whom Hutton hoped to soon replace with a younger imperial officer.[57] The two branches of the mounted forces were reorganised into units of this brigade, which in each case were soon commanded by a major.

More significant in terms of the development of Australia's mounted troops was that the Mounted Infantry Regiment was renamed the

Mounted Rifle Regiment as Hutton believed that the former title was 'a misnomer in the sense that it is understood in the Imperial Service'.[58] Hutton had long-standing views of the relative roles and places of mounted rifles and mounted infantry. He had told the Royal United Service Institution in 1891:

> Mounted or Mobile Infantry are infantry soldiers *pur et simple*, who are so organized, equipped, and trained as to be capable of receiving any available means of rapid locomotion to enable them to act as infantry soldiers with the greatest rapidity and mobility. Mounted Rifles, on the other hand, are defined as horsemen trained to fight on foot, men who are mounted and intended to perform all the duties of cavalry, except that which may be best described as 'the shock'. It is expected of them that they should perform all the outpost, reconnoitring, and patrolling of an army in a manner similar to cavalry; the only difference being that they must rely solely upon their fire powers for defensive and offensive action.[59]

These definitions should be noted because they would have long-term and profound implications for the future development of Australia's mounted troops. Taking the opposite view to his Queensland counterparts, he decided that the men of the now Mounted Rifles Regiment, being recruited as horsemen and horse owners, should not be classified as infantry able to ride but who would fight like infantry, but as horsemen trained in certain cavalry and dismounted duties. It was an organisational and operational template that would have a long influence in Australia.

The New South Wales Mounted Brigade was formed in July 1893. More than just an administrative arrangement, the two mounted regiments were also supported within the brigade by elements of the field artillery, engineers and service corps. The balance between the mounted rifles and the cavalry was maintained with each contributing equally to the brigade. Despite his advocacy for mounted infantry and mounted rifles, there was never any suggestion that Hutton considered the cavalry a useless part of his forces. His report for 1893 lauded the mounted troops in general but particularly noted the 'degree of practical efficiency [which] has been reached... in the Lancers'.[60] In his writings Hutton had never advocated the disposal of traditional cavalry and had generally seen other types of mounted troops as being complementary to British cavalry, fully replacing them in colonial situations only where regular cavalry could not be obtained.[61] New South Wales's regiment of lancers (as they were increasingly being known) was, with more than 400 men on the books,

Photo 3 A British artist's 1890 vision of the Victorian Mounted Rifles (VMR) on manoeuvres. By the 1890s most colonial governments had opted to support mounted rifle corps in preference to cavalry. The VMR was one of the most successful units, although it is unlikely that its field training was ever as picturesque as this. (AWM ART19712)

decidedly viable as far as colonial units went and was the only successful body of cavalry in the Australian colonies. Without any doctrinal or administrative reason to dispose of it, the future of the New South Wales cavalry was assured until after Federation.

Hutton's attempts at reforming Australian mounted troops were not just confined to New South Wales, and at his instigation the officers from a number of the colonies soon met to consider the creation of a training manual that could be used by all Australian mounted troops. Hutton considered that the 'want of a Manual for drill and interior economy suited to the Mounted Troops of Australia had for some time pressed itself upon the attention of all the Commandants of the Australian Colonies'.[62] Colonel Joseph Gordon, late Royal Artillery and commander of the South Australian forces, agreed and told his government that the preparation of a common 'Drill Manual for Mounted Rifles is *very necessary* and it is most desirable'.⁶³ Major-General Alex Tulloch, the Victorian commandant, was in agreement; especially as, he noted, the relevant imperial mounted infantry manual was out of print and unobtainable.⁶⁴ The committee, made up primarily of Hutton, Gordon and Tom Price of the Victorian Mounted Rifles, met at the conclusion of the Inter-Colonial Defence Conference in Sydney in October 1894.⁶⁵ Hutton forwarded the report of the committee to the New South Wales government in late 1894, and the manual was prepared for printing shortly after the New Year.⁶⁶

The resultant *Manual of Drill for the Mounted Troops of Australia* contained, like the earlier Queensland mounted infantry manual, a preface in which a conception of the role that mounted troops would play if they were required was stated. This time, however, it was written by Hutton, and it represented a clear statement of what he considered the function and place of mounted troops, not just in New South Wales but also in Australia as a whole. The opening paragraph stated:

> In no country in the world will a mounted force be found more necessary for military operations than in Australia. Distances are so great, transport away from the great lines of rail so difficult, that, as in America at the commencement of the great war of Secession, 1862–65, so in Australia would success be to that force which had the best and the most completely equipped mounted force... So will, undoubtedly, be the result of any warlike operations which may in the future be conducted on this continent. Success will be to that army which can turn to account the splendid inherent resources which the Colonies of Australia possess in the supply of horsemen, who, while hardy and of an independent character, have all those British characteristics which have made and are now making an Empire and race without parallel in the history of the world.⁶⁷

Despite the fairly simplistic summary of the American Civil War and the expression of the idea that Australians made excellent natural horse-soldiers, this was a succinct summary of Hutton's views on mounted troops and how he saw them in the Australian context. As the comments on the American Civil War indicate, the manual's preface showed a significant influence of the thinking of George Denison, as did his advocacy of the strategic use of self-sufficient mounted formations capable of independent operations through their use of rifle-based dismounted tactics and field artillery support.⁶⁸ The manual was written so that it was suitable for all the forms of mounted troops in Australia. Cavalry, mounted rifles and mounted infantry were all given tactical roles, although the basic drill for all was essentially the same, and the focus was on dismounted tactics rather than mounted action.

Hutton was not the only person to be pushing mounted riflemen as the ideal Australian mounted soldier. One New South Wales parliamentarian, Edward O'Sullivan, produced a pamphlet in 1894, *The Power of Mounted Riflemen*, to support the development of mounted rifle formations in Australia. Although his pamphlet revealed a Denisonian influence, he did not consider only the example of American mounted riflemen in the Civil War as being worthy of emulation, and he also displayed a keen interest in the performance of the Boers against the British in 1880–81,[69] for social as much as military reasons. His pamphlet is perhaps the clearest expression from this period of the parallels that could be drawn between the Boer farmer and his Australian counterpart. For him the Boers were 'graziers and farmers, who correspond almost in every particular to our selectors'.[70] Thus, for O'Sullivan, in the mobile warfare that was likely to take place after the landing of any enemy expeditionary force, it was mounted riflemen who would be of great value owing to the skills in horsemanship and shooting that they, like the Boers, supposedly possessed.[71]

Others seemed to share his views, or at least some of them, and Major-General Sir Charles Holled Smith, an imperial officer and Victoria's commandant from 1894 to 1899, believed that the colony wanted 'as many mounted rifles as we can get', and that they were second only to the guns at the harbour's heads in terms of defence importance. Reflecting on the fighting in the Transvaal in 1880–81, he noted that the 'Boers were practically mounted rifles and as such were, of course, able to outmarch our infantry everywhere. They were what mounted rifles should be – good shots and good riders.' His enthusiasm did not extend to cavalry, though, contending that there was 'any amount of wire fences and other obstacles to' their effective local use, presumably meaning that cavalry charges would prove impossible in the Australian countryside.[72]

Hutton's successor in New South Wales, Major-General George French, imperial officer, artilleryman and late commandant of the Queensland Defence Force, held a similar view on the relative utility of cavalry and mounted rifles in Australia. In his report to the government for 1897, after pointing out that Australian horses were generally suited to mounted rifle but not cavalry work, he explained his preference for mounted rifles over cavalry in detail. Cavalry, he felt, were unsuited to the type of country to be found along the coast and, because no invader could bring any substantial number of cavalry with them, there was no requirement for Australian *arme blanche*–wielding horsemen to counter foreign *arme blanche*–wielding horsemen. Any invading force would, however, be predominantly infantry, and he believed they would be 'sorely pressed if mounted men with magazine rifles, and well able to use them, attacked them at pleasure in front, flanks or rear'. Moreover, it was clear that New South Wales could produce thousands of excellent mounted riflemen at short notice, but the same could not be said of fully trained cavalry, which would always be few in number. In conclusion he made it clear that he had 'no hesitation in advising that any extension of our Mounted Forces should be in the direction of Mounted Riflemen'.[73] He then went on to exhort the government to encourage the formation of mounted rifle volunteer corps to supplement the existing partially paid regiment, as well as request that the existing body should be 'enlarged and extended'.[74] What the origins of French's pro-mounted rifles views were is unclear, but it could have been based on his experiences in Canada where, in 1873, he had been appointed the first commissioner of the paramilitary North West Mounted Police, the forerunner of today's Royal Canadian Mounted Police.[75]

That Australia was a good source for mounted riflemen was a view also shared by the Governor of Victoria of the late 1890s, Lord Brassey.[76] An enthusiastic publicist on naval and maritime affairs, he wrote to Joseph Chamberlain, the Secretary of State for the Colonies, in 1897 advocating the establishment in Australia of a partially paid reserve force of 5000 mounted rifles, to be paid for by the British Government on condition that the force be available for service anywhere in case of war.[77] Evidently impressed by the contingent that the Victorian Mounted Rifles had recently sent to Queen Victoria's Diamond Jubilee celebrations, and probably influenced by his colony's commandant, Smith, as well as those in other colonies,[78] Brassey wrote to Chamberlain claiming that 'there can be no question as to the efficiency of the men, especially for irregular warfare and in hot climates'.[79] In support of this he pointed out that the 'military spirit here is strong, and horses incredibly cheap'.[80] The Colonial Defence Committee considered the proposal, and there was a general warmth for the whole idea of getting a colonial contribution to imperial defence, but a number of problems ensured that the scheme foundered. First, there was concern about the costs involved, in particular as to whether Britain would get value for money from a non-regular colonial force. There was also a feeling that regular cavalry was still more valuable, 'even in native wars', than 'irregulars' serving under officers and non-commissioned officers whose training may well be deficient in comparison. Finally, the committee was worried that forming an Australian corps, and possibly using it in an unpopular campaign, could be detrimental to the broader aims of imperial cooperation, not to mention Australian Federation. Lord Brassey was asked to consider his proposal further, but the idea never came to fruition.[81] This was the first plan to use Australian mounted troops for imperial service since 1885 when Victoria, trying to match New South Wales, had unsuccessfully offered 400 mounted infantry to London for service in the Sudan, but it was not to be the last.[82]

While mounted rifle and mounted infantry units were receiving particular encouragement during the 1890s the few remaining cavalry units in the Australian colonies were, with some notable exceptions, finding it difficult to survive. In Victoria the last remaining troop of cavalry, at Sandhurst, had been removed from the establishment in 1892, and there seemed no inclination on the part of the Victorian Government or its military officials to encourage any other bodies of cavalry. An attempt was made to establish a volunteer cavalry troop in Melbourne in October 1890 but, despite the remaining men at Sandhurst, the colony's Department of Defence saw no value in the idea; one official dismissing it as 'an arm of the service which was not likely to be valuable'. What the colony needed, he noted, was 'was an efficient and well-drilled body of men able to move rapidly about from place to place for purposes of locomotion' but which fought on foot; a role that the Victorian Mounted Rifles clearly fulfilled.[83] Thus when the last remnants of the Adelaide Lancers were incorporated into the South Australian Mounted Rifles in 1895 only New South Wales continued to maintain any cavalry.

As pointed out above, the New South Wales Lancers (an evolution of the New South Wales Cavalry), having become partially paid, were able to maintain their numbers and their viability through the 1890s. In 1892 a New South Wales royal commission into military affairs had commented that the 'high state of efficiency to which this force has attained is a strong inducement to the Colony to maintain it'.[84] Yet, as Major-General French's comments in his 1897 report above highlight, it was not without its detractors. The *Sydney Morning Herald* commented that those remarks had 'hurt the feelings of cavalrymen'.[85] Even Hutton, who had praised the lancers for their enthusiasm in his 1893 report, had not been totally content with their approach to training and attempted to modernise their methods. In the same report he pointed out that he had to make 'some necessary changes in the method of carrying the firearms, and some alteration in tactical training, so as to develop the power of dismounted action'.[86] It seems this reform had little effect as French later complained that 'with fine contempt for the carbine, they were not expert riflemen'.[87]

Some within the lancer regiment itself evidently did not share this scepticism about their value. Detachments of the lancers had sailed to England to compete in the Royal Military Tournaments in 1893 and to take part in the Queen's Diamond Jubilee celebrations in 1897, on both occasions exciting considerable comment at home and in Great Britain. After the 1897 trip there arose within parts of the regiment a desire to build on these experiences by going on active service.[88] In 1897–98 the regiment's commanding officer, Lieutenant-Colonel James Burns, sought to give his regiment some realistic overseas experience by offering a lancer force of about a hundred for service in India where Britain was then engaged in one of its intermittent wars on the North-West Frontier.[89] Opinions about this offer have been mixed and variously marked down as merely the natural and expected next step in achieving military efficiency or, alternatively, as little more than 'naked militarism'.[90] Major-General French seems to have been broadly of former opinion at the time, urging the government to pass the offer on to London, and he drafted a suitable cable to facilitate this.[91] The then Premier, George Reid, perhaps reflecting the latter view, was more concerned about the idea, commenting when he rejected the proposal that he 'did not wish to see a spirit of unrest and military adventure grow up in this country'.[92] Reid's obstruction of the plan was enough to kill it off, and the lancers instead began to focus on sending a training detachment to England in 1899. They would have to wait for a conflict in South Africa for a chance to try their hand at war.

A sense of military adventurism also pervaded another pre–Boer War proposal by a New South Wales cavalry officer to use Australian mounted troops on imperial service. Lieutenant-Colonel James Mackay had started his citizen soldiering in 1885 when he had been involved with the raising of the West Camden Light Horse, but in 1897 he took the opportunity of the revival of volunteer units in New South Wales to found his own unit, the 1st Australian Horse. Mackay drew on the remote country districts not then utilised by the New South Wales forces to recruit his regiment, and he was always keen to promote it as a force of bushmen, all of whom were, he claimed, 'natural riders and good shots... accustomed to roughing it'. Despite the general preference for mounted riflemen, Mackay took an opposing view when forming his regiment and chose to fashion his new unit as cavalry. Then, in July 1899, Mackay made a proposal to the New

Photo 4 Detachments of the New South Wales Mounted Rifles and the New South Wales Lancers parade through London as part of Queen Victoria's jubilee celebrations in 1897. These small contingents excited considerable interest, which contributed to the increasingly frequent calls for the use of Australian mounted troops for imperial defence. (AWM P01208.004)

South Wales and British governments to establish a mounted regiment 'in Australia to be subsidized by the Imperial Authorities, and to be used for the defence of the Empire when and where required', and he was firmly of the view that it should also be cavalry. The model he suggested was really one of the cavalry hybrid, using both sword and rifle, but in examining this proposal it is difficult to escape the conclusion that form, in the superficial sense, was as important to Mackay as military utility. To him rifles and pistols were obviously necessary, but it was the sword and 'the prestige and pride which belongs peculiarly to that weapon ... which appeals in a singular degree to all men who love their horses and know how to ride them'.[93]

Mackay was always one for self-promotion and hyperbole, and his offer of imperial service, and perhaps his taste for cavalry over mounted rifles, should be seen in this light. When not soldiering he was a pastoralist and New South Wales parliamentarian, a horseman of some repute (and an amateur jockey) as well as something of an author, producing numerous short stories, ballads and novels, among which was a novel about a Chinese invasion, *The Yellow Wave*.[94] As one recent scholar has put it, his imperial service proposal 'was a scheme proposed by a colonial swashbuckler who fancied himself at the head of a cavalry charge on the plains of India or the veld of southern Africa'. In pushing this proposal Mackay seems, typically, to have completely bypassed the colonial commandant, French, and taken the idea directly to the Premier, George Reid, and the Governor, Earl Beauchamp.[95] This might have been a reflection of French's dim views on cavalry or simply the way a self-promoting politician might approach the matter, but either way it was apparently well judged, and it received a warm welcome from the latter two. Reid gave it his 'hearty support', and when passing it on to London the Governor asked for it to be given 'the most favourable consideration'.[96] Reid's earlier opposition to military adventurism was probably overcome in this case by the prospect of there being no requirement for his treasury to foot any of the costs for the regiment.[97] In London the Colonial Defence Committee considered the proposal, and despite evidence that they considered it a 'much more detailed and practical looking scheme than [Lord] Brassey's', it was felt in London that any such proposal should wait until after Federation and until the lessons about using colonial troops in the now-raging war in South Africa had been digested.[98]

By the late 1890s a degree of confidence and perhaps brashness had become evident among some of the mounted troops of Australia's military establishment, certainly in New South Wales at least. The desire to get detachments overseas to train with the regulars at Aldershot, or, better still, fight some of Britain's enemies somewhere, was certainly symptomatic of this. Such a development was not surprising as by then mounted troops, in one form or another, had been part of the local military landscape for nearly a hundred years and perhaps restlessness – or, more generously, a search for purpose – had to come with age. After all, one of the colonial era's most successful early military (or paramilitary) establishments, the Mounted Police, had a clear and definite purpose. They and other mounted men had had a profound effect on the often blended roles of policing and warfare on the colonial frontier. In doing so they had become, along with a large number of like organised units elsewhere, one of the empire's exemplars for the employment of mounted troops in the colonies. None of the multitude of colonial units raised for defence in the years that followed would have so direct a purpose (there being no clear enemies) but when, in the latter part of the century, military-minded colonials and their imperial commanders began to give some serious thought and attention to the mounted corps they were raising and maintaining, the mounted arm certainly developed a vigour.

The corps raised between 1840 and the mid-1880s were not spectacularly successful by any worthwhile measure. Most were small, loosely organised, lacked sustainable resources and were usually bereft of systematic higher military direction. They were also utterly dependent on the whims of the men who enlisted, their officers and their only half-interested colonial societies and governments. It is difficult to conclude that these early corps were much more than passing military fancies. From 1885, however, a confluence of factors meant that these earlier limitations were overcome strongly enough for the new mounted corps raised thereafter to become broadly successful. Fundamental was the willingness of governments to make arrangements for larger, better organised units in which the men who joined often, although by no means always, were paid for their time spent in uniform. This factor combined with a growing view that fortifications were not the only viable form of defence and that some form of citizen soldier field force was worthwhile. In such forces mobility was vital and the military horseman became increasingly attractive. What form that horseman should take, however, was not so clear. Cavalry remained part of the military establishment, particularly in New South Wales, until Federation, but by the beginning of the 1890s it was clear that mounted rifles were gaining increased favour. As the American Civil War and the First Anglo-Boer War had demonstrated, it was a model that seemed to offer everything the colonies needed; it was militarily useful (witness Majuba Hill), was better suited to the skirmishing tactics of the citizen soldier the colonies had, was in favour with the imperial authorities – at least for colonial wars – and was easier to produce than full-blown cavalry. When Edward Hutton came to New South Wales and set out to establish such a model more firmly, he found fertile ground for his ideas. These military factors combined with the increasingly noticeable social ones about bushmen and natural soldiering, evident in the views of Edward O'Sullivan and others, to produce a growing view that the mounted arm, particularly the mounted rifleman, was not only the arm best suited to Australia's defence, it was also the quintessential Australian arm. It was a notion that was to face a stern test in South Africa.

CHAPTER | 2

TOUGH LESSONS
South Africa, 1899–1902

Although the figures are subject to dispute, the Australian colonies and, after 1901, the new Federation, sent approximately 16 000 men to fight in the Boer War of 1899–1902.¹ New South Wales alone sent perhaps 6200 men and Victoria sent less than half this, about 3500 men. The smallest colony, Tasmania, sent just 800.² As many men volunteered more than once for different contingents and others made their own way to South Africa to join one of the many units raised there, or were there when the war started and did much the same thing, such figures are indicative only. The most recent and authoritative history of Australia's involvement in the war estimates that perhaps 20 000 Australian men were involved in fighting it in one way or another.³ Almost all of them did so as mounted soldiers.

The war that broke out in South Africa in 1899 came at a time when the mounted troops of the Australian colonies, for all their faults and weaknesses, had become relatively mature. The confused and hesitant steps of the mid-nineteenth century had been left behind, and the mounted corps of the late colonial period generally possessed, with or without justification, a surety about themselves, their military role and their martial abilities. Every mounted corps – be they cavalry, mounted rifles or mounted infantry – was imbued with ideas of the bushman as natural soldier, and South Africa would provide an acid test for both these social ideas and broader military theories about mounted troops in modern warfare.

Despite the predominant colonial view favouring mounted rifles and mounted infantry, a detachment of the New South Wales Lancers would be the first Australian mounted troops to go to war. Unable to get to India's North-West Frontier, the regiment had instead sucessfully sent a contingent of a hundred men to train with the regular cavalry in Britain. The colonial government had had no interest in this proposal either, but when Earl Carrington, the colony's ex-governor and the regiment's honorary colonel, obtained practical government support in London and enough money was raised to underwrite the venture, the New South Wales government allowed them to go provided it did not have to meet any of the costs, and the lancers arrived in England in late April 1899. The trip was an imperial public relations triumph, but it seems that its value as a training experience was limited.[4] Nevertheless when the political situation in South Africa began to deteriorate mid-year some of the detachment, particularly its commander, Captain Charles Cox (who would go on to command a light horse brigade in the First World War), began to think of volunteering their military services.

There was some tension within the detachment about who would and would not go on active service, and it seems that a number of the waverers were pressured to sign up. Despite this, not all the men proved willing to volunteer, and because others were not medically fit enough, or were too young for the New South Wales government to let them go, in early November only 69 lancers disembarked at the Cape to fight the Boers.[5] Those who returned home were subjected to a regimental inquiry and such public and press opprobrium, regardless of how valid had been their reasons for not going, that all who could subsequently volunteered for later contingents for South Africa. One of them reportedly told another lancer that he had to come back to South Africa because the pressure on him had been such that 'a man couldn't live in Sydney'.[6]

The lancers would not, however, remain Australia's only military contribution to the war for long. Queensland had been the first Australian colony to offer troops to London, and had done so as early as July 1899 when pre-war tensions had started to rise. Although not all of them were so enthusiastic, the other colonies soon began to think along similar lines, and the telegraph cables between London and the colonial capitals saw more military traffic than usual over the next few months. At the urging of the Victorian government the colonial commandants met in Melbourne in September to discuss the possibility of sending a combined Australian contingent. They suggested sending a combined arms force of more than 2000 men, but this hesitant step towards military unification was soon overtaken by events in South Africa and succumbed also to growing intercolonial rivalry. London sealed it by clarifying that its requirement was

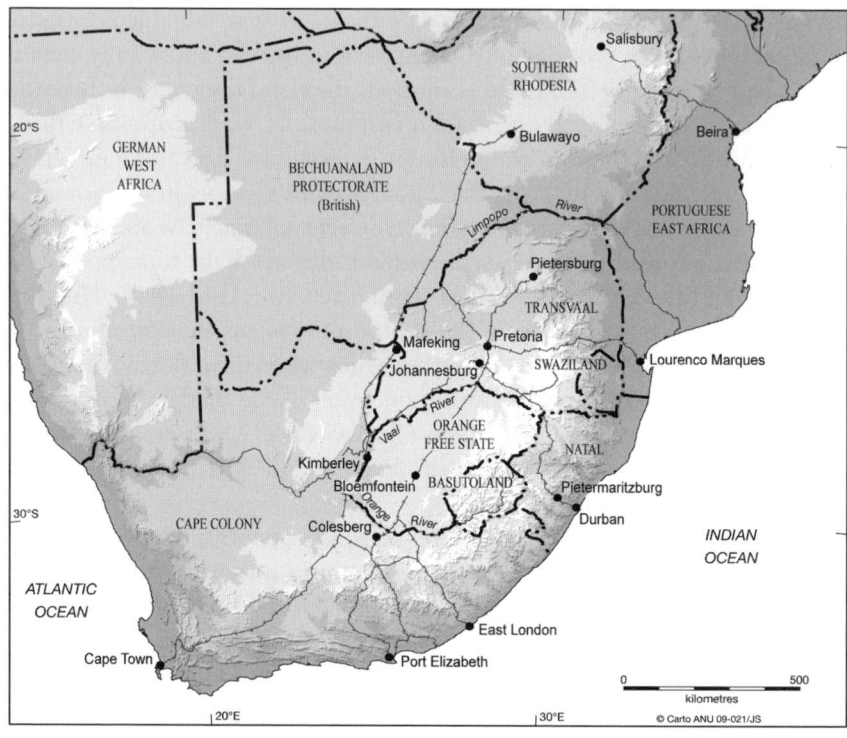

Map 1 South Africa, 1899

for smaller contingents that could be subsumed into the larger imperial forces.[7] The now infamous cable of 3 October told the colonies: 'Firstly, units should consist of 125 men; secondly [they] may be infantry, mounted infantry, or cavalry; in view of numbers already available, infantry most, cavalry least serviceable.'[8]

The subject of much later criticism, this cable appears to have been largely the result of a hasty decision in London by a busy General Sir Redvers Buller (who was trying to get the British Army to South Africa) rather than British obtuseness about what was already established as being Australia's supposed military forte.[9] The cable had little effect on Queensland's plans as its offer of a contingent of 250 mounted infantry had already been accepted. New South Wales included the lancers already on their way to war in its contingent and recruited more to supplement the small numbers already committed.[10] The 1st Australian Horse and New South Wales Mounted Rifles were also allowed to raise contributions (eventually increased to squadron size) for the force, and a company of infantry provided the arm that London seemed keenest on. Victoria raised a squadron from the Victorian Mounted Rifles and added it to an infantry company for its first contingent. South Australia, Western Australia and Tasmania provided contingents of infantry as per London's request.[11]

There proved to be enough enthusiastic militiamen to fill the ranks of these first units except in South Australia and Queensland where men outside the forces had to be recruited.[12] Major Percy Ricardo could find only 123 members of the Queensland Mounted Infantry who were willing to join and, after scouring another 25 men out of the artillery, had to resort to 'men who said they were, or had been, members of the Queensland Defence Force'.[13] Men enlisting in the New South Wales contingent had to pass an exam concerning discipline, be pronounced medically fit, pass shooting and riding tests, be older than 21 and not be articled or apprenticed to a profession.[14] Similar conditions applied in the other colonies.

These first contingents embarked for the war in November and began arriving in December just in time to greet the news of Boer victories at Colenso, Stormberg and Magersfontein, the reverses collectively known as 'Black Week'. The new arrivals were sent forward to where the army wanted them, but back home the defeats brought out a swelling imperial loyalty that soon produced another series of colonial contingents. London's taste for infantry had disappeared, and now they were happy to accept mounted men, but still only relatively small bodies of them. Raised and despatched to the war through December 1899 and January 1900, they generally joined, and in some cases subsumed, the smaller first contingents already campaigning.[15]

Black Week also spurred on a number of wealthy men to approach both London and the local colonial governments about raising a new force of colonial soldiers recruited from the bush; the sort of men who could, theoretically at least, match Boer farmers on their own terms. An empire-wide movement with its eventual equivalents in Britain, Canada and New Zealand, the resultant mounted Australian contingents became known as the Bushmen. Financed in part by public subscription, their ranks were filled not by pre-war citizen soldiers (although there were probably a few), but by what one historian has termed 'a curious blend of gentlemen's sons and roughnecks'.[16] The numbers of volunteers for these new contingents were huge, but this round of contingents, and those that followed, were hampered by a lack of suitable officer material, many of the best permanent and citizen soldier commanders having already been sent across the Indian Ocean.[17] London, keen for manpower seemingly regardless of its military quality, sought more such material and asked the colonies to produce more Bushmen (to be known this time as the Imperial Bushmen) for which it would carry the costs. Like the Bushmen before them, who had left in February and March 1900, they were largely intended for service in Rhodesia, although in the event many would disembark at the Cape or Durban when they arrived in May and June 1900. Later, in early 1901, the new states of the Australian Federation stepped in where the new national government could not as yet, and they raised another round of contingents (generally referred to as the draft contingents), again as agents for the imperial government.[18]

These loose waves of volunteers, roughly linked by little more than the methods of their raising and financing and the timing of their despatch, were also separated by colonial loyalty and origins, as well as by a certain degree of organisational idiosyncrasy, as is evidenced by the confusing array of unit and contingent titles used to label them. To learn their names and track their respective movements takes considerable time and a very reliable reference work. It would not be until the new federal government was able to organise its own contingents of what was titled the Australian Commonwealth Horse in early 1902 that organisational uniformity would characterise Australia's military contribution to the war in South Africa. For this reason this chapter will adopt not the broadly chronological approach of the others but a thematic approach.

The war that these men fought has traditionally been separated into two distinct phases. The first commenced on 12 October 1899 when the Boer commandos of the South African Republic (the Transvaal to Britons) and the Orange Free State crossed into Natal and the Cape Colony. After the difficulties and defeats that year British fortunes began to recover the following February with the appointment of their new commander, Field Marshal Lord Roberts, and by mid-March they had taken Bloemfontein, capital of the Orange Free State. There followed a pause during April, but Roberts again commenced an advance on 3 May and took Johannesburg at the end of the month before entering Pretoria in early June 1900. President Kruger of the South African Republic had fled and, although there had been no surrender, Roberts and others thought the war effectively over at this stage. The Boer commandos had withdrawn eastwards from Pretoria towards Portuguese East Africa and were gradually dispersing under continuing British pressure. Kruger left Africa for European exile in October and, despite some significant fighting into the second half of the year, the war was changing into a guerrilla campaign. Roberts went home in November, convinced that little more than tidying up and policing remained to be done, and left his ex-chief of staff, General

Photo 5 Mounted units, such as the Tasmanian Bushmen pictured here in 1900, were considered far and away the most valuable units in South Africa and predominated on both sides. Australia's contingents were patchy in their quality, although as experience was gained so their competence and efficiency increased. (AWM P00175.058)

Lord Kitchener, to carry out this work. Until the final peace settlement on 31 May 1902, there followed an increasingly bitter guerrilla war in which mobile columns swept the countryside occasionally sparking a pitched battle, but more often small skirmishes. Lines of blockhouses sprung up alongside the railway lines, then across the countryside, to provide something for the British to pin the mobile Boers against, and a policy of enforced relocation of Boer women and children to camps was pursued in order to remove one of the enemy's key logistic and moral supports.[19]

The various Australian contingents found themselves involved in both phases of the conflict. The first small arrivals were dispersed to various parts of the Cape Colony as circumstances required. The New South Wales Lancers found themselves split on arrival with the bulk joining the regular cavalry under General Sir John French at Colesburg. A smaller detachment of 29 men was sent to join Lieutenant-General Lord Methuen's division further to the west as it worked up the railway line towards Kimberley. The first contingent of the Queensland Mounted Infantry was entrained for Belmont and took part in a small battle at nearby Sunnyside on 1 January 1900, which, as the first notable victory after Black Week, became a moment of some public and military celebration. It was notable also because Victor Stanley Jones, a soldier with the Queenslanders, became the first man in an Australian uniform to die in battle.[20] It was also the first battle for a captain with the Queenslanders, Harry Chauvel, who would later to go on to command the Desert Mounted Corps in the First World War.

The infantry companies sent by the colonies soon found themselves mounted on horses and unhappily amalgamated into the Australian Regiment under the command of a Victorian permanent soldier, Colonel John Hoad, as part of Lord Roberts' plan to drastically increase the number of mounted troops at his disposal. All these early contingents served as part of Roberts's dual advance on Bloemfontein.[21] Here the Australian Regiment was disbanded and, along with all the other Australians, except the lancers and 1st Australian Horse, who stayed with French's Cavalry Division, were reorganised into part of an imperial mounted infantry brigade under the command of the ex-New South Wales commandant, Major-General Edward Hutton. Hutton thought it a portentous moment in imperial history and wrote to his wife that the 'responsibility is very great, quite as much political and imperial, as it is military'.[22] So organised, the Australians took part in the advance into the Transvaal and on to Pretoria before the last operations of 1900 and returned to Australia at the end of the year.[23]

Many of the Bushmen and Imperial Bushmen contingents, when they arrived, were put into the new Rhodesian Field Force and, leaving Beira in Portuguese East Africa, moved down through Bulawayo and into the Transvaal from the north where some Queenslanders were present at the relief of Mafeking. At Elands River in the first half of August 1900, 500 men, 300 of whom were Australian Bushmen, withstood a siege for 12 days.[24] These men and the contingents that followed found themselves involved in the guerrilla war that had replaced the more conventional fighting in which the first contingents had taken part. They became part of the mobile columns that conducted the incessant 'drives' across the Transvaal, the Orange Free State, Natal and the Cape Colony, which sought to eliminate the Boer commandos, until the end of the war.

Mounted troops and the war

On the other side were the citizen Boer riflemen of the two republics, along with a few foreign idealists and those Boers in the British colonies of the Cape and Natal who were inclined to throw in their lot with them.

Again it is impossible to know how many fought, but one South African source estimates that the two republics put 90 000 men into the field during the course of the war.[25] These men were organised around the commando system that was both a social and military feature of Boer life. A relatively loose military organisation, it was officered by landholders and other local notables who were elected to their posts and dependent on the willingness of the lesser farmers and *bywoner* (men with no land but movable property such as cattle), who made up its rank and file, to go on campaign. Much of its military heritage stemmed from the sort of colonial warfare against black Africans that had characterised conflict in the region since the arrival of white settlers, but the victory against the British in the short war of 1880–81, and which was such an influence on Australia's citizen soldiers, had been a recent military triumph.[26]

Apart from a small force of permanent artillery, most Boers fought as the archetypal mounted riflemen. Using their small hardy horses for mobility, they dismounted to fight with their rifles, were more inclined to skirmish than close for the assault and, like many citizen armies, were disinclined to incur too many casualties.[27] Although men with forceful personalities and proven battlefield nous could command great respect and loyalty as leaders, many commandos had loose standards of discipline, and Boers could leave their comrades and head home without apparent concern if they were so inclined.[28] Perhaps their greatest asset was their knowledge of the country in which they were fighting and their ability to exploit it.[29] Captain John Antill of the New South Wales Mounted Rifles reported that their defensive positions were very good, 'being almost impregnable', and were 'very difficult to see'.[30]

The countryside where much of the fighting took place was the South African veld, a high, open grassy plateau between 1500 and 2200 metres above sea level. The summer months were wet and provided useful pasture, but rivers were frequently flooded and virtually impassable. During winter the rivers became passable and the ground hardened as there was little rain, but pasture disappeared and drinking water became scarce.[31] The clear air and open terrain allowed the observer wide, uninterrupted views as well as allowing the possessor of a weapon to begin firing at his mark at extreme range. To consider such long-range rifle fire as genuinely aimed would be overly generous, but at 2000 metres a Boer bullet from a high-powered rifle could still kill, and the experience of men being hit by unseen riflemen at long range contributed to a belief that Boers were excellent marksmen.[32] Boer shooting could be very accurate and was enhanced by their knowledge of the country and practice at judging distances. The Australians defending at the Elands River post in August 1900 found the shooting of de le Ray's commando very accurate indeed.[33] But in a military system that relied on the attitudes of individuals as to how much they should practise their skills, Boer shooting standards were inevitably uneven. Queensland's Percy Ricardo noted in a letter after one skirmish near the Vet River that 'we were within 500 [yards] when he opened fire on us with shrapnel and Mauser, luckily the fire was very wild'.[34] During the peace negotiations following the First Anglo-Boer War in 1881 a British cavalry regiment, the 14th Hussars, had challenged a group of Boers to a shooting match and found they outshot them at 300 and 500 yards.[35]

To counter the Boers Britain sent just over 5500 mounted men to South Africa in 1899, about 2 per cent of the total force deployed. This was made up of about 4500 regular cavalry and 1100 mounted infantry, composed of men drawn from the regular infantry line regiments who had largely received instruction at the mounted infantry schools before the war. To this it hoped to add about another 8000–10 000 hastily raised irregular horsemen at the Cape and in Natal.[36] The demands of the campaign, however, meant that this number was soon considered deficient. Faced with a mobile enemy organised as mounted rifles and forced to patrol vast tracts of territory just to properly secure their own forces, let alone secure the British colonies, meant that more mounted troops were soon needed. Despite the logistical problems that increasing the numbers of horsemen would bring, the disasters of Black Week had been caused in large part by poor British reconnaissance due to a lack of mounted men.[37] The result was a call for more mounted men that overturned the 'infantry most, cavalry least serviceable' attitude of the early days.

The regular cavalry had an early success of the traditional kind in October 1899 when the 5th Dragoon Guards managed a charge against a withdrawing Boer force at Elandslaagte. As the war progressed most of the cavalry was organised into the Cavalry Division under Major-General John French. At Klip Drift it charged through defending Boers to lift the siege of Kimberley. But charging was not all that the cavalry could do and, as the Boers withdrew from here towards Bloemfontein, they were overtaken by one of French's brigades, which dismounted and, through the effects of its fire, forced the Boers to dig in and endure a siege at Paardeberg before surrendering about ten days later.

The regulars of the mounted infantry proved, at least in the early stages of the war, a mixed blessing. Products of the pre-war theory and practice of improvising mounted troops from the ranks of plentiful infantry, they provided the extra numbers that were wanted, but poor horse-riding and horse management skills meant that their value, at least in the early months, was debatable.[38] The vast bulk of the mounted troops eventually raised and used in South Africa were best referred to as mounted riflemen. They were differentiated from the mounted infantry by the fact that generally they were not regular soldiers and were also horsemen to start with. In earlier wars, but also frequently in this one, they would have been referred to as 'irregulars' or 'auxiliaries'. They took on all the roles of cavalry from scouting to skirmishing, to closing with the enemy, and did so, not with the *arme blanche* but by using rifle fire. There was no clear organisational or doctrinal template for these mounted units, and the term 'mounted rifles' covered everything from the Imperial Yeomanry, which shared part of its name and some of its personnel but none of its organisation with Britain's Yeomanry Cavalry, to the full range of colonial mounted units, be they the Imperial Light Horse, the New South Wales Mounted Rifles or New Zealand Rough Riders.

What happened on campaign, however, was that the distinctions between these forms of troops eventually disappeared. Cavalry, their valuable, large and powerful horses destroyed by poor logistics and poor horse management, were, after the first months, unable to contrive to charge and thus use the *arme blanche*.[39] Regular mounted infantry, through the necessity of campaigning and the difficult process of on-the-job training, learnt how to ride and make use of mounted tactics rather than simply use their horses for mobility. Their title of infantry largely became token, and they took to the traditional light cavalry/mounted rifle/irregular tactics of patrolling, skirmishing, surprise attacks, and mounted fire and manoeuvre. Like the Boer enemy, all British and colonial mounted troops effectively became mounted riflemen for most of the war. After the war, the report of a royal commission into the war, the Elgin Commission, noted that 'there was no real distinction between the use of "Mounted Infantry" and "Mounted Rifles" and, in the later part of the war, the cavalry were armed and employed in much the same way'.[40]

Just as French's cavalry had manoeuvred around the Boers at Paardeberg so too had the mounted infantry and mounted rifles under Edward Hutton at Vet River when, in a long outflanking move, followed by an attack across the river, they restarted Roberts' advance on Bloemfontein. The value of mounted riflemen for the British Army was not so much their tactical model, however, but their sheer numbers.[41] The large increase in mounted troops required after Black Week, a need that the drives of the guerrilla war only amplified, could be adequately provided only by large numbers of hastily raised units made up mostly of men who had, until a few months previously, been civilians. Such men, with little military training, could not be brought up to the standards of regular cavalry but, reflecting contemporary ideas about citizen horse soldiers, they could be organised into the sort of rough military material that was good enough to patrol, skirmish with and harry an enemy who was, in many ways, much the same thing.

This rough military equation rather than tactical obsolescence saw traditional cavalry eclipsed. As noted above, cavalry had successfully charged Boers at Elandslaagte and at Klip Drift. They also did so successfully, led by Major-General French himself, against Boer riflemen at Zand River. At Diamond Hill 85 men of the 12th Lancers successfully charged uphill only to lose 16 of their number to flanking fire while rallying after the charge. Charges continued to be part of the war and were even used in a modified form by the Boers themselves towards the end of the war. Boer 'rifle charges' made no use of the *arme blanche* but usually consisted of an open-order charge towards their objective with men firing from the saddle. Typically they dismounted at close range and commenced a firefight, but on more than one occasion Boer horsemen rode into or through their British opponents.[42] One observer noted that British cavalry leaders eventually 'used to gallop any position [sic] with mounted troops in loosely extended order, and almost invariably with success'.[43] What was something of a revelation to cavalrymen was that they, using their firepower like mounted riflemen, could charge at a point, dismount there and hold ground.[44] By combining mounted and dismounted tactics, and more fire and manoeuvre, cavalry were developing greater tactical flexibility and learning new ways.

This flexibility, however, was usually undermined by the quality of the horses they were riding. Cavalry came to fight like mounted rifles not, as indicated above, so much because of tactical developments but because, after the first few months of the war, their horses were not up to the effort required of them. Despite the believed necessity, the decision to expand the number of mounted troops put a severe strain on an already creaky logistic system, and this, when combined with poor horsemastership and the general difficulty of trying to keep horses in a climate not suited to them, soon led to such horse casualties that the efficiency of all mounted troops was affected.

Most of the horses used by the British Army in South Africa, including those used by the Australian contingents, were imported for the war. Many of them were of excellent quality. British cavalry took their trained and groomed troop horses. The New South Wales Lancers drew their horses from the New South Wales Mounted Police, and they were probably as good as anything that came with the regular cavalrymen. Some officers of the New South Wales Mounted Rifles took their own, and their men had the best mounts that could be bought from men in the regiment at home.[45] It should be noted, however, that as the war progressed the Australian contingents found it increasingly difficult to get good horses at home.

Yet whatever their quality it was necessary for them to begin their war service by being transported by ship to South Africa. Life aboard ship could be treacherous for horses, and their introduction into a new climate proved to be a decidedly difficult process. Australian horses sent to India as part of the imperial remount trade required up to a year to recover from the voyage and acclimatise to their new surroundings, a process that required long, continuous and graduated exercise together with appropriate feeding.[46] That process was a luxurious peacetime one, but it was generally accepted in South Africa that at least two to three months acclimatisation was necessary and that four to six months was better.[47] No horse that either accompanied an Australian contingent or was sent as a remount ever received anything like this sort of treatment on arrival in South Africa. Horses sent with a contingent, like their riders, generally found themselves sent into operations at the first opportunity. The horses of the New South Wales Lancers despatched from Sydney were being used in action within a week of their arrival in 1899,[48] those of the 1st Australian Horse within five days of theirs.[49] The time allowed each contingent varied, but it was never enough for their mounts.

Thus disadvantaged from the start of their work in a new country, horses had little hope of dealing with the difficulties they would face. Perhaps the greatest of these challenges was finding enough to eat. The veld offered poor grazing, and the onus thus fell on the logistic system to provide enough horse fodder. The system was unable to cope, and as early as November 1899 British commanders were forced to cut horse rations in order to reduce the burden on the supply services and South Africa's relatively primitive rail system.[50]

Roberts' decision to dramatically increase the number of horsemen in his army thus proved to be a logistical gamble. It would provide him with the mobility he wanted, but the time for which it could be

Photo 6 As this photograph testifies, the British Army killed horses at a staggering rate in South Africa. The environment was not well suited to horses on campaign, but deep systemic faults in the army made a poor situation dire. Australian contingents proved just as lethal to their mounts as those from elsewhere in the empire. (AWM P00295.840)

maintained would be limited, and when his supplies ran out the effect on the mounted arm would be catastrophic. Captain John Antill of the New South Wales Mounted Rifles noted in a report to Sydney in February 1900 that, although the men were well fed, thanks to captured stock, the horses were restricted to six pounds (less than three kilograms) of mealies and six pounds of chaff each day. This, he believed, was good enough for the smaller local horses but was only about half what his large walers needed.[51] A month later he noted that this had been reduced to just four pounds of grain a day (less than two kilograms); the result being that the horses were 'becoming very weak and [there is] a good deal of loss from starvation, the grazing being very bad'.[52]

The demands of campaign on horses were considerable as they were required to work all day carrying rider, food and military equipment, and were expected to gallop if the situation demanded it. If a rider was required for night-time outpost duty, even this period of rest was denied to them. When in the horse lines they were usually tied so that the opportunity to stretch or lightly graze was also withheld.[53] Even if they could graze, it could not make up for the lack of regular feeding of more substantial fodder. For a horse to graze nearly six kilograms of grass as a substitute for grain took five hours of every day, and such spare time was not to be found on campaign.[54]

The decision to expand the mounted arm meant that well before the army reached Pretoria 'horse wastage', a term for equine death and debility, along with the generally poor condition of the horses, meant that the mounted forces were effectively collapsing. At Poplar Grove the two Boer presidents were able to escape the British Army because the cavalry were unable to get their horses up to the speed needed to conduct a pursuit. The change to a guerrilla war made it impossible to reorganise the remount and logistical system to address the problem as the need to keep columns on the move, often well away from the rail lifelines, militated against the necessary pause in operations. The result was that horses continued to die at staggering rates. It was not until late 1901 that the remount system was able to recover from the collapse of early 1900 and start to again provide useful horses to the army.[55]

Exacerbating this already dire situation was the fact that South Africa was an unhealthy place for horses. As mentioned, the grazing was poor and, in any case, most imported horses, not properly acclimatised, seemed to dislike the peculiar South African grass.[56] Some of the grazing was deadly, and Lieutenant Granville Ryrie, a New South Welshman with the Rhodesian Field Force, noted in a letter home that eight horses died in one night near Mafeking from eating a poisonous weed.[57] More dangerous was what one man described as the 'mysterious horse sickness'.[58] Now known to be an insect-borne viral disease, African horse sickness, spread by midges, is common in the African tropics and often spreads south into low-lying temperate regions during summer. After incubating for a few days, an infection of the lungs can kill a horse as quickly as half an hour after the first outward signs of infection.[59] With a mortality rate of 95 per cent for respiratory infections, such a disease could, and did, decimate a regiment's mounts with alarming rapidity. The chaplain with a New South Wales Bushmen contingent, James Green, wrote of the dangers for horses in one of their early camps in Rhodesia where water was 'within two feet of the surface [and] consequently it was very fever stricken'. There the 'dreaded horse sickness was common... Every morning a truck-load of dead horses was taken up the line to be burnt. Amongst these was the very best, which had been given to the Bushmen by their friends in Australia. Unfortunately my own horse died here before he had been used at all.'[60]

In a counter to these problems most units had a veterinary officer or two, and these men no doubt did much in difficult circumstances despite the fact that the support veterinary services were poorly organised.[61] Of more importance on a day-to-day basis was the individual and collective practice of horsemastership – the horse soldier's art of horse management, described by one historian as 'a mixture of country wisdom and veterinary science'.[62] Its routine covered everything from knowledge about saddling to rest, feeding, watering and load-carrying – all that was required to keep a horse alive and working well on campaign. A key practice was regularly getting off the horse and walking beside it so that its load was relieved. Horsemastership was a skill, however, that most British and colonial soldiers knew little about before they were committed to operations, and learning it thereafter proved difficult and costly in horseflesh.[63]

The net result was astounding equine death rates. A veterinary history of the war noted that in each month of 1901 the British Army in its entirety killed 11 600 horses and 1200 mules, and that another 41 400 were so sick, debilitated or tired as to be considered useless for military purposes. During the whole war the army took on about 520 000 horses and, with a death rate of nearly 67 per cent, destroyed 326 073 of them.[64] Although an inadequate logistic system, a rushed remount system and overwork were the root causes of it all, the general ignorance of horsemastership made matters far worse. It was generally held after the war that the regular cavalry regiments, thanks to limited pre-war training, maintained the best practices, but they were the best of a very bad lot. One regular regiment, the Inniskilling Dragoons, took on 4290 horses during its two and half years of active service and managed to expend 3750 through death, destruction, abandonment or return to the veterinary or remount services. The result was 'the equivalent to the whole regiment being rehorsed ten and a half times'.[65] Such figures were not exceptional, and the regular mounted infantry was worse. At least those

Photo 7 The result of equine death and debility on campaign was that most columns soon had to contend with many dismounted men, who were a hindrance to operations and an administrative headache. (AWM P00175.171)

who had been through the mounted infantry schools before the war could ride reasonably well, but the mass of improvised units could not, at least at first, and neither class were much good as horsemasters.[66] One such unit in 1901 received 1048 horses over a five-month period and at the end of it had only 43 fit for service.[67]

Nor was there any comfort to be drawn from the horse management skills of the colonial troops, including the Australians. Despite the idea that bushmen could take their civilian skills to war, Australians proved just as capable of destroying horseflesh as their imperial cousins. The Inspector-General of Remounts noted in early 1900 that 'the MI [mounted infantry] go through ponies at a fearful rate, colonial corps especially – 15 per cent has been the average per month so far'.[68] The Marquis of Tullibardine, who recruited many Australians for his unit, the Scottish Horse, noted: 'The Australian knew most about horses, but owing to their being accustomed to getting a large supply of horses in their own country were apt to use them up too quickly. Had they been less good horsemen they would have been better horsemasters, but the best Australians left nothing to be desired in this respect.'[69] Colonel Douglas Haig, Chief of Staff of the Cavalry Division, similarly believed that the 'over-sea Colonials were good horsemen, but bad horsemasters'.[70] His commander, Sir John French, agreed and noted how the squadron of the 1st Australian Horse was reduced to just ten fit horses after its first month of campaigning but that, during the same period, the squadrons of the regiment to which it was attached, the Scots Greys, had each kept at least 30 horses fit.[71] That the 1st Australian Horse had been in action so soon after landing may have skewed these figures, but certainly French was not impressed by Australian horsemastership.

James Green recalled how upon their arrival in Rhodesia one Bushman pointed to walking infantry and commented, '[We] couldn't do that; it would break our hearts.'[72] But to save their horses they should have been doing it regularly and, because they did not, they would eventually do a lot more walking than planned. Similarly one of the causes of dissatisfaction among the men of the 5th Victorian Mounted Rifles was orders requiring them to walk when horses with sore backs were found in their column.[73] Such orders were needed as, in just over a month's trekking in early 1901, this unit had reduced its number of fit horses from 1038 to just 450.[74] The surviving orders books of the Queensland Imperial Bushmen are replete with instructions trying to improve the treatment of the unit's horses. Men were told that sick horses had to be reported, that their mounts should be tied properly so that animals were not injured, that saddle fitting had to be checked and that grazing and feeding be properly conducted. But it was to no avail. Poor management and horse illness soon meant that the daily preoccupation of these orders books was how to administer an ever-growing number of dismounted men.[75]

Some, of course, were better than others. Captain John Antill of the New South Wales Mounted Rifles made his men get off their horses and walk up to a third of any given march they had to make.[76] Major George Lee of the New South Wales Lancers wrote home that, on reaching Pretoria in 1900, they still had about a dozen of their original horses with them. He believed that 'not many of the squadrons that started work at the same time as we did can say this'.[77] Attrition and the arrival of remounts soon meant that a unit's horses became a motley bunch. Percy Ricardo wrote to his son that the Queensland Mounted Infantry 'have got all sorts of horses now, ponies and draught horses and all colours, this is a frightful country for horses, the mules are the only thing that do well here'.[78] All big horses proved ultimately to be unsuited to South Africa as they ate too much and required too much work to keep them fit. By the end of the war the ones most desirable, and not incidentally the ones most likely to have survived thus far, were the small, compact ones, not dissimilar to what the Boers rode. It was small Australian horses, known locally as 'nuggets', not the big walers, that were considered the most useful Australian mounts, but they were not very common.[79]

Australians in the Boer War

Just as Australian soldiers in South Africa proved indifferent horsemasters, so too did their general military skills prove patchy. It became commonplace at the time – and the idea has continued – to express an opinion of the great value of colonial troops in South Africa. One New South Wales officer wrote to the military authorities in Sydney in early 1900: 'There seems to be a general opinion that our Colonial mounted men are the very class required. They appear to be able to fight the Boer with his own weapons. The Boer will not come into the open and have a straight fight. He changes position under cover and sits down and smokes and waits. When forced out he retires independently to another the range of which he has fixed.'[80] The same man believed that they were 'sadly in want of mounted troops, and are sighing for mounted rifles... I have worked my men up very well. Pity there is not 1000 of them.'[81] Both implicit and explicit in expressions of this sort were criticisms of regulars and a faith in the looser military model of the citizen soldiers of the British empire, Australia included. A few years after the war Colonel John Lyster, who had commanded Australians in South Africa, wrote of regular soldiers that they were 'pliable, and obedient machines', in which 'the cultivation of individuality, and intellectual training, has been overlooked'; something that, he believed, meant they were often to be found lacking on the battlefield.[82]

There is a strong sense of self-congratulation in utterances of this sort, but the supposed strength of Australia's mounted men rushed into military service was by no means completely mythological. As the Elgin Commission noted, many British officers spoke highly of their 'physique, intelligence, courage, instinct for country, and powers of individual action and initiative'.[83] But their value was often described as their military potential rather than what they actually achieved. Lord Roberts believed that if they could be better trained 'they would be still more valuable, for they are most valuable material'. Colonel Rimington, one of the most successful column commanders in South Africa, would have liked to 'take good Australians and make them into very good Cavalry in a month if one were allowed to work there in Australia; they are good horsemen'. It was generally noted, however, that their value increased after they had gained

Photo 8 Small horses, like the Cape pony this Australian soldier is astride, were widely regarded as being among the most desirable in South Africa. Although Australia supplied to the war exactly what the War Office wanted in terms of contingents, virtually all were beset with problems of inadequate training and inconsistent officer standards. (AWM P00492.005)

enough experience not to embarrass themselves. So poor was the military performance of some of the Imperial Yeomanry that it was joked that their abbreviation, IY, was said to stand for 'I'm yours', a reference to the supposed ease with which the more skilful Boer could capture them.[84] No Australian contingent was as poorly viewed as the British townsmen of the later Imperial Yeomanry contingents, but it was a common observation that all the specially raised mounted rifles corps took the better part of a year to become genuinely efficient, at which point they were usually lost to the army through their limited enlistments.[85]

A key criticism of the Australian contingents, particularly the later ones, was the virtually untrained nature of so many of their officers. The early contingents drew on the best of the permanent and militia officers each colony had at its disposal, but this small pool was quickly exhausted. Even with these men performances were inconsistent. Some, like Harry Chauvel of the Queensland Mounted Infantry, did well; others like the ex-Indian Army officer Henry Airey of the New South Wales Citizen Bushmen, did not.[86] Granville Ryrie wrote to his wife complaining of how his colonel, the New South Wales permanent officer Haviland Le Mesurier, was 'very weak... and afraid to say boo to any of those over him. It is very sickening to have to be under [him] when you know he is incapable of leading men...'[87] Even so Lieutenant-General Sir Ian Hamilton testified to the Elgin Commission on the 'difference between the first contingents under Colonially trained officers and the latter contingents which came out with untrained officers'.[88] In May 1900 Granville Ryrie was incredulous at news that there were more Australian contingents on the way: 'I don't believe it. I don't know where they are to get their officers from. I think we pretty well exhausted the supply.'[89] Senior officers remembered that the efficiency of colonial troops tended to improve greatly if they were attached to formations under the command of a regular officer.[90] Appointing virtually untrained men to command, of course, had its consequences as the Reverend James Green candidly admitted of his Bushmen contingent in which, with the 'exception of a small but efficient nucleus, his officers were civilians who had to learn everything military by experience, and in the face of the enemy'. The inevitable result, he noted, was that they had to learn their officering 'at the expense of the health and the lives of the men under their charge'.[91] Latter contingents often had officer appointments unfilled when they departed Australia so that men considered suitable and already serving in South Africa could fill them on arrival, although this source also often proved indifferent.[92]

Not coincidentally, those later contingents with such questionable leadership were often not as useful as the earlier ones with more qualified commanders. The early contingents drew heavily on the militia and volunteer regiments at home and, even if their skills were at times questionable and they were naive, at least they knew something of soldiering and approached their new duties with a certain amount of professional vigour under the command of men who had some idea of what they were doing. The latter contingents tended to recruit adventurers and opportunists, few of whom had much military experience. Although elementary training was conducted in camp in Australia, it was usually brief and, despite more work being done aboard ship across the Indian Ocean, there was usually little opportunity once in Africa to further hone individual and collective skills. Quickly sent into the field, the relatively undisciplined and untrained rankers, and undertrained and untried officers, were often not up to the task.[93]

This had its consequences in battle at places like Koster River where 300 Bushmen under Airey were clearly bested by the Boers, or at Wilmansrust where a squadron of the 5th Victorian Mounted Rifles was surprised and defeated at night by a commando.[94] More mundanely, it meant that such troops required constant supervision. The Queensland Imperial Bushmen had to appoint one officer and four men each day when on operations simply to pick up significant amounts of ammunition left by careless men in camp each night.[95] One similar camp inspection conducted by the NCOs of the same unit in 1902 collected four horses, three saddles, 23 pairs of spurs, a bandolier full of ammunition and 17 mess tins, among other things.[96] Such simple neglect did not augur well for military efficiency in more demanding circumstances.

Problems of this sort were never totally overcome, and even the quite well-organised units of the federally raised Australian Commonwealth Horse contingents of 1902 were similarly beset. Despite the large numbers of veterans who could be recruited, most of the men of these last units (three in four) were new to the military, and finding enough competent officers remained a problem.[97] These last units mostly arrived in South Africa too late to see the war, but they are worth noting because, in their organisation of about 500 men divided into four or four and a half squadrons of mounted riflemen, it is possible to see an organisational stepping-stone to the post-Federation light horse. This structure had been set out by Britain's War Office, and the colonial commandants had taken the first steps towards their creation, but from early 1902 the responsibility for their raising and despatch belonged to a man who had already had a marked influence on Australia's mounted troops, and who would soon have an even greater one, Edward Hutton.

The Australian military experience in South Africa was one of contradictions. What was seen by many as Australia's military niche, the citizen mounted soldier, was both vindicated and questioned. Tactically there was no doubt that mounted soldiers had proved to be the most useful form of troops during the war. Mounted riflemen had come to dominate operations on both sides of the conflict, and this fact would come to be used by advocates of this form of soldiering and fighting to support their case in the years ahead. That cavalry, too, had become mounted riflemen was seen by many as further proof that they were a military anachronism that should be drastically reformed or perhaps even abolished. Conversely, cavalry defenders and reformers would remember the successes they had, including the mounted ones, the tactical lessons they had learned and the logistic failures they had been forced to endure, and take a strongly differing view. Its sequel in Britain was to be a tempestuous process of cavalry reform that would last until the eve of the First World War. In Australia, too, it would have its consequences for the remaining cavalry units, although the results would be far less contested.

The outcome of the test of the ideas about bushmen as natural soldiers proved far more ambiguous. Despite the shortcomings of the undertrained Australian contingents, the idea that men could be taken from the farm or shop, given a rifle and a uniform, and be sent to fight was a persistent one and did not disappear with the end of the war. Upon returning home the New South Wales Mounted Rifleman John Antill told a crowd that 'in my opinion so long as we have men who are good riders and shooters we do not want any defence force at all... Teach them to ride and shoot, and that is all you want to do. That is all the Boer can do.'[98] Perhaps what made such mythology so persistent was that, like all good myths, it had some basis in fact. Despite all their shortcomings and difficulties the Australian contingents had, broadly speaking, been good enough to do what was required of them. For all the misgivings of British officers about the quality of the colonial troops, what the colonies and the new Federation sent to South Africa was exactly what the War Office had asked them to send. Australia's contingents were rough instruments, but in the end it was a colonial war with a colonial enemy, and such wars had often been fought with rough instruments.

Nevertheless it was clear that hastily raised mounted soldiers, including Australia's, had faced numerous problems in South Africa. Problems of poor training and discipline, severely exacerbated by poor officer standards, had shown anyone interested in investigating it that units made up of such material were not the most reliable of forces. Should the enemy be more determined or more militarily competent the consequences could be dire. Australian horsemastership had proven to be weak, and any future mounted force that the country raised would have to pay serious attention to this or its military value would prove to be merely a fraction of its potential. This was a problem not easily fixed, and definite organisational and training steps were needed as the corrective for Australia's forces as well as Britain's. Despite a common view that Australia's men had done what was required of them, and done it admirably, there were numerous officers who had seen their weaknesses and took a different view. Many of them would take steps in the next decade or so to ensure, even if with some difficulty, that the new Australian forces relied on more than mythology to shape their character. Yet, in part, because mounted riflemen had proved so valuable in South Africa, and because the man who would have charge of Australia's military in the next few years keenly supported them, mounted soldiers would come to assume a key position in the post-war Australian military. How that came to be so is the subject of the next chapter.

CHAPTER | 3

THE HUTTON ERA
Founding the light horse, 1901–05

While soldiers from Australia were still fighting in South Africa the six Australian colonies formed a new Federation on 1 January 1901, and the responsibility for defence passed to the new Commonwealth Government, then temporarily established in Melbourne, on 1 March 1901. In defence terms the key matter at hand was taking the disparate colonial military establishments and creating a new national force. A profound development in Australian military history, rather than the mere developmental stepping-stone it is sometimes portrayed as being, the ensuing years were to be ones of major change. For the mounted branch this would mean a period of remarkable reform as the colonial units were brought together under the direction of an officer who had long held views on the form and role of modern mounted troops.

Australia was, literally, on the far side of the world and a military backwater, so the government of Sir Edmund Barton had some trouble finding someone to take on the job of commanding its forces, but it eventually announced in December 1901 that Sir Edward Hutton, the British officer who had commanded the New South Wales forces in 1893–95, then commanded Australians and other colonials in the Mounted Infantry Brigade in South Africa, had accepted the appointment of General Officer Commanding of the Military Forces of the Commonwealth of Australia.[1] Hutton arrived in Australia in January 1902 and, moving quickly, presented his plans to the government the following April in his *Minute Upon the Defence of Australia*. In strategic terms he reiterated what British military men had largely been telling the colonies for decades; that is, that with the Royal Navy on side and being geographically remote there was not much chance of a major attack by a foreign power. Similarly Hutton also noted there was always the possibility that one of Britain's enemies might launch a raid or, if the Royal Navy was tied up somewhere else, might try something more serious with some warships and a landing force. Where he did differ from his predecessors was in advancing the ambitious idea that perhaps Australia should also prepare itself to defend its 'interests', even if they might be found outside Australia's waters.[2]

With these two matters in mind Hutton intended that the nation's nascent army (although it was not called that) would have three elements. As before Federation, there would be few regulars and the Permanent Force, as it was titled, was to hold just a few technical troops, such as the garrison gunners and submarine miners, as well as the instructional and administrative cadre that would oversee the part-paid militia and unpaid volunteers who would make up of the bulk of the military. The more numerous part-time soldiers were to be split. First were the mostly unpaid volunteers of the Garrison Force, which would be responsible for defending the 'strategical centres and places of commercial importance'; that is, the capital cities and selected ports. More numerous and important was the part-paid militia Field Force, which was intended to be highly mobile, well trained and prepared to move to threatened areas to engage the enemy wherever they might appear. It was this which, Hutton intended, could also be embarked and used to defend Australia's 'interests' should it be necessary.[3]

The Garrison Force, being tied to the defences of cities and ports, had little requirement for mounted troops, and Sydney was allocated just two half-squadrons; the other stations would have to make do with just one each.[4] The mobility required of the Field Force meant that a very high proportion of it would be made up of mounted troops. The full force was to be nine brigades strong at war establishment (26 019 men), but only three of these were to be infantry (15 534 men), and the remaining six brigades (10 485 men) were to be made up of mounted troops. By traditional military standards this was a high proportion of mounted men, but Hutton justified it on the grounds of the recent experiences in South Africa, a war that he believed any Australian campaign would be likely to resemble.[5] Like the mounted brigade he formed in New South Wales in the 1890s, these new brigades were to be well-rounded, self-sufficient combined arms forces that included artillery, engineer and service branches. The intention was that the Field Force, or a component of virtually any size drawn from it, could operate independently or in concert to counter

Photo 9 Major-General Sir Edward Hutton had a deep interest in mounted troops, which reflected his experiences with Britain's mounted infantry at home and on colonial campaigns. The establishment of the light horse, although reflecting wider imperial and local thinking, was in many ways due to him. (AWM P03875.002)

any enemy incursion or attack on Australian interests.[6] Its units were to be organised on a cadre basis and, during peacetime, would have nearly their full complement of officers and non-commissioned officers but only half the necessary other ranks. This fulfilled what was always the government's paramount requirement, that of keep defence spending as low as possible, but it was rationalised that on mobilisation the cadre of trained and experienced men, stiffened with the few permanent soldiers, could quickly bring new drafts of recruits up to the necessary standard.[7]

Hutton's plans, as evidenced by his desire to defend the nation's 'interests', had in part been motivated by a desire for Australia to contribute to the empire's defence. The calls for Australia to make a military commitment to the empire, which had been common in the late 1890s, had not abated with Federation or the Boer War. Lord Brassey, who had called for an Australian mounted regiment to be raised for imperial service when he was Governor of Victoria, had continued with more of the same in the House of Lords after returning home.[8] In 1901 the Colonial Defence Committee had also been hoping that Australia might do something along the same lines and, when it saw Hutton's plans for a Field Force, concluded that it could be designed only for potential imperial use. The Australian Government was not of Hutton's, Brassey's or London's mind, however, and at the Imperial Conference of 1902 the Prime Minister, Sir Edmund Barton, quickly told London that, although Australia could be counted on in an emergency, earmarking any Australian force for imperial use was contrary to the principles of self-government so recently attained. When the *Defence Act 1903* was finally passed it made it clear that none of Australia's citizen soldiers could serve outside the nation's boundaries unless they specifically volunteered.[9] This foiled Hutton's plans, but he had little choice except to accept the decision and continue preparing for continental defence.

Apart from his imperial intentions, Hutton's scheme had differed little in principle from the plans first put forward by Major-General Edwards in 1890 and which the various colonial commandants, including Hutton in New South Wales, had loosely pursued as policy throughout the 1890s.[10] Still, whereas Edwards had merely proposed the creation of formations that could be employed anywhere throughout the country, Hutton would have to try to create such a force, and this challenging process would take up much of the following years.

The mounted forces that Hutton inherited from the pre-Federation colonies, despite being established along widely varying lines, were not very different in kind from the forces he had seen when he had served in New South Wales, although they were presently far more numerous.[11] Just as the wars and scares of the nineteenth century had caused men to flock to the colours of the citizen regiments, so too had the recent war in South Africa. Because that war had been fought largely by mounted men Australia's horsed regiments had also proven very popular, both with the men who were keen to enlist and with the governments that maintained them.[12] Western Australia, having struggled with a number of small and unsuccessful mounted corps through the 1890s, raised a new mounted detachment at Bunbury in 1900 that soon formed the basis of the Western Australian Mounted Infantry.[13] The local commandant thought it 'eminently suited to the country', and by mid-1901 it had 300 men on the books, easily making it the most successful mounted corps in the colony's history.[14] Tasmania, without any mounted corps since 1883, had gazetted the Tasmanian Mounted Infantry four weeks after despatching its first troops to South Africa in 1899.[15] It was not all that might have been hoped for, however, as in mid-1901 it had only 137 men on strength, despite being authorised to have more than twice as many.[16] An attempt to raise a detachment in the colony's north in 1900 had failed completely owing to its not being able to gather any local support.[17] South Australia had expanded its mounted arm and nearly doubled the establishment of the South Australian Mounted Rifles between 1898 and 1902 (and was the only colony to match the expansion of its mounted troops with one for the infantry).[18]

In Queensland the clamour to join the horsed arm was so great that the Queensland Mounted Infantry had to be thoroughly reorganised to accommodate the opportunity presented to it, resulting in an expansion of the establishment from 619 men in 1898 to nearly 1200 men in 1901.[19] The value of this organisation was such, and the recent example of South Africa so persuasive, that in late 1899 Queensland went out of its way to cancel the appointment of a new imperial officer as its colonial commandant and requested instead the services of a cavalry officer. In doing so Queensland's representative in London asked the Colonial Office to consider that the mounted infantry were 'not only the most important, but the most popular branch of the service', got the best recruits and, 'as recent events are proving[,] are the most suitable auxiliary forces for the defence of the Empire'.[20] For their trouble they received Colonel Henry Finn, late of the 21st Lancers.

In Victoria the expansion was more modest. The government there had been inundated with more than 60 applications to form new mounted corps in late 1899 and early 1900, but the Victorian Mounted Rifles was limited to expanding it ranks by 250 men, enough for one new company and a fleshing out of the others.[21] To channel popular martial energies the government tried to encourage the men left out to join the curious experiment of what were described as un-uniformed 'Mounted Rifle Clubs', which required government funding only for their rifles.[22] Still, the two battalions of the regiment could together maintain more than 1100 men on their books, and it remained one of the most successful mounted units in the country.

More anomalous was its cousin, the Melbourne Cavalry, a small corps of less than 50 men, which had been raised in 1901. Its most noteworthy aspect was the way it had been formed, which perhaps constitutes the most remarkable episode of buck-passing in Australian military history. Although the corps had first been suggested to the Victorian Government in 1900, it was not until 28 February 1901, *the day before* all pre-Federation forces would become part of the new Commonwealth Military Forces, that a deputation from the proposed unit managed to arrange a meeting between themselves and the Victorian Minister for Defence. At that meeting the minister, displaying plenty of care but little responsibility, and apparently ignoring the advice of senior officers, agreed to their idea and later that day facilitated the passing of an order in council authorising the corps' establishment.[23] The new Commonwealth Government thus found itself, the next day, in possession of a small, marginal military organisation with fewer than 50 soldiers and no administrative authorisation or support other than a hastily organised order from a government that had released its defence responsibilities within 24 hours of passing that order! When he arrived Hutton was, not surprisingly, unimpressed, noting that it was 'of little military value'.[24]

New South Wales had continued the maintenance of its lancer and mounted rifles regiments throughout the Boer War. The 1st Australian Horse, having been raised as a volunteer regiment, had been converted to part-paid troops in 1900 and remained under the command of the state parliamentarian and invasion novelist James Kenneth Mackay. Aside from the small Melbourne Cavalry, the New South Wales Lancers and the 1st Australian Horse were the only colonial mounted units established as traditional cavalry equipped with the *arme blanche*. New South Wales's two cavalry regiments also benefited from the enthusiasm brought on by the Boer War, and the lancers had their establishment raised from 428 men in 1898 to 678 by 1902; the 1st Australian Horse had been allowed 628 men in 1900. The New South Wales Mounted Rifles was perhaps the only major colonial unit not to benefit from the Boer War. In 1902 its commanding officer had noted a degree of demoralisation in the regiment owing to recruiting and promotion limits placed on it while the new Commonwealth system was being introduced, something that, he felt, exacerbated earlier 'disorganisation' in the unit when many of its officers and best men had been absent in South Africa.[25] Perhaps this was the reason why, despite the authorised expansion elsewhere, the regiment was restricted to an establishment of just over 400 men throughout the entire Boer War period.[26]

Photo 10 Hutton inherited from the six colonies a disparate range of mounted units. This trooper was from the 1st Australian Horse, a cavalry unit in New South Wales. This colony was the only one to maintain cavalry units of any size, and there was considerable disquiet from the regiments about their conversion to light horse. (AWM 01890.001)

Reflecting its experiment in 1888, the New South Wales Government had also gazetted an instructional corps, known as the Permanent Cavalry, in mid-1900. It did not last long, however, and was disbanded in December 1901.[27] Similarly the Border Scouts, a small unit raised along the Queensland–New South Wales border solely for the purpose of scouting, was gazetted in January 1901 and had a commanding officer nominated in April the following year, but did not survive the coming military reforms.[28]

Aside from these differing colonial organisational models, there were also considerable differences in regard to the conditions under which the men in the various colonies served. All mounted troops in New South Wales were paid for the time they spent in uniform, and a private soldier in the lancers could receive up to £6 annually for his service

Table 3.1 Strength of the mounted troops of the Commonwealth (inherited from the six colonies), 1 July 1901

		NSW	Vic	Qld	SA	WA	Tas
Cavalry	Part-paid & permanent	1269	–	–	–	–	–
	Unpaid volunteer	–	55	–	–	–	–
Mounted rifles/ infantry	Part-paid & permanent	430	12	1185	728	–	–
	Unpaid volunteer	50	1132	–	–	449	137
State totals		1749	1199	1185	728	449	137
Total		5447					

Source: Strength of the Commonwealth Forces, 1 July 1901, Federal Military Committee, 1901, NAA B168, 1901/4532.

with another £2 horse allowance paid to those deemed efficient. A lieutenant of the same regiment received £15 annually plus an uncommonly generous £52 horse allowance.[29] In Queensland a private, if he attended all his scheduled training commitments, received £6.10.0 in base pay, £1.2.0 of uniform allowance and an additional £3.15.0 in horse allowance.[30] South Australia's soldiers also received pay in compensation for their time, but to their east the Melbourne Cavalry and Victorian Mounted Rifles got virtually nothing from the government aside from some of their military equipment (excluding horses or saddlery) and uniforms.[31] Tasmania's and Western Australia's newly raised mounted troops also defended their colony *gratis*.[32]

The attention and resources allocated to defence forces in general also varied widely from colony to colony. For example New South Wales was willing to spend nearly £24 for each soldier in its forces *per annum* in 1901, but Tasmania spent only just over £7.[33] Victoria's defence budget was the largest of all the colonies in 1900–01 with an annual expenditure of £244 747, but with that sum the government chose to maintain only 6657 men in uniform (of whom only about 2500 were permanent soldiers or part-paid militia) alongside a further 21 000 in un-uniformed rifle clubs. In contrast New South Wales spent £232 821 in 1900–01 to keep 9905 men in uniform (more than two-thirds of whom were paid), but decided to maintain only 1908 men in rifle clubs.[34] Policy decisions such as these meant that the numbers, and (as will be seen) the quality, of mounted troops contributed by each of the colonies to the new federal mounted forces would, in most cases, be very different. That the larger and more populous colonies would necessarily provide many more was not, however, a given. Queensland, with far fewer economic and population resources, was able to provide nearly as many mounted troops to the Commonwealth as Victoria (see table 3.1).

To the forge

How these pre-Federation mounted forces would be integrated into the new army organisation quickly became clear. As Hutton's plans were being formulated there were calls for Australia to maintain more than one type of mounted troops, and at least one journalist with connections to the cavalry advocated the raising of a third cavalry regiment in New South Wales so that a complete brigade could be maintained there.[35] Australia's first Minister for Defence, Sir John Forrest, did not favour this course and – probably with regularity and economy at the forefront of his mind – he had written to Hutton asking for advice on the practicability of there being just 'one uniform organisation and equipment for Mounted Troops in Australia'.[36] In considering what form Australia's mounted troops should take there were several factors at play. First, there was an imperial aspect. Following the war in South Africa, and what was seen to be the relative performance of mounted rifle over cavalry units, there followed an empire-wide movement that did away with citizen soldier cavalry units and replaced them with mounted rifles. In Britain the yeomanry, after decades of resistance, were forced to discard their swords and apply themselves to rifle training, while much the same happened in Canada and New Zealand.[37] Second, and related to the first idea, there was the long-standing principle, which was well understood in Australia before Federation, that it took far less training to create an effective mounted rifleman than it did to create a cavalryman. Thus it was widely believed that part-time citizen horse-soldiers were more suited to being trained as mounted rifles.[38]

The third factor was Hutton's own views and, as a long-standing proponent of mounted infantry and mounted rifles theories, he had certainly formed a strong view that the war in South Africa had highlighted the power of the rifle in modern war, particularly in the hands of non-regular soldiers.[39] Similarly he was dismissive of the idea that traditional cavalry armed with the *arme blanche* would easily defeat mounted troops intent on using firepower, and it was his view that 'success in the next great European struggle will belong to that nation which first adopts the principle of mobile fire power'.[40] Always a studied and regular contributor to service journals and the like, he had written an article in 1901 extolling the virtues of the mounted rifles and mounted infantry that had served the empire in South Africa and called for increases to the mounted infantry schools in Britain as well as the official establishment of three regular mounted rifle regiments, as part of the cavalry, for the purposes of training Britain's yeomanry and the empire's colonial mounted corps.[41] In Australia he soon published a small book in which, apart from expounding on his other interest of imperial defence cooperation, he reiterated his thinking on the central importance of rifle-equipped mounted troops backed by adequate artillery and support troops in Australia's defence.[42]

Hutton was not necessarily dismissive of modernised cavalry that could use either mounted or dismounted attacks as the situation demanded, and he rejected as 'enthusiasts' those who argued for the replacement of well-trained regular cavalry with rifle-equipped mounted men, even if the latter might form a valuable adjunct to the former.[43] When commandant in New South Wales Hutton had seen a place for cavalry and had been generally supportive of the lancer regiment, even if he did encourage them to pay more attention to their carbines. His public pronouncements and articles before the Boer War had always made the proviso that the *arme blanche* should not be done away with entirely. Upon hearing of Field Marshal Lord Roberts's March 1903 order for the lance to be abolished as a weapon in the British Army (it was restricted to ceremonial functions, but the decision was reversed after Roberts' tenure as Commander-in-Chief), Hutton wrote to Roberts asking that the Australian lancers be able to continue using it: 'The essential element however in the case of the Australian Militia Cavalry is that the retention of the lance establishes the principle, hitherto not recognised by Australian mounted men, that our ... Regiments must be prepared to charge and close with the enemy whether armed with a lance or a pistol.'[44]

What happened to this sentiment is not clear, but there is no evidence that Hutton followed through with this and attempted to ensure a continuation of the lance as a weapon in Australia, at least in peacetime. It was not proscribed completely, and soon manuals, as well as provisional regulations issued in 1904, allowed it for ceremonial use and mentioned that the lance and pistol were to be considered secondary wartime weapons that 'will be hereafter specified for certain corps'.[45]

Although Hutton would continue to pursue the pistol for his mounted troops (reflecting a contemporary idea that a pistol could be used in a charge), he does not seem to have persisted with the lance. It seems probable that the minister's desire for regularity and economy militated against the idea of continuing with the lance and – given Hutton's attitudes to mounted riflemen, the training limitations of a militia system and the imperial trend of encouraging the rifle at the expense of the *arme blanche* – that the idea was simply abandoned. Whatever the reasons, Hutton soon ensured that the new mounted units of the Commonwealth Military Forces, christened the Australian Light Horse, would be raised based on his own long-prepared mounted rifle template.

When Hutton had conceived this new title for the Australian mounted arm is not clear, but he communicated his desire to use it in a minute in late-March 1902, not long after his arrival in Melbourne.[46] 'Light horse' was not a new name by any means. A number of pre-Federation Australian corps had used the term in their title, the Queensland Light Horse and the Prince of Wales's Light Horse Hussars being just two examples. Nor was it a particularly Australian appellation. The Imperial Light Horse and South African Light Horse had been two well-known units in South Africa, and some of Britain's volunteer mounted units of the mid-1800s had used the title of Light Horse Volunteers.[47] The American Confederate General Robert E. Lee's father had carried the nickname of Harry 'Light Horse' Lee after his association with a mounted body in the American Revolution. Although not a common title, it had been used regularly enough for it to have an increasing association with the 'irregulars' of mounted rifle units and, more generally, light cavalry, which had long performed the roles of reconnaissance, screening, foraging, patrolling and protecting communications. Not coincidentally, activities of these types had taken up much of the time of mounted riflemen in South Africa and, apart from a vision of grand strategic mounted raids and turning movements, this was much the role that Hutton had in mind for the new Australian mounted force. Later that decade one Australian officer highlighted the lineage and the light horse's form, writing that Hutton 'always held that the irregular horsemen of Australia were capable of, and would have to perform, duties of more extended nature than those within the power of Mounted Infantry, and he gave them, therefore, the title of Light Horse'.[48]

As this quote highlights, the light horse were not to be mounted infantry but a form of cavalry differing only in their lack of a bladed weapon that could be used from horseback, the archetypal mounted riflemen that Hutton had long been promoting. If used in the defence of Australia they were a replacement for cavalry; if used imperially they could be either a replacement for, or an auxiliary to, regular cavalry.[49] The infantry organisational terms of company or battalion used for the mounted troops in some colonies before Federation were banished for the light horse, and they were now to be organised into the traditional cavalry bodies of squadrons and regiments. Anyone holding the

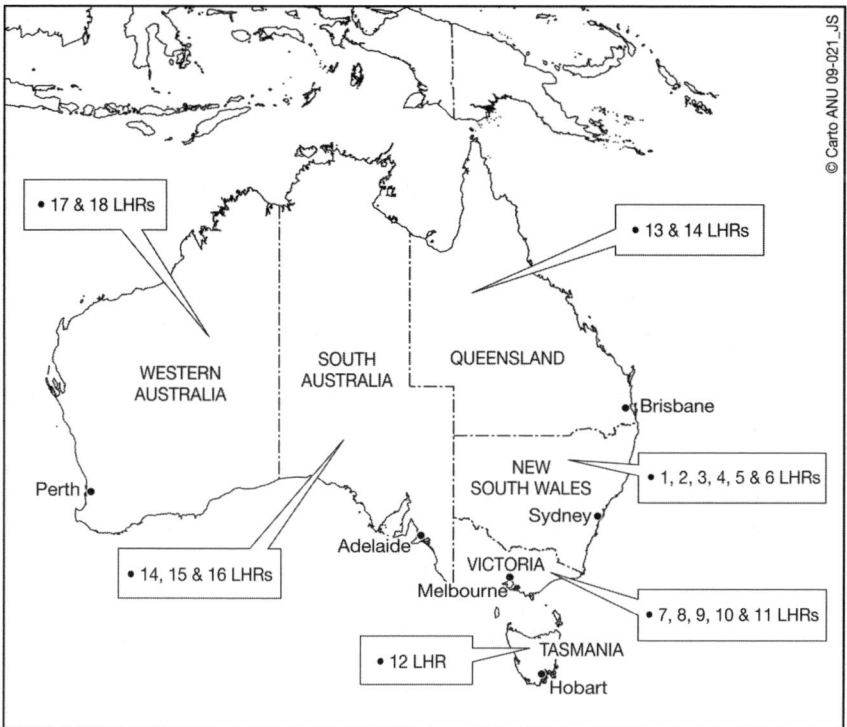

Map 2 Distribution of light horse regiments, 1903

appointment of bugler now found themselves given the cavalry rank of trumpeter. Although large by British standards, at four instead of three squadrons, light horse regiments were still only just over half the size of a new Australian infantry regiment (later battalion).[50]

These mounted regiments were all to be partially paid, even the half squadrons of the largely volunteer Garrison Force, and were established on a regional basis. The squadron was to be the basic 'tactical and administrative unit, capable of independent service at all times'. These were further divided into four troops, again required to be able to serve independently, and these troops then divided into sections of four men (a now well-established basic organisational building block for rifle-equipped horsemen).[51] Under the scheme troops were to be recruited in the same locality with the intention that the bonds of community would be replicated on the battlefield.[52] In peacetime, regiments could be commanded by either a major or a lieutenant-colonel, but if war broke out regimental command would go to a lieutenant-colonel. A commensurate arrangement was made for captains and majors as squadron commanders.[53]

Regimental and permanent instructional staffs were intended to guide and assist, but not interfere unnecessarily with a unit's day-to-day operation. Decentralisation and the pushing of responsibilities down the ranks were intended to foster individual action and the independence of thought of commanders.[54]

Officers and non-commissioned officers were to exercise these responsibilities at least 16 days per year, which was the annual training requirement for the light horse, infantry and most supporting arms except for the artillery and engineers, who would do more.[55] While city units, mostly infantrymen, would do much of their training at night and at weekends, those in the country, effectively most of the light horse, were expected to conduct their training mainly in continuous periods, and one eight-day continuous camp per year was prescribed. The remaining time was to be broken up into a series of whole-day and part-day parades conducted in local areas where nothing greater than squadron concentration, if that, was to be expected. Musketry courses and an annual inspection by the relevant state commandant were also part of the calendar.[56] To foster the skills of the officers Hutton instituted 'Schools of Instruction' for all branches of the service and saw that passing examination for promotion was made a requirement for advancement. Also introduced was a system of 'Staff Rides upon Field Conditions' that required officers to consider and provide solutions to tactical problems presented to them in the field.[57]

To provide the guidance for this training Hutton had printed in late 1902 a new training manual for mounted troops. His *Mounted Service Manual for Mounted Troops of the Australian Commonwealth* was based on a manual he had prepared for the yeomanry in Britain the year before, which was in turn 'to all intents and purposes a revised edition' of the 1895 manual of which he had overseen production in Australia.[58] The manual had been modified for use in Britain, somewhat to Hutton's disgust, but he found no impediment to its publication in Australia.[59] With fire action at the centre of his thinking, Hutton believed that the preliminaries of 'every skirmish and every engagement' had to depend on the actions of mounted troops and that those mounted troops must be trained to fight on foot with the rifle. He did not completely dismiss the role of *arme blanche*–carrying cavalry but asserted that their opportunities would be limited and implied that their effective use required a high level of training beyond the capabilities of Australia's part-time soldiers. He attached great importance to 'strategical' operations that would see mounted troops organised as self-sufficient all-arms formations striking at an enemy's flanks, rear or lines of communication. These troops had to be a 'complete fighting unit and be capable of dealing in dismounted action with an enemy's infantry in a manner which no cavalry, organised and trained as modern European cavalry, can ever hope to do'.[60] By definition these troops had to be mounted riflemen or mounted infantry in a formation organised along the lines of the Field Force brigades.

Aside from the cavalry-styled mounted riflemen of the light horse, the manual did note a place for mounted infantry in Australia, and it is clear that Hutton saw the infantry brigades of the Field Force as equally suitable for either traditional dismounted use or use as mounted infantry.[61] His manual was also published under the alternative title of *Mounted Service Manual for Australian Light Horse and Mounted Infantry* and, although it may have been in use earlier, in 1904 the manual (under one or both of its titles) was issued to selected companies of the Field Force infantry regiments.[62]

The necessity to adopt drill suited to men on horses reportedly caused some dismay among town-based infantry who suddenly had to imagine the presence of horses in their ranks.[63] Hutton was, however, clear that the two forms of mounted troops were distinct in their nature and military roles. Mounted infantry was limited in its conception and characterised merely as normal infantry 'temporarily provided with increased means of mobility or rapid locomotion'. They were not true horsemen, simply infantry with extra mounted training, and their duties were no different from their duties when dismounted. Although intended to be made up from the best-shooting, hardiest and smartest troops in the infantry, and suitable for use either as the small mounted component of a largely dismounted infantry force or for concentration as a large mounted infantry body, their utility outside their assigned role was limited. He stressed that they could be used for more demanding, light horse–type tasks only '*after prolonged training and practice in the field*'. Alternatively, the mounted riflemen of the light horse had to be 'daring and bold horsemen' who possessed the 'cohesion and individuality which are only begotten of a sound organisation and of true discipline'. As a type of cavalry they were tasked with fighting on foot as required in the offence and defence, the performance of reconnaissance and screening duties, as well as to provide protection from surprise for all bodies of troops.[64]

MUTTERINGS IN THE RANKS

With the defence scheme formulated and the mould for the light horse made, there remained the job of actually creating the regiments and brigades that would play such an important role in Australia's defence. In his *Minute* Hutton had pointed out that the large proportion of mounted troops required by his scheme meant that a significant number of country-based infantry units would have to be converted into light horse. Hutton was not concerned at such a change, believing that it was 'consistent with the characteristics of the Australian people' recently highlighted in South Africa.[65] In pure defence terms it was hardly controversial, given the lessons of South Africa and the military tenor of the time. In terms of the Australian character, however, Hutton, was tapping into the long-evident belief that men from the bush made excellent natural material for horse soldiering. One journalist and recent war correspondent thought Hutton was on the right track, believing that converting country infantry units would be easy, given that most country men owned horses anyway and rode them into town to attend their infantry parades.[66]

Not everyone was so convinced that Australian horsemen were martial wonders, however. The New South Wales senator, defence pundit and volunteer infantry lieutenant-colonel J.C. Neild bemoaned what he called 'Horsetralia' and the advocates of 'gallop and shoot': '[T]he people of Australia have now an ingrained belief that an Australian, astride anything with four legs, is, if possessed of a rifle and a pillow case full of cartridges, a match for an indefinite number of the best trained soldiers of any nation under heaven. This unhappy mania is shared and propagated by Members of Parliament and Ministers of the Crown.'[67]

This was perceptive, but Neild's views were of little consequence and Hutton's changes would go ahead. They would have the greatest effect on Victoria and New South Wales as they had to support two light horse brigades each, which was considerably more than the roughly one brigade of mounted troops that each had maintained before Federation.[68] In New South Wales the plan was to reduce the number of companies in the infantry regiments, then convert the surplus infantrymen in the remoter country areas. In Victoria the scheme called for the conversion of much of an unpaid volunteer infantry regiment based in rural centres, the Victorian Rangers. One of its detachments had already applied to become a mounted one and, because many of the rangers had already served mounted in South Africa, Hutton was sure this conversion in particular would be successful.[69] This view proved to be unduly sanguine, however, and the conversion process became a fraught one – not everyone wanted to be a light-horseman.

In Victoria the change began in July 1903 when the affected infantry company commanders received orders to disband their commands and ask their men to enrol in the light horse regiments now being raised in their place. Particular opposition to this change was heard from the ranger detachments at Echuca and Kerang, where the men were not of the opinion that the pay of a light horse soldier, at £7.8.0 a year, was much compensation for the costs of owning a horse and, while other detachments contentedly signed up for the mounted branch, these two did not.[70] By September the *Kerang Times* had taken up the cause, and the local member had spoken on their behalf in the Commonwealth parliament.[71] During a visit to the area the new Minister for Defence, James Drake, heard complaints that the conversion, particularly the financial impost of owning horses, was unfair to men who had already rendered effective service as infantry and who wished to continue to do so. In the end their objections paid off, the minister was sympathetic and, after some resistance, Hutton was forced to relent and allow these two companies to continue as infantry, but it was not the only trouble spot.[72]

The Echuca company had been earmarked for conversion partly because it was isolated from other companies of the regiment and was far from its wartime concentration place in Melbourne. In New South Wales an infantry company in Cooma was in a similar position, being more than 400 kilometres from its concentration point in Sydney. Lacking a qualified commander and with few of its soldiers judged efficient, it was planned to combine its men with existing detachments of the 1st Australian Horse in the Monaro region to form a new light horse squadron. Once again, however, the affected men did not seem to be impressed, and local politicians and press became animated in their defence. The *Cooma Express*, giving the affair a democratic bent, cried that it was an effort by the 'Aristocratic Hutton' to favour the elites in the cavalry over ordinary working men. Once more the crux of the matter was whether men who were serving in infantry units were able or willing to afford the purchase and maintenance of horseflesh in order to continue soldiering. Despite the complaints the Cooma company was disbanded, but 30 to 40 of its men put their names forward to join the light horse, of whom about 20 actually took the step of buying horses.[73] Unfortunately for many of them, the officer commanding the light horse squadron, Major Granville Ryrie, an ex-officer of the 1st Australian Horse and Boer War veteran, had more applicants from the full squadron area than he needed and was hence able to judge some of the Cooma men as unsuitable. Moreover in Sydney the state commandant, Brigadier-General Henry Finn, was worried that, although two were needed, only one suitable troop leader could be found in Cooma.[74] In the end, and despite further loud complaints, Ryrie accepted only one troop's worth of men from Cooma, all from the

Photo 11 There was much reform and change during Hutton's tenure, and one of the ways to keep the sometimes unhappy regiments more content was to recognise their traditions. This, the proposed full dress uniform of a trooper in a descendant unit of the New South Wales Lancers, includes adornments that most other units would not have worn. (AWM A05617)

original infantry company, and established the other troop in Bredbo, which seemed to have some promising candidates.[75]

It was not only remote infantry companies that were unhappy with conversions. Disquiet was also heard about Hutton's plans from the cavalry units of New South Wales and from the small Melbourne Cavalry. The Melbourne Cavalry became fractious in June 1903 when it had aired complaints in the *Age* about delays in confirming the unit's officer appointments. The newspaper reported that the corps had 'not merely [been] neglected but snubbed' and 'discouraged to the point of disbanding'.[76] The delay was really just an example of the bureaucratic hold-ups that came with implementing the new Commonwealth scheme, but Hutton, ever one for military propriety, pointedly noted the unit's unorthodox creation and contended that it 'could only end in discontent and irregularity among the personnel of the detachment'.[77] Not to be dissuaded from expressing their views, however, the Melbourne Cavalry's commander then wrote to the military authorities the following month outlining the corps' ambitions. Aside from continuing their complaint about officer appointments they also expressed a desire to remain cavalry, to remain volunteers, to remain 'under their own distinct command' and to expand the size of the unit to more than 70 members.[78] The minister wondered whether, as the small corps were already in existence and were willing to continue as unpaid volunteers, then perhaps their wishes might be accommodated.[79] Victoria's commandant disagreed and rightly pointed out that doing so would create a unit that effectively existed outside the whole scheme of organisation.[80] Evidently irritated by the whole affair, Hutton held much the same opinion, and he brought the episode to an end by slating the unit for inclusion in the local Garrison Force, where they would neither be cavalry, under their distinct command, nor volunteers, although they could keep their old uniforms and their old unit name as a subtitle for the time being.[81] The minister was somewhat dismayed that instead of getting a free squadron of cavalry he now had another partially paid light horse squadron to fund, but the matter rested there.[82]

The Melbourne Cavalry's desire to continue serving as cavalry was echoed loudly across the border in New South Wales. There the lancer regiment was unhappy about a number of things. Partly they were concerned about the change in title to light horse and the fact that the regiment was to be split to facilitate the creation of two mounted brigades in the state, but loud concerns were also aired about their armament.[83] The regiment's commander, the prominent Sydney businessman Colonel James

Burns, expressed his strong views on these matters to Hutton in 1902 and wrote to his officers expressing his hope that they would be able to 'follow the English lancer regiments in the carrying of the rifle' in a bucket on the saddle, thus allowing the lance to be carried in hand, which would then allow its members to 'loyally adhere to the regiment' to which they belonged.[84]

The lancers and the sword-carrying 1st Australian Horse found public support for their cause from a number of sources. The imperial cavalryman Henry Finn, Queensland's last commandant, who had stayed on in Australia after Federation, apparently expressed his views in support of the lance in some quarters, although how influential he was is not clear.[85] Other support came from the same journalist who had advocated the maintenance of a separate cavalry brigade in New South Wales. Frank Wilkinson, picking up on the anti-cavalry sentiments expressed during the Boer War, produced a small history of the two New South Wales cavalry regiments in 1901 that defended the military utility of cavalry. He attacked those who had come to the 'unsound conclusion that because Cavalry – *qua* Cavalry – have not been a pronounced success in this campaign, therefore the days of Cavalry are numbered... as though one could transplant the kopjes of South Africa to all future battlefields'. Repeating a then popular refrain among pro-cavalry polemicists, he argued that any form of mounted soldier without a sword or lance would quickly find himself at the mercy of traditional European cavalry.[86]

Not everyone was of the same mind. The leader of the Labor opposition, John Watson, derided the lancer regiment in parliament, wondering why they were allowed to 'prance around in fine uniforms with a pig-sticking instrument on their arm'? When informed by Forrest that Finn, who had been with the 21st Lancers in their charge at Omdurman in the Sudan in September 1899, thought the lance very useful, Watson continued that that might have been all very well against 'the black fellows whom the British had to fight there', but it would be 'very different from fighting the white people whom we might expect to invade us, and who would not be foolish enough [to] allow us to stick them with lances'. He then suggested that Hutton's dictums on rifle-equipped mounted troops seemed the most sensible.[87] By the end of 1902 it was clear even to the lancers that, despite Hutton's contemplation of retaining the lance, that they were not going to get their way and it was decided that the light horse were to carry their rifles slung on their backs, being allowed their lances only for ceremonial occasions and perhaps if a war broke out.[88] Some seem to have taken the decision with more equanimity than others, and one historian has claimed that the lancer half-squadron at Lismore lost 23 men through resignation in one day in protest at the decision.[89]

Other changes caused more problems in Victoria. In 1903, just after the interstate transfer of the long-serving permanent commander of the Victorian Mounted Rifles, Colonel Tom Price, Hutton planned to use the upcoming camp to combine the two existing battalions of that regiment with an artillery battery to create for the first time a *de facto* light horse brigade, thus introducing his new mounted system. To command this brigade he brought in a recently promoted New South Wales permanent officer with Boer War experience, Lieutenant-Colonel George Lee. By placing Lee in command Hutton had passed over the services of the now senior officer of the Victorian Mounted Rifles, Lieutenant-Colonel William Braithwaite who, although popular with his regiment, had no war experience and was decidedly overweight.[90] Hutton and the state commandant, Brigadier-General Joseph Gordon, thought him incapable of commanding a light horse brigade.[91] Not surprisingly, Braithwaite objected to his being superseded and to what he saw as the quashing of a citizen officer's right to command his own unit. He wasted little time appealing to the minister, Sir John Forrest. This was all 'in-house', but things were soon aggravated when an article appeared in the Melbourne *Herald* decrying the decision to replace Braithwaite as 'the most insulting order... that has ever seen the light since the Mounted Rifles Regiment was formed... For the order implies that the senior officers of the Regiment are not fit for their posts.'[92] When it came to Hutton's attention that the news editor of the *Herald* was none other than Lieutenant-Colonel W. Reay, commander of the Victorian Mounted Rifles' 2nd Battalion, he demanded of Reay whether he had anything to do with the article. Reay refused to give a clear answer. Hutton immediately placed him on leave and demanded that he tender his resignation.[93]

With the problem in the public domain it quickly became an issue for all and, within a week of the article appearing, the matter had gone before federal cabinet and the official correspondence had started filling the files. Hutton, for his part, was outraged at the possibility that cabinet might overturn his appointment of Lee and wrote a heated private letter to the minister to express his indignation, telling him he would 'not answer for the consequences either to the discipline and well being of the forces generally or for the indignation which the men themselves will feel at being made fools of by an incompetent and ignorant leader'.[94] For his part Forrest wondered why the lancer Colonel James Burns, who was 'not an expert', had been left to command his brigade under similar circumstances in New South Wales and whether Hutton could 'not avoid all trouble by [following] a similar course in Victoria'.[95] Ultimately Forrest and the Prime Minister, Sir Edmund Barton, considered that Hutton was right to have appointed Lee and upheld his decision, but were not impressed by his handling of the matter. Hutton was reprimanded on the grounds that he should have gained ministerial approval before appointing Lee and that when dealing with citizen officers 'exceptional tact and discretion are required, particularly during the inauguration of a new system'.[96] Certainly 'Hutton' and 'tact' were not two words to be usually associated – although capable, he was inclined to righteous priggishness and ill-considered outbursts over military matters – but the issue died away when Braithwaite and Reay asked to be put on the retired list and the camp proved a success.[97]

Teething troubles

These camps were a vital aspect of Hutton's plans. As the organisational difficulties of 1902–03 were left behind Hutton's reforms for the mounted troops at last began to take shape, and training became the focus of activity. Hutton undoubtedly saw the eight-day continuous training camp as the centrepiece of light horse training. Since his first command in Australia he had held the view that a reliance on theoretical training without adequate field training, particularly for officers, had been a serious deficiency.[98] Now that the first eight-day camps had been successfully held, he believed that the decision to hold them had been vindicated, especially for the light horse, 'as the most important portion of the cavalryman's duties can only be learnt when concentrated in considerable bodies'.[99]

With the war in South Africa in the recent past it is not surprising that its influences dominated training at this time. As early as 1900, following a visit to South Africa, the Victorian commandant had organised a local exercise that specifically sought to demonstrate the capacity of a relatively small group of mounted men with rifles to hold a position and keep a larger force at bay. This trend was continued on Hutton's arrival, and the 1903 Victorian camp was held at Sunbury because of its resemblance to Natal.[100] Once more in 1904 the Victorian camp was held in a location that 'lent itself by appearance and physical configuration to illustrate the South African high Veldt, which was the scene of many similar combats during the war'. The tactical operations there were 'intended to illustrate the tactics pursued by the Mounted Troops during the recent campaign against the Boers'. South Africa's influence was felt in other areas, too, and in the concluding report for the 1904 Victorian camp Hutton expressed his pleasure that most of the tasks given to the light horse brigades had been carried out effectively owing to the competence and experience of the officers and men present who had served in South Africa.[101]

Still, the same report revealed that the light horse was not without problems. The South Africa veterans were of considerable value, but Hutton noted that without them things might have been much less successful, particularly as 'the great bulk of troops... possessed but small experience and only elementary knowledge'.[102] While the general adoption of an eight-day camp for the light horse represented a significant improvement on the usual pre-Federation, four-day Easter camp, it was hardly a period in which to create truly knowledgeable or competent soldiers. The problem was exacerbated by the generally low level of skills held by most officers and soldiers in an organisation that had undergone rapid change and expansion in the previous few years. Hutton always praised the zeal and general determination of the Australian citizen soldiers under his command, but in a military system in which the vast majority of soldiers were part-time, training opportunities limited and the government intent on keeping a tight rein on spending, there were always going to be deficiencies.

Aside from soldier training at the 1904 Victorian camp Hutton complained of a variety of problems in implementing his new scheme. Some of these were merely the teething problems of a new system while others highlighted that the Field Force still had a long way to go. Hutton thought the squadron-based system was working quite well but noted that regimental administration and routine left 'much to be desired'. The supply system was effectively nonexistent and without that it would be 'useless to suppose that the... troops can be effectively utilised for Field Operations'. Men had attended the camp in a wide variety of uniforms, and many were in fact soldiering in their plain clothes. Not enough of the modern 0.303-inch magazine-loading rifles were issued to the light horse brigades present (most had the old single-shot Lee Enfield), and at least two squadrons had arrived at camp without any rifles at all. No machine-guns were available, a deficiency considered grave for mounted troops.[103] These problems were largely generic and could well have been repeated anywhere throughout Australia in regard to any troops of any arm at this time, but additional problems noticed at this camp were peculiar to the light horse, although not necessarily peculiar to Victoria.

Hutton noted with evident concern that a significant number of horses brought to camp were too small and below the standards set out. He reminded his mounted arm that small horses that were 'incapable of carrying out the role of Light Horse and of doing quick and rapid work are useless for the purpose for which Light Horse exists'.[104] This was followed by a reminder that they were no longer mounted infantry and that their role, as light-horsemen, had been extended considerably. Compounding this concern was that the civilian colonial-pattern saddle widely owned and used by the men was unsuitable for military use. After just one and a half days of vigorous peacetime manoeuvring at this camp 'a very considerable proportion of horses were incapacitated for further use during the camp by reason of sore backs and galls'.[105] The implications for any real wartime use of the force were obvious. Hutton could do little about this until the government approved the funds to provide suitable military saddles, a planned but expensive and unprecedented step for any Australian government, so the pre-Federation practice of men using their own saddles had to continue.

An effort to keep Boer War veterans, particularly officers, in the ranks of the citizen forces was one of the ways seen to improve the general situation. As early as 1902 the Minister for Defence had tried various ways to keep the skills and experience of veterans at the force's disposal. Men who had maintained a connection after returning home were given encouragement by having their South African promotions confirmed as honorary rank. Hutton, who was well aware that promotions granted in South Africa were often made for 'local reasons and quite apart from any personal efficiency or any meritorious service', had mixed feelings about this and unsuccessfully tried to have this rule applied only selectively.[106] But, as his replacement of Braithwaite in 1903 and his assessment of the 1904 Victorian camp had shown, Hutton clearly felt that in this largely inexperienced force some returned officers were very valuable indeed.[107]

If Hutton and the government were hoping that the leavening of South African veteran officers was going to provide the much-needed boost to the citizen soldier light horse, as well as the other arms, they were hoping for much from a very few. Even in 1904, with the war only just over, the number of officers serving in light horse regiments who had war experience was small. In New South Wales the 1st Light Horse Regiment, for example, had just four out of 20 officers who had active service experience, none of them presently holding a rank higher than captain, and the 2nd Light Horse Regiment had just two out of 25 officers. The 3rd Light Horse Regiment fared best in that brigade with six out of 21, including one squadron commander and the commanding officer. Overall the 2nd Brigade fared no better, and in these two New South Wales brigades just 17.5 per cent of the officers had seen active service.[108] These figures, in themselves, may have been a cause for some optimism, but the numbers were not evenly spread, many had gained their war experience in the ranks rather than as officers, and in a system in which citizen officers lost interest in their martial pastime, had civilian commitments that overcame their military pursuits, got sick, were retired through age or moved their homes outside recruitment areas, these small raw numbers could be eroded quickly. Given that not all officers who served in South Africa had performed well, the value of this sprinkling is even more open to doubt. Hutton believed that New South Wales and Queensland had the best of it in quality and numbers when it came to the veteran officers, which did not bode well for the forces in some of the other states.[109]

The inequalities between the states dating from before Federation were a constant source of consternation for Hutton, who believed that in New South Wales and Queensland the pre-Federation system of organisation and instruction was 'far in advance of that in the other states'.[110] In his 1904 annual report he complained about the comparative spending and instructional standards that had been allowed the mounted troops of the various colonies.[111] Upon his initial inspection of South Australia in March 1902 Hutton had been alarmed to discover that the whole state, owing to colonial government spending, had only two permanent instructors to instruct non-commissioned soldiers. He immediately ordered the despatch of another ten instructors from other states that could better afford the loss, including three for the mounted rifles, to rectify the situation.[112] Victoria, with its long reliance on unpaid volunteers, was also deficient in Hutton's eyes and, when criticising the poor performance of most officers and soldiers at the 1904 manoeuvres, he made the qualification that not much could be expected given 'the limited knowledge and small extent of military training which the Light Horse Regiments of Victoria have hitherto received'.[113] Similarly, emphasising again that the light horse were not mounted infantry, he criticised Tasmania's light horse officers following a 1904 staff ride because they had yet to 'grasp the enlarged scope of their duty as Cavalry'.[114]

Problems with equipment also played their part in making life in the light horse difficult. Within months of his arrival Hutton had noted that 'there is little if any satisfactory equipment for Light Horse available in the Commonwealth'.[115] In an attempt to get a useful uniform saddle Hutton's first draft estimate for expenditure in 1903–04 had proposed

Photo 12 Essential to Hutton's scheme was the introduction of hitherto unexpected standards of officer instruction. The senior instructor of this 1904 light horse school of instruction (centre, looking to his right) is Lieutenant-Colonel John Antill, who had served in South Africa and would have a controversial career with the light horse during the First World War. (AWM 01208.003)

spending £10 263 on saddlery. When told by the minister that his total budget was not to exceed £50 000 for that year, he was compelled to reduce the saddlery expenditure to just £90 for the production of 12 sample saddles.[116] The reduction in spending affected more than just the mounted arm, and in 1903 Hutton made it clear that it was 'impossible now to state any definitive date by which the Military Forces... are likely to be effectively equipped'.[117] Also affected was Hutton's decision that the light horse must, after their rifles and a bayonets, have a secondary weapon.[118] As mentioned above, he had wanted a pistol for the light horse but thought the imperial Webley revolver unsuitable and instead sponsored the local production of a double-barrelled pistol prototype. The prototype was eventually made, but the pistol never made it to general issue, and the matter of secondary armament for the light horse would be an ongoing concern right up to the outbreak of the First World War.[119] Even finding bayonets for the light horse proved a problem, and in 1905 consideration was given to converting old triangular bayonets held in stocks to a more modern rapier bayonet, which could be issued to the light horse, but as this would have been more expensive than new bayonets it was never undertaken.[120] Other complaints about unsuitable belts and bandoliers were heard from Queensland, and one Western Australian regimental commander, presumably feeling the chill on camps, was still waiting for the issue of greatcoats in 1905.[121] Uniform supply was a recurring problem, and some New South Wales light horse commanders ruefully wished for the return of their old system whereby they organised and paid for uniforms out of allocated unit funds rather than having to wait on a centralised bureaucracy to deliver their needs.[122]

Other complaints flowed from the nature of the new post-Federation army uniform itself. Units that had previously had more colourful uniforms disliked the new plain khaki affair, and those who had plain pre-Federation uniforms were disdainful of the necessity to add coloured facings, braid and aiguillettes to make it presentable for occasions requiring full dress.[123] The selection of white uniform highlights for the light horse, who generally worked on dusty country roads, was scorned within the military and in the press as a particularly foolish decision.[124] Although the infantry managed to have their scarlet coats and white helmets reintroduced for full-dress occasions in 1905, the efforts to have the mounted uniforms changed were to no avail.[125] Certain New South Wales regiments, desiring to maintain their traditions, simply continued to wear their pre-Federation uniforms. Paying for the uniforms out of regimental funds, the 1st Light Horse Regiment continued to wear a variation of the old lancer uniform for full-dress occasions, and the 3rd Light Horse Regiment continued to wear the myrtle-green affair of the 1st Australian Horse for both service and full-dress occasions at least as late as 1908.[126]

Hutton faced plenty of difficulties when serving in Australia, and the above problems were just some of them. He had, however, run out of time to address them. Hutton's tenure in Australia finished at the end of 1904, and he sailed from Melbourne that November. For the mounted troops of Australia there had been much change since Federation. Brought, not without difficulty, into a uniform structure, they were now organised and trained to a single plan. Hutton had been pleased with what he had achieved with the light horse and had told London so, noting that the mounted troops had 'responded in the most enthusiastic manner to the increased demands made upon them'.[127] An article by him in a 1906 edition of the *Cavalry Journal* expounded the virtues of the light horse and, not surprisingly, highlighted what he saw as its strengths: its territorial organisation, its establishment around independent brigades and its use of both peace and war establishments as a basis for expansion when required.[128] Whether these facets of the light horse's organisation were the strengths that Hutton thought they were would be tested in the years ahead. Certainly there could be little doubt that the light horse, beset with the problems of brief, unequal and sometimes mediocre training, poor or non-existent equipment, and devoid of any true logistic system, was not yet the force it was meant to be.

Despite the myriad problems, there was no doubt that Hutton had achieved a great deal in the three years he had been General Officer Commanding, and his creation of the light horse was perhaps one of his greatest successes. The remarkable nature of what Hutton created with the Australian Light Horse should not be underestimated. Restricted only by the broadest of government guidelines and the depth of his government's exchequer (which was not very deep), he was, to all intents and purposes, handed the opportunity to create a distinctive mounted force that reflected what he had been thinking and writing about for nearly a quarter of a century. The Field Force brigades, and specifically the light horse, imperfect though they were, were the direct result of Hutton's experiences as a proponent of mounted rifle and mounted infantry theory. Animated by his own position on mounted firepower and, in his view, vindicated by recent events in South Africa, he created a force that owed its heritage to certain interpretations of mounted warfare in the late nineteenth century and Britain's recent colonial warfare experiences. By way of Hutton the theorising of men like George Denison, analysed through the prism of South Africa, had borne fruit in one of Britain's most remote dominions. The light horse, trained and equipped as the archetypal mounted riflemen, organised into permanent self-sufficient brigades capable of both tactical and grand strategic use, was, on paper at least, a force that was unique in many ways.[129] This was of no concern to Hutton as he believed that South Africa had confirmed what he saw as the direction of modern warfare and that any wars to come would find his mounted rifles of great value. Helped by the empire-wide trend to make all citizen soldier mounted forces into mounted rifles and the decision by Lord Roberts to allow him a free hand in local mounted doctrine, Hutton went a fair way to creating an Australian force in many ways unique in the British empire. In doing so, however, he had also set the stage for a number of problems.

CHAPTER | 4

UNFULFILLED PROMISE
The militia light horse, 1905–20

Looking back more than over a century later it is perhaps easy to underestimate the magnitude of the changes that Hutton had brought to the nation's military forces. A collection of quite small, parochial and disparate colonial forces had, within a few short years, been largely broken up and rearranged to conform to a new national scheme guided by a new national government working through the agency of a new national commander. This deep and thorough reform would be followed by one almost as fundamental in the years just before the First World War with the introduction of a military service scheme that was compulsory for most of the country's able-bodied males. In doing so, however, they continued to use the traditional citizen soldier (militia or unpaid volunteer) as the basis of the nation's forces. Combining this with limited defence budgets and a military scheme that owed a great deal to the sense of mission that Hutton had brought – especially for the light horse – meant that the years in the decade and more ahead of the mounted branch were to be troubled ones.

THE POST-HUTTON HANG-OVER

Hutton's efforts in Australia had not been without controversy. The government, for one, had found that dealing with a powerful and opinionated general could be difficult. Keen to broaden the sources of advice available to it, and echoing the reforms to the British Army's control then being undertaken, which led to the creation of the Army Council, it decided it would not replace Hutton. Instead they opted to create a committee to be known as the Military Board of Administration, which would, with the exception of an interregnum during the Second World War, oversee the army's administration and advise the government until the mid-1970s.[1]

It was not long before the Military Board had to begin to deal with the problems that were becoming increasingly obvious among the nation's new light horse regiments, which were in many ways still trying to find their feet. One of these problems was dealing with low peacetime establishments, which had reflected the need for the defence budget to be kept as small as possible. Light horse units soon found that the restriction placed on them by having small numbers of men in the ranks was a real problem and that, unless units were concentrated for larger-scale collective training, little could be achieved.[2] The dispersed local 'home training' was also a problem and could compound the problems relating to establishments. As one officer noted, 'if there were only sixteen men in a Troop and four were away, it was only a farce'.[3] Perhaps this had been anticipated to some extent as the *Mounted Service Manual* instructed squadrons to have their men train holding extended ropes as 'by this means four men can be made to act as a Troop', a suggestion that was certainly utilised but which can hardly have been very satisfactory.[4]

The problems caused by the difference between war and peace establishments was exacerbated by the government continuing to keep a tight rein on defence spending, which meant that the authorised establishments of units did not, in many cases, even approach the restricted levels that Hutton had proposed. A reduction in the defence estimates for 1903–04 meant that light horse squadrons in New South Wales and Queensland were restricted to three instead of four troops.[5] In Tasmania the 12th Light Horse Regiment was restricted to two squadrons of two troops and one squadron of one troop, and South Australia's regiments also faced similar restraints.[6] Things did not necessarily improve as time progressed, and in 1907 Tasmania's light horse regiment was still restricted to a peace establishment of 256 men of all ranks, which was still 40 men short of what Hutton had wanted in 1902, although, as will shortly be highlighted, this was perhaps not too great a problem for this troubled regiment.[7] Similarly the 5th Light Horse Regiment in New South Wales was limited to just 152 men during the same period.[8] Not surprisingly, complaints were heard, and there were frequent calls for the establishments to be increased. In 1905 one regiment's commanding officer, apparently chafing at his limits, advocated the raising of the peacetime establishment of a squadron to what would have been a quite handy 100 men.[9]

Photo 13 A New South Wales trooper of the post-Federation period (still in his colonial uniform) astride his horse. The military authorities would have frowned upon this horse due to its light colour, which would have stood out on the battlefield. As men provided their own mounts, however, there was little that could be done. (Mitchell Library, State Library of NSW, BCP_02369)

Not all units could have met such an expansion easily, and in several areas around the country units were encountering recruiting difficulties. Tasmania's lone unit, the 12th Light Horse Regiment, for example, had been created from the Tasmanian Mounted Infantry, which would, in wartime, round out the 4th Light Horse Brigade in Victoria. Tasmania had always been a marginal area for recruiting mounted troops, and the record of the nineteenth century was one of unsuccessful and failed units. Despite the best wishes and efforts of the Commonwealth military authorities, such inherent limitations could not be overcome, and in 1904 the regiment could boast a strength of only 146 soldiers.[10] In 1905 the Military Board sought to correct this deficiency (and echo the events in 1902–03 with the Victorian Rangers) by recommending that the state's 12th Australian Infantry Regiment give up two of its country-based companies in favour of raising extra light horse detachments. Not surprisingly, the infantry commanding officer objected to losing two companies on the grounds that they were among his best and that most of the affected men had no means of meeting that most fundamental requirement of joining the mounted arm, the ever-present matter of having to own a horse. In his view the two company areas were 'essentially infantry and not light horse districts', and trying to recruit light horse squadrons would be a time-consuming and difficult process.[11]

What the result of this exchange was is not clear but, as this incident highlights, the characteristics of recruiting areas after Federation could, as they had before, have a significant impact on the viability of local detachments and units as a whole. Although not perhaps as traditionally strong an area as Queensland or New South Wales, even South Australia, with its successful record of viable units in the nineteenth century, had difficulties reaching its light horse manning requirements. In mid-1904 both the 16th and 17th Light Horse Regiments reported from there to Melbourne that many of their squadrons were still far below their establishment.[12] In other areas it proved necessary to abort efforts to maintain detachments entirely. In 1904 the authorities were forced to disband a squadron at Gunnedah, for example, as 'attendance at parades has dropped to less than [20] and is likely to get lower as there is an absence of life in the Squadron'.[13] Similarly at Casterton in Victoria in 1905 a detachment of the 11th Light Horse Regiment faced disbandment owing to poor recruiting. The officer commanding, Captain Little, wondered why his brigade headquarters had stopped recruiting efforts for his detachment as he felt it 'was one of the best in the Regiment'.[14] This was either hyperbole or a backhander to the rest of the regiment because a check of the records revealed that the detachment had only been able to get, on average, two soldiers of all ranks, of the 23 enrolled, to attend local half-day parades in the last quarter of 1903. In early 1904 this non-attendance had been followed by a flood of discharges, which meant that only Captain Little, one troop leader and one sergeant could be said to be regularly attending parades.[15] No new men were forthcoming and, not surprisingly, Captain Little's pleas fell on deaf ears; he was placed on the unattached list and his detachment wound up. Other proposed detachments could not even be raised in the first place, and in South Australia a plan to establish a troop at Georgetown in 1906 was abandoned as 'the anticipated response from the young men of the District [was not] forthcoming'.[16]

Beyond administrative matters of this sort there were also deeper problems with how the light horse was going about its training, and within a few years of his departure Hutton's *Mounted Service Manual* was proving a particular cause of concern. The infantry, forced to use it in anticipation of their being required to act as mounted infantry, had never taken to it, and the outspoken infantry officer and senator, J. C. Neild, had dismissed its contents in parliament as the 'bastard mounted drill'.[17] By 1906 the government had agreed with London on a process of imperial standardisation, and the infantry and other arms returned to imperial manuals for their guidance.[18] With this there followed the effective demise of any notions of continuing with mounted infantry training in Australia and, although there would be occasional proposals to create a corps of 'bushmen' or cyclists for some role or another, the light horse now became the sole mobile arm of the Commonwealth Military Forces.[19]

The light horse manual had been exempted from the process of standardisation, but Hutton's work was now proving troublesome. A 1906 committee convened to consider military organisational matters believed that the *Mounted Service Manual* was 'unsuitable for the Light Horse of Australia' and recommended the immediate compilation of a new manual based 'as far as possible on Imperial text-books'.[20] The primary concern seemed to be that Hutton's drill and ideas, having been permitted by Lord Roberts for use in Australia, but not without modification in Britain, were so far removed from imperial practice that any attempt to combine the two was overly difficult. Lieutenant-Colonel Charles Cox, commanding the descendant of the lancer regiment, the 1st Light Horse Regiment, found it so difficult to cross-reference with imperial sources that he, noting that the many corrections and additions made for confusion, strongly recommended adopting the imperial *Cavalry Training*.[21]

Cox's brigade commander was the old lancer commanding officer, James Burns, and he forwarded Cox's letter in favour of *Cavalry Training* to the Secretary of Defence with his strongest support.[22] The state commandant did not agree, and he thought that what was needed was 'a Manual more on "Mounted Infantry" lines than "Cavalry"'.[23] A board convened to consider what should be the training text for light horse noted the observations from New South Wales but did not consider them convincing, and in 1907 came the publication of the *Light Horse Manual for the Drill Training and Exercise of the Light Horse Regiments of Australia* (hereafter the *Light Horse Manual*).[24]

A significant departure from Hutton's doctrine, it was also a much thinner volume than its predecessor. Gone was his preface and its dictums on mounted firepower, and gone also were his ideas of grand strategic strokes by mounted forces. The new manual restricted the light horse to the more traditional roles of cavalry, except the charge, which had been in the previous manual but did not contribute to its grandiosity. One officer, referring to the imperial manuals, later described it as 'more or less a compromise between "Cavalry Training" and "Mounted Infantry Training"'.[25] Restricted to 'skirmishing', 'information' and 'protection' duties, the manual outlined general principles of action, but it was surprisingly vague about many of the duties that would be undertaken when light horse took the field. In the end it was not much more than a manual of mounted drill.[26]

BEYOND HUTTON

The development of the new light horse manual was not the most pressing matter then confronting the military authorities, however, and the rise of Japan as a Pacific power was a particularly troubling development. The signing of the new Anglo-Japanese Alliance in 1902 (which had been greeted with alarm in Australia), Japan's victory in the Russo-Japanese War of 1904–05 and the continuing rise of German naval power gave rise to fresh fears in government and military circles that the traditional guarantee of protection by the Royal Navy may not have been as sure as it once was. London, as always, was unconvinced by Australian anxieties and maintained its long-standing view that no dominion was less likely to be attacked than Australia. The second Deakin ministry remained sceptical, and in 1906 a committee formed under the Inspector-General, Major-General John Hoad, recommended that the protection of the Royal Navy should not be solely relied on, that Australia should be prepared for at least the temporary loss of British sea supremacy and the possibility that a foreign power could subsequently attack with a large and well-trained expeditionary or raiding force.[27] This was little different from what Hutton and Bevan Edwards before him had said, but in the circumstances the idea carried more weight, and soon the government was beginning to contemplate the introduction of a system of military training for all able-bodied males. Steps in this direction were made over the next few years, but it was not until 1910 that a scheme was finally settled on. Against this backdrop the existing light horse organisation was left to try to overcome the problems that it had hitherto faced. The results were mixed.

Some equipment concerns were gradually being solved, and in 1907 automatic weapons were finally added to light horse establishments. By 1908 regiments were able to conduct their first live firings with their new pom-pom and Colt machine-guns, which would be the arm's automatic firepower until Maxim guns were introduced in 1912.[28] The history of the New South Wales Lancers records that the first firing practice

Photo 14 Soldiers of the 4th Light Horse Regiment's machine-gun section with a Colt 1895-pattern machine-gun in 1910. Introduced in 1908, machine-guns filled a deficiency in Australian mounted troop firepower that had been recognised since the 1890s. (AWM P01796.002)

by the 1st and 2nd Light Horse Brigades in 1908 left much room for improvement, but it was a start and the issue of the guns rectified a long-standing deficiency.[29] Standardised bandolier equipment was issued in 1907, but the supply of saddles had not yet been addressed and would not be until 1913. The provision of a secondary weapon for the light horse also remained a significant problem despite periodic calls for bayonets, side arms or something else to be issued. Still, given these and the other difficulties they faced, Hoad was generally content with the light horse. Writing in 1907 that they did 'not as a rule, bearing in mind the number of days training and the instruction available, leave much room for criticism, and all ranks are keen to improve their efficiency'.[30]

This proviso of training quality was the key to the overall usefulness of the light horse and continued to trouble the arm. In late 1904 the then Minister for Defence, James McCay, himself a citizen soldier, had made a series of decisions aimed at placating the sizeable number of citizen officers unhappy with Hutton's reforms. Among them had been a decision that it was no longer necessary for light horse units to spend a full eight days in camp, a requirement that had been a problem for many units but particularly so in Western Australia.³¹ As a result of McCay's decision Western Australia's only light horse regiment no longer did the eight-day camps that Hutton had thought so essential and restricted themselves to the pre-Federation habit of four-day Easter camps, a practice that the Victorian units seem to have emulated.³² Most other units and formations continued with the eight-day activities but, as always, these could be subject to a variety of disruptions. In 1908, for example, the two New South Wales brigades found that their planned May camp had to be aborted when a severe drought saw their rolling stock assigned to move cattle starving in a drought. This proved a major disruption to officers and men who had long laid plans to attend, but a camp organised later that year to coincide with the visit of the great American fleet at least fulfilled the annual requirement. This longer camp (17 days owing to the fleet visit) used up all the training funds for that financial year and, as the funds from the previous year had not been carried over, it was January 1910 before they could go into camp again. One of these brigades, the 1st, again found their plans disrupted in 1913 when the Minister for Home Affairs, King O'Malley, got wind of their intention to hold camp in the 'Federal Capital Territory' and had them co-opted into the ceremonies to be held in connection with the foundation of the new national capital.³³

When camps went ahead without such disruptions, as they usually did, attendances often proved another impediment. At the 1908 fleet visit camp most of the regiments could field about 300 men, reasonably close to their establishment. The long break to the 1910 camp must have had its effects as at that camp the 2nd and 3rd Light Horse Regiments could attain only an average daily attendance of 262 men against their respective establishments of 346 and 310.³⁴ Things were considerably worse in Victoria in 1909 with only one regiment, the 10th, being able to achieve an average daily attendance of 80 per cent of their actual strength; most were well below 70 per cent.³⁵ In the same year the 18th Light Horse Regiment in Western Australia, with just a four-day Easter camp to be concerned with, could get only 163 of the 245 men enlisted to attend. Again, the figures look inauspicious when compared to the authorised establishment of 310 men. Of the 82 who did not attend only 13 had managed to obtain leave for the camp.³⁶ There was some good news from Queensland where most of the regiments managed attendances of more than 90 per cent that year.³⁷

Good attendances were not always what they seemed, however, and there were complaints about the tendency to conduct recruiting drives in the lead-up to camps. Such drives boosted numbers, but the high number of new recruits meant that the training for all concerned had to be limited in its complexity and usefulness in order to accommodate the new men. There were those who hoped that the habit of mixing recruits and more experienced men could be done away with, but one of the reasons why the 1st Light Horse Brigade decided to camp near the eventual site of Canberra in 1913 was that the high percentage of new recruits in the ranks made attending a larger multi-brigade concentration at Albury not worthwhile.[38]

Despite the deficiencies in extended camp training, it was the best chance the light horse regiments had of moulding themselves into something like the military organisations they were meant to be. The 'home training' of evening, half-day and full-day parades was increasingly being perceived as a decided weakness of the training scheme. The regional organisation of units and formations had been meant to provide organisational strength, but the reality was that many light horse units, spread out over large areas of sparsely populated rural areas, did not experience the anticipated cohesion. Echoing concerns expressed earlier in the decade, the inescapable consequence was that it was 'not often possible to get together sufficient men to make work as valuable and instructive as could be wished'.[39] In these circumstances the quality and training of officers, who had in turn to manage the training of their subordinates, was a continual worry. There were criticisms of the variable attention, interest and energy displayed by citizen officers and exhortations that commanders had to stamp out 'perfunctory performance'.[40] The mounted arm was not exempt, and one light horse brigade major professed concern in 1909 that while the men available could be quickly trained to be good soldiers, 'the trouble all the time [was] to get properly trained officers to lead them'.[41]

These criticisms were undoubtedly justified in many ways. Militia officer training was far from being a thorough process, but it should be borne in mind that it was now far better than before Federation when any form of systematic approach barely existed. Hutton had instituted the uniform schools of instruction and, although relatively brief affairs, they at least gave officers who could afford the time to attend them (and attendance was a prerequisite for promotion or confirmation in rank) some instruction on basic tactical, administrative and logistic matters. These courses varied in length and could be as long as three weeks, but the officers who attended a light horse course for promotion in Tasmania during this period spent a busy nine days learning squadron and regimental drill, the use of light horse in attack and defence, map-reading, musketry instruction, field engineering and troop movement before taking part in a two-day 'tactical scheme' designed to test their knowledge.[42] Officers were expected to build on this base with private and unit-based study and, when conducted, take part in the staff rides that Hutton had also instituted. Although seldom attended by more than a dozen officers at a time, these staff rides provided an excellent opportunity for senior commanders to assess the quality and training of officers under their command. Unfortunately they often revealed as many deficiencies as reasons for contentment but at least, in some cases, they were being used to broaden horizons. Whereas South Africa had long dominated local military minds, the 1908 Queensland staff ride, for example, organised by Harry Chauvel, was based on operations in the Shenandoah Valley during the American Civil War.[43] This level of training, scant though it was, was really all that could be achieved under the existing defence system. Further improvements in officer training would require a drastic reformation of the defence scheme and its training plans so officer training would remain an imperfect system, and expressions about its inadequacy would continue.

The barbs about officer quality were not all directed one way, and complaints from citizen officers about their permanent counterparts were not uncommon. Although they generally respected and appreciated the large amount of work that permanent instructors put into their work, citizen officers were periodically moved to vent frustrations about the often variable knowledge and skills of the men who guided, organised and conducted so much of their training. The Royal Military College at Duntroon was not founded until 1911 and did not produce its first graduates until after the start of the First World War, so permanent officers of this period were something of a grab-bag who had either served in the British or another dominion's army or the pre-Federation colonial forces (which in turn had irregular sources) or had joined following some service in the militia. That there were also far too few of them did not help.[44] Major-General John Hoad, as Chief of the General Staff, had worried that their staff appointments and the lack of exposure to regimental life meant their understanding of private soldiers and leadership was not as good at it might have been.[45] One infantry officer, apparently tired of dealing with presumptuous permanent officers, publicly complained about a tendency among staff officers to interfere with the higher command responsibilities of militia officers.[46] Tension between the citizen soldiers who served in and led the regiments of the forces, and the permanent officers who administered them, undoubtedly grew. In 1912 the Minister for Defence felt the need to bring about an annual militia officer conference partly so as to develop 'a better understanding between the permanent officers and the citizen officers'.[47]

In addition to the problems outlined above, there is evidence that the light horse was experiencing a degree of uncertainty towards the end of its first decade of existence about what its actual role on the battlefield was meant to be. With Hutton's departure the trend in defence thinking, particularly since 1906, had been to follow the example and form of the British Army more closely. Yet the military authorities had made no effort to explicitly update or clarify the light horse role and, despite some changes, technically the Field Force was much as Hutton had left it in both structure and intent. Hutton had placed the mounted rifle light horse at the centre of Australian defence and potential imperial military contributions, but with the following of British examples this central role seemed less and less viable. The tone and methods in the *Light Horse Manual, 1907* had seemingly placed them more in the traditional supporting role of cavalry than as the centerpiece of a mobile strike force, but this conflicted with the defence structure as it stood. Moreover, the continued lack of a secondary weapon was proving a vexing matter and leading to uncertainty. One officer, at a well-attended lecture at the New South Wales United Service Institution, contended that without a bayonet or sword the light horse was neither beast nor fowl: 'We are trained up to a certain point as Cavalry, but have no secondary weapon... Let us understand exactly what we are, properly equip us, and make us feel we are really part of the defence force, ready to take our place with Imperial troops in the Empire's defence whenever called upon.'[48]

This officer, Major W. Everett, strongly believed that although fire tactics were undoubtedly the essential action of all mounted troops in modern war, the light horse should be equipped with a sword so that its role was confirmed and the 'cavalry spirit' could be fostered locally.[49] The comments made by other officers following his lecture indicate that he was not the only one thus concerned, although even the supply of a bayonet would have satisfied some.[50] Lieutenant-Colonel George Lee, who attended the lecture, summed up the officers' sentiments by pointing out that at the very least the light horse role had to be better defined for only then would they 'know what training is necessary to bring about the efficiency required'.[51] If nothing else this sort of discussion was some evidence that Hutton's mounted rifle template had not been as firmly embedded in the Australian military as he had hoped.

Perhaps these men felt they received some sort of answer the following year with the publication and issue of a new light horse manual in which large portions were taken 'word for word' from the imperial *Cavalry Training*.[52] It meant that in the 1910 edition of the *Light Horse Manual* training principles were closer than ever to those followed by British cavalry. Reflecting this, the manual outlined three types of cavalry operations, those of the independent, protective and divisional cavalry, of which only the actions of 'independent cavalry' could be considered analogous to what Hutton had in mind earlier in the decade. More generally the new manual also represented a substantial improvement over the 1907 version and rectified many of the oversights of that rather lightweight edition. One interesting development was the inclusion of appendices dealing with sword and lance practice, making it the first manual used in Australia since 1902 to find a place for the *arme blanche* in the mounted branch. It was not a blank cheque for wholesale lance and sword training, however, and it was directed primarily at training for participation in tournaments and skill-at-arms competitions.[53]

This inclusion was not without controversy, and there had been some debate about the inclusion of sword and lance training in the manual (and more specifically as to how much it should be allowed) when the manual was in production. Some apprehensive comments had also been made about the possibility that imperial drill inappropriate to Australia's citizen soldiers had been imported,[54] but the new edition remained a manual aimed at mounted rifle–style tactics, which, given that was what British regular dismounted cavalry tactics were anyway, was entirely suitable.

The universal training era

As the 1910 manual was being released and adopted for general use, the formula for the long-awaited reform of Australian defence was finally arrived at. Since Hoad's 1906 review of defence there had been a number of reports and attempts to introduce a new compulsory military service scheme. In 1910, following an inspection and report by Field Marshal Lord Kitchener, the Fisher government introduced a bill that called for mandatory military service for all able-bodied males to commence in the junior cadets at age 12 and conclude at age 26 in the citizen forces.[55] For the light horse, Kitchener's report and the consequent adoption of Universal Military Training (as it was called) would have a variety of consequences.

Kitchener's report was an organisation-wide review and, for the first time since the visit of Major-General Bevan Edwards in 1889, Australia's mounted troops hardly rated a mention in an imperial officer's comments. Given his brief to comment on the suitability of the whole new defence scheme, this was not in itself surprising, but it did emphasise that the time of the light horse being the arm of choice for local and imperial defence was coming to an end. Mention of the light horse was confined to propositions of its organisational structure, and its relegation to a traditional supporting arm role, foreshadowed for some time, was to all intents and purposes complete. The high proportion of mounted troops that Hutton had established would, in effect, be inverted. Under Kitchener's proposals the unpaid volunteer forces were to be removed from the order of battle and Australia would aim to support 84 battalions of militia infantry fed by universal training and organised into 21 brigades. The number of light horse was to be increased but, with a proposed 28 regiments organised into seven brigades, they were now clearly slated to be used in support of infantry formations.[56]

Following agreements between the Australian Government and London at the 1907 and 1909 Imperial Conferences, all Australian forces, with only minor local modifications, were to comply with the organisational templates set by the British Army.[57] The existing light horse structure of four squadrons to a regiment was brought to an end, and regimental commanders would now have three larger squadrons to field.[58] The surplus squadrons thus produced would, when combined with those released from the garrison forces, provide a basis for the new regiments. As these units were raised existing squadrons could anticipate that the regiment they belonged to might change as territorial recruiting and unit boundaries were altered.[59] Hutton's unique Field Force brigades, structured with their own integrated artillery and departmental support, which had been withering on the vine since 1906, were given their death knell.[60] Similarly the large discrepancy between peace and war establishments was reduced, and units could at last recruit to a target nearer to their wartime strength.[61]

The use of local military manuals was also ended and, despite the recent publication of the updated 1910 version, the *Light Horse Manual* was replaced by the imperial *Yeomanry and Mounted Rifle Training* in mid-1912.[62] This was a significant development, and the imported text brought to the light horse a manual of detail and thoroughness not seen since Hutton's manual had been withdrawn. As the rest of the nation's forces had been using imperial manuals since at least 1906 and the light

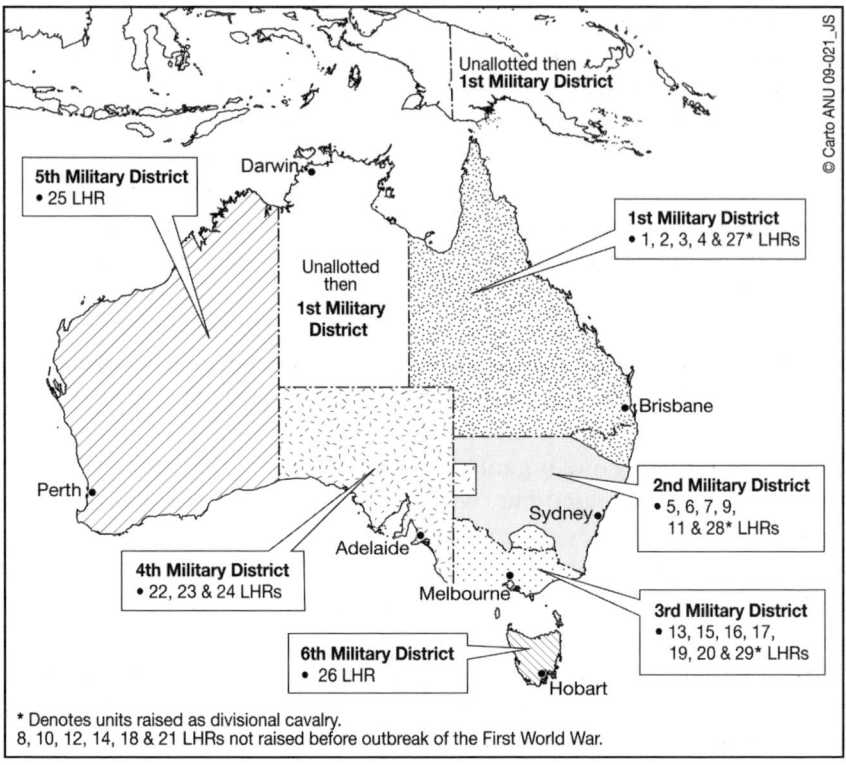

Map 3 Distribution of light horse regiments, 1913

horse was now explicitly taking up a traditional cavalry role identical in many ways to the yeomanry, and even regular cavalry (except shock action), in Great Britain, the change from the local manual was a positive step. It gave Australia's mounted arm a firmer basis that had been missing for some years and which now made more sense when read in conjunction with the overarching principles set out in the imperial *Field Service Regulations*. Those regulations currently defined the role of the light horse and other mounted rifle units around the empire thus: 'Yeomanry and Mounted Rifles... act chiefly by fire but may, when they have received sufficient training, employ shock action in special emergencies... Mounted Rifles, when cooperating with cavalry assist the latter to combine fire with shock action; when cooperating with other arms their mobility enables a commander to transfer them rapidly from one portion of the field to another, and thus to turn to account opportunities which he would be unable to otherwise achieve.'[63] The new training guidance was implemented at the same time Universal Military Training was to commence, and the light horse regiments were issued a new, centrally created training syllabus and schedule in April 1912.[64]

The expansion of the light horse was, however, to face a severe restriction. Universal training, based on a regional system in which units were allocated a number of areas from which their compelled recruits would come, was not to apply fully to the light horse. The compulsory training areas set out by the scheme were of necessity based on cities and significant towns that could support the infrastructure as well as provide the men for training. Light horse regiments existed largely outside these designated training areas, and men in these localities were exempted from the scheme because of their distance from training centres. The government took a fundamental decision that it would not buy horses for the light horse and, as it could not compel men to buy them, this meant that the mounted branch would effectively have to continue with a reliance on voluntary recruiting.[65] Only men obligated under the scheme by living within the training areas, and who owned horses and were willing to volunteer their horses for military service, would be able to serve their commitment in the light horse. To supplement what was always going to be a relatively small number from this method regiments were permitted to continue with voluntary recruitment from men exempted from the general scheme. No particular inducements were offered for men to join the light horse, and new recruits were offered as compensation for their time only half the pay (four shillings per day) that soldiers enlisted under the old system had received. Men already in the force continued to get their eight shillings per day (which had been thought very generous in 1903) but, if their engagement ended and they wished to re-enlist after 1 July 1912, they would have to take a pay cut to the new rate, which was well under civilian rates of pay for the time. Moreover the men still received only the token one pound per year horse allowance, which had been a periodic source of complaint since Federation. These conditions of service were not to prove helpful to the light horse in the years ahead.[66]

Other organisational changes were also required, and all light horse units and formations were to undergo a renumbering process. The old state command system was abandoned in favour of new military districts, which nevertheless conformed roughly with state boundaries. The system started with the 1st Military District based on Queensland and part of northern New South Wales. Most of New South Wales made up the 2nd Military District and so on around the country; each state was given a number and formed the basis of a military district.

Photo 15 Members of the 1st Light Horse Regiment at the 'Kitchener Camp' of 1910. Lord Kitchener's tour of inspection capped the Australian Government's moves towards the introduction of a compulsory military training scheme, which had significant effects on the militia light horse. (State Library of South Australia, PRG1364/1/74)

Regiments and brigades would reflect this system, and the 1st Military District supported the 1st Light Horse Brigade, made up of the 1st, 2nd and 3rd Light Horse Regiments, which were in fact renumbered Queensland units. Again this system flowed around the country so that a unit's number roughly reflected its place on the national clock face.[67] This caused some consternation around Sydney and southern New South Wales where the old 1st Light Horse Brigade suddenly found itself renamed the 3rd Light Horse Brigade, and the old 1st, 2nd and 3rd Light Horse Regiments – the direct descendants of the lancers, New South Wales Mounted Rifles and 1st Australian Horse – found themselves the 7th, 9th and 11th Light Horse Regiments respectively. James Mackay, commanding the brigade, thought this an affront to the state that had long maintained the largest and most effective military forces and made his displeasure at the change known. Whether it occurred to Mackay that Queensland's mounted units could trace a lineage at least as far as those of New South Wales (and somewhat further than Mackay's 1st Australian Horse) is not known, but the Military Board, more worried about managing a massive reorganisation, were unmoved by such sentimentality, and Mackay's pleas were politely rejected.[68]

Perhaps of some consolation to those offended by renumbering was the official implementation of Kitchener's recommendation that units be allowed to adopt the titles of their antecedents or the region they were from. Many units had continued to use pre-Federation titles in a semi-formal fashion after 1901 but now, advocated as a way to foster unit and regional loyalty, the practice was officially encouraged for use as unit subtitles. By 1913 all light horse regiments had adopted such a title, and the practice sometimes filtered down in a semi-official way to squadron and troop level. Some old titles found new life and, for example, the 7th Light Horse Regiment became subtitled the New South Wales Lancers, the 22nd Light Horse Regiment the South Australian Mounted Rifles. Other units looked to their region for something distinctive and new, and the 19th Light Horse Regiment took the title Yarrowee Light Horse, the 23rd Light Horse Regiment the Barossa Regiment.[69]

All this did little to change problems with training, and the raising of new units may have been as much a hindrance as a help as the limited pool of energetic and knowledgeable officers, and reasonably trained men, was further diluted by the new organisation. Concerns about the quality of local home training had not changed, and by 1912 the military authorities had effectively given up on the idea for the light horse. The Inspector-General, Major-General G.M. Kirkpatrick, an imperial officer, summed up the problem in his annual report that year by noting that 'most squadrons arrived in camp practically untrained' because of the poor standards of home training attainable in country districts. It was a system that he and many officers felt would 'always prove unsatisfactory'.[70]

Some units did better than others, and Kirkpatrick's observations when touring the country reflected this. Visiting the 8th Light Horse Brigade in South Australia he noted numerous problems with equipment maintenance, weapon care, standards of 'interior economy' and training, but he could nevertheless see the benefits and promise of work done in the regiments and gave some encouraging comments. In contrast a visit to some units in Victoria revealed both poor standards of equipment serviceability and military competence because of the poor standard of home training.[71] Local experimentation sometimes helped, and in 1908 one commanding officer abandoned brief home training parades in favour of small two- and three-day camps that allowed better use of the eight days not used by the annual camp, and reportedly achieved improved results.[72]

The efforts of enthusiastic officers were, however, often for nought. The frustrated pleas of one Western Australian commanding officer for more funds to visit parts of his regiment during this period may represent an extreme example but gives such a clear expression of the problems facing many units that his minute is worth an extended quote:

A. The regiment is scattered over an area of 180 miles by 140 miles.
B. In only two cases do two officers reside in the same town, the remainder many miles apart.
C. I have no officers in the regiment, not even Squadron Leaders capable of teaching, the majority being 2nd Lieutenants and provisional appointments.
D. Although I have visited all Squadron centres on several occasions since assuming command, have carefully inspected all books, assisted with all Squadron training, and done what teaching I could in the limited time at my disposal, and recognise my duty as Commanding Officer to see all officers are taught, and have given up nearly three months in the year to regtl. duties cheerfully, to try and get the necessary time and money privately to train my officers individually.
E. Unless the officers are trained the expenditure on the upkeep of the regiment is wasted and it might as well be disbanded.
F. The officers could not be taught to lead their men in eight weeks, the time in which the men could be made nearly fit to take the field.
G. By regimental tours only can officers be quickly and practically taught duties other than drill.
H. Nearly all the officers are busy men, attending to their own businesses, and cannot afford to leave their duties and go away to schools of instructions as often as they would wish...
I. I now hold the resignation of my best Squadron Leader because he is not learning as he would wish, and stays on only because I promised to see he was given assistance in his training; two other of my best officers and bushmen have given expression to the same thoughts and intention.
J. I cannot remain in Command of the Regiment unless it progresses satisfactorily, and if I am not assisted in my efforts to train my officers my own time is wasted as an unpaid administrator.[73]

It was not only officers who faced difficulties, and reports criticising the quality of non-commissioned officers in light horse regiments, although not as common, are not hard to find.[74]

Kirkpatrick reported in 1912 that the consensus of opinion among light horse commanders was that what was needed was not a rejigging of home training but its virtual abandonment and the extension of the amount of time spent in camp.[75] Steps in this vein had already been taken, and in 1910 all light horse units were again compelled to make their camps eight days in length.[76] From 1913, 12 of the 16 days allocated to annual training were to be used in camp with the remaining four being split equally into quarterly one-day parades at which the military authorities hoped, perhaps a little optimistically, that time would be well spent teaching officers and men the finer details of fire discipline.[77] Reflecting the problems with citizen soldier leaders of all ranks, the plan stipulated that light horse camps should take place at different times of year from those of the infantry so that they could be properly supervised. This seems to have been quite successful, and in his report for the following year Kirkpatrick believed that, although there were still many areas of weakness, it had improved the standards in the light horse regiments.[78]

Echoing Hutton and others, Kirkpatrick reiterated that compared to the infantry 'mounted troops have so much to learn in the short training period, and their efficiency is so vital to success in the field that every effort should be made to extend the period of training'.[79] Accordingly he advocated that the light horse should have its training commitment increased, yet again, to equal that of the field artillery at a total of 25 days per year, of which 17 days should be spent in a continuous camp, four days in a continuous musketry course and four dedicated to local home training. Asked to comment on this proposal, a 1913 militia officers conference thought the idea had merit but, probably worried about trying to get light-horsemen to attend such a long camp, recommended that the idea be put off for further consideration and no action was taken before the war.[80]

The training problems facing the light horse were compounded by a worrying trend of the arm falling increasingly short of its establishment. Exacerbated by the expansion required from the new defence scheme, the most likely cause identified by all concerned was the pay received by men under the new system and in particular the perpetuation of the paltry one pound per year horse allowance.[81] Complaints about the horse allowance had been long-standing but had been exacerbated by the pay cut that had come with the introduction of universal training. The issue had received renewed attention at a conference of militia officers held in Melbourne in October 1912 at which the representatives, attuned to the complaints of the men they commanded, recommended that the allowance be increased to five pounds per year.[82] One representative, pointing to the costs of forage, horse-shoes and the like, thought that nothing less than the continued existence of the light horse was at stake.[83] The Military Board, with a worried eye on the number of men enrolled, considered the proposal in late 1912 and supported an increase to four pounds per year.

Table 4.1 Establishments and strengths of the light horse, 1906–13

Date	Establishment, all ranks	Strength, all ranks	Deficiency	Percentage of strength to establishment
31 Dec 1906	5184	4723	461	91.0
31 Dec 1907	5734	4664	1070	81.3
31 Dec 1908	5712	5467	245	95.7
31 Dec 1909	5712	5405	307	94.6
31 Dec 1910	6403	5373	1030	83.9
31 Dec 1911	6384	5687	697	89.1
31 Dec 1912	9138	6630*	2508	72.5
30 Jun 1913	9194	6401#	2793	69.6

* Includes 931 trainees under the universal training scheme.
# Includes 1064 trainees under the universal training scheme.
Source: correspondence regarding light horse allowances, NAA A2023/1, A229/1/1.

Through 1913 there was an animated correspondence in the Department of Defence about the matter and in particular how the proposed rise could be accommodated in the always tight defence budget.[84]

Following an endorsement from the 1913 militia officers conference it was finally approved late that year, but there were restrictions, namely that it applied only to those soldiers who had enlisted since 1 July 1912 under the universal training scheme (those who enlisted before that date continued to receive the old rate of one pound per year) and was to be paid at a rate of five shillings per day, up to a maximum of four pounds per year, for mounted parades only.[85] Rather than truly addressing the expenses associated with owning a horse, the pay rise was really an imperfect attempt at equalising the discrepancy in pay between those men who had enlisted before mid-1912 and those who had done so after.

The raise in allowances was no doubt welcome, but the delay in its introduction made a significant contribution to continuing problems in recruitment, and in mid-1913 the arm was nearly 3000 men short of what the government wanted from the regiments it had raised thus far (see table 4.1).

Kitchener had thought 28 regiments of light horse necessary, and the Australian authorities had quickly raised this objective to 31 units.[86]

Defence headquarters, focused on achieving the massive expansion of the infantry and other arms, and perhaps showing continuing faith in the enthusiasm of Australian horsemen, seemed to think the light horse increase would pose few difficulties. By 1913, however, only 23 regiments had been raised and, considering the difficulties, the immediate likelihood that the remainder would be raised seemed unlikely at best.

When, in 1914, the next imperial officer came to visit and inspect the Australian forces his verdict on the light horse could not be anything but mixed. General Sir Ian Hamilton, who would soon command Australians at Gallipoli, agreed with almost all previous observers and enthused about the raw material in the light horse ranks.[87] In an oft-quoted line he wrote to the Minister for Defence that 'they are the pick of the bunch... they are real thrusters who would be held up by no obstacle of ground, timber or water, from getting in at the enemy.'[88] Less well remembered are the numerous and grave deficiencies he highlighted. There were, he noted, severe problems with standards of training, unit cohesion and the control exercised by men in command. Tactical planning was elementary and execution often poor, and he concluded that in most cases attempted manoeuvre by anything larger than squadron-sized bodies would quickly degenerate into 'disarray and confusion'. Against these weaknesses could be balanced the reassuring assessment that any invader of Australia would of necessity be 'very weak in the cavalry arm' and the light horse 'would have the time of their lives with [the enemy's] communications and with his scouting and foraging parties. When battle was joined they would also play their part...'[89]

Hamilton was perhaps being diplomatic and no doubt thought his remarks encouraging, but he had in fact driven to the heart of the matter in pointing to the value of the light horse chiefly lying in its ability to harass enemy scouts. Despite the considerable collective efforts that had been expended on the mounted branch since Federation, what the government now had in the light horse was in many ways what the pre-Federation colonies had despatched to South Africa: a force of irregular citizen soldier horsemen that no doubt possessed individuals with drive, knowledge and warlike talent but that, as an organisation, in its current state was capable of engaging only in minor warlike activities with any hope of efficiency. The basis was there, but it would take a long and intense period of continuous training on mobilisation for the regiments and brigades to reach the efficiency required of them in war. George Lee, the man whom Hutton had placed in command of the Victorian *ad hoc* brigade in 1903, had said as much to a grouping of officers at a lecture in 1909:

108   UNFULFILLED PROMISE

> It is absolutely impossible to train our mounted troops up to the standard of Imperial cavalry. I don't think it will be possible for a considerable time to aim for such a standard. We can put into the field first-class irregular light horse. If the force is well organised, excels in fire discipline and marksmanship, is thoroughly trained in horse management... then I have no hesitation in saying that with the material we have in Australia an exceedingly useful force can be made available.[90]

That was all well and good for the last war, but not everyone was so convinced about the next one. Another officer noted that despite 'all the good work done in South Africa by both our officers and men, it must be remembered that we will not have Boers to fight again, and much higher training will be required against European troops'.[91]

THE MILITIA LIGHT HORSE AT HOME, 1914–20

On the outbreak of the First World War in August 1914 the government called out 10 000 militiamen to man the forts and bolster local defences.[92] Light horse units were part of this effort, and selected squadrons found themselves mobilised to assist with it. In order to ensure that light horse and other militiamen took their commitments seriously orders were issued in November that men obligated to military service by the universal training scheme were to be prosecuted for offences under the regulations.[93] Such steps proved largely unnecessary, however, and Japan's declaration of war on Germany in August effectively removed any potential threat to Australia. By the end of December 1914 most citizen units had been stood down, although some would occasionally be called on to undertake patrols or other protective duties for a while yet. The three squadrons of one New South Wales regiment, for example, each spent a few weeks protecting Sydney's water supply in March and April 1915 from an enemy raid that never eventuated.[94] Activities of this sort proved to be the high point of warlike activity for the light horse at home during the war. By mid-1917, when there were 89 officers and some 3000 other ranks on duty for home defence, the sum of the contribution by the light horse appears to have been just three men on duty at Fremantle.[95]

It is probably just as well that such an effort was all that was required of the militia light horse in 1914, and the warnings about the militia light horse in Hamilton's report proved prescient. An assessment of the militia's

Photo 16 On the outbreak of war in 1914, selected militia light horse units were mobilised to patrol and protect key centres around Australia. These militiamen, apparently unarmed and with some in civilian clothes, are moving around Sydney in 1915. (State Library of South Australia, PRG280/1/27/54)

competence for war in 1914, made in 1917 by a Military Board wizened by war, could only come to a similar view. It realistically concluded that at 'the outbreak of war it would not have been possible to take a Militia Regiment as it stood and put it in the field at once against an efficient enemy, without disaster'.[96] This did not mean, however, that efforts were not continuing towards the goal of trying to improve things (at least at first), and during the first years of the war the government and military authorities planned to maintain the citizen forces at home alongside the AIF overseas.[97] The training commitment of the light horse regiments in 1914–15 highlighted this determination, and when the 2nd Light Horse Brigade went into camp at West Maitland in June of that year, for example, they followed Kirkpatrick's direction of a few years earlier and did so for the extended period of 12 days.[98]

There had also been a continuing effort to expand the light horse, a project perhaps helped by the enthusiasm of men who proved keen to join the local forces upon war breaking out, just as their forebears had during the war scares and imperial conflicts of the nineteenth century. In the last months of 1914 and up to mid-1915 the Department of Defence received at least 23 applications to form mounted detachments or squadrons.[99] How many similar approaches were made to local commanding officers or the commandants of military districts is unknown, but it seems likely that this martial enthusiasm helped boost the numbers of the men serving in the light horse. In 1912 and 1913 the light horse had about 6500 men on the roll books, but by the end of 1914 there were 8604 men and by the end of 1916 the number had risen to an unprecedented 11 103.[100] The traditional reliance on voluntary enlistment for the mounted branch means that most of these men were probably volunteers, but it seems likely that a significant proportion were men who had opted to serve their universal training commitment in the light horse.[101]

This seems to have facilitated a degree of organisational expansion. In late 1914 there were 70 light horse squadrons serving around the country, which was equivalent to the 23 regiments raised up to the middle of 1913, but by the end of 1916 there were 78 squadrons. This was equivalent to 26 regiments but, as there had been no increase in the number of regimental headquarters, the expansion evidently took place within the existing units. An increase in the number of units did eventually occur, however, and by 1919 the light horse order of battle included 30 separate regiments, a figure close to the target of 31 regiments that had been set with the introduction of universal training in 1912.[102]

By the end of the war these regiments had undergone yet another renumbering process designed to align them territorially with their AIF brethren overseas. Thus, just as the 1st Light Horse Regiment of the AIF came from New South Wales, so now did the 1st Light Horse Regiment of the militia, and so on around the country. The government, which was behind the idea, saw it as a way to foster the *élan* and spirit of the AIF in the troubled units of the militia. The Military Board, looking at the practicalities, had some misgivings about the plan as there were more militia than AIF units and the territorial recruiting areas of the two forces did not always neatly overlap, but the plan was approved in mid-1916 and took effect in 1918.[103] The change also saw another abolition of the territorial subtitles adopted after 1912 as a way of strengthening the ties of regiment and community. Although the plan did have some merit, it also tended to reinforce the notion that the militia was the AIF's inferior,[104] especially as it was the third renumbering process undertaken since Federation, and one that went against the rationalist approach adopted with the introduction of universal training. If nothing else it certainly represented a cavalier attitude to the traditions and community associations of some long-serving citizen units.

Higher-level changes were also considered, and during the war some steps were made towards the adoption of a divisional organisation for the militia, including the light horse. The possibility of a divisional structure had perhaps been implicit in the militia organisation after the introduction of universal training (the number of proposed units and brigades closely correlating with that needed to form divisions), and some moves had been made towards suitable war establishments in 1912, but it was not until the beginning of July 1914 that the Military Board authorised the first definite steps towards the creation of the first two infantry divisions as part of the peace establishment. A little over a month later, though, Australia was at war, and it seems that whatever was being arranged was left unfinished. It was not forgotten, however, and in 1915 new peace establishments were issued outlining the creation of six infantry divisions (which included divisional mounted regiments) and two light horse divisions.[105] The establishments allocated every unit then existing in the citizen forces as well as those that were planned but had not yet been raised; but all of this was highly optimistic. Although the paper establishments were periodically updated and reissued over the next few years (and it is possible this framework provided a basis for post-war deliberations), there is no evidence that this grand divisional scheme ever progressed beyond the drawing board. Indeed, given the true state of the light horse and the rest of the forces at home during most of the war, such a plan can only be described as fanciful.[106]

Despite the increase in numbers of men serving and the number of units raised during the war, the reality was that the light horse (and the other arms) at home during the war quickly became a hollow force. Chief among the reasons for this was a persistent and debilitating drain on manpower from the militia to the AIF. By December 1914, 10 000 soldiers out of the 56 000 then serving in the citizen forces had agreed to join the AIF, and by 1917, 75 per cent of militia officers and 50 per cent of the other ranks had done the same.[107] What proportion of these men were light-horsemen is unclear, but the impact on the units they left must have been considerable, particularly as those who left were often the keen, fit and interested officers, non-commissioned officers and men who had made soldiering a passionate pastime and who were the backbone of their units.

The high percentage of officer transfers meant that most units were soon under the command of quite junior men. Before the war unit command had been a lieutenant-colonel or major's appointment, but by early 1915 many were passing to the command of captains and by 1917 six light horse regiments or infantry battalions were under the command of a lieutenant.[108] Command of brigades was similarly falling to majors, and men who would normally have been retired through age were granted extensions of service.[109] Given the criticisms of pre-war militia officers, one can only wonder at the command qualities of many of these junior men suddenly found in important appointments.

Men who did not volunteer for the AIF did so for their own reasons, and it seems likely that many light-horsemen who had family and farm or business commitments were not in a position to volunteer without bringing hardship on their families.[110] The fact that more than 80 per cent of the men who enlisted in the AIF were unmarried serves to reinforce the point.[111] Others tried to volunteer but were rejected on medical grounds, a factor given much less consideration when men undertook to serve in the citizen forces. Some, as the Military Board discovered in 1916 when it tried to comb out more officer volunteers from the citizen forces, were simply not inclined to join the AIF and go to war. The Inspector-General, with evident distaste, noted the sometimes vague reasons given and wondered 'of these officers what they conceive to be the moral obligation of a holder of the King's Commission'.[112] Such men soon found their commissions withdrawn and their military services dispensed with. It seems reasonable to assume that similar situations and attitudes could have been found across the full spectrum of the ranks.

The loss of quality manpower was exacerbated by a general rundown of support given to the citizen forces as the war progressed. The determination to maintain militia training and resources while also meeting the requirements of the AIF quickly faded, and by July 1915 units were informed that many of their rifles and all of their pistols were to be returned to store. Three months later they learned that no new uniforms would be issued them.[113] That September the Military Board decided that training would be suspended for six months and, although this decision does not seem to have affected units until the beginning of 1916, the suspension was extended until 1917.[114] The support of permanent instructors was also drastically reduced as most of these men found their way to war, and by late 1915 there were only sufficient permanent staff to maintain basic administrative functions.[115] When training did take place, the circumstances were sometimes unusual, and in 1917, for example, the 26th Light Horse Regiment found itself supervising and training a large number of infantry recruits.[116] Home training, although of little use to the light horse before the war, continued to be in abeyance through 1917. Twenty-four days were allocated to training in 1918–19, of which 16 days were to be in camp, but many camps were never held owing to the influenza epidemic. Again in 1919–20 training was suspended, by which time the Military Board concluded that 80 per cent of the men in the citizen forces were non-efficient.[117] Proving how empty was the expansion of the number of units at home during the war, in 1918 the government gave consideration to the idea of temporarily amalgamating units so that some useful training could be achieved.[118]

War had offered those who served at home some opportunities, however, even if they were not always what the government had in mind. The permanent adjutant of one light horse regiment found himself the custodian of a large amount of cash left over after paying one of the unit's squadrons following a period of mobilisation early in the war. Temptation eventually got the better of him, and he soon graduated to creating fraudulent pay sheets and forage contracts, eventually defrauding the government of more than a staggering £67 000. The scandal that accompanied the discovery of the crime became grist for the mill of a royal commission into lacklustre defence administration held between 1917 and 1919. The liquidation of his estate recovered just £19 726.[119]

With the end of the war the light horse at home was in poor shape. Universal trainees whose service obligation had expired during the war were allowed to discharge or voluntarily re-enlist in 1919, but it was June the following year before the men who were voluntarily enlisted in the light horse were released from serving under the war provisions of the Defence Act and allowed either to discharge or to re-enlist. Those who had been fortunate enough to have enlisted before the introduction of universal training were now informed that if they re-engaged they would finally have to do so at the lower, post-1912 pay rate of four shillings per day instead of the eight shillings they had been getting.[120] The immediate post-war period remained as *ad hoc* as the years before. Training again took place in 1920–21, of which eight days were in camp, but it proved impossible to do anything but the most basic military work.[121]

The difficulties of the war years were in many ways simply a reflection of earlier problems brought to their natural conclusion. The militia light horse had always been likely to face problems. Hutton's scheme owed perhaps too much to his own mind to last long. Reflecting his long-standing views on mounted troops and influenced by the experiences of South Africa, they were too idiosyncratic and detached from broader imperial trends to endure. With Hutton's departure the military authorities, increasingly interested in London's views on military organisation, were unsure whether they liked the mounted force they had inherited. As a result the light horse and the Field Force of which it was part were left largely to drift under the initial impetus from Hutton. Hamstrung also by general uncertainty about the whole direction of defence thinking, the light horse was forced to continue with a system that possessed many inherent weaknesses and under a guiding doctrine that was regarded as increasingly irrelevant by the military authorities.

When a new defence scheme was at last unveiled in 1910 and introduced in 1912, the light horse was given some badly needed doctrinal direction, but the other problems were given no correction and were exacerbated by the need to suddenly expand the number of mounted troops available. It was an expansion effectively beyond the organisation. As shown in table 4.1 (page 106), Hutton had inherited about 5500 mounted soldiers from the colonies, and the strength of the light horse, surprisingly, regardless of the desired establishment, hovered between 4600 and 5500 for much of the Federation period until the introduction of universal training in 1912. Total light horse strengths for 1912 and 1913 went up to about 6500 men, but these figures required an injection of about a thousand men each year under the new scheme. With the desire to further expand the number of light horse regiments, even this increase was not enough.

One of the perverse strengths of the pre-Federation mounted forces was that they were dependent on the demand from citizens themselves to be included in the defence forces. Colonial governments largely restricted their role to stabilising the offers, shaping their form and administering what the citizenry gave. The new Commonwealth Government and the military bureaucracy inverted this relationship and, particularly after 1912, sought to dictate what forces they would have. This was deemed necessary and was not in itself the problem but, unaccompanied by any changes to the way the light horse was recruited, organised, paid, trained and led, it meant that the military authorities would have great trouble escaping the unwritten limits set by men they relied on to give their own free time and labour to the mounted branch. These limits were evident before the war but were made alarmingly clear during the war years when the men and resources that had propped up the system quickly disappeared.

CHAPTER | 5

THE LIGHT-HORSEMEN I
Citizen mounted troops and Australian society

With the exception of the men who served during the First World War, the light-horsemen and their colonial predecessors were almost all part-time soldiers. Only the few permanent instructors and staff officers employed by the colonies, and later the Commonwealth, thought about and carried out their military duties as full-time professionals. Australian governments, shielded by the empire, facing no real threat, and loathe to raise and pay for any permanent forces apart from the small groups of technical troops who manned the guns of the forts or the submarine mines, were quite content with this. Only when the threat of Japan began to animate defence thinking after 1905 was a serious effort made to alter the way the country was defended, but even then under the universal training scheme the militia model was merely expanded rather than replaced and had only limited application to the mounted branch. By making these choices governments and their military commanders wedded themselves not just to a military training system but also to a complex interaction between the way their part-time soldiers trained to defend the country, then went home to lead normal and varied lives. To some extent armies are products of the society that begets them, and this is rarely more true than when considering the volunteer and partially paid men of the mounted forces of late colonial and post-Federation Australia.

The early volunteer mounted corps established around the Australian colonies between the 1850s and the mid-1880s had had a difficult time remaining viable organisations. Few of these bodies lasted long and, once the spurt of enthusiasm that had brought about their conception had spent itself, they usually collapsed under the weight of the problems that beset them. Uneven and poor standards of leadership, the financial strain of being a volunteer, negative attitudes from bystanders and repetitive or boring training all made their contribution to the high rates of discharge – and thus eventually corps failure – that characterised the early mounted units of the Australian colonies. After 1885 the larger mainland colonies adopted larger and more thorough plans to maintain their mounted forces and, with Federation, an even more complete plan was adopted. These organisational changes made little difference, however, to many of the broader characteristics of citizen mounted units themselves or to the way they interacted with the society from which they came.

Social interactions

Certainly the way in which colonial governments obtained the services of mounted troops – applications from local communities – changed little throughout the entire pre-Federation period. An 1890 application to the New South Wales Government from Lismore provided a typical example, informing the government that following a local meeting a number of local men were offering their services to make up a troop of cavalry that would 'drill into a most efficient and enthusiastic body of men'.[1] In such applications the alleged suitability of the men was, not surprisingly, a recurring theme and was often pitched as a key selling point. An 1888 application to form a mounted infantry company in Cooma emphasised that 'the nature of the country and climate in this district has resulted in a race of particularly hardy men calculated to provide an efficient Corps... and that a similar description is applicable to the horses'.[2]

Whether such applications were to prove successful was another matter and depended on various considerations. If made during a period of military fervour, such as that which followed a war scare, the number of offers could easily exceed the requirements (really the budgetary limits) of governments. When the Victorian Mounted Rifles was first raised in 1885–86, for example, the authorised establishment of a thousand men was easily reached and a number of applications to form detachments had to be turned down.[3] Similarly in New South Wales between 1886 and 1889 the government received 19 separate applications from districts to form a variety of mounted detachments, but most had to be turned down because to accept all of them would have cost 'upwards of £37 000'.[4] Practicalities relating to location, resources and instructors always played a part in which districts would get to raise their detachment, but a degree of luck often played a role. Applications from Liverpool and Camden to form mounted infantry detachments in 1891 proved successful as the government at that time desired to raise the establishment of the mounted infantry to make it roughly equal in size to the colony's existing cavalry establishment.[5] The 1890 Lismore application was accepted as the existing Sydney troop was proving incapable of maintaining attendance, and this opened up a space on the establishment.[6]

Although Sydney was able, with varying degrees of success, to maintain mounted elements both before and after Federation, most urban detachments rarely lasted long. The inherent requirement of mounted troops having to provide their own horses effectively ruled out most town and city dwellers, for whom keeping a horse implied the possession of considerable wealth in order to keep it stabled and otherwise attended to. Hiring a horse from a livery stable when required, as was sometimes done in earlier years, also implied considerable personal expense,[7] and military authorities became wary of this practice for the obvious reason that access to a horse in a military emergency could not be guaranteed. Colonial authorities generally agreed with those in Queensland when they asserted that 'in the case of Mounted Infantry, the suburban and country districts supply the best men'.[8] Perhaps the distractions of town played some role in this, but fundamentally it was only in country areas that sufficient men owned and kept horses in the course of their normal lives. Although the revival of mounted units in New South Wales in 1885 had started with the Sydney Light Horse Volunteers it was no accident that by the mid-1890s their successors, the New South Wales Lancers, became centred on the more suburban environs of Parramatta rather than Sydney proper. In 1903 the New South Wales commandant, when trying to raise a half-squadron of light horse for the Sydney Garrison Forces, had to admit that 'suitable men with horses are most difficult to get in and near Sydney'.[9] Even provincial Brisbane proved unable to support more than one troop of light horse in 1909.[10]

City units, when they existed, thus tended to be something of an oddity. Of the 69 men engaged with the Sydney troop of the New South Wales Cavalry Brigade Reserves between 1885 and 1889, it included 11 men, of apparent means and leisure, who simply stated on the muster roll that their employment was 'gentleman'. Other prosperous middle-class professions were suitably represented, and the rolls included one barrister, four solicitors, three auctioneers, two architects, one surgeon and one newspaper proprietor with the propitious surname of Fairfax.

The remainder was a cross-section of typical urban employment of the time with clerks being the most represented after the 'gentlemen'.[11]

More representative of most mounted detachments was the rural make-up of the Illawarra troop during the same period. Here the troop was more successful to begin with and was able to recruit 90 men into its ranks between 1885 and 1889. Of these men 47 described themselves as farmers and a further four as graziers, while the remainder of the men enrolled represented a cross-section of small town professions of the time. Only two men described themselves as 'gentlemen'.[12] Again, because of the requirement to own a horse and have enough spare time available to go soldiering, membership of rural detachments also required an indefinable but real level of financial comfort from the members. Many lowly but respectable township employment categories, such as drapers or tinsmiths, found themselves in the ranks, but the rolls reveal fewer men enlisted who could be considered rural labourers, such as shearers or station hands. This possibly reflected the itinerant nature of many of these workers or perhaps the radical labour politics of the time, which was often dismissive of citizen soldiering.[13] The real reasons were probably more prosaic, however, and after Federation one permanent officer thought that the lack of station hands in the light horse was simply due to their employers not releasing them for military service.[14]

Thus, although many men involved may well have possessed an air of colonial hardiness and been worthy of the vague title of 'bushmen', the composition of most detachments was more of a rural and respectable middle-class than the stereotypical rough and ready stockman or boundary rider more often brought to mind. In the Casino troop of the Upper Clarence Light Horse of the late 1880s, for example, 38 per cent of the men were small landowners or local merchants. In the Ulmarra Light Horse 31 of the 46 men described their occupation as farmer.[15] Of the 88 men who put their names forward to enlist in the proposed Lismore troop in 1890, 49 were farmers.[16] A sample of the 6th Light Horse Regiment in 1907 similarly reveals that farmers and graziers outnumbered stockmen and labourers by two to one.[17] When the Tasmanian Mounted Infantry was raised at the end of the nineteenth century, the colony's commandant, summing up the requirements, proposed to start it 'on the North Coast, where the farmers are well-to-do, and have the horses necessary for the service'.[18]

No doubt attractive to many of these men was the nature of mounted service in Australia during the pre-Federation period, which, like everywhere else in the world, carried with it a certain military cachet. In

Photo 17 In colonial Australia, military endeavours were frequently accompanied by flights of martial fancy. This 1872 engraving imagines Victoria's Prince of Wales's Light Horse moving to deal with the colony's enemies. (State Library of Victoria, IAN23/04/72/88)

1858 one South Australian parliamentarian proposed to the house the establishment of a corps of horsemen and offered that there was a 'class of persons... who, though... not prepared to go and shoulder the musket would if properly mounted and armed, prove a most effective means of defence'.[19] Similarly, when a New South Wales parliamentarian provided support to an 1895 application to raise a mounted rifle company in Glen Innes, he contended that there would be a number of farmers' sons and others 'who would be very glad... to join a Mounted Corps, and who would never dream of serving in an Infantry force'.[20]

Much of the differentiation between potential cavalrymen and potential infantrymen was related to horse ownership and the costs associated, but simply to belong to a mounted corps usually entailed considerable other expenses. Even those corps eventually put on the partially paid establishment during the 1890s in colonies such as New South Wales, South Australia and Queensland started out in the mid-1880s as unpaid volunteer units. In these corps, and sometimes also in the part-paid units they became, men were required to meet the costs of their uniforms, saddlery and perhaps some of their military equipment. These expenses quickly added up and were a particularly steep requirement on enlistment. A trooper of the New South Wales Lancers (undoubtedly Australia's most socially and economically patrician regiment) in the 1890s received perhaps £10 in pay and allowances per year from the government for his services, but was also expected to own and maintain a suitable horse, provide his own saddlery, pay for some of his equipment, including a dress uniform (a £10 cost by itself, although service dress was now provided by the government), meet his out-of-pocket expenses and make a contribution to support the regimental band.[21] Also expected of him was paid-up membership to the New South Wales Lancer Association, a body that organised social functions including the annual ball, assisted injured soldiers and engaged well-known Sydney chefs to cook food in camp.[22] No other regiment expected as much of its men as did the lancers, but, in any unit, to be a mounted soldier was not a poor man's pursuit.

The social standing of, and affluence in, mounted units was emphasised in the officer ranks. The costs involved for these men were considerable, particularly if their unit chose to adopt one of the more glorious uniforms. In 1885 when the Sydney Light Horse Volunteers converted to lancers they adopted a uniform based on that of the 5th Royal Irish Lancers, which was made in England and cost £60. Such dazzling uniforms were rare by the late 1880s as the realities of modern warfare permeated even the forces of the Antipodes, but the costs of being an officer remained high. Many of these were, nominally at least, voluntary (or more likely the simply expected, but not strictly compulsory, kind of contributions that officers' messes excel in collecting) and reflected a mixture of patrician attitudes and a kind of military philanthropy that benefited the corps they belonged to. The New South Wales Lancer band, for example, made its first appearance in 1891 on 24 horses supplied at the complete expense of the officers of the Hunter River troop of the regiment. When the band required some revitalisation in 1898, fresh horses, saddlery and music were provided, and the costs were again borne by the regiment's officers.[23] By the end of the century the officers were collectively contributing about £200 per year in order to maintain the regimental band.[24]

The wealth and military largesse of some officers became somewhat famous, and perhaps the best-known example was the command of the New South Wales Lancers by Colonel James Burns. A prominent Sydney businessman, he was the Burns half of the Burns Philp business empire founded in 1893, and the regimental history records that his involvement with the regiment 'was his main non-business interest and he spent lavishly on it'.[25] As an indication of what prominence and enthusiasm could bring a man in the right circumstances, he had enlisted in the Parramatta troop as a trooper in early June 1891 but was promoted to captain by the end of the following month. By 1897 he had attained the rank of lieutenant-colonel and taken command of the regiment. He involved himself closely in all aspects of the regiment and used his wealth to help it wherever he could.[26] Undoubtedly a popular man in the unit, his military philanthropy was, in certain circles at least, held up as an example of selfless patriotism: 'Colonel Burns, although a very busy city man, has always found a good deal of time to devote to the fine Regiment of which he is so justly proud. Few men in the military world of Australia have proved more unselfishly patriotic, where patriotism spells £. s. d. and loss of valuable time. The Regiment owes its present Commanding Officer more than it will be able to repay within the next decade or two.'[27]

Burns was a rare example of the confluence of extreme wealth and citizen soldier activity, but men who could be described as financially comfortable and perhaps prominent in some other way, typical pillars of society, were part of the fabric of many mounted units. Large landholders were involved with many units and often commanded detachments, squadrons or even regiments themselves. In the late 1880s Captain Goodger of the Ulmarra Light Horse and Captain Fanning of the Casino troop of the Upper Clarence Light Horse were both prosperous graziers.[28] Charles Chauvel, founder of the Upper Clarence Light Horse, was also the patriarch of a prominent pastoral family of northern New South Wales. As an indication of how the civilian relationships of landholders could transfer to the military sphere his son, Harry Chauvel, was able to form the basis of a company of the Darling Downs Mounted Infantry in Queensland when the family's employees, who had made up a troop of the Upper Clarence Light Horse, crossed the border with their employers in 1890.[29]

This does not, however, mean that the well-to-do were universally interested in military affairs. In 1884 the completely unpaid volunteer Victorian Forces, then coming to an end of a period of degeneration, were moved to issue as a general order a lament that 'the wealthy mercantile, professional and leisured classes... have ceased for many years to belong to or take any active interest in the force'.[30] Things did not change with Federation, and in 1909 another officer complained: 'Of the men who have most to lose, the large graziers and farmers, with few exceptions, show the least active sympathy with the defence movement, and I can safely say that not more than one per cent of the Light Horsemen in the country are station hands...'.[31] Nevertheless politicians also regularly found their place, and in 1855 the South Australian forces had four parliamentarians serving in their ranks. Two of these served in the Adelaide Mounted Rifles and one, Captain Edward Gwynne, was its commander.[32] The 1st Australian Horse included among its officer ranks no fewer than three parliamentarians. The services of the colony's Governor were secured as the regiment's honorary colonel, and his private secretary, Captain Ferguson of the 2nd Life Guards, took on the appointment of regimental second-in-command with a local rank of major.[33] The regiment's founder, James Mackay, was an influential pastoralist from Gundagai and held enough political clout to gain a place as vice-president of the colony's Executive Council in 1899.[34] Showing again what social or political prominence could do, he had previously held the rank of captain from an earlier association with the West Camden Light Horse but, on being given permission to raise his own unit, he immediately gained a promotion to major and in 1898 was promoted lieutenant-colonel.

The financial burdens on officers meant that only those men willing and able to meet the expenses could be seriously considered to receive commissions. Men who might have otherwise had leadership skills but did not have the wherewithal to meet all the outlays could not consider, or be considered for, officer appointments. Many detachments failed because their officers were unable to continue with their service and no suitable candidates could be found to take their place.[35] Suitability had economic as well as military considerations, and one officer claimed that 'many of our best young officers are far from being independent, and the cost of providing for themselves with a complete kit often deters good men from joining our Australian Mounted Service'.[36] Edward Hutton was of much the same opinion and, after Federation, hoped that the introduction of a plain uniform would encourage potential officers 'who have in the past found it extremely difficult to supply themselves with expensive uniform'.[37] He also took a dim view of the New South Wales tradition of officers paying for bands, complaining that it added considerably to officer expenses, making it difficult to find candidates 'for vacant Commissions in mounted regiments'.[38]

After Federation various attempts were made to keep the costs of being an officer down, but the efforts seem to have had only partial success. In 1909 one senior officer thought the problem of expensive uniform was a 'hardy "bogey" which no amount of substantial facts and solid figures seem to effectively allay'.[39] That one year's service would provide enough pay to return the investment seemed a suitable balance to him. Yet his view was counter to that of the inspector-general who, just two years previously, had again raised the problem in his annual report and pointed out that to buy all the uniforms and accoutrements a new light horse officer would be out of pocket by more than £41.[40] The costs were even higher for a man taking a commission in the engineers or artillery. Messing was another expense, and one Queensland light horse officer voiced concern that to attend camps in that state in 1911–12 cost 10 shillings more than they were paid in allowances. In the same forum Harry Chauvel, then adjutant-general, pointed out that it was worse for permanent officers who had to attend multiple camps – his attendance at six camps in Queensland in one year had left him £20 worse off.[41] Maintaining horseflesh remained a key burden. In the first years after Federation officers of the light horse, emphasising that they must have some means, received no horse allowance. This deficiency was corrected at some point before the First World War, although the allowance remained a token amount: £1.17.6 for a lieutenant, £5.12.6 for a colonel in 1913.[42]

The costs associated with command never disappeared entirely, and between the two world wars there were complaints from officers who had to pay for their own travel to visit their dispersed detachments.[43] Accordingly many men who were willing and able to serve as citizen officers made sacrifices to do so. Such men perhaps felt they were giving something to their society by making the sacrifices necessary to pursue citizen soldiering,[44] but the demands on time, effort and finances meant that most officers did not serve long and the effects had to be carried by the units they served.

Regiments having to change their organisational structure to accommodate the location and skills of the men who were willing to serve was not an uncommon event. In 1888, for example, the commander of D Company of the Victorian Mounted Rifles, Captain Fawcett, transferred to the reserve, and as his replacement, Lieutenant Nethercote, lived in Moe the company headquarters had to be moved there. When he in turn received a promotion in 1889 the new commander lived in Warragul, and the headquarters again moved. In 1890 the headquarters of C Company had to be similarly relocated from Heyfield to Sale when a new commander was appointed.[45] In 1903 Hutton was amazed to discover that, although the 2nd and 3rd Light Horse Regiments were established in rural New South Wales, their respective headquarters were to be set up in Sydney. The state commandant responded to his queries that as Lieutenant-Colonel Onslow (2nd LHR) was in Sydney two to three times a week and that Colonel Mackay (3rd LHR) actually lived in town it was easiest to have their headquarters there.[46]

Photo 18 To be an officer, like this unidentified gentleman of the South Australian Mounted Rifles, required considerable outlays to meet the associated expenses. Despite the popular image, the financial commitments even to be a ranker meant that most mounted militiamen were more likely rural landowners than stockmen. (AWM A03853)

The social function of such units for the men enlisted in the often remote communities in which the corps existed should not be overlooked. When men went into camp they did so not only to train but also for the opportunity to socialise. The usual Easter camps held by the Victorian Mounted Rifles included not just military training and tactical manoeuvring but also time, usually on the Sunday, to relax and enjoy sports. Martial sports such as tent-pegging and lemon-cutting they may have been, and hence another form of military training, but sports nonetheless. Viewing activities at the camps was a popular pastime for Melburnians looking for a day out, and for these onlookers as well as the men enlisted horse-jumping competitions and camp concerts were often organised.[47] The men of the regiment regularly competed for prizes, and in 1896, for example, the Victorian Minister for Defence offered £10 in prize money at the North Gippsland Agricultural Show for the men of C Company of the Victorian Mounted Rifles competing in riding skills.[48] Similarly, in 1905 the commander of the 12th Light Horse Regiment encouraged his men to enter a military sports competition at the Elphin Show Grounds.[49] Detachments of cavalry in northern New South Wales during the 1890s often hosted dances or smoking concerts, and most held annual balls.[50] A Victorian newspaper recorded that the ball held by one light horse troop in 1913 was 'the very top rung of the ladder of social life as far as Minyip was concerned'.[51] Displays by detachments on significant days, such as the Anniversary Day (now Australia Day) cavalry tournament by the Lismore and Casino troops in Lismore in 1892, were a regular part of local celebrations.[52] Communities sometimes got more than simple viewing pleasures, and in 1899 the Young and Cootamundra hospitals received £23 donated by a half-squadron of the 1st Australian Horse from funds raised from a sports day and ball.[53] In the 1890s, an age of growing labour unrest, some hoped that activities of this sort would have a soothing effect in their communities, and the New South Wales Commandant, Major-General French, thought that the formation of the 1st Australian Horse was 'bringing masters and men into close intercourse, class prejudice and distrust [are] being supplanted by a feeling of camaraderie and esprit de corps'.[54]

In spite of these at times prominent communal interactions, the mounted corps of the late nineteenth and early twentieth centuries were not free of the same sort of negative comments from bystanders that had bedevilled the volunteer bodies of earlier decades. The representative of one application to form a cavalry detachment in the 1880s wrote to the authorities asking that their case be expedited so that he and others on the committee no longer would have to 'suffer a great amount of annoyance, [and] unpleasant remarks etc. at the hands of a section of the community who are always opposing persons or movements of a military character'.[55] The parliamentarian Edward O'Sullivan supported the New South Wales Mounted Rifles 'not withstanding the sneers of those who are apt to try to belittle our citizen soldiery'.[56] Colonel Tom Price congratulated one of his companies of the Victorian Mounted Rifles for remaining dignified and disciplined 'while being harassed by a lot of people, who are apparently too idle to serve this country themselves and consider it a generous action to annoy those who do'.[57] Another Victorian officer summed up the dual attitudes to citizen soldiers of the time, noting that '"Playing at Soldiers" has been the most general expression applied to the really effective work of the volunteers and the partially paid forces'.[58]

These views owed much to an attitude – held with some justification – that citizen soldiers, with what in reality constituted only a small amount of military training, were not much in the way of a defence force. The *Adelaide Observer* commented on the South Australian Mounted Rifles after a review that, despite their flair, 'it could readily be seen where regular drill came in and where it did not'.[59] War in South Africa may have ameliorated attitudes of this sort as complaints about derisive comments are scarce after Federation, but this did not mean that communities were always supportive. One of the reasons behind the failure of a light horse troop at Gunnedah in 1904 was that the trustees of the local School of Arts would not entertain the idea of allowing a small room to be added to their building for use as an orderly room. As a result the men had to drill in the street by moon- or lamp-light.[60]

Views such as these are unlikely to have made service in the late colonial or post-Federation mounted corps more pleasurable. Nor were the other sacrifices men had to make. The time alone required to be an active mounted soldier was often considerable. If living near a town, regular attendance at short local night- and day-time drills was the norm. In the late 1890s the men of the Parramatta half-squadron of the New South Wales Lancers were required to parade two nights a week and to be available for the many public events to which the detachment was committed.[61] Members of rural detachments, although facing perhaps fewer requirements to parade, often had to make long trips by foot, horse or train to make it to their destination to attend local or unit training – a round trip that could amount to perhaps 30 kilometres. On top of that, if the unit was further concentrating, for an Easter Camp for example, there was usually a further train trip to where the camp was to be held, and by that stage some men would have travelled almost 300 kilometres with their horse and their equipment just to train for four days.[62] The obstacles to make it even to the train could be considerable, and in the early 1890s the Casino Troop of the New South Wales Cavalry had to ford three rivers simply to get to their nearest railhead.[63]

Difficulties of this sort, combined with the demands that the men faced from their civilian employment or business interests, meant that many men soon became disillusioned and unhappy with their military lot. All these factors, in combination, meant that the Victorian Mounted Rifles, despite having an on-paper strength of between 800 and 1000 men for much of its existence, achieved a camp attendance of 400 men on only two occasions. In some years the regiment could not even muster 200 men at camp.[64] Even at local parades attendances for this regiment were often poor. In the final quarter of 1897 most detachments could get, on average, only a third of their men to attend such gatherings. In B Company the detachment in Shepparton could only get 10 of its 27 enrolled men to attend; in Murchison 12 of 25; Broadford eight of 19 and Avenel six of 15. These figures are entirely representative of the other companies.[65]

The changes to conditions of service with Federation proved a mixed blessing for the men who made up the rank and file. The new base pay rate of eight shillings per day meant that, in combination with the one-pound horse allowance, soldiers who attended all their training commitments could receive up to about eight pounds per annum.[66] This meant that the mounted men of Queensland and New South Wales were slightly worse off under the new regime than they had been before Federation. The previously unpaid men of Victoria, Western Australia and Tasmania were, of course, much better off. The horse allowance that enlisted men received after Federation was purely token and reflected the idea that sacrifice was part of the contract of service. However, what men had to provide themselves did gradually improve under the federal system. They would always have to provide their own 'quiet, active, compact, well-built horse',[67] but uniforms were simplified and, even if they were sometimes difficult to get, at least the government paid for them. From 1913 all light-horsemen were finally issued a set of saddlery, thus fulfilling a long-standing need. From 1905, if a man's horse was injured or killed when being used for military training, he was compensated, although the amount was 'not intended to make good the full amount of loss sustained'.[68]

Other changes in conditions had their own effect, and the time required to be a mounted soldier remained appreciable. After Federation Hutton emphasised that only men who could attend his eight-day camps should even contemplate joining the light horse.[69] This change caused considerable consternation among some soldiers who had served in the pre-Federation forces, and the reorganisation of part of the New South Wales Mounted Rifles into the 2nd Light Horse Regiment was hampered by poor attendance 'ascribed to the lengthened duration of parades and other of the new regulations'.[70] Despite the pay, getting men to parade in the light horse was an apparently insurmountable problem. One officer, echoing earlier experiences, noted that it was not uncommon for light-horsemen to have to ride more than 15 kilometres, although some might have ridden up to 50, to attend a half-day parade. Such demands, he noted, meant that getting men to the drill hall or training paddock was often difficult.[71]

Although social interaction was an important part of local parades, the focus more often tended to be purely military in character, particularly after Federation. In November 1906 the Hamilton troop of the 11th Light Horse Regiment spent two half-day parades training in mounted drill and dismounted outposts, as well as two night parades doing a firing exercise, and practising saluting and marching.[72] The program of half-day parades for the 12th Light Horse Regiment two years earlier was a long list of military training activities ranging from the occupation of a position to reconnaissance duties and field firing with blanks.[73] Because Australian soldiers were 'naturally... indifferent horsemaster[s]', and highlighting one of the lessons of South Africa, men in longer camps now spent a large amount of their time learning how to tend to their horses properly.[74]

Distractions from these routines were to be purely wholesome, and the sale of cigarettes and alcohol at light horse and other continuous camps was strictly prohibited. An unpopular regulation, this restriction was generally opposed by most officers, who believed that as long as the men were 21 years of age they should be able to partake. One Tasmanian medical officer even warned that 'it was dangerous to keep some away from their beer'.[75] Leisure was thus largely restricted to sports or perhaps a concert by the regimental band.

Men who did attend their parades often found the training dull or repetitive after a while. This was largely the result of uneven leadership standards, poor attendances and the high turnover of men in the ranks. With men missing, or with many new men in the troop or half-squadron, the training rarely moved beyond a basic level. Frustrated men soon left their units, but this exacerbated the problem for men left behind who had fewer comrades to train with or had to contend with the new recruits who replaced them. Thus a cycle of boredom and discharges was often begun. The ordinary discomforts of military life no doubt also made their contribution. One lancer officer wrote to another that the 'drought still continues, but I expect when we go to Camp in a few days, the heavens will be likely to open out'.[76]

Retention of men in the ranks hence remained much the same problem that it had been since the inception of colonial defence forces in the 1850s. The Adelaide Mounted Rifles found that all the 101 original names on the roll books in 1877 had been struck off by 1881.[77] Individual detachments collapsed as regularly and completely as did the disparate volunteer corps of earlier decades, but this fact has been somewhat hidden by the larger organisational structures that the successful mainland colonies had adopted after the mid-1880s. In order to maintain its strength throughout the pre-Federation period the Victorian Mounted Rifles established a staggering 105 separate detachments between the regiment's raising in 1885 and its being subsumed into the federal organisation in 1903. Of this massive total only 13 were of sufficient integral strength to survive the whole period without interruption.[78] A high turnover of men and officers was an inescapable characteristic of Australia's mounted regiments. The orders book of Tasmania's 26th Light Horse Regiment warmly records that it took 22 men onto its books in July 1913, but also noted that on the same day 31 were to be struck off as non-efficient. The roll books of the 6th Light Horse Regiment indicate that about 40 per cent of men enlisted in 1907 had left or been discharged by 1910.[79]

When the number of discharges began to exceed recruiting, as it so easily could in the thinly populated rural areas where the only interested men were the ones already leaving, the failure of detachments was not far off. After Federation the new Commonwealth Government continued to receive applications from enthusiastic citizens to raise detachments but, as time went on, the role of finding and raising new light horse elements began to fall increasingly on state and military district commandants, then on to unit commanding officers who had to ferret out new sources within their existing unit boundaries The process sometimes led to peculiarly circular recruiting patterns and, in 1908, for example, the 4th Squadron of the 13th Light Horse Regiment, formed in the Lockyer Valley west of Brisbane, maintained troops at Gatton, Helidon, Laidley and Blenheim. In that year and the following, both the troops at Laidley and then Blenheim were disbanded and replaced by troops at Forrest Hill and Ma Ma Creek. By 1912 the troop at Helidon was also in serious decline, and the then commanding officer, having made enquiries, discovered that now there were again 20 men in Laidley who were willing to enlist. Laidley thus again became a troop centre within four years of being closed down as unviable.[80]

Detachments failed for plenty of reasons, many of which have been outlined. The troop leader of the above Blenheim troop attributed its failure to the 'fact that the young men of the district take no interest in military matters'.[81] As in earlier decades, the performance or interest of the officers played an important, often crucial, role in how successful a detachment was. The loss of a commander for the Liverpool half-company of mounted rifles was a key reason, for example, why the New South Wales commandant sought to have it removed from the establishment in 1895.[82]

More generally the 1890s, a decade of economic depression, proved to be particularly hard years for retention and unit viability. The difficulties were twofold in that men, faced with the problems of trying to get by, were less likely to give up the time, effort and money to join military organisations, and governments, faced with diminishing revenues, were soon forced to reduce the amount spent on defence. In 1893 the Victorian Government slashed the establishment of the Victorian Mounted Rifles from 1000 to 800 men and disbanded the lone troop of cavalry at Sandhurst in order to reduce costs.[83] In 1894–45 further cuts were made that reduced the number of companies and instructors as well as the pay of the permanent officers.[84] In New South Wales cuts were also contemplated, and five cavalry and mounted infantry detachments considered too remote from the metropolis were facing disbandment in 1893, although in this case the cuts did not apparently take place.[85] In Queensland the mounted infantry were saved from cuts owing to their proven reliability during the Shearers' Strike in 1891.[86]

Aid to the civil power

The role of the Queensland Mounted Infantry in the Shearers' Strike pointed to one reason, aside from the basic one of defence, that colonial governments chose not to cut deeper into their mounted defence forces in the mid-1890s. The role of mounted units as defenders of the colony carried not only the responsibility of seeing off an invader but also the traditional function of aiding the authorities in maintaining good order. Perhaps the first instance in which colonial mounted troops were used to help restore order had occurred at Kyneton, Victoria, in 1861 when the local magistrate called out the 60 men of the Kyneton District Mounted Rifles Corps to help disperse a crowd of railway gangers disgruntled over a pay cut.[87]

Mounted units dealing with labour unrest became a relatively common sight in the early 1890s. During the maritime strike of 1890 two troops of cavalry and two companies of mounted infantry volunteered themselves for service as special mounted police in New South Wales. Sworn in as special mounted constables and given police uniforms, they were used to escort non-union labour and wagons to the wharves, but were involved in no serious incidents.[88] To the south 200 men of the Victorian Mounted Rifles were called out owing to concerns that a planned mass meeting might turn into a riot. The night before the meeting the men were issued live ammunition, but the event proved peaceful and their services were not required. The regiment became a subject of considerable controversy, however, when a newspaper reported that on the issue of the ammunition Tom Price had addressed his soldiers and exhorted them that should it prove necessary they were to fire 'low and lay them out – lay the disturbers of law and order out'. Price contended that he had been misquoted, and his defenders have pointed to the Queen's Regulations of the time, which stated that when firing during a civil disturbance soldiers were to aim low in order to lay out the leaders, and opined that he was doing nothing more than reciting the rules.[89] Unionists tended to cast it, rightly or wrongly, as another Peterloo narrowly averted.[90] What Price actually said remained a moot point but, not surprisingly, many from the working class and labour politics came to view Price and the regiment with some suspicion.

Labour politics grew more suspicious of the place of the colonial military the following year during the Queensland Shearers' Strike when the men of that colony's defence forces were called out to assist. The first troops called on had been the Moreton Mounted Infantry, and they were soon joined by elements from all the Queensland Defence Forces, including most of the rest of the mounted infantry. Responsible for escorting non-union shearers and transport, protecting remote property and providing communications in remote districts, the mounted infantry quickly gained a reputation for endurance, fortitude and reliability.[91] The government was so pleased with their service that after the strike the establishment of the mounted infantry was expanded by 180 men.[92] When, later in the decade, the government had to consider defence cuts owing to a poor economic outlook, reductions to the mounted infantry were strongly resisted by those who remembered their service. One anonymous bureaucrat wrote, 'The Mounted Infantry although more expensive than the infantry are, far and away, the most dependable and best soldiers we have to rely on for internal protection... The reduction in numbers should, therefore, be principally made in outlying country corps which are certainly not needed either for defence purposes proper or for internal protection.'[93]

When the shearers struck again in 1894, 50 members of the mounted infantry volunteered for service as special constables and were sent to Rockhampton as a police reserve.[94] Their reliability, and that of the men in New South Wales and Victoria, probably stemmed from the social origins of the men who made up the ranks. Originating mostly from the rural and suburban middle class, few of them would have held much sympathy for the political radicals in the trade union movement. Unionists were certainly wary of the soldiery and, after Federation, the Defence Act, which relied on Labor Party support for its passage, made law the still extant principle that citizen soldiers cannot be used by governments to break labour disputes.[95]

HORSE SOLDIER MYTHOLOGY

The usefulness of mounted troops in helping solve internal disruptions only served to reinforce the growing idea that mounted troops were a particularly useful form of soldiery for colonies to raise. This idea had a firm military basis in the colonial experiences of the British Army in the second half of the nineteenth century and the related efforts to redefine the role of horse-mounted soldiers in an age of rapid technological change. Encouraged by recent wars, in particular the First Boer War of 1880–81, the idea that mounted troops were useful in colonial situations grew into a resilient notion that Australians, particularly those from the bush who could ride and theoretically shoot well, with only minimal traditional training, would make excellent soldiers. The idea received its first airing in the 1850s when the newly self-governing colonies, spurred by war scares, began considering some form of self-defence. Not everyone was excited by the idea, but after the First Boer War the idea that mounted men from the bush were the best form of defence that the Australian colonies possessed gained particular currency.

Perhaps the clearest written enunciation of this idea was in *The Power of Mounted Riflemen,* by the New South Wales parliamentarian Edward O'Sullivan. In this small book he drew a clear parallel between the performance of the Boer farmers and the Australian men serving in mounted rifle units. His book was published 'with the object of showing what colonial soldiers can do when fighting in mountain or bush country'. Pointing to the superior shooting of the Boers at the battle of Majuba Hill, and their mounted rifle style of fighting, he argued that Australia's mounted riflemen and mounted infantry should be given strong encouragement. 'It utilises two of the strongest natural habits of the young Australian – love of horse-riding and shooting – and they, therefore, take to the training of

Mounted Riflemen with a vim and vigour which promises to make them formidable foes to any body of invaders who may have the temerity to land upon our shores.'[96] This was a representation of a growing idea that an ability to ride and shoot, combined with a small degree of military training, would provide all that colonial and imperial authorities could want. The idea had a strong element of myth but became a persuasive idea among concerned citizens and military men in the colonies.

Imperial officers serving in Australia also subscribed to the idea to some extent, although they would generally have asserted that the proper military training of their men should not be overlooked. The Victorian commandant in the late 1890s, Major-General Sir Charles Holled Smith, contended that mounted rifles were 'essentially the arm for Australia. They know the country to be operated over, and they can ride.'[97] The commandant of New South Wales in the early 1890s, Major-General Edward Hutton, actively promoting mounted rifles and mounted infantry in the British Army and empire as a whole, enthused loudly about the mounted men of Australia:

> Good as the Infantry and Artillery are, the arm of the country is undoubtedly the mounted branch. The Australian is a born horseman. With his long, lean, muscular thighs he is more at home on a horse than on his feet, and is never seen to greater advantage than when mounted and riding across bush or difficult country. The mounted troops (Cavalry and Mounted Infantry) are recruited from the small farmers, the stockmen, and boundary riders who, living in the saddle, seem to take naturally to their military duties. Fine horsemen, hardy, self-reliant, and excellent marksmen, they are the *beau ideal* of Mounted Riflemen, and as such are the equal, if not the superior, of the best that South Africa can boast... Accustomed to shift for themselves in the Australian bush, and under the most trying conditions of heat and cold, they would thrive where soldiers unaccustomed to bush life would die.[98]

He included similar, although less emotively put, sentiments in his preface to *The Manual of Drill for the Mounted Troops of Australia, 1895*.[99] Such views were, potentially anyway, more than just hyperbole. In 1896, during the tensions in South Africa over the Jamieson Raid, Hutton wrote to General Sir Redvers Buller: 'Don't forget if you want men to lick the Boers... you have a magnificent description of Mounted Troops here in Australia, but especially in NS Wales.'[100]

Such notions made a significant contribution to the efforts of some to have an Australian mounted regiment formed for imperial service should

Photo 19 By the mid-1880s the idea that Australia's bushmen were excellent natural material for citizen mounted units already had wide currency. Scouting, which this 1889 engraving depicts, was one of the skills for which bushmen were supposed to be well prepared, although the experience of fighting in South Africa did much to quash such romantic ideas. (State Library of Victoria, IAN06/04/89/supp)

they be required. One enthusiastic New South Welshman, Neil Moffat, wrote to the Premier of his colony in 1896 of the futility of British authorities trying to raise mounted infantry at home when 'we here have some of the finest fighting material in the world going to waste':

> For rough and tumble, bush, jungle, or mountain warfare there is nothing to beat our Kangaroo and Brumby shooters, nomadic Shearers, Stockmen and Bush bred youths in general. Clean built, wiry fellows used to roughing it, hard as nails, all of whom can ride well and shoot straight... There is much too much Starch and Pipeclay, look well on Parade, about the British Soldier, while his riding is wooden and mechanical, that is why he goes down before the Boer every time.[101]

Mr Moffat most likely received a polite rebuff, but comparable sentiments were behind the efforts of more prominent men to achieve a similar outcome. The efforts of the Governor of Victoria in the late 1890s, Lord Brassey, to have a regiment of mounted rifles raised and maintained in Australia ready for imperial service had similarly met with no success, but he too had been partly motivated by the traits of the bushmen he had seen in Victoria's mounted men. Rejecting the War Office view that Indian cavalry were better trained and more reliable, he objected that they 'would not be as reliable as Australian horsemen in irregular warfare, where all would depend on individual energy, resources, and courage'.[102]

Lieutenant-Colonel James Mackay, founder and commander of the 1st Australian Horse, also had ambitions to promote an Australian mounted regiment for imperial service, and the idea that hardy bushmen were an ideal basis also permeated his proposals to London.[103] His idea similarly met with little success, but the regiment he did raise in New South Wales was perhaps the most remarkable example of the combination of the mythology of the martial skills of the bush horseman and official military sanction. In 1895 James Mackay had published a novel titled *The Yellow Wave*, in which an *ad hoc* unit of mounted bushmen, the fictional Hatten's Ringers (armed with lances, the blades of which had been fashioned from plough shears), had bravely fought against a Russian-officered Chinese invasion of Queensland. In that novel the Asiatic hordes, superior in numbers and military technology, if not race, had found the under-trained and ill-equipped militiamen and volunteers of Australia's colonies easy pickings. The cavalry of New South Wales and the Queensland Mounted

Infantry, although brave and active, never seem to have the same battlefield presence as the men of the bush led by their natural and charismatic leader, Hatten.[104]

The line between fantasy and military reality blurred somewhat when in 1897 Mackay began raising the 1st Australian Horse, and he went to great pains to form what he felt was 'a distinctly bush force'.[105] The motto of his new regiment – 'For hearths and homes' – was even the same catchcry that had run through his novel. The link between Mackay's fantasy and what he was now doing was not lost on his more perceptive contemporaries, one newspaper noting his unit was 'based on the lines of 'Hatten's Ringers'.[106] Enlisting men from the hitherto untapped recruiting grounds of the more remote parts of New South Wales, Mackay stressed that the natural skills of the bush horsemen he was recruiting provided the ideal basis for the unit.

For this regiment the adjutant Lieutenant R.R. Thompson prepared a new manual, *The Bushman's Military Guide*. Like some of its colonial antecedents, it was essentially a reproduction of extracts from a number of imperial manuals, mostly *Cavalry Drill*, but with a new cover and a locally written preface in which the supposed parallel between bush and military skills was most actively put forward.[107] Thompson pointed to the bushman's love of horses and sport as well as his adaptability and contended that, 'with a small amount of consistent training, these qualities could be diverted into Military channels'. The preface outlined four key areas in which the bushmen of New South Wales, at least, were already on the verge of tremendous military utility. First, because as bushmen they could already ride well, there was no requirement to teach them military equitation. Second, because they often shot kangaroos or other game, their marksmanship was already good and they therefore needed only instruction in military musketry principles to make them excellent military shots. Third, as real bushmen already had great skill in finding their way through the country with no artificial aids, they already had the essential skills to become scouts. Finally, because most knew how to handle a stockwhip with great skill, they were well on their way to wielding a sword from horseback with equal skill.[108] As events in South Africa would soon prove, the idea that bushmen could become soldiers without extensive training was somewhat fanciful, but that tough lesson had yet to be learnt.

The hard lessons of the veld did, in certain quarters at least, put a dampener on such mythologising. It is not difficult to find instances after Federation of writers enthusing about the skills of the bushmen in the light horse. One journalist and veteran of the 1st Australian Horse and

Boer War, John Abbott, wrote just before the First World War that lighthorsemen had 'all the civil training which South Africa was able to prove to be such advantage in the making of efficient, hardy and resourceful soldiers'.[109] Even Edward Hutton, writing in Britain and who in fact knew better, could enthuse in 1906 about the remarkable natural abilities of Australia's horsemen as soldiers.[110]

Such comments were, however, remarkably rare after the Boer War compared to before it. Never again would Australia's mounted troops be provided with an authorised manual anything like the *Bushman's Military Guide*. Comparisons of Australia's bushmen with Boer farmers, perhaps because they were now a beaten foe, became a less common part of the Australian military experience. The notion that bushmen could be sent to war without significant training was not an idea taken up by the post-Federation military authorities, and every effort after 1902 was aimed towards the elusive goal of making the light horse (and the other arms) as efficient and well trained as possible. Hutton, belying his public comments, had stressed the importance of the light horse training as hard and realistically as they could, and later military authorities pushed for further extensions to the time spent in training. Comments by officers during this period served repeatedly to highlight deficiencies and seek ways to correct them, not to rest on the supposedly innate military traits of the men who filled the part-time regiments of light horse. The concept that Australia's men of the bush made excellent natural soldiers remained part of the cultural backdrop and would find a new voice after the First World War, but the realities of the campaign in South Africa gave the idea a certain amount of rest in the years after Federation, at least among those who were most closely associated with soldiering in Australia.

Regardless of when these ideas found their expression, there had been a tendency to consider that the apparent utility of frontiersmen making excellent natural horse soldiers was a uniquely Australian development, although many of the same sentiments could be found across the English-speaking world in the late nineteenth and early twentieth centuries. The same principles applied to cowboys as well as to bushmen, and Theodore Roosevelt's Rough Riders of the Spanish-American War were a good example of the same notions having their sway in North America. Even where there was no frontier the same ideas had their voice, and Britain's foot and mounted volunteers of the nineteenth century had also been praised for their individuality and commonsense approach to soldiering.[111] Similarly the military forms that Australian horse soldiers adopted were not confined to Australia, and all were more or less directly imported ideas. Local cavalry corps based themselves on British regulars and yeomanry in everything from uniforms and armament to the manuals they used to train themselves. Mounted rifles and mounted infantry bodies could trace their origins to the model of the seventeeth-century European dragoon (foot soldiers made mobile by horses), which had found new life and refinement in the Cape Mounted Rifles of South Africa, the American Civil War and a variety of Britain's colonial conflicts. As noted, the example of the Boers was a particular influence and acknowledged by some, if not all. The Queensland Commandant in 1892, Major-General John Owen, apparently forgetting the other armies of the empire, contended the khaki dress worn by mounted infantry units throughout the colonies was 'not only smart and soldierlike, but it is a distinctive national dress'.[112] Edward O'Sullivan, who deliberately and enthusiastically sought to highlight the potential similarities between the men of the veld and the bush, was more perceptive: 'They [the Boers] wear soft felt hats with bands around them, and carry their rifles slung across their backs and their cartridges stuck in belts... The uniforms and equipment of our Mounted Rifles is, in fact, an imitation and improvement of the Boer costume and equipment.'[113]

Many of the men who played significant roles in the development of Australia's mounted corps had, of course, received their training in other armies or were imperial officers. Captain F. Fawcett, who formed Western Australia's Pinjarrah Mounted Volunteers, then commanded them for nearly 20 years, had once been a cornet in the 6th Dragoon Guards.[114] Malcolm Macdonald, prominent in the mid-1880s raising of cavalry in New South Wales and later the commander of the New South Wales Mounted Brigade, had started soldiering in India and commanded the Poona Horse in frontier fighting there.[115] Henry Lassetter, long-time commander of the New South Wales Mounted Infantry/Rifles, had been trained at Sandhurst and served in a British infantry regiment on campaign in the Sudan before coming to Australia.[116] Tom Price, credited by some as the father of the mounted rifle movement in Australia, had similarly learned his soldiering in the Indian Army and reportedly been impressed there by the Queen's Own Corps of Guides Cavalry.[117] Colonial commandants like Charles Holled Smith, George French and particularly Edward Hutton, who did so much to shape and encourage mounted units, were all imperial officers and had brought their ideas and experiences from other parts of the empire.

The connection with, and influence of, officers and men who were current or past serving members of the British Army or its offshoots should not be underestimated, as it was in men such as these that Australia's mounted units often found their genesis and their champions. They brought to Australia a whole series of experiences and views on mounted troops from around the empire and, even if those experiences were somewhat removed in time, they had a profound influence on the shape and nature of Australia's mounted units. That the local pre-Federation units and post-Federation light horse had their overseas equivalents in Britain, New Zealand, Canada and South Africa was not coincidental. In this regard Australian mounted soldiers had their overseas citizen soldier contemporaries whose experiences must, in many ways, have been quite similar.

Probably not unique to the local experience were the long-standing problems of uneven leadership and its consequences: of getting men to parade with their units and fulfil their commitments, and of having to deal with the financial and social burdens of spending one's spare time mounted soldiering. The mundane and apparently inescapable tribulations that faced Australia's mounted men were considerable, and meant that all their units and organisations had their share of serious problems. Given the multiplicity and seriousness of those problems, it is remarkable that the militia light horse and its predecessors were as successful as they were. It is testimony to the industriousness and keenness of that minority of men who made citizen-soldiering an earnest pastime, and stayed in the ranks beyond the brief interlude of so many others, that mounted soldiering continued as strongly as it did for so long. That many of those men were local notables and relatively prosperous farmers, rather than their working-class employees, gave most units a noticeably rural middle-class flavour. In the more extreme cases, such as the New South Wales Lancers, it was capable of breeding an atmosphere verging on the patrician. It is little surprise, then, that when they were called upon to do so there was little apparent concern in taking up the mounted soldier's long-established secondary role of helping to put down civil disturbance.

Of little surprise also is that such rural units proved able to both draw on and provide the exemplars for a contemporary train of thought that hardy countrymen could, with a minimum of training, take to horseback with rifle on their back and provide all that their society needed in its defence. The Boer War had undermined that myth to a considerable degree, and in the years following there had been a serious effort to move beyond the mythology and train as hard as could be expected given the limitations.

CHAPTER | 6

MOUNTED RIFLES
The light horse at war, 1914–17

The outbreak of the First World War in August 1914 meant that the light horse as an idea and organisation, although not the militia units already in existence, was to face its test in war. The last despatch of Australian mounted troops to a war had been a mixed experience, but since then Australia's mounted branch had undergone significant change. Brought together under a single national scheme, it had trained accordingly and, even if there had been significant problems, matters had clearly improved overall. The militia light horse bequeathed to the regiments of the Australian Imperial Force (AIF) its organisational template, role and many of its men. The demands of war, however, meant that it soon developed a competence and efficiency far beyond what the militia had ever come close to achieving. By 1917 light horse regiments had fought in three theatres in which the British Empire was engaged and in one of them, Egypt, became the centrepiece of the force that campaigned against the Turks in the second half of 1916.

FORMATION TO GALLIPOLI

The Defence Act, which had frustrated Hutton by forbidding the sending of Australia's militiamen overseas, meant that on the outbreak of war attention quickly turned to the raising and despatch of a separate expeditionary force composed entirely of volunteers. Accordingly, on 10 August 1914, the new AIF commenced recruiting to a plan set out by the then inspector-general, and soon to be AIF commander,

Table 6.1 Territorial origins of AIF light horse regiments

State	Military district	Contribution
Queensland	1st MD	2nd, 5th and 11th LHRs
New South Wales	2nd MD	1st, 6th, 7th 12th and 14th LHRs
Victoria	3rd MD	4th, 8th and 15th (1 × sqn) LHRS
South Australia	4th MD	3rd (2 × sqn), 9th and 15th (1 × sqn) LHRs
Western Australia	5th MD	10th and 15th (1 × sqn) LHRs
Tasmania	6th MD	3rd (1 × sqn) LHR

Source: Territorial basis of light horse regiments, undated, AWM27, 303/19

Brigadier-General William Throsby Bridges. Reflecting the existing military structures, the forces raised by the Commonwealth Government were meant to be roughly commensurate with the existing militia contribution of each state to fulfil the initial offer of an infantry division and a brigade of light horse, both with the necessary support elements. Half the rank and file was to be recruited from the militia, the remainder from men who had previous war or militia service but were not presently serving.[1] The immediate goal was the raising of the four light horse regiments of the first contingent – three to constitute the 1st Light Horse Brigade, the fourth to be the divisional mounted troops for the infantry 1st Division – but the demand to enlist was so high that by the end of the year Australia's total offer of mounted troops to London had increased to three full brigades and two divisional mounted regiments.[2]

Despite the conscious decision to draw on the existing militia structures, the somewhat contrary decision was taken not to reflect the rationalised unit numbering system introduced with universal training, and few regiments of the AIF would have a number that unambiguously reflected any clear militia or military district origin (see table 6.1).[3] Each regiment of the first contingent received, as Hutton had intended more than a decade before, stiffening by the inclusion in their ranks of four permanent senior NCOs from the Administrative and Instructional Staff: the regimental sergeant-major, the regimental quartermaster sergeant, the sergeant of the machine-gun section and the sergeant of the signal section.[4]

As the units began to form those men who were coming to the new expeditionary force from the militia were ordered to bring all the 'personal and public clothing on issue to them'.[5] The new regiments looked much as their militia counterparts were meant to look once the peacetime recruiting limits had been removed, and each regiment was initially raised with 23 officers and about 500 other ranks. Unit size would change throughout the war, and through 1915 the establishment was 25 officers and 511 men. By late 1916 this was down to 24 officers and 450 men and, although there were some fluctuations, this was roughly the regimental establishment until the end of the war.[6] Soldiers of the lowest rank were initially enlisted as privates but appear to have been referred to from the start by the honorific cavalry title of trooper, a practice formalised in Egypt in 1915.[7] Each regiment, in line with the establishment revisions of 1911–12, consisted of three squadrons of four troops and possessed a machine-gun section equipped with two Maxim guns. As had been the intention since Hutton's day, unit commanders were lieutenant-colonels, and squadron command was given to majors. Brigade commanders were only colonels, but these men were later given a step to brigadier-general in order to bring the AIF into line with British practice. Although later in the war all AIF officers were promoted from the ranks, in these early years the reliance was on the variable skills of citizen officers from the militia who volunteered. As in South Africa, it is clear that the appointment of these officers sometimes had as much to do with political influence, social standing or simply long, loyal service in the militia as with genuine, or at least imagined, military skill.[8] The history of one British mounted regiment, the King Edward's Horse, which was raised from dominion and colonial residents in Britain, later noted that in 1914 the unit enlisted a number of 'young Australians, who for reasons of their own, did not wish to compete in the political influences pervading their own contingents'.[9]

Although some preliminary training was undertaken in Australia, the intention had always been to send the AIF to Britain at the earliest opportunity, where training was to be completed before its commitment to battle across the English Channel. The first four light horse regiments sailed from Australia in November, and on this voyage the untrained nature of the forces meant that time on board ship, as it had been on the way to South Africa more than a decade before, was largely dedicated to training. Despite the effort to draw on men with previous military experience, it was clear that the collective military skill level was low and that all units and formations had to be constructed virtually from the ground up. On board ship officers attended lectures on their professional duties and basic tactical principles as well as on a multitude of basic but essential tasks, such as how to navigate or write a field message.[10] The men they commanded were similarly occupied in learning their new trade and attending to the horses that accompanied them.

Instead of England the AIF found itself disembarking in Egypt, largely owing to the work of Colonel Harry Chauvel who, after inspecting the inadequate facilities on Salisbury Plain had, with the help of the Australian High Commissioner to London, persuaded the War Office that the desert was a better place for the AIF than Salisbury Plain in winter.[11] The 1st Light Horse Brigade disembarked in Egypt and went into camp at Maadi just south of Cairo. The 4th Light Horse Regiment, as the divisional mounted regiment, accompanied the 1st Division to its camp at Mena.[12] At almost the same time the new commander of the 1st Light Horse Brigade, Harry Chauvel, the only permanent force officer to be given a brigade, arrived from England to take up his appointment, and training began almost immediately. It was a process that the 2nd and 3rd Brigades were to repeat in the coming months.

Building on the work done on the ships, training started with elementary individual work, such as musketry or sentry duties, and gradually built up to squadron and regimental programs, generally preceded by a series of lectures for officers and NCOs, who often learnt their job just ahead of the men they commanded.[13] In contrast to the experience in South Africa, and in a demonstration of how both the British and Australian military authorities had learnt from their mistakes, detailed and thorough horse care became an abiding characteristic of life for the men in the mounted arm. As the horses were unloaded their acclimatisation and return to fitness after the long sea journey became a carefully managed process. At first they were simply watered, fed and led for brief walks, then, as their fitness improved, taken for brief rides.[14] Eventually they were ridden for longer periods, then used in the increasing number of unit and eventually brigade training activities. It was not until the very end of 1914 that the 1st Light Horse Brigade began to use their horses in their training.[15]

Despite the bush origins of most men and their familiarity with horses, it was clear that making light-horsemen good horsemasters was as important as anything else they learnt. Men were taught how to saddle their horses, to check that saddlery was properly adjusted, and to dismount and lead their horses regularly so that they were not constantly under load.[16] This early training and its maintenance as a field discipline, along with a number of other factors, would do much to ensure that the horses of the AIF would earn a reputation for endurance and reliability in the campaigns to come. Contributing also was the establishment of the remount units, which were raised in response to the demands of maintaining the light horse's mounts during the Gallipoli campaign. Arriving in Egypt in December 1915, they were made part of the Imperial Remount Service, and over the following years it contributed a steady stream of properly acclimatised, broken and trained horses to the Australian formations.

The eventual despatch of the light horse to Gallipoli also gave the horses that they left in Egypt a very extended period of minimal work during which they were properly acclimatised, and this, the exact opposite experience of the horses sent to South Africa, meant that in 1916, when they were again used, they were thoroughly accustomed to their climate and food.[17] Once in the field the imbued horsemastership lessons were observed, and light-horsemen ensured that their horses were properly rested whenever tactically feasible. Officers who had to ride their horses hard were allowed multiple horses so that none was overworked. In 1917 a brigade commander was entitled to five mounts and all regimental officers except the chaplain, quartermaster and medical officer were allowed three, although whether the allowances were always catered for is less clear.[18] Perhaps most significant, however, and often ignored when discussing the performance of walers in the Palestine campaign, was the maintenance of an efficient logistic system that kept fodder flowing forward. When conditions militated against effective logistic support, such as after the capture of Jerusalem in the winter of 1917–18, the horse formations were often relieved to ease the supply situation. The net result of all this was that, in direct contrast to the experience in South Africa, horses in the British and dominion forces in Palestine performed extremely well.

Much has been written and said of the alleged superiority of walers over the other mounts,[19] yet, although they undoubtedly did well, there is little to suggest they were innately superior. Just as there are many recorded instances of Australian horses performing extraordinary feats of endurance so too are there similar tales from British yeomanry regiments riding more diverse stock, and from the New Zealand Mounted Rifles riding predominantly New Zealand–sourced horses. Moreover, with the cessation of Australian horse shipments in late 1916, light horse units also received remounts from widely varied origins, which generally seem to have done just as well as the walers.[20] Without discounting their genetic constitution, it is clear that what made the waler such a reputation was a thorough horse management system that benefited all the horses of every formation in the theatre.

In the meantime, on the arrival of the Australians and New Zealanders in Egypt both forces were reorganised into the new Australian and New Zealand Army Corps (ANZAC). The 1st Light Horse Brigade found itself part of the New Zealand and Australian Division under the command of Major-General Alexander Godley, a British regular in command of the New Zealanders. The newly arrived 2nd and 3rd Light Horse Brigades, still in the process of creating themselves, were left outside the new divisional organisation and were allotted as corps troops.

In April 1915 the Australian and New Zealand infantry formations, but not the light horse regiments, began to leave the camps in Egypt in preparation for the Gallipoli landings on the 25th. By early May the offensive had gained little ground, and casualties among the infantry meant that the light horse in Egypt was soon being considered for reinforcements at Anzac Cove. Senior commanders in the Dardanelles considered that breaking up the light horse formations and using the personnel as individual reinforcements for the infantry was the best course open. Key among their concerns was that bringing in the relatively small light horse regiments was not wise as they would not be interchangeable with the infantry battalions and that if they came as brigades there would be no clear role for the extra number of brigade staffs. The senior light horse commanders were, not surprisingly, strongly opposed to their units being broken up for reinforcements and found an ally in the senior commander in Egypt, General Sir Archibald Maxwell, who gave orders to despatch the 1st Light Horse Brigade and New Zealand Mounted Rifle Brigade (about 3000 men) as complete entities. These two brigades arrived in a dismounted condition at Anzac Cove from 12 May, and the 2nd and 3rd Light Horse Brigades embarked in Egypt for the same location a few days later.[21] The 4th Light Horse Brigade, which formed in Australia in mid-1915, never deployed to Gallipoli as a formation and, after its arrival in Egypt in July, its regiments were broken up and the squadrons deployed to Gallipoli in August to reinforce light horse units already there.[22] So that they could go to Gallipoli to take up a dismounted role, it was necessary for the regiments to leave approximately a quarter of their men behind to care for the horses, but reinforcements were taken on before embarkation to bring the numbers up so that they went into battle close to full strength. The 5th Light Horse Regiment, for example, marched out for Gallipoli with 455 men and left another 227 in camp to look after the horses and other equipment.[23] Leggings, spurs and other mounted accoutrements had been handed in, and infantry webbing, some of it improvised, was issued instead.[24]

On their arrival the 1st Light Horse Brigade, under Harry Chauvel, and the New Zealand Mounted Rifles, under the New Zealander Brigadier-General Andrew Russell, who would later go on to command the New Zealand Division on the Western Front, having well-regarded commanders, being relatively well trained and composed of the best officers and men that the first contingents had been able to recruit, were easily absorbed into the local arrangements. The respective brigade staffs were given sections of the line to run, and the regiments soon took their place in the line. The 2nd and 3rd Light Horse Brigades, when they arrived, being much newer formations, were of more concern. The commander of the 3rd Brigade, Colonel Frederick Hughes, a pre-war militia officer, businessman and local politician from Victoria, was thought too old for his appointment. However, as he was assisted by a well-respected, if prickly, brigade major, the permanent forces soldier and veteran of the Boer War Lieutenant-Colonel John Antill, the brigade was left as it was and given a section of the line to defend. The commander of the 2nd Light Horse Brigade, Colonel Granville Ryrie, a New South Wales pastoralist and politician who had fought in South Africa and served in militia mounted regiments since the late 1890s, was also deemed an unknown quantity. However, as his brigade major was also of concern the brigade was broken up soon after arrival and was not re-formed until mid-June with a new brigade major to support Ryrie.[25]

In the line the light horse regiments took up the same duties as the infantry and were involved in the fighting in much the same way. Aside from the periodic major operations by either side when the fighting was at its fiercest, the routine at Gallipoli was one of continually improving positions by digging and wiring, carrying rations and water to the front lines, observing the enemy's lines, night outposts, night patrolling and sniping. As there was barely any place within the Anzac Cove position for units to rest, it was not unusual for light horse regiments to have spent their entire time on the peninsula in the front trenches.[26] Like the infantry, they suffered heavy casualties, the most notorious episode being the costly charge of the 8th and 10th Light Horse Regiments at the Nek during the 7 August attack, a day that also saw a costly failed attack by the 2nd Light Horse Regiment from Quinn's Post and another by the 1st Light Horse Regiment from Pope's Hill.[27] The daily dangers of trench warfare at Anzac Cove could have much the same effect over a longer period, and the association of the regiments of the 1st Light Horse Brigade with Quinn's Post and the head of Monash Valley was a long and bloody one. The 5th Light Horse Regiment spent a costly three

Photo 20 The disastrous attack at the Nek in August 1915 is the best-known light horse episode of the Gallipoli campaign, but these 40-odd men were all that remained of the 200 who took part in the failed attack by the 1st Light Horse Regiment from Pope's Hill on the same day. (AWM H00356)

weeks securing Wilson's Lookout, in October and November 1915, by which time evacuations caused by illness were often more numerous than evacuations caused by fighting.[28]

The light horse regiments, greatly under strength, withdrew from the peninsula with the rest of the expedition in late 1915 and returned to Egypt via Mudros before the end of the year. The mounted men, like the cavalry of the same period on the Western Front, had been put in the trenches as an expedient to cover heavy infantry losses. There had been much concern that the small light horse units were a poor substitute for infantry but, given the broken terrain of the Anzac position and the weakened state of many infantry battalions when the light horse arrived in May, there do not seem to have been many complaints about this once they arrived. More generally the campaign at Gallipoli had given the light horse units and formations considerable experience, even if it was not in their mounted role.

It had also allowed the abilities of the commanders to be appreciated, for the less capable ones to be replaced and for others to come to the fore. Frederick Hughes proved incapable and too old for his brigade command and, after the bloody failure at the Nek, was evacuated sick later in the campaign before being sent home. Of the other brigade commanders,

Chauvel did well enough to be given a temporary divisional command at Gallipoli, and Granville Ryrie was confirmed as suitable for his position leading the 2nd Light Horse Brigade, if not perhaps for any higher appointments. Vigorous and competent junior commanders also made their mark. Major Lachlan Wilson, for example, a solicitor and militia officer from Queensland, arrived at Gallipoli as a squadron commander with the 5th Light Horse Regiment and became its commanding officer in August after the death of the previous incumbent; by mid-1917 he would be a light horse brigade commander.

REORGANISATION: EGYPT 1915–16 AND THE WESTERN FRONT 1915–18

The units at Gallipoli had not been the only light horse in battle, and the Composite Australian Light Horse Regiment, an *ad hoc* unit formed from reinforcements and other 'odds and ends' left in Egypt during the Gallipoli fighting, had been involved in fighting the Senussi tribesmen of the Libyan Desert who, partly stirred up by Turkish and German agitation, had triggered a frontier conflict west of the Nile in late 1915. The regiment had been hastily thrown together in November 1915 when relations between the Senussi and the British had broken down, and its three squadrons had been drawn from reinforcements in Egypt. Placed under the command of a British officer, it had immediately joined the just as hastily raised Western Frontier Force. From mid-December 1915, when the first serious fighting occurred, this anomalous light horse regiment fought in the sort of small colonial expedition that was part and parcel of maintaining the British Empire but which is now largely forgotten. Although the natural elements were perhaps the biggest challenge, the Senussi had formed bodies of troops, artillery and machine-guns at their disposal, and there was a series of stiff, if one-sided, fights involving the Australians. The unit ended its turn in the desert in early February 1916 when the last of the composite regiment was disbanded and returned to Egypt in favour of properly formed units. Its deployment was followed by that of the 1st Light Horse Brigade after its return from Gallipoli, when it was quickly brought up to establishment, horsed and despatched to the western approaches to the Nile Valley so as to prevent raids by the Senussi.[29]

After the strains of Gallipoli most of the light horse regiments were in a greatly weakened state. Before departing for Gallipoli the 10th Light Horse Regiment, for example, had numbered 520 men of all ranks, but by the time it awaited its return to Egypt at Mudros in mid-December 1915 it had been reduced to 285.[30] The huge number of reinforcements awaiting the AIF in Egypt (61 000 men had enlisted between July and September 1915) soon changed that deficiency. While awaiting reorganisation and the establishment of new training depots, some units, especially in the 3rd Light Horse Brigade, soon found themselves stuffed with a large number of new men for training, disciplinary and administrative reasons – although in the circumstances none of these demands was adequately attended to. It took several months and a huge expansion and reorganisation of the AIF for these men to be redistributed and the regiment to return to something near its normal size.[31]

Gallipoli had given all the existing light horse regiments and formations a not inconsiderable amount of battle experience but, as one regimental history notes (perhaps with a touch of romanticism), many had looked upon 'their dismounted role there as some sort of diversion'.[32] Required to again become proficient on horseback, training and re-equipment became the highest priority for the mounted branch in early 1916. The training routine became much as it had been for the new regiments the year before, with a particular emphasis on musketry.[33] It was hampered, however, until the mass of reinforcements, and a training system to cater for them, could be properly organised.

The AIF had left Australia without any training arrangements apart from that which could be found within the regimental environment. During the Gallipoli campaign a number of training units had been improvised in Egypt but, short of experienced officers, they were now groaning under the strain of holding and trying to train the huge number of reinforcements.[34] Accordingly, in January 1916, it was decided to establish light horse training regiments to provide trained reinforcements for each brigade. Each line regiment was linked to one of the squadrons of these training units,[35] effectively creating a depot system for the light horse to draw on as required.

Not all the personnel policies were to the immediate advantage of the light horse. Exploiting the huge pool of manpower in Egypt, the number of infantry divisions was being expanded from two to five, all of which were imminently destined for France. The expansion saw the light horse raided for men, of all ranks, to make up the numbers in the new formations. There was no shortage of volunteers for transfers as it was widely believed that the light horse was being left in a military backwater and that promotion prospects were better in the new formations headed for France. Harry Chauvel, having been in temporary command of the 1st Division,

Table 6.2 Organisation of the Australian and New Zealand Mounted Division, March 1916 – March 1917, with commanders

A & NZ Mounted Division (Chauvel)

1st LH Brigade (Cox)
2nd LH Brigade (Ryrie)
3rd LH Brigade (Antill, later Royston)
NZMR Brigade (Chaytor)
Inverness, Ayrshire, Somerset and Leicester Batteries, RHA

Source: The division was formed on 16 March 1916. Chauvel, 'The Australian Light Horse in the Great War', NAA A1194, 33.68/15152, p. 1; Foster, 'Operations of the mounted troops of the EEF', p. 8.

was approached about his willingness to go to France in command of one of the new infantry divisions, but he instead opted to remain in Egypt and take command of the new Australian and New Zealand Mounted Division (usually shortened to Anzac Mounted Division but more correctly abbreviated to A&NZ Mounted Division), formed in March 1916.[36]

A proposal to form a mounted division from the Australian and New Zealand mounted troops had first been suggested in late 1914 but had not then been taken up by the War Office.[37] Now it was decided to form the 1st, 2nd and 3rd Light Horse Brigades, along with the New Zealand Mounted Rifles (NZMR) Brigade, into this new division for the defence of Egypt and the Suez Canal.[38] No Australian or New Zealand artillery being available, British territorial horse artillery batteries were attached, and British gunners would support the light horse in the Middle East for the remainder of the war (see table 6.2).[39] The signals, engineer, logistic, ambulance, medical and veterinary elements required to support this formation were raised and their training commenced.[40] The 4th Light Horse Brigade, not fully raised when its members were sent to Gallipoli as reinforcements, was not reformed, but its 11th and 12th Light Horse Regiments continued on in Egypt as independent units. The once divisional mounted unit of the 1st Division, the 4th Light Horse Regiment, was expanded to four squadrons and split. Two of the squadrons then continued on in what appears to have been something of an administrative netherworld in the Middle East, training and involved in general patrol duties around Egypt until the unit was reconstituted and a new brigade home found for them in early 1917.[41]

The other two squadrons were destined for France, as was the 13th Light Horse Regiment, which had originally been raised in Australia as the divisional mounted troops of the 2nd Division. The nature of the fighting on the Western Front meant that the former divisional cavalry were now better utilised at the corps level, and changes were made to reflect this.[42] The 13th Light Horse Regiment was broken up at first and its squadrons were allocated to the 2nd, 4th and 5th Divisions, but it was brought back together in France in mid-1916 as the mounted troops of the new I Anzac Corps.[43] The two squadrons of the 4th Light Horse Regiment, along with the regimental headquarters, also went to France where they were combined with a squadron of the Otago Mounted Rifles in mid-1916 to become the 2nd Anzac Corps Mounted Regiment, the corps cavalry for II Anzac Corps.[44] Following the reorganisation of the Australian and New Zealand troops in late 1917 and early 1918, this unit was kept by General Godley when he assumed command of XXII Corps. Thus they fought most of the last year of the war away from their compatriots as part of a British and New Zealand formation with the title of XXII Corps Mounted Regiment.

The 13th Light Horse Regiment spent much of 1916 doing the unenviable but necessary work that often fell to cavalry on the Western Front – the provision of orderlies, work parties, escorting prisoners or as infantry reinforcements – but through 1917 it had opportunities to operate as a divisional mounted unit, particularly before the battle of Bullecourt. The conditions at Third Ypres (Passchendaele) in 1917 hardly suited anyone, let alone mounted troops, but by 1918 the regiment had developed its skills, partly by intensive training alongside British cavalry earlier that year, to such a degree that it played a noteworthy role during the German spring offensive, then later in the advances of the Australian Corps and other formations in summer and autumn. The requirements for cavalry during these final advances were such that the regiment was heavily in demand, and Australian and British commanders alike praised its good work.[45]

Similarly for the men of XXII Corps Mounted Regiment the more mobile operations of 1918 saw it heavily engaged as a mounted unit, first in the fighting that blunted the German spring offensive in April and May, then in support of the French 5th Army's offensive on the Marne in July. When the Allied armies began their major offensives in August, the regiment was used for cavalry reconnaissance and screening duties, often well in advance of the infantry. Because the Australian Corps was

Photo 21 Despite the generally negative depiction of cavalry on the Western Front, recent research shows that it did play a noteworthy role. Here the 13th Light Horse Regiment moves up to support an infantry attack near Bray, France, in August 1918 – a year in which the more mobile fighting had meant it was often in demand. (AWM E02979)

in reserve after its attacks on the Hindenburg Line in October 1918, the XXII Corps Mounted Regiment was one of the few Australian units still in action on the armistice that November.[46]

Back in Egypt in 1916, other changes were also being made, among them the creation of new camel-mounted formation, which had formed in January 1916 when each Australian infantry brigade was required to provide a section (equivalent to a platoon) to it.[47] With the dispatch of the infantry to France, most of the men for the new Imperial Camel Corps were ultimately drawn from British yeomanry regiments, the light horse and the New Zealand mounted rifles and by direct recruiting in Australia and New Zealand.[48] Later in 1916 the remnants of the 4th Light Horse Regiment, along with the 11th and 12th Light Horse Regiments, were earmarked for conversion to cameleers, but this did not take place, which would probably have been a relief for the affected light-horsemen as, in Chauvel's later words, there was 'no doubt that service in the ICC is very unpopular with most Australians'.[49] The unit was not especially popular in France either, and when General William Birdwood, commander of the AIF, heard of its establishment he tried, unsuccessfully, to have the Australian component broken up and forwarded to France, along with the 11th and 12th Light Horse Regiments, as infantry reinforcements.[50]

Despite the origins of many of its men in the horse-mounted regiments of the empire, the Imperial Camel Corps bore little resemblance to the light horse, and it is worth briefly outlining its creation to highlight its differences from the light horse. Initially it was organised under the command of a lieutenant-colonel and contained ten companies,[51] which were employed as needed, mostly against the Senussi in the Western Desert. By the end of the year operations against the Turks were of increasing importance, and it was expanded to a brigade of four battalions (each of four companies) and generally came to be referred to as the Imperial Camel Brigade.[52] Its training and organisation were based on the pre-war imperial manual, *Camel Corps Training 1913*, but this book was largely confined to the drill and handling skills to be used by cameleers.[53] For instruction regarding the tactical role of camel troops, readers of this first manual were told that in battle they would 'usually employ the tactics of mounted infantry'.[54] Thus Australian soldiers, for the first time since Edward Hutton had left Australia and the infantry had divested themselves of this unwanted role, again became mounted infantrymen. Training notes made it quite clear that there was considerable tactical difference between the mounted infantry cameleers and mounted riflemen, such as the light horse:

> It must be remembered that there is a radical difference between the fire tactics of mounted riflemen and those of the Camel Corps which are infantry [sic]. The infantryman moves comparatively slowly, and once committed, he can rarely be disengaged. He attacks in depth, moving in successive waves.
>
> The mounted rifleman, on the other hand, relies principally on his mobility. He makes no attempt to advance in depth, except when attacking an immobile enemy in position, which, except in small affairs, is not his usual role. He seeks to obtain a decision by surprise and, by catching the enemy at a disadvantage, endeavouring to bring a crushing fire to bear at once by putting in every available rifle at the start.

He avoids, above all, becoming tied down to a face-to-face fire fight, for by doing so he loses his mobility. He keeps his horses as close as possible, so that if he does not secure success at the outset he can break off the fight, to renew it under more favourable conditions.

On the other hand, once committed, Camel Corps can be disengaged only with difficulty.[55]

Light horse operations, 1916–17

For the British Empire the defence of Egypt was really the defence of the Suez Canal. Initially the inclination had been to rely on the difficulties that would face a Turkish army if it tried to cross the Sinai Desert, and British defensive arrangements had therefore been arrayed on the western side of the canal. A Turkish attack in February 1915 managed to reach the canal, however, and even put pontoons in it before being driven off. Throughout that year parties of Turks managed to get to the canal and on occasion laid mines, interfering with navigation. Therefore in about October 1915 it was decided that the defence had to be moved eastwards. Once the concept had been authorised by London, the first of the new defensive positions east of the canal was occupied in February 1916, but the ultimate goal was to move out of the difficult desert country and establish a more secure position on the firm ground in the eastern Sinai or even southern Palestine. For much of 1916 the immediate objective was the establishment of a position at El Arish, about 140 kilometres from the Suez Canal along the Mediterranean coast.[56]

The Anzac Mounted Division therefore commenced its first significant operations against the Turks east of the Suez Canal about a month after its formation, in April 1916. It began a long series of reconnaissances, raids and patrols in the Sinai Desert aimed at dominating the area and denying the Turks another chance at attacking the canal. These activities were often conducted at brigade strength, especially at first, although augmented squadron and regimental missions were more common as experience was gained. These missions regularly required demanding night marches across the desert followed by short, sharp actions with Turkish outposts in order to bring about their capture or retirement, and the aim of many of them was either to secure water supplies or to deny them to the enemy by their destruction. A reconnaissance, for example, led by a squadron of the 9th Light Horse Regiment to Jifjaffa in April 1916 was launched at an objective more than 80 kilometres from its start point, and the subsequent attack resulted in 16 Turks killed, 15 wounded and

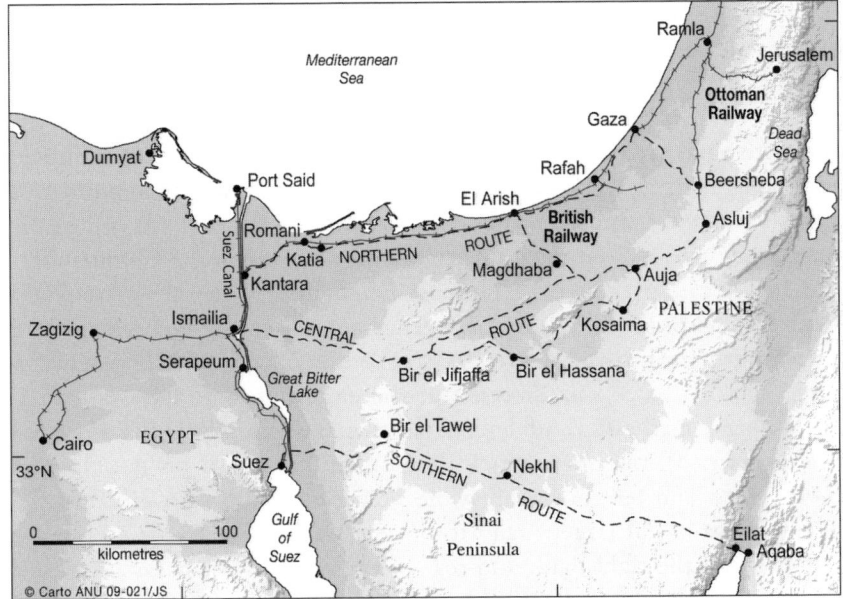

Map 4 The Sinai Desert and southern Palestine, 1916–17

34 captured and the destruction of the Turkish camp and water-boring equipment located there.[57]

Mastering the desert proved a key challenge, and a patrol of the 6th Light Horse Regiment to Bir el Bayud, nearly a hundred kilometres from their start point, in temperatures higher than 50°C across soft sand, found by 10 o'clock in the morning that it was unable to continue and had to retire to rest under palms. No men were lost to heat exhaustion, but four officers and 30 troopers required evacuation and 500 horses were rendered unfit for use for 'some time'.[58]

With the 1st and 3rd Light Horse Brigades detached on duties up the Nile and on other parts of the canal, much of this early work in the Sinai fell to the 2nd Light Horse Brigade, which was still under the command of Granville Ryrie, and the New Zealand Mounted Rifles Brigade, under the New Zealand permanent force officer who had taken over the formation at Gallipoli, Brigadier-General Edward Chaytor. It was not until late May that the 1st Light Horse Brigade returned to the division from west of the Nile. Since Chauvel's elevation to divisional command on Gallipoli it had been commanded by Brigadier-General Charles Cox, who had been a militia light horse officer and infamously commanded the first Australian contingent of lancers to Aldershot and the Boer War in 1899. The 3rd

Light Horse Brigade, which had passed to the command of Brigadier-General John Antill in September 1915 on Gallipoli, would not return until later in the year.[59]

From late April much of this patrolling activity took place in the northern Sinai in the Katia–Bir el Abd oasis area, which had been occupied following a strong Turkish attack in April that had overrun a number of British-manned outposts. Centred on Romani, at the western end of the oasis, the division continued its active patrolling while the Commander-in-Chief of the Egyptian Expeditionary Force (EEF), General Sir Archibald Murray, consolidated his logistic arrangements by pushing a railway and water pipeline into the desert.[60] This continued until 19 July when a large Turkish force was detected at the eastern end of the oasis area. Following a methodical advance from there (which Chauvel's mounted troops harried), the main attack on Romani developed on the night of 3–4 August and fell, not against the prepared infantry positions of the 52nd Division, but largely against the 1st and 2nd Light Horse Brigades deployed on the right flank and rear of the Romani defences. The result was that the Turks had to fight for what they had intended to be the starting point of their attack. This led to delays and changes of approach for the Turks and meant that, as the day wore on, the desert heat and the resilient light horse defence increasingly debilitated the Turkish attackers. By mid-morning the attack had petered out, but not before the Turks had captured several key positions and given Chauvel a few anxious moments.

Chauvel counter-attacked with the New Zealand Mounted Rifle Brigade, the 5th Mounted Brigade (yeomanry) and light horse later in the day, and there was an expectation that on the following morning the mounted troops might be presented with an opportunity to cut off the Turks, who were now exhausted and badly strung out around Romani. A poorly arranged and uncommunicative command system on the British side, however, combined with an unimaginative plan by Major-General H.A. Lawrence, who was commanding that section of the canal's defences, meant that the advance was straight at the Turks, who were falling back on Katia, a few miles south-east of Romani, rather than around their flank. Antill's 3rd Light Horse Brigade was the only formation sent to attack the enemy's exposed westernmost side, and it initially did well, but when it withdrew unexpectedly (and for reasons that have never been adequately explained) soon after coming into action, the Turks were able to fight their pursuers to a standstill at Katia and ultimately make good their withdrawal, despite their heavy losses at Romani. They then

Photo 22 Light-horsemen move out to Jifjaffa in the Sinai in April 1916. The recently formed Australian and New Zealand Mounted Division spent much of 1916 working to ensure the Turks could not use the desert to again make an approach on the Suez Canal. The battle of Romani in August marked the Turks' last attempt to do so. (AWM A00221)

skilfully retired through a series of defended positions prepared during their advance across the desert, frustrating Chauvel's attempts at a more decisive pursuit. After the battle senior officers in the EEF were critical of the way the pursuit had been conducted and felt that the Anzac Mounted Division had not tried hard enough to get around the Turkish flank. The assertion that the mounted troops were still relatively inexperienced and might have done better was not unreasonable, but given the circumstances of a pursuit across a hot desert with little water, these criticisms were largely unfair.[61] By 12 August the pursuit was exhausted and the enemy was clear of the oasis.[62]

The battle at Romani had been the first large-scale victory for the light horse and, coming as it did on the heels of the unsuccessful Somme offensive of 1916 on the Western Front, was a fillip for British spirits in general. Congratulations poured in from all over, and among them was a message from Edward Hutton, with whom Chauvel had maintained a warm correspondence over the years. Hutton noted that all 'the world has complimentary remarks to make upon the Australian Light

Horse, whether as Infantry at Gallipoli or as Light Horse in Egypt'.[63] There followed for the light horse an extended period of rest, training and relatively minor operations during which the Anzac Mounted Division, along with most of the other troops involved in the fighting thus far, was detached from the canal defences. They were made part of the new Desert Column, itself part of the new Eastern Force, under the command of the British regular cavalryman Lieutenant-General Sir Phillip Chetwode.[64]

Thus arranged, the light horse again took part in major operations in late 1916, supported now by the railway and water pipeline, which had been inching its way across the desert and which dictated the pace of operations in the Sinai. The Anzac Mounted Division, after occupying the abandoned Turkish position at El Arish on 21 December, then moved two days later on a strongly held position at Magdhaba, about 30 kilometres to the south-east up the Wadi el Arish. Here the Turks had developed a strong position, and the lack of water nearby meant that the attackers would have to take it within the day or fall back on El Arish. After a night approach the division commenced its assault on the morning of 23 December, quickly surrounding the Turks. A well-planned defence frustrated them, however, and Chauvel, worried about the lack of water for the horses, had decided on a withdrawal when the 1st Light Horse Brigade took a major Turkish redoubt, precipitating further gains and eventually the surrender of the garrison.[65]

A little over a week later this was followed by an attack on a position at Rafah, south-west of Gaza on the Egypt–Palestine frontier. Chetwode thought this isolated position 'a gift' and, on the night of 8–9 January 1917, the mounted troops of the Desert Column set out from El Arish to take it. A long, difficult and at times confused night march was followed by another difficult day of fighting. The Turks were surprised to find themselves surrounded in the morning, but their position, on a small rise surrounded by ground that gently sloped away, was a strong one. As the day and the slow advance of the Desert Column's units ground on, Turkish relief columns began to threaten, and Chauvel and Chetwode began, once again, to be worried by the impending need to water the horses. They had decided on a withdrawal and just issued the necessary orders when the New Zealand Mounted Rifles Brigade and the Imperial Camel Brigade launched near-simultaneous assaults on the Turks from the north and south respectively. They carried the redoubts to their front, and the assault became general as the light horse and then yeomanry brigades joined in, forcing a Turkish collapse.[66]

The battles at Magdhaba and Rafah highlighted both the strengths and the weaknesses of the light horse during the Sinai campaign. The requirement for the attacks on both these places to be made by striking across tracts of desert from more firmly established bases meant that, in effect, only the horse- and camel-mounted troops of the Desert Column could be successfully used. The infantry had, since Romani, largely been used to follow up the advances and secure the gains. At Magdhaba and Rafah, however, the light horse had largely been used like mounted infantry rather than cavalry-like mounted rifles, being required to make dismounted assaults against Turkish strongpoints. They had been successful, but on both occasions the battles had been close-run things, with the attackers being on the verge of retiring when bold unit action had saved the day. The range, flexibility and fortitude of the mounted troops was evident, but so also was their relative lack of striking power against well-prepared static defences. A dismounted light horse brigade, working within an establishment designed with mounted work in mind, and facing a need for one in every four men to act as horse-holders, was barely equivalent in strength to an infantry battalion. This meant that in dismounted action this 'slender striking force', as the official historian later put it, found it impossible to develop the depth of formation or firepower of their infantry equivalents.[67]

The light horse adapted as best it could, largely successfully, but a fighting structure designed to facilitate skirmishing, surprise attack, and the rapid overwhelming of an enemy with rapid fire and manoeuvre in open warfare was not well suited to sustained assaults in front of the enemy's trenches. At Rafah in particular the Turkish defenders dominated the firefight for most of the day, forcing the attackers to edge their way forward slowly until their fire discipline and field artillery support was able to effect a local dominance that could be exploited. The mounted riflemen of Australia and New Zealand, and British cavalry in general, could and did act to fulfil the role of mounted infantrymen when it was required of them, but doing so was always a balancing act. Against an enemy in the open the mounted rifles could exploit their strength of mobility to sway the fight, but set-piece actions against prepared defences were always a more difficult proposition. Artillery could have compensated to some extent, but the horse artillery batteries were also arranged for mobile operations, being provided with small ammunition reserves (at Rafah some batteries ran out of ammunition, and a logistic error meant the resupply was not immediately forthcoming) and relatively light field guns: 18-pounders in 1916 and most of 1917. These were not the sort of battery that, in the small numbers generally available, could drastically make up the deficit in combat firepower. It is testimony to the enterprise of the Australian light horse and the New Zealand mounted riflemen that these battles went as well as they did. Whether the lesson was learnt, however, must be open to some doubt as the mounted troops would continue to be used in this way throughout much of the campaign.[68]

Having secured the Sinai–Palestine frontier, the defensive scheme embarked on at the end of 1915 had been completed, but it was not long before an advance to southern Palestine was being contemplated. During February 1917 a number of minor operations were launched to clear the last remaining Turkish outposts from the Sinai and, the railway and pipeline having been brought up as far as Rafah, in March an attack was mounted against Gaza.

Here the mounted troops of the Desert Column, aided by the camel brigade, were to circle around Gaza and position themselves north and east of the town, cutting off the Turkish defenders' withdrawal route and halting any attempt at relief that might be made. The infantry of the 53rd Division were then to attack the town itself. This plan was executed on 26 March, and the horsemen of the Desert Column did as they were required, but the infantry assault proved ponderous. A morning fog had delayed the reconnaissance, but even when it was completed the division was slow in disseminating and executing its plan. Inadequate artillery support and the open approaches to the town further slowed things and made the assault costly; three thousand infantrymen became casualties during the afternoon. To help the infantry and save the situation Chetwode removed the Anzac Mounted Division from its duties beyond town and threw them into the assault, too. By the end of the day the light-horsemen, the New Zealand mounted riflemen and yeomanry had entered the town, and the infantry had also gained a key objective.

Substantial Turkish relief forces were threatening, but the Gaza garrison seemed largely intact to the British (although this was an overestimation) and, as always, the matter of watering the troops and horses came into play. Chetwode, with the agreement of the commander of Eastern Force Lieutenant-General Sir Charles Dobell, therefore decided to break off the action after dark, the infantry were required to conform and during the night Gaza was left to the Turks.[69] The decision was puzzling to many of the mounted troops as they were in the town and thought the battle won (and the Turks certainly thought it lost). The EEF's command was worried about the fresh Turkish troops who threatened to join the

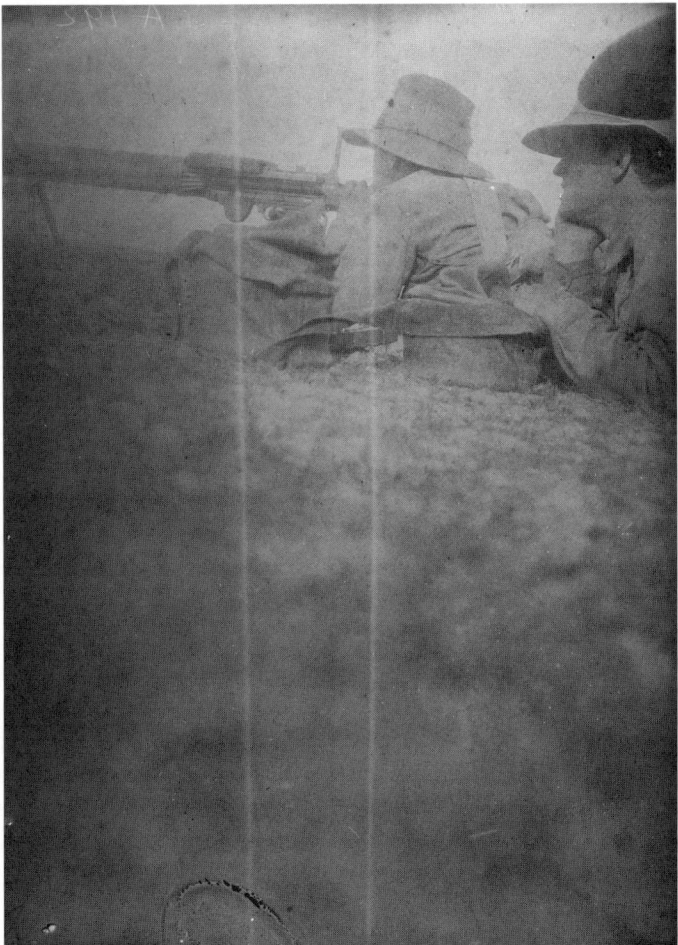

Photo 23 A Lewis gun of the 9th Light Horse Regiment in action at Rafah in January 1917. With only three such guns per regiment at this point of the war, and with one in every fourth man required to take care of the horses in action, the light horse had difficulty generating enough striking power in the set-piece fights demanded of it in the eastern Sinai. (AWM A00192)

battle on the morning of the 27th, but these troops actually stopped short of town and this threat did not materialise. Failures of communication in and between the overly numerous and very understaffed British headquarters also meant that not all the successes of the day were understood; victory was effectively handed to the Turks.

Heartened by their victory, the Turks then set about improving and reinforcing their defences at Gaza and extending them out to the southeast towards Beersheba. Sir Archibald Murray had sent a misleading dispatch to London suggesting that the Gaza assault had been more successful than it actually was, and he was instructed to exploit his successes at the first opportunity. The EEF therefore attacked again in April and had even less success than in March. This time three infantry divisions went up against Gaza, but with little result. The six worn-out tanks sent from France were scattered too widely among the attackers and were of no benefit. The first use of poison gas during the campaign went unnoticed by the Turks as it quickly dissipated in the hot Middle Eastern air. More importantly, the artillery fire plan was completely inadequate. There were virtually no heavy guns available, and the too brief and insufficiently dense bombardments by the light field guns of the infantry divisions did little to trouble the well-entrenched defenders.

As an example of a mismanaged, poorly planned and costly battle against prepared defences it would not have been out of place on the Western Front in 1915 or 1916. Official British casualties for the day amounted to about 6500 (of which 5000 were in the infantry divisions), but with about 1500 men missing the real number was much higher, and the strength that might have supported an advance into Palestine was gone. Rather than fall back on the firm bases of Rafah or El Arish the British opted to dig in on an advanced line secured during the April battle, and a trench stalemate in the harsh environment in front of Gaza developed.[70]

THE EXPANSION OF THE MOUNTED TROOPS

At Second Gaza, as it became known, the Anzac Mounted Division had played a relatively minor, if busy, role securing the right flank of the attack. The recently created Imperial Mounted Division had been heavily engaged, having been sent to make dismounted attacks, which proved fruitless, on one of the Turkish positions south-east of Gaza. It was not the division's first operation; it had been used at First Gaza to help with the encirclement of the town and, along with the cameleers, had successfully held off the Turkish relief forces – something for which, the commander noted, they 'got a nice pat on the back from the Corps Commander'.[71]

This new division owed its existence to the successes of the mounted troops from Romani to Rafa, which had led to a decision in early 1917 to expand and reorganise the horse mounted troops in the theatre. Two

Table 6.3 Organisation of the EEF's mounted divisions, March–June 1917, with commanders

A & NZ Mounted Division (Chauvel, later Chaytor)	Imperial Mounted Division (Hodgson)
1st LH Brigade (Cox)	3rd LH Brigade (Roytson)
2nd LH Brigade (Ryrie)	4th LH Brigade (Meredith)
NZMR Brigade (Chaytor, later Meldrum)	5th Mounted Brigade (Wiggin)
22nd Mounted Brigade (Fryer)	6th Mounted Brigade (Pitt)
Inverness, Ayrshire, Leicester and Somerset Batteries, RHA	Berks and Notts Battteries, RHA; A and B Batteries, HAC

Source: Chauvel, 'The Australian Light Horse in the Great War', NAA A1194, 33.68/15152, pp. 10–11; Browne, 'Operations of the Mounted Troops of the EEF (continued)', p. 223.

additional yeomanry brigades were brought in from the moribund front in Salonika, and this, along with the reconstitution of the 4th Light Horse Brigade with the 4th, 11th and 12th Light Horse Regiments,[72] meant that there were now eight mounted brigades in the EEF.[73] The Anzac Mounted Division lost the 3rd Light Horse Brigade and gained instead the yeomanry of the 22nd Mounted Brigade. The new Imperial Mounted Division, which had first been proposed in January, started forming in February and been formally established in mid-March,[74] was made up of the 3rd and 4th Light Horse Brigades and the 5th and 6th Mounted Brigades. British territorial horse artillery again made up the new formation's fire support (see table 6.3). Reflecting these changes the Desert Column was reorganised to include the two new mounted divisions, the Imperial Camel Brigade and the infantry of the 53rd Division.[75]

The yeomanry had hitherto been patchy in its performance and in 1916 there had been a need to weed out poorly performing officers and send them home, but by early 1917 its quality was approaching that of the Australian and New Zealand mounted troops. Murray intended that this trend should be reinforced by mixing the British mounted brigades in with the more experienced dominion troops.[76] This decision, along with one to appoint a British cavalryman, Major-General Sir Henry Hodgson, to command the new division raised the hackles of a number of Australian officers.[77]

When the division had first been mooted in January the question of command had been the subject of some discussion. The New Zealand brigadier Edward Chaytor was highly regarded and seems to have been the first choice at headquarters EEF where Murray's chief of staff, Major-General Arthur Lynden-Bell, thought him 'an exceedingly good man and a real soldier – far better than any of the other Brigadiers'.[78] His appointment seems to have been blocked by Chetwode, and Hodgson, who had performed well in the Western Desert against the Senussi, was given the command instead.[79] Chaytor soon got his chance, however, and within months took over the Anzac Mounted Division.

Still, the creation of a mixed imperial brigade commanded by a British officer fuelled a degree of disruptive national enthusiasm from some in the light horse that dragged on for some months, although the disquiet appears to have been limited largely to a vocal but influential few. A number of officers, including Granville Ryrie, wrote to Lieutenant-General Sir William Birdwood, commander of the AIF, expressing their belief that the four light horse brigades should together make up an exclusively Australian division.[80] The commander of the AIF Administrative Headquarters in London, Brigadier-General Robert Anderson, acting as a conduit for the discontent and doing more than his bit to fan it, also lobbied Birdwood on the matter.[81]

Chauvel's biographer, Alec Hill, has suggested that Ryrie, at least, was partly motivated by personal ambition as the removal of the New Zealand Mounted Rifles Brigade and its commander, Chaytor, to another division would improve his chances of advancement, and this might well have been the case.[82] Ryrie certainly harboured a desire for promotion and, as he stayed in command of his brigade for the entire war and received a higher command and rank only after the armistice, was inclined to be resentful about his situation, blaming Chauvel for blocking him.[83] In an oft-quoted line Chauvel, reflecting on Ryrie's background as a politician, thought him 'a Member of Parliament first and a soldier afterwards', a view that was probably not without substance.[84] Birdwood, who also seems to have thought that none of the Australian brigadiers in Egypt was up to the required standard, saw it as essentially a local decision made by men with better understanding of the situation than he and was loathe to intervene in the matter.[85] For its part the Australian Government, fired up in part by Anderson's agitation, signalled disapproval of the new arrangements and cabled that they 'strongly urge that these Brigades should be kept together in one Division'.[86] Although this was resisted in Egypt, the whole affair was kept alive by dissatisfaction at the appointment of predominantly British officers to Hodgson's staff and a simmering belief that, although the Australians had been doing much of the fighting, they had not been receiving the credit due to them.[87]

Chauvel, who had ascended to the command of the Desert Column just after Second Gaza on Chetwode being given the command of Eastern Force (a shuffle that also gave Chaytor the Anzac Mounted Division), became increasingly concerned at the tensions. He cabled Melbourne that the 'agitation for Australian Mounted Division is running risk of breaking up Anzac Mounted Division which has earned honourable distinction as such'.[88] Anderson suggested that taking the Australians from the camel corps would free up enough men for another Australian brigade, which could then be used to create an Australian division, thus preserving the Anzac Mounted Division. Chauvel rightly pointed out that this would unacceptably weaken the Imperial Camel Corps and that, in any case, there was insufficient horses to mount a new Australian brigade.[89] The whole affair was brought to a merciful end in June when the arrival of more yeomanry brigades gave Murray the opportunity to further reorganise his mounted troops.[90]

Having learnt that it would be wise to consult the Australian Government when reorganising its troops, this time he cabled Melbourne asking for its concurrence before he contacted the War Office with his proposals. Accordingly in June the mounted troops of the Desert Column were again reorganised into three mounted divisions, each of three brigades. The Anzac Mounted Division lost its yeomanry and, with the remaining Australian and New Zealand brigades, would see out the rest of the war with the same structure. The Imperial Mounted Division, which included the 3rd and 4th Light Horse Brigades, was renamed the Australian Mounted Division. Murray expressed a desire to form, in time, another light horse brigade from further reinforcements and make this formation truly Australian, but the manpower surpluses of early 1916 had dried up and the idea remained unfulfilled for the time being.[91] Instead it was rounded out with the yeomanry of the 5th Mounted Brigade, who had been campaigning alongside the light horse since early 1916, and the other three yeomanry brigades were formed into the new Yeomanry Mounted Division.[92] The 7th Mounted Brigade, although allotted as army troops, became a regular attachment of Chauvel's command (see table 6.4, page 166).

This reorganisation must have been among Murray's last acts in Egypt as later that same month he was replaced as Commander-in-Chief of the EEF by the British cavalryman General Sir Edmund Allenby. This resulted in further reorganisation. Eastern Force was done away with as Allenby moved his headquarters eastward to be with his army, and Chetwode was moved to command one of two new infantry corps. The Desert

Table 6.4 Organisation of the EEF's mounted divisions, June 1917 – April 1918, with commanders

Desert Column/Desert Mounted Corps (Chauvel)		
A&NZ Mounted Division (Chaytor)	Australian Mounted Division (Hodgson)	Yeomanry Mounted Division (Barrow)
1st LH Brigade (Cox)	3rd LH Brigade (Wilson)	6th Mounted Brigade (Godwin)
2nd LH Brigade (Ryrie)	4th LH Brigade (Grant)	8th Mounted Brigade (Rome)
NZMR Brigade (Meldrum)	5th Mounted Brigade (Fitzgerald)	22nd Mounted Brigade (Fryer)
Inverness, Ayrshire, and Somerset Batteries, RHA	Notts Battery, RHA; A and B Batteries, HAC	Berks, Hamps and Leicester Batteries, RHA

7th Mounted Brigade made army troops, but usually attached to the Desert Mounted Corps
Source: Chauvel, 'The Australian Light Horse in the Great War', NAA A1194, 33.68/15152, pp. 13–14; Egypt 1917: Composition of Force, 6 March 1917, Murray papers, IWM.

Column also underwent a name change. Allenby proposed to call it the 2nd Cavalry Corps (the first being in France) but was prevailed upon to maintain a reference to a formation that earned a reputation for itself, and hence it became the Desert Mounted Corps on 12 August 1917.[93] The new corps, in keeping with its definition, lost its integrated infantry division, and the Imperial Camel Brigade was detached to become army troops.

While all this had been going on the units and formations in the field had continued a process of consolidating the lessons learned from the work of 1916 and early 1917. Of this process perhaps the most important change at the regimental level was a significant augmentation of the firepower available to the light horse. Although each regiment, following pre-war practice, had gone to war with two medium machine-guns (Maxims or from mid-1917 Vickers machine-guns), the light horse, as part of a general British policy that affected both the infantry and cavalry, had concentrated them into new machine-gun squadrons in mid-1916, one to each brigade.[94] As a degree of compensation each regiment was given instead three of the lighter and more portable Lewis guns, one being distributed to each squadron. Although no doubt useful, the Lewis gun appears not to have been entirely successful as a cavalry weapon and, following what had been done for the cavalry on the Western Front in 1916, in early 1917 they were traded in for 12 Hotchkiss guns (one to each troop), which were more robust, slightly lighter and more amenable to horse carriage. Given the limitations that dismounted riflemen faced in terms of thin firing lines, this represented a substantial and important increase to regimental firepower, which was first used by the light horse at Second Gaza.[95]

During the stalemate following that battle the three divisions of the Desert Mounted Corps began a process of rotation, training and rest. One division was kept busy patrolling forward while another, in reserve a few miles back, would be training, the third resting on the coast.[96] With training there was considerable work to be done and, despite the experience of the light horse formations, no resting on laurels. The value of continued training was well understood and regularly reinforced for any who tended towards sloth.[97]

There were also deeper tactical lessons to be learned and, while senior British officers readily acknowledged the many strengths of the mounted troops, it was felt that their ability to coordinate their actions, make use of the weapons available to them and generally make the most of their tactical strengths was not what it might have been. As a regular cavalryman, Chetwode thought, among other things, that their 'movements are "heavy" and they have no snap about them'.[98] Perhaps reflecting this, Chauvel and Chetwode pointed out to their subordinates in mid-1917 that, previous good performances aside, some things needed to be better done. First, leaders needed to make up their minds more quickly and travel well forward in their commands so that they could make a rapid appreciation if the enemy was contacted. A general inclination among the men to dismount too soon and engage in long-range rifle firefights had to be reformed as it both wasted ammunition and aided the Turks if they were attempting to delay. Second, there was too much extension of units when in contact in an effort to cover too much frontage and maintain 'actual hand to hand touch'. Chetwode made it clear that 'gaps in the line during offensive operations by mounted riflemen are of no importance provided all know the general plan and work to it under one command'.[99] It was not just junior leaders who were learning, and in May Chetwode had admonished Chauvel when he discovered that, with the EEF now establishing a defensive posture, he was setting to digging trenches – a needless waste of mounted troop mobility.[100]

Aside from such tactical lessons there was a huge amount of more applied work for regiments to get through, and units spent much time working at their grenade-throwing, signalling, conducting gas drills and training with the Hotchkiss guns. Shooting, as always, remained a vital skill, and Chauvel's staff held up the already legendary musketry of the British Expeditionary Force in 1914 as the standard to which their men should aspire.[101]

The training program stretched all the way back to the work done with new recruits in Australia, although in this regard there had been substantial unhappiness in Egypt that the efforts in Australia were misguided or mismanaged. The commander of one training area complained that the efforts to provide elementary training to light horse reinforcements in Australia was undermined by a lack of good instructors in touch with recent developments, a remarkable prevalence of absence without leave and an overgenerous allowance of official leave. It was his opinion that when they arrived the 'men were very backward in musketry instruction and drill and a comparatively large percentage of the men were bad horsemen... I am of the opinion that a large number are drafted to Light Horse units without having gone through a riding test.'[102] This complaint and others eventually secured assurance from home that all that could be done would be done and that riding tests would be enforced for light horse recruits.[103] The problems with poor horsemen were not new, however, and it seems that not all light-horsemen were the natural riders of the martial legend. The previous year another training officer in Egypt had noted that the riding syllabus in the training regiments, based on the assumption that the recruits had passed the riding test and were competent on horseback, was 'too advanced for most of the men' and that they were doing troop and squadron drill 'before they have been taught how to ride'.[104] Accordingly the light horse training regiments had a busy time of it both training new men and conducting advanced specialist courses for officers, NCOs and men coming to them from the front. One such training unit, supporting just one brigade, trained 16 officers and 1290 men in the first six months of 1917 alone, with an average of 400 men being in the camp at any one time.[105]

The results of this training regime were to be put to use in late 1917 as the EEF again went on the offensive. The force that would undertake that offensive was, however, in many ways quite different from the one that fought across the Sinai and twice tried to take Gaza. The advance across the Sinai had, apart from the logistic arrangements that underpinned it, largely been an affair for the mounted troops. In early 1916 they had increasingly demonstrated their competence and ability to dominate in the desert and, once the Turks had been turned back at Romani, were able to use their strengths to strike out eastwards. Magdhaba and Rafah had demonstrated the light horse's ability to cross an expanse of inhospitable terrain, then exploit their flexibility as mounted riflemen to attack fixed positions. At both places the fighting had been difficult, and the limitations of using mounted riflemen like infantry had also been evident. Although they were notable and important successes, they had also been relatively small affairs by First World War standards, the attackers being no greater than divisional strength. At First and Second Gaza the EEF was, for the first time, required to operate like an army, and the inexperience showed, with poorly conceived and planned attacks being repulsed. From mid-1917 the EEF underwent a transformation to fight the next part of the campaign. How the light horse evolved and adapted in response to the changes and the campaign is the subject of the next chapter.

CHAPTER | 7

CAVALRY
The light horse at war, 1917–19

The light horse had played a prominent role in the advance across the Sinai and, although the infantry and other arms had become more important from First Gaza onwards, it was still an important part of the Egyptian Expeditionary Force (EEF). So far the employment of the light horse had roughly conformed to pre-war notions of how dominion mounted troops might be used. Organised as mounted rifles, the light horse's employment was based on mobility and rifle firepower. Mobility had been proven in the ability of the mounted troops to get at the enemy across tracts of desert, but rifle firepower, despite successes on the day, had been proven to have limitations. Sending mounted troops alone against prepared defences was risky business. With changes to the EEF's structure in 1917, however, as well as learning how to employ mounted troops, through 1917–18 the light horse would, with some exceptions, be better and more properly exploited as a mobile arm of an all-arms army. This development would also lead to a significant change to the light horse's form, and by the end of the war most of the light horse had undergone a conversion from mounted riflemen to full cavalry.

Following the failure at the second battle of Gaza the EEF underwent a dramatic overhaul. General Sir Archibald Murray's command had maintained control in Egypt (which was a paramount requirement), secured the Sinai and extended the essential logistic arrangements to the Palestine frontier, but his inability to grapple with the requirements of fighting his army there had been manifest. The morale of the EEF had ebbed, and London had lost confidence in him. The despatch of General Sir Edmund

Allenby to replace him at the end of June 1917 marked a change in the EEF's fortunes. Partly this was owing to the effect of Allenby's arrival, which, as much through his frontline tours and changes to command arrangements as anything, gave the men of the EEF an impression of confidence and competence – a contrast to the general impression held of Murray.

More tangible was that the British Government of Prime Minister David Lloyd George was seeking alternatives to the fighting on the Western Front and began to consider that attacking Germany's allies might do something to undermine Berlin. The belief that this was a good way to defeat Germany was a dubious strategy as Germany was doing more to prop up its allies rather than the other way around, but the new British intention to gain a notable victory in the Middle East – specifically the capture of Jerusalem in the near future – meant that the EEF was given military resources previously denied it. Allenby did not get all he asked for,[1] but another infantry division was transferred from Salonika, more artillery, including essential heavy guns, was supplied and new aircraft types able to deal with the hitherto superior German machines were introduced (Bristol fighters, Royal Aircraft Factory RE8s and improved Martinsyde G102s among them).[2]

The EEF was also reorganised and, besides the establishment of the Desert Mounted Corps, the infantry was arranged to establish XX and XXI Corps. The staffs were shaken up, the new formations trained hard and the intelligence-gathering effort on the Ottoman forces was reorganised to improve things.[3] In short the EEF changed from what had been in many ways an *ad hoc* colonial expeditionary force to a modern army. The light horse remained an essential component of the Desert Mounted Corps, but its days of being the EEF's primary striking arm were over and it was a genuinely imperial all-arms force that would advance into Palestine.

BEERSHEBA AND ITS CONSEQUENCES

By October 1917 Allenby, drawing on an appreciation and outline plan first drafted by Lieutenant-General Sir Phillip Chetwode around the middle of the year,[4] was ready to again attack the Turkish defences in southern Palestine. These ran from Gaza near the coast and stretched out southeast to their leftmost position at Beersheba. The plan, as adopted, called for a feint to be made against the main defensive position at Gaza, then for a rapid strike by infantry and mounted troops at the Turkish left at

Photo 24 Men of the 9th Light Horse Regiment seek cover during the second battle of Gaza, where the British infantry bore the brunt of the fighting. With the shift into Palestine and the reorganisations of mid-1917, the Egyptian Expeditionary Force became a modern all-arms army in which the mounted troops were no longer dominant. (AWM A0223)

Beersheba, with the mounted troops circling around to attack it from the east. With Beersheba in British hands the main assault on Gaza would commence, and the entire Turkish position in southern Palestine could be threatened from behind by the possibility of a thrust north-west from Beersheba by the Desert Mounted Corps and XX Corps.[5] The mounted troops faced a difficult problem of crossing a large tract of near waterless country in order to get at Beersheba, but some good intelligence work, a series of thorough reconnaissances and some industrious work by field engineers meant that sufficient water was found west of Beersheba for the plan to become a reality.[6]

On 27 October the guns of XXI Corps commenced a bombardment of Gaza, and on the night of the 30th the Desert Mounted Corps, less the Yeomanry Mounted Division, which was detached to cover the gap between XX Corps at Beersheba and XXI Corps at Gaza, left the watered staging points and commenced the final approach on Beersheba.[7] On the morning of 31 October, XX Corps opened its bombardment of the Turkish positions on the west and south-western approaches of Beersheba and, following up with a well-executed infantry assault, secured its objectives by mid-afternoon, incurring more than 1100 casualties in the process.[8] The Desert Mounted Corps had approached the town from the south and south-east during the night and, getting around to the east of Beersheba, commenced its attacks later in the morning. The 2nd Light Horse Brigade quickly got astride the Beersheba–Hebron road, and the New Zealand Mounted Rifles Brigade was sent to deal with the key Turkish position on a small but prominent steep-sided hill east of town called Tel el Saba. Here the deficiency of mounted troop striking power against prepared positions, which had been evident at Magdhaba and Rafah, was again highlighted.

The New Zealanders moved against the tel just after 9 a.m., but were held up by Turkish artillery firing from closer to town and by well-concealed machine-guns firing from north of the Hebron road. It was nearly midday before these machine-guns were located, and the horse artillery, of which there were now two batteries in support, was brought to bear. Although these machine-guns were slowly suppressed, generally speaking the horse batteries had an insufficient weight of fire to trouble the well dug-in Turks. This was all the more so now as, despite the objections of Chetwode earlier in the year (although Chaytor seems to have been involved as an advocate in their adoption), the horse batteries had swapped their 18-pounder guns for the more mobile but very light 13-pounders in September, which were arranged in small batteries of just four guns.[9] It was not until about 3 p.m. that the New Zealanders, having been reinforced by the 1st Light Horse Brigade with the 3rd Light Horse Brigade also on its way to assist, was able to work their way forward, effect local fire superiority with the help of the artillery and machine-guns, and take the tel.

As a defensive position Beersheba was now untenable and, unknown to the attackers, a withdrawal was ordered. Beersheba's main importance to the EEF, however, was as a water source to support further operations, and the wells had to be captured intact. With Tel el Saba secured the Anzac Mounted Division was closing in on the town from the east, but night was coming and Chauvel ordered the 4th Light Horse Brigade to attack across the open ground to the south-east of the town to seize it and its wells. Under Brigadier-General William Grant, a pastoralist and surveyor from Queensland who had been a pre-war militia light horse officer and recently commander of the 11th Light Horse Regiment, the 4th and 12th Light Horse Regiments formed up side by side in squadron ranks and, supported by two batteries of horse artillery, galloped at the

Map 5 Palestine and adjoining territory, 1917–18

trenches ahead of them. The first squadrons dismounted on the trenches and engaged in a fierce close-quarter fight while successive squadrons wheeled on to other objectives or charged on into town to capture the water sources.[10] In a later report the commanding officer of the 4th Light Horse Regiment, Lieutenant-Colonel Murray Bourchier, summed up the effect of the charge:

> In commenting on the attack I consider that the success was due to the rapidity with which the movement was carried out. Owing to the volume of fire brought to bear from the enemy's position by Machine Guns and rifles, a dismounted attack would have resulted in a much greater number of casualties. It was noticed also that the morale of the enemy was greatly shaken through our troops galloping over his positions thereby causing his riflemen and machine gunners to lose all control of fire discipline. When the troops came within short range of the trenches the enemy seemed to direct almost all his fire at the horses.

He also noted, most importantly, that this 'method of attack would not have been practicable were it not for the absence of barbed wire and entanglements',[11] something that was known to be the case before the charge due to aerial photography. For the remarkably light casualties of 31 killed and 36 wounded, most of which fell in the fighting in the trenches rather than during the charge itself, the brigade had secured the wells and captured more than a thousand Turks and nine guns.[12]

The charge was a remarkable feat of arms and secured its objectives, but periodic assertions that it constituted a 'turning point' in the campaign are generally overblown for several reasons. First (aside from the historically dubious exercise of trying to find a 'turning point'), the Turks had already been on the defensive since Romani and were in no position to trouble the British in Egypt – so making the charge a 'turning point' indicates a poor appreciation of its place in the wider campaign. Second, Beersheba was already doomed by the time the charge took place, and capturing its water did not prove to be the anticipated boon once the EEF pushed north. Third, Allenby had amassed a clear preponderance in forces over the Turks, which would undoubtedly have had their effect sooner or later. Finally, the Beersheba attack was but just one element of the greater third battle of Gaza, which, in its totality, decided the outcome in southern Palestine. Indeed taking Beersheba was but a preliminary operation on the Turkish left flank, and Allenby foresaw that the most important fighting would take place north-west of the town around Hareira and Tel

Photo 25 Three Australians look over the old Turkish trenches on Tel el Saba, the hill east of Beersheba that took the New Zealand and Australian mounted troops most of the day to secure during the battle. Without its capture, the charge by the 4th Light Horse Brigade, over the flat ground behind the men (going from left to right), would likely have been impossible. (AWM B03068)

el Sheria, which largely turned out to be the case.[13] Partly in order to keep it fresh and organised for this fighting XX Corps was given only limited objectives around Beersheba on 31 October.

The left of the Turkish defensive line thus secured, Allenby's plans to dash into the flanks and rear of the Turkish army seemed set for success, but a combination of dispersion, fatigue, lack of water and determined rearguards, supported by German and Austrian artillery and German machine-guns, meant that although the enemy forces were pressed, disaster did not overtake them. The Turks fell back northwards on a relatively strong position around Tel el Sheria, and this, together with a stiff stand at Tel el Khuweilfe and a general lack of water in the country which caused the mounted troops to spend much effort dealing with their horses' thirst, meant that the strength of the British advance was dissipated. (The experience in the Sinai notwithstanding, during this period the endurance of the EEF's mounts was established as lore.)[14] Chetwode's XX Corps eventually broke through at Tel el Sheria on 6–7 November, but by now the Desert Mounted Corps, dispersed along the front and tired and weakened by the lack of water, was in no shape for a decisive pursuit. The Turks at Gaza, in spite of having lost heavily, escaped Allenby's encirclement.

The victory was not a complete one, but it was a victory nonetheless and the advance continued well into November as the EEF pushed north. Jaffa fell to the New Zealanders in mid-November, and Jerusalem, Lloyd George's 'Christmas present for the British nation', fell to XX Corps, with the 10th Light Horse Regiment attached to represent the Australians, on 9 December. The Desert Mounted Corps alone had taken more than 9000 prisoners and captured 80 guns before the new front stabilised across central Palestine.[15] Winter having set in and a Turkish counter-attack towards Jerusalem having been defeated in late December, largely by XX Corps, the Desert Mounted Corps was withdrawn to locations along the main railway lines to ease the supply situation.[16] The corps' pause in operations allowed time for the events at Beersheba and of late 1917 to be taken into consideration. In particular there was an enthusiastic discussion about what the Beersheba charge meant for mounted troops in modern war, which would eventually lead to a significant change to the light horse's tactics and form.

British cavalry in particular, having undergone a thorough period of reform since the Boer War that emphasised both effective mounted and dismounted action, had proved a very valuable and flexible force in 1914 on the retreat from Mons.[17] That experience was, however, soon forgotten as the open warfare of the first months of the war was supplanted by trench fighting dominated by artillery and infantry. In 1915 the commander of the New Zealand Expeditionary Force, Major-General Alexander Godley, who was a pre-war proponent of mounted infantry, had written from Egypt that this was 'an infantry and artillery war – exactly the opposite of the South African Campaign [and] it is very difficult if not impossible to find a place for mounted men'.[18] This was a common view and when, for example, in late 1914 the 4th Light Horse Regiment charged Australian infantry during training, umpires declared that it had suffered nearly 100 per cent casualties from machine-gun fire.[19] Even Phillip Chetwode, who had commanded a cavalry brigade and then the 2nd Cavalry Division in France before coming to Egypt, had concluded that 'modern firepower has gradually, for some years, and now almost finally put an effective check on the mounted employment of masses of cavalry'.[20] As Henry Gullett, official historian of the AIF in Palestine, later put it, 'with occasional exceptions, the cavalry leaders were inclined to accept the view established by the struggle in France, that trench warfare and machine guns had... greatly curtailed the possibility of cavalry shock tactics'.[21]

Light-horsemen, inheritors of the pre-war militia at home and largely products of the mounted rifle model that Hutton had introduced, appeared to have a variety of opinions on the issue. Hutton's post-Federation regulations had suggested that during war at least part of the light horse should be equipped with lances, but this point had not, apparently, remained part of the collective memory. Light horse training and experience did not encourage expansive mounted action in battle, but still some seem to have been considering the options. After its return from Gallipoli the Anzac Mounted Division reportedly carried out trials with a type of lance, but for some reason it proved unsuitable and was not adopted.[22] Training records for 1915 include part of a South African mounted rifle manual, published in 1906, which included a section on fixing bayonets and using them mounted in the pursuit.[23] How much this was practised in training by any of the light horse, if at all, is unclear, but evidently it was of interest and in various actions across the Sinai light-horsemen had in fact used this expedient on occasion. Such thinking remained well in the background, however, as dismounted skills and mounted rifle mobility remained the centrepiece of training. During 1915–17 practice in such things as shooting, grenade-throwing, bayonet work and Stokes mortars dominated individual training – just a few weeks before Beersheba the Anzac Mounted Division went out of its way to rationalise and improve its dismounted work for what it thought the coming battle would require.[24]

Nevertheless, a number of events showed that the usefulness of mounted action was under serious consideration. At Katia, in August 1916 during the pursuit of the Turks after Romani, brigades of the Anzac Mounted Division, perhaps reflecting the influence of the South African manual, had fixed their bayonets while mounted and charged a Turkish position. Intended more for moral effect against an enemy thought demoralised than a desire to get home with cold steel, the charge, the first by the light horse in action, was unsuccessful as it petered out in boggy ground. A similar charge by the 5th Light Horse Regiment and Auckland Mounted Rifles at a hod thought to contain a battery of guns later the same day was deflated by the belated realisation that there were in fact no enemy at the objective.[25] A few days later at Bir el Abd squadrons of the 3rd Light Horse Brigade had attempted to push forward against the Turks with a series of mounted rushes.[26]

More notable were other efforts by several regiments at Magdhaba in 1916. Early in that battle there had been a brief charge by the 1st Light Horse Brigade that soon ran into heavy fire and went to ground in a wadi, but later the 10th Light Horse Regiment, under its acting commander, Major Horace Robertson, a young permanent officer graduated early from Duntroon in 1914, encircled the enemy position and opted not to advance on foot at the redoubts, but instead 'went forward in a succession of mounted rushes, galloping from cover to cover'. By doing so they demoralised and confused the Turks, captured a number of redoubts and eventually took more than 700 prisoners. A squadron of the 2nd Light Horse Regiment later galloped over some of the same ground into another Turkish redoubt to capture it.[27] Many years after the war, and in light of subsequent events, Robertson thought the success at Magdhaba important because it highlighted the potential in mounted attacks and made it clear that the light horse 'must become cavalry if they wished to reap the full harvest of mounted action'.[28]

More generally it was being found by early 1917 that the rapidity and surprise inherent in well-executed mounted manoeuvre or attack made it a valuable tactic. Notes on 'cavalry fighting' circulated in April 1917 reflected on the actions mentioned above and a few others, and pointed out:

(d) Advances were made successfully over exposed ground moving at the gallop, extended.
NOTE – Both at QATIA [Katia] and OGHRATINA by the 2nd LH Bde and WMR [Wellington Mounted Rifles] and at MAGDHABA by the 1st LH Bde an advance at a gallop under fire was made. In both cases the losses were practically nil. At RAFA also Bdes galloped up to 2000 yards before beginning the dismounted attack . . .
(f) When attacking, a sudden opening of hostile machine gun or rifle fire from a flank may be dealt with by detaching a troop or Squadron to gallop at the gun or rifle men while the main body continues its advance.[29]

This last point, given the widespread belief that it was the machine-gun that spelt doom for cavalry, is particularly significant. A yeomanry officer recalled that for months before third Gaza 'the possibility of having to carry enemy trenches at the gallop had been urged upon us'.[30]

Some accounts of Beersheba like to stress the improvised or 'devil may care' nature of the mounted attack by the 4th Light Horse Brigade.[31]

In light of the expressions and experiences in the preceding months, however, the Beersheba charge does not so much seem like an inspired one-off as the culmination of a series of tactical experiments and lessons over which the Desert Mounted Corps had been mulling throughout much of 1917.[32] This rumination was certainly evident among the light horse officers, and the 12th Light Horse Regiment's commanding officer, Lieutenant-Colonel Donald Cameron, had apparently remembered mounted rifles charging Boer sangers in South Africa and remained convinced of the ability of mounted men to gallop at Turkish defences if the conditions were correct.[33] One can only wonder whether the fact that he had started his military life before Federation as a cavalryman in the 1st Australian Horse was important. More significant was the view of the divisional commander, Sir Henry Hodgson. A British cavalryman with a concomitant belief in the value of mounted action, he had unsuccessfully attempted before Beersheba to have the two light horse brigades of his command equipped with the sword.[34] Frustrated in this course, he instead issued a detailed order on mounted action to his formation just before the battle on 26 October:

(i) It is to be noted that the country is built for mounted action, whereas any dismounted attack is handicapped for want of cover. The Divisional Commander hopes that all brigades will endeavour to profit by their knowledge of these facts.
(ii) To manouevre an attack mounted an *arme-blanche* weapon is necessary. The Divisional Commander suggests that the bayonet is equally as good as the sword, if it is used for pointing only; it has the same moral effect as a sword as it glitters in the sun and the difference could not be detected by the enemy.
(iii) If used in this manner, the point only should be sharpened, to ensure the men point instead of striking.
(iv) The Divisional Commander suggests that the bayonet, used thus, will be more effective as an *arme-blanche* weapon than the rifle with bayonet fixed, as he fears that the latter method would leave the control of the horse too difficult in manoeuvre, and would leave the right arm too tired to give the final thrust.[35]

As one history notes, the utility of the bayonet as a substitute for the sword was probably overstated, but the armourers were detailed to suitably sharpen all bayonets.[36] Assuming that the 4th Light Horse Brigade did as it was ordered, the men who charged at Beersheba had blades thus prepared and the senior officers at least must certainly have known their divisional commander's views. That the men who charged at Beersheba carried their bayonets rather than fixed them to their rifles, as had generally been done across the Sinai, is some indication that Hodgson's order, or at least the thinking behind it, was noted among his regiments.

After the charge those within this same brigade could not help but compare their relatively cheap success at Beersheba with their involvement in Second Gaza. There 'this Brigade made a long advance on foot, with two Regiments (11th and 12th) and the Machine Gun Squadron, and had 187 casualties without any satisfactory result being obtained'. Lessons were being learned, and a week after Beersheba a squadron of the 4th Light Horse Regiment, conducting a reconnaissance, galloped in open order for more than two miles under heavy rifle and howitzer fire and suffered no casualties.[37] The lessons were sometimes hard learned, however, and an ill-judged attempt by the 11th and 12th Light Horse Regiments to conduct a charge at Tel el Sheria in November 1917 had quickly come undone when they emerged from a wadi into heavy Turkish rifle and machine-gun fire. The regiments dismounted rather than press on, but one troop of the 11th Light Horse Regiment missed the order and reached the enemy line before they dismounted and were then shot down.[38]

Nevertheless the open fighting north of the Gaza–Beersheba defences in November and December provided more examples of what charges could do. On 8 November at Huj a mixed group of yeomanry from the 5th Mounted Brigade drew swords and charged a series of strong positions made up of riflemen, machine-guns and Austrian artillery. Hastily organised and conducted without any fire support, the charge was relatively costly. The figures proffered vary, but it seems that of the 120 or so men who took part in the charge somewhere between 70 and 90 men became casualties. For that cost, however, they took a remarkable 11 field guns, four machine-guns and a number of prisoners (the numbers offered again vary).[39] The commander of the 60th Division, whose own formation had benefited from the charge and undoubtedly had been saved considerable losses by not having to deal with the enemy artillery, expressed regret at the casualties but was pleased that the cavalry 'completely broke the hostile resistance and enabled my division to push on to Huj'.[40]

Following this, on 13 November, a charge by the 6th Mounted Brigade at El Mughar – which had been preceded by a thorough reconnaissance, had good fire support and was generally well executed – was very successfully carried out. As well as clearing a long ridge from which the Turks had held up the 52nd Division most of the day, the brigade killed an unknown but large number of the enemy, took nearly 1100 prisoners and captured two field guns and 15 machine-guns.[41] For that it had lost 16 men killed and 113 wounded.[42] Other successful charges by the yeomanry that November were made at Khuweilfeh, Yebnah and Abu Shusheh.[43] During the same period two regiments of the 1st Light Horse Brigade galloped about six kilometres to capture the village of Ameidat, nearly 400 prisoners and a large amount of stores. The 1st Light Horse Regiment captured Ludd on horseback and galloped down an enemy infantry column beyond the town under artillery fire to take more than 300 prisoners and two machine-guns.[44]

The charge at Beersheba, although arguably the most impressive (El Mughar was at least as spectacular), was but one of a rapid series of events that pointed to the continued utility of sensibly executed mounted tactics carried out under the right circumstances. During the quiet period that followed Beersheba and subsequent operations, there was a flurry of communications around the Desert Mounted Corps about tactical lessons learned, and key among them were queries about the judged value of mounted attack.

The experiences of mounted work by the 1st Light Horse Brigade not withstanding, there was a degree of ambivalence about the whole idea from the Anzac Mounted Division. There was a general expression that because they had done nothing like the charge by the 4th Light Horse Brigade they could not pass any worthwhile comment, although it was noted that advancing mounted under shellfire in suitable artillery formations did not present a good target to the guns, and therefore casualties were generally slight.[45] The responses of the Australian Mounted Division to these queries have not been found but, writing a year later, Grant, commander of the 4th Light Horse Brigade, highlighted the limitations of mounted rifles tactics when pursuing the Turks after Beersheba, which had required large and comparatively slow turning movements, and noted that the 'sword permits a far more direct line of attack and brings quick decisions'.[46] Brigadier-General Lachlan Wilson, a pre-war Queensland solicitor and militia officer, appointed to command the 3rd Light Horse Brigade from the 5th Light Horse Regiment just days before Beersheba, expressed similar views later in the war and noted how, during the attempted pursuit of late 1917, the mounted riflemen could only attempt long outflanking movements in an attempt to bring a decision by rifle fire: 'If we had had swords, I am sure we could have ridden on and captured thousands; as it was we stood off and shot hundreds only.'[47]

In January 1918 Desert Mounted Corps set out its thinking on the matter. Referring to some of the charges of October and November, it stated:

(i) Mounted troops are capable today, as in the past, of crossing a fire swept zone, so long as they move quickly and extended. In most of the attacks the Squadrons of each Regiment followed on another in a succession of waves. They were carried through at the gallop.
(ii) The moral effect of a mounted attack has lost none of its potency. On one occasion the horses were so exhausted, after the gallop, that the enemy, if he had stood his ground, could have shot down our men with ease as they topped the crest.
(iii) It is in close cooperation with infantry and not when acting independently, that mounted troops may expect to find the most favourable conditions, and to gain the most far-reaching results.

It also counselled against deciding on dismounted attack too readily, noting that once men were off the horses the delaying effect of enemy machine-guns was noticeably greater.[48]

For the light horse to begin to consider the advantages of mounted attack did not, in the end, mean much of an extension of its existing role. The difference between British cavalry, in the form of the yeomanry in Palestine, and the light horse or New Zealand mounted rifles had not been great to start with. The yeomanry had spent most of the years since the Boer War training to much the same mounted rifle template as the light horse. Since 1912 both had used the same *Yeomanry and Mounted Rifle Training* manual and occupied virtually the same doctrinal ground under the *Field Service Regulations*. Never very content as mounted rifles, and reflecting a 1912 Army Council decision to allow them the *arme blanche* on hostilities, the yeomanry had taken up the sword in 1914.[49] Yet the dismounted tactics – which it should be emphasised were generally the most commonly used form of battle tactics for all mounted troops – of the yeomanry and light horse were identical, and they were taught without differentiation to every yeomanry, Indian cavalry, light horse and New Zealand mounted rifles officer in the theatre who required instruction at the Cavalry School of Instruction at Zeitoun in Egypt.[50] Within the theatre the term 'cavalry' was habitually used to describe all the horse-mounted troops, as Allenby's proposal to retitle Chauvel's formation the 2nd Cavalry Corps demonstrates. By 1917 the distinction between cavalry and mounted rifles, which had always been one of degree rather than kind, had become largely a technical one.[51]

The increasing focus on mounted tactics did not mean that the light horse was beginning to subscribe to a doctrine of hell-for-leather, close-order charges. Reforms carried out before the war meant that British cavalry tactics called for relatively dispersed formations (unless charging cavalry, when tighter formations were called for), the use of concealed approaches, comprehensive use of fire and manoeuvre, and the judicious use of shock tactics in a modern and tactically adept way.[52] The description 'mounted attack', as opposed to 'cavalry charge', perhaps better explains the tactical approach, and the emphasis was on combining mounted action with dismounted and alternating between the two to best suit the circumstances, which is borne out in corps training notes used in 1918:

1. (i) In [an] enemy's position one locality may appear most valuable tactically.
   (ii) Take special precautions [to] get to this point by
       a – sweeping it with fire
       b – arrange that successive lines should sweep over it
       c – let your last line halt on it
       d – send up Hotchkiss battery at once to consolidate.
2. (i) Give an objective to each attacking squadron.
   (ii) Squadron[s] will probably have to dismount to complete job; keeping one troop mounted as reserve.
   (iii) Hotchkiss battery [to] follow squadron close, come into action close behind melee ready to –
       a – shoot if things go badly in melee
       b – if melee successful at once consolidate position.
   (iv) Having consolidated with Vickers, Hotchkiss etc, rally all horsemen with a view to attack.

If Hodgson had been keen to have the light horse of his division equipped with the sword before Beersheba, he was now, not surprisingly, thoroughly animated on the issue. In March 1918 the regiments of the Australian Mounted Division were informed that mounted training with the bayonet, using lightly modified sword drill, was 'to be at once taught to all ranks',[53] and Hodgson continued to agitate for his light-horsemen to be given swords. Even in the Anzac Mounted Division, a formation generally much more ambivalent about mounted action, the 1st Light

Horse Brigade was telling its regiments to 'always look out for a chance for a mounted attack'.[54]

1918

Before Hodgson's plans could come to fruition, operations against the Turks again commenced in early 1918. The pursuit of the Turks after Beersheba eventually came to a halt in December 1917 just north of a line between Jaffa on the coast and Jerusalem further east. In an adjustment of this line the following February, the Anzac Mounted Division, attached to XX Corps, attacked east from Jerusalem to capture Jericho and secure the British flank on the western bank of the Jordan River.[55] In March the Anzac Mounted Division, along with the cameleers, was attached to the 60th Division to take part in an operation across the Jordan aimed at taking Es Salt and destroying the rail viaduct and tunnel on the Hejaz Railway near Amman, thereby providing some assistance to the Arab Revolt under Emir Feisal.[56] It was also hoped that the local Arab population around Amman might be encouraged to rise up against their Ottoman rulers.

Although the Jordan was in flood, the force got across the river and took the town of Es Salt, but the tracks to Amman were narrow, in poor repair, over mountainous terrain and further degraded by the rain that fell throughout. The advance was consequently slow, and there was great difficulty in getting the guns forward. The Turks, with ample forewarning, rushed reinforcements to Amman, and once again the EEF's mounted troops, under Major-General Edward Chaytor, lacked the combat power to dislodge a numerous and resolute enemy in prepared defences. With just a few light camel-borne pack guns at their disposal, the Anzac Mounted Division and the camel brigade, later reinforced with British infantry and a few extra guns, fruitlessly attacked the Turkish positions in wet and bitterly cold conditions for several days, taking substantial casualties. The hoped-for Arab support largely failed to materialise. The EEF managed to cut the railway both north and south of Amman, but this was of little compensation as the viaduct and tunnel, the destruction of which would have been longer lasting, were too heavily defended to be threatened. On the last day of the month the attackers withdrew from Amman and within two days were back in the Jordan Valley, keeping the bridgehead across the river.[57]

This operation, it turned out, had coincided with the launch of the major German spring offensive of 1918 in France and Belgium. The severe strain this placed on the British in France led to Allenby's army being required to fulfil its role as a strategic reserve for the empire, and it was raided for badly needed troops to reinforce the battered British Expeditionary Force. As a result Allenby was required to despatch about 60 000 of his troops to France over the next few months, including the bulk of the Yeomanry Mounted Division, two complete infantry divisions, five and a half siege batteries, and much else besides.[58] In compensation the Desert Mounted Corps received from France the experienced Indian 5th Cavalry Division and a further five unallotted Indian regiments, all of which were destined for the EEF anyway and had embarked at Marseilles for the Middle East just days before the German spring offensive (much to the eternal disgust of General Sir Douglas Haig, who sorely missed their battlefield mobility during the crisis), but which would not be immediately usable by the EEF.[59] The infantry replacements were mostly drawn from largely untrained Indian units.

All this change required a substantial reorganisation, but that would have to wait until Allenby's second effort across the Jordan, which was aimed at Es Salt and a new strong Turkish defensive position established facing westwards between the Jordan River and Amman, called Shunet Nimrin.[60] The operation was designed to take the town of Es Salt, from which the Turks at Shunet Nimrin might be imperilled by the possibility of a thrust southwards into their rear by the EEF's mounted troops. With the 5000 or so Turks there and their guns captured or destroyed, then another advance on Amman might be tried, the whole Turkish position east of the Jordan annihilated, Arabia removed from the Ottoman Empire, and the possibility of further advances northwards towards Deraa along the Hejaz Railway opened up. If Deraa was taken, the Ottoman rail communications in Palestine would be completely severed.[61] The operation subsequently came to be known to Australians as the Es Salt raid (and is generally given the blander title of second trans-Jordan operation elsewhere), but Allenby's thinking, even allowing for the immediate focus on Es Salt and Shunet Nimrin, was considerably greater than what could accurately be called a raid.

The whole scheme, which was given to Chauvel to command, had been brought forward in an effort to assist local Arabs who had joined the anti-Ottoman uprising and promised assistance. The overall conception of operations from Allenby was ambitious, and Chauvel certainly seems to have had his reservations about the whole enterprise.[62] He was not alone, and Chetwode later thought that it, along with the earlier Amman operation, 'the stupidest things he [Allenby] ever did'.[63] Nevertheless

Chauvel's command, made up primarily of the remaining parts of the Desert Mounted Corps, the 60th Division and the Imperial Camel Brigade, attacked on 30 April. The 60th Division moved to take the Turks frontally at Shunet Nimrin while the Australian Mounted Division, less the 5th Mounted Brigade but with the 1st and 2nd Light Horse Brigades attached, was to attack through Es Salt and around the Turk's northern flank.[64] The men of the Australian Mounted Division, some of whom at least (the 3rd Light Horse Brigade was under orders to) were wearing the steel helmets that were compulsory on the Western Front, but which are not normally thought of as light horse head dress in Palestine,[65] further demonstrated the value of mounted tactical movement by galloping over the line of outposts east of the Jordan and moving rapidly in open formations under artillery fire for few losses.[66] When the division swung east towards Es Salt and the northern flank of Shunet Nimrin, the 4th Light Horse Brigade under Brigadier-General William Grant was left to protect its left flank and overlook the Jordan.

This thinly arrayed brigade soon bore the brunt of a strong Turkish counter-attack. Unknown to Allenby and Chauvel, the Turks had made a number of improvements to key tracks and bridges not far from where the 4th Light Horse Brigade had taken up its position. Unknown also was that the Turks had been planning their own foray down the Jordan and hence had at their disposal several extra divisions to send against Chauvel. On the morning of 1 May the Turkish 24th Division and 3rd Cavalry Division fell upon Grant's brigade, soon turning his left and seizing the vital ground at a location known as Red Hill, which dominated the area. Grant was forced to withdraw his brigade hurriedly and, although most personnel were brought out, nine 13-pounder guns had to be left to the enemy. Major-General Sir Edward Chaytor and all available mounted reinforcements were sent to stabilise the situation on the left, but by the time this was achieved the whole enterprise at Es Salt and to the rear of Shunet Nimrin under Major-General Sir Henry Hodgson relied on a single threatened track (little more than a 'goat track') from the bridgehead for its survival. This was the most troubling situation of a battle that was generally not going well. The 60th Division had been unable to reduce Shunet Nimrin, which was getting reinforcements, and, apart from the threat to his rear, Hodgson was now being pressed by attacks around Es Salt. With air reports of large Turkish reinforcements massing at Amman the whole operation was brought to an end on 4 May. The Arabs, perhaps wisely (although it did little to impress their British Empire allies), had dispersed as soon as it was evident that the initial 60th Division attack had made little headway at Shunet Nimrin and played no part in the fighting.

The old bridgehead across the Jordan being maintained, Chauvel's force withdrew.[67]

Little recalled today, the Es Salt operation was perhaps the most 'close run thing' to occur to the EEF in the whole campaign and, indeed, with the exception of the Gallipoli evacuation, the AIF in the whole war (the capture of 1100 Australians at Bullecourt in April 1917 not withstanding). The Turkish attack on 1 May quickly overwhelmed the 4th Light Horse Brigade, and the fact that it managed to withdraw in as good an order as it did, in confused and dangerous circumstances, is testimony to the experience of the troops and the quality of the junior, squadron and regimental leadership, which seems to have had more sway in the situation than the brigade headquarters. The battle casualties of the 4th Light Horse Brigade on 1 May were remarkably light with just two men killed, 51 wounded and 48 missing (these being largely the wounded and the ambulance men who stayed with them),[68] but it would not have taken a dramatically different set of circumstances for the brigade to have been completely destroyed or captured. If that had happened, the same fate would almost certainly have befallen the rest of the Australian Mounted Division, the 1st Light Horse Brigade and the 2nd Light Horse Brigade at Es Salt. In a few days virtually the entire AIF in the Middle East could have been lost. Having tested their fortune, however, for the light-horsemen and the rest of the Desert Mounted Corps there followed a long, hot, dusty and disease-plagued summer in the Jordan Valley as Allenby's army rebuilt itself with its new Indian troops and further campaign plans were developed.

ARMAGEDDON

The despatch of much of the yeomanry to the Western Front and the arrival of the regiments of Indian cavalry had started a process of reorganisation in the Desert Mounted Corps, which was still underway when Allenby ordered the Es Salt raid. With enough troops now to rearrange the corps into four divisions, the remaining yeomanry, including the 5th Mounted Brigade of the Australian Mounted Division, was redistributed. Following the traditional practice in India, one British regiment was brigaded with two Indian regiments to make one of the new cavalry brigades, which were then arranged into the 4th and 5th Cavalry Divisions (see table 7.1).[69]

To replace the yeomanry in the Australian Mounted Division it was decided to reduce the Imperial Camel Corps and use the Australians and New Zealanders so released to create a new light horse brigade. The

Table 7.1 Organisation of the Desert Mounted Corps, April 1918 until the armistice, with commanders

Desert Mounted Corps (Chauvel)			
A&NZ Mounted Division (Chaytor)	Australian Mounted Division (Hodgson)	4th Cavalry Division (Barrow)	5th Cavalry Division (Macandrew)
1st Light Horse Brigade (Cox)	3rd Light Horse Brigade (Wilson)	10th Cavalry Brigade (Godwin)	13th Cavalry Brigade (Kelly)
2nd Light Horse Brigade (Ryrie)	4th Light Horse Brigade (Grant)	11th Cavalry Brigade (Gregory)	14th Cavalry Brigade (Clarke)
NZMR Brigade (Meldrum)	5th Light Horse Brigade (Macarthur-Onslow)*	12th Cavalry Brigade (Wigan)	15th (Imperial Service) Cavalry Brigade (Harboard)

*Not formed until August 1918 after disbandment of the Imperial Camel Corps.
Source: Chauvel, 'The Australian Light Horse in the Great War', NAA A1194, 33.68/15152, p. 25.

decision to convert the cameleers led, however, to a series of difficulties. Although camel troops had played their part in every major action since Magdhaba in 1916, generally their value had diminished since the EEF had left the desert and crossed into Palestine. Still, it was thought prudent to maintain a few companies, and the yeomanry cameleers stayed with their unconventional mounts, которые were mostly used for patrolling or sent to assist the Hejaz uprising beyond the Dead Sea.[70] For the released dominion troops Allenby proposed, in June, to form a new mounted brigade with one New Zealand and two Australian regiments. The War Office, perhaps cognizant of the long-standing desire for a purely Australian division, differed and told Allenby to form the brigade with three Australian regiments and use the New Zealanders to create its machine-gun squadron. Allenby, looking at the diminishing Australian reinforcement pool (just 25 officers and 867 other ranks in early July) objected that the plan was not feasible, but when the New Zealand government, apparently holding its own manpower concerns, fell in with the War Office view, he had to give way.[71]

All efforts to this end were being undermined by the spread of disease among the cameleers in the Jordan Valley. Despite the vigorous efforts of the troops in draining marshes and the medical services in preventing disease, the camel brigade was so depleted by malaria and other illness that, when they were combined with the available reinforcements, there were only enough Australians to form two regiments.[72] The new 14th and 15th Light Horse Regiments soon joined the Australian

Photo 26 Evident in this photograph of the 10th Light Horse Regiment preparing for an inspection just before the Megiddo offensive are the swords with which the Australian Mounted Division had recently been equipped. Reflecting the lessons of the campaign, the swords gave the equipped regiments greater tactical flexibility. (AWM J02468)

Mounted Division as the 5th Light Horse Brigade, under the command of Brigadier-General George Macarthur-Onslow, a scion of the Rum Corps soldier and pastoralist John Macarthur, pre-war militia light horse officer and recently commander of the 7th Light Horse Regiment, at the beginning of August.[73] The 16th Regiment was on hold until more men could be found, and the new brigade was rounded out with a mixed French regiment of Spahis and Chasseurs d'Afrique (French colonial troops from North Africa, Spahis were recruited from the Arab population and the Chasseurs d'Afrique from the white settlers there). The War Office asked Australia to increase the light horse draft to 400 men per month, but even if this number could have been found, a difficult proposition in 1918, it would take time for the men to filter through.[74] The actual conversion proceeded smoothly enough but, as many of the new light-horsemen had gone to the camels from the infantry in 1916, it was a busy ten weeks learning the horse-riding and cavalry trade.[75]

Training the new formation was made all the more complex by the fact that Hodgson's agitation to be allowed the *arme blanche* had finally borne fruit, and the cameleers had to master this weapon as well. Hodgson had continued to assert his views on the sword throughout the year,[76] but it was not until an event in mid-July that his arguments began to hold sway. On 14 July a Turkish attack by two divisions, spearheaded by two and a half German battalions who soon found the Turkish allies on their flanks unwilling participants, was launched at the Anzac Mounted Division at Abu Tulul in the Jordan Valley. They were quickly defeated by a rapid counter-attack by the 1st Light Horse Brigade, and this battle proved to be the last Turkish offensive of the campaign.[77] Further south, as part of the same general battle, the three Indian regiments of the 15th (Imperial Service) Cavalry Brigade took part in a series of mounted actions around El Hinu where they employed their lances to deadly effect, spearing about 90 Turks, capturing another 90 and taking four machine-guns.[78]

This relatively small fight produced more discussions within the Desert Mounted Corps about the evident value of the *arme blanche* and mounted action in Palestine.[79] Hodgson took the opportunity once again to push to obtain the sword for the light-horsemen of his division. Claiming support from his two Australian brigade commanders, and pointing to the pursuit after Beersheba, he reiterated his view that 'the conditions in this theatre of war are particularly suited to the employment of a steel weapon' and that he could 'expect greater and more rapid results from my Light Horse brigades if they are equipped with a sword'.[80] He contended that the dash shown on the move to Es Salt was a reflection of the mounted training with the bayonet he had ordered and dismissed objections about the extra weight of the sword on already burdened troop horses or the potential limitations related to the light horse manual *Yeomanry and Mounted Rifle Training* (which had no sections on sword training). Promising to overcome any training obstacles, he argued that he could produce light horse cavalrymen in a month.[81] Chauvel, apparently finally swayed by the actions of the three Indian regiments on 14 July, now agreed to his request.[82]

The staff of the Australian Mounted Division had already been preparing for such an eventuality and, once authorised, they quickly swung into action. Rifle buckets and swords (the British 1908 cavalry sword) were procured and issued, and training commenced in mid-August, continuing until the middle of the following month.[83] Whatever the passions for the *arme blanche* among the senior officers of the division, the move raised a few eyebrows further down the ranks. One regimental history recalled that the news was met with 'the delight of all ranks', but another brigade recorded that at 'first the new arm for Light Horse was looked upon with a certain amount of doubt, but once the troops had become accustomed to it, and commenced training in earnest all feeling within the Division against its use soon vanished'.[84] Things were eased by the mounted bayonet training that Hodgson had instituted earlier in the year as the regiments had then gone through a vigorous period improving their mounted manoeuvring, including mounted attacks, melees and rallying.[85] The Hotchkiss gunners too had already been trained to operate in machine-guns groups at squadron level, as was necessary for mounted actions, rather than as part of each troop as had been done previously.[86]

Unfortunately, what was being discussed at this time in the upper echelons of the Anzac Mounted Division about the sword is largely unknown. Earlier in the year the commander of the New Zealand Mounted Rifles Brigade, Brigadier-General William Meldrum, had expressed his opposition to equipping with swords, asserting that the ability of the mounted riflemen in the Anzac Mounted Division was based on 'tried and true methods' and that the sword might in fact merely upset the system so much as to invite a tactical disaster. He had expressed similar views as early as 1914, and it seems likely that this officer, at least, still felt this way in mid-1918.[87] What the other two brigade commanders, Charles Cox and Granville Ryrie, thought as men with backgrounds in the pre-Federation militia cavalry of New South Wales is not known (Ryrie was also hospitalised during this period and might not have had a say). That the divisional commander shared the same outlook as Meldrum was perhaps borne out after the war when one of Hodgson's staff officers, writing one of the first histories of the campaign in the early 1920s, noted that the Anzac Mounted Division was 'content to remain a mounted rifle division, as it had proved itself of magnificent quality at mounted rifle work, and the Divisional Commander [Chaytor] was by no means certain it would gain anything by adopting the sword'.[88] With the two light horse divisions having thus taken somewhat divergent tactical approaches, the final preparations for the next offensive were being made.

Facing the EEF in mid-1918 were three weak Turkish armies. The Fourth Army was astride the Jordan River with most of its strength on the eastern side. The rest of the Turkish line out to the Mediterranean Sea north of Jaffa was held by the Seventh Army in the centre and the Eighth Army near the coast. Although continuous trench lines had been constructed closer to the coast, the Turkish line was not particularly strong, lacking depth and generally also barbed wire. Furthermore, the defence had been developed such that every inch of ground had to be fought for when a more flexible system would have better suited the situation. Moreover the Ottoman armies were under strength, overstretched, suffering greatly from an increasingly strained supply system and outnumbered by the EEF by about two to one,[89] a situation reflected by the steady stream of deserters flowing into the British lines.

Following the two British excursions across the Jordan earlier in the year, the Turks seem to have considered that it was here that Allenby would again attack, a belief reinforced by Allenby at every opportunity and by the location of the Desert Mounted Corps, his well-established striking arm, in the Jordan Valley throughout the summer. Instead Allenby developed a plan that called for the Turkish Fourth Army to be held on the Jordan while his infantry and artillery near the coast punched a hole in the Turkish defences, through which the Desert Mounted Corps would move and strike deep into the enemy's rear, cutting off his withdrawal routes across the Plain of Esdraelon (or Armageddon). The Turkish Seventh and Eight Armies would be trapped by Chauvel's corps, and the Fourth Army on the Jordan would have to withdraw towards Damascus or risk being cut off.[90]

Broadly speaking, it was a similar concept of operations to the Gaza–Beersheba attack the previous November; that is, a cavalry envelopment of the Turkish flank, but steps were taken so that the problems that had hampered that mounted thrust and pursuit did not reoccur.[91] The most important of these was that the mounted troops would not be required to take part in the assault on the Turkish lines and thus dissipate their powers, but would instead be concentrated in a position where they could more properly exploit the gap created by the artillery and infantry – in the military parlance of the time a 'G in Gap' plan (a word play on a British map referencing system used early in the war, which used printed words on maps as if they existed, thus the cavalry would 'ride for the G in Gap'; that is, get through the enemy lines).[92] Covered by a thorough and well-executed deception plan, the 4th and 5th Cavalry Divisions, along with the Australian Mounted Division, moved at night from the Jordan Valley into an assembly area in the orange groves north of Jaffa behind XXI Corps. The Anzac Mounted Division remained in the Jordan Valley as part of a mixed force, known as Chaytor's Force because he commanded it, which would 'demonstrate across the Jordan [and] attack the [Fourth] Army should the main operations be successful'.[93]

One history of the campaign has contended that some members of the Anzac Mounted Division were disappointed that they were not to be part of the cavalry effort on the coast and muttered that they were being prejudiced because they had opted not to equip with the sword.[94] Whether this was so remains unclear but, as outlined above, there had been concerns about the use of mounted rifles in the pursuit, and it is possible that this might have been part of the reason why they were used as they were. This division was, however, one of the most experienced and capable formations Allenby had at his disposal, having proven itself in more that two years of warfare. The proposed operations against the Fourth Army in mountainous terrain were by no means simple, as the two operations there earlier in the year demonstrated, and the bestowal on Chaytor of a force nearly equivalent to two divisions and this important mission was in itself an expression of confidence.[95]

On the morning of 19 September the attack commenced with an artillery barrage, which, although not quite up to the intensity then employed on the Western Front, was ferocious by the standards of Palestine, with roughly one gun allotted to every 50 yards of front to be attacked (on the Western Front the ratio would have been more like a gun to every 10 yards, with many more heavy guns employed).[96] Within three hours the infantry of XXI Corps had gone forward under the barrage and smashed open the Turkish defences near the coast. Now, with the 4th and 5th Cavalry Divisions leading and the Australian Mounted Division in reserve, the Desert Mounted Corps was headed towards its objectives in the Turkish rear. Important also were the airmen of the Palestine Brigade of the Royal Air Force (including No. 1 Squadron, Australian Flying Corps) ranging ahead of the advance, and the men of the service corps driving behind with their lorries to keep the whole operation supplied.[97]

The advance was so rapid that the 5th Cavalry Division had reached Nazareth, more than 80 kilometres from their start point, by 5 a.m. the next day. The 4th Cavalry Division covered more than 130 kilometres in 34 hours to reach Beisan, and Chauvel's headquarters had reached its initial destination at Megiddo (Lejjun), nearly 70 kilometres from its start point, by midday on the 20th. By the end of the first day Chauvel could keep touch with his leading troops only by wireless and aircraft.[98] Chauvel was elated and wrote to his wife that he had 'a glorious time. We have done a regular Jeb Stuart ride... It is the first time in this war that the G in GAP Scheme has really come off and I am feeling very pleased with myself.'[99] Allenby noted later too that 'all my Cavalry leaders are delighted with themselves'.[100]

There followed a rolling series of cavalry actions in the Turkish rear, and by 25 September the Australian Mounted Division had been pushed as far as Lake Tiberias where that morning at Semakh, at the southern end of the lake, the 11th and 12th Light Horse Regiments fought a tough action against German and Turkish defenders around the village's railway buildings. Reflecting the flexibility that the sword and the ability to change between mounted and dismounted action gave the light horse, the Australian attack had commenced in the pre-dawn darkness with a charge, swords drawn, which overran the enemy outposts. The German machine-gun fire soon became more effective, and the horsemen dismounted not far from the buildings and commenced a firefight at close range. With dawn and the support of Australian machine-gunners the attacking squadrons closed on the buildings and killed or captured the defenders.[101] Later the same day the 3rd Light Horse Brigade secured the town of Tiberias after dealing with the Turkish rearguard there.

The reaching of Lake Tiberias could be said to be the end of what is now known as the battle of Megiddo, the neat title given to the infantry and artillery breakthrough of 19 September and the subsequent cavalry actions. Although the cavalry battles traditionally garner the most attention, it was, in reality, an excellent example of a well-conducted all-arms offensive, and the cavalry's success depended on the efforts of the whole EEF. The victory was remarkable and, through the combined efforts of the infantry to the south and Chauvel's cavalry and the airmen in their rear, the Turkish Seventh and Eighth Armies had effectively been destroyed by the end of 21 September – an eventuality that astounded everyone. Allenby wrote home that he was 'absolutely aghast at the [excellence] of the Victory'.[102] By the time it had reached Lake Tiberias the Desert Mounted Corps alone had taken about 33 000 prisoners.[103]

To the east, meanwhile, Chaytor's Force had met stiff Turkish opposition in the hills east of the Jordan for the first few days, but by 21 September the Turks, realising the threat to their rear from Chauvel, began a withdrawal that quickly turned into something of a collapse as the enemy sought refuge and escape at Amman. This city and its rearguard fell to the 2nd Light Horse and New Zealand Mounted Rifles Brigades on 25 September. The 2nd Light Horse Brigade captured the last Turkish force of any consequence east of the Jordan at Ziza a few days later. About 10 000 prisoners were taken at Amman, although the remainder of the Fourth Army escaped north towards Damascus in reasonable order.[104]

With two Turkish armies destroyed and what remained of the third dislodged and headed north, Allenby moved to exploit the success and, at a meeting with Chauvel on 25 September, outlined his intention to push on immediately. The Desert Mounted Corps, except the detached Anzac Mounted Division, which had now, unknown to it, fought its last battle, was now directed to Damascus. The 4th Cavalry Division was sent eastwards towards Deraa where it joined the Hejaz forces there, then

Photo 27 The cluttered streets of Jenin after its capture, along with thousands of Turkish and German troops, by the 3rd Light Horse Brigade in September 1918. The ferocity of the Megiddo offensive and the cavalry exploitation completely shattered the Turkish forces in Palestine. (AWM H02981)

headed north to Damascus in pursuit of the fleeing Turkish Fourth Army. The Australian Mounted Division and the 5th Cavalry Division marched north from Tiberias on 27 September, and there followed another series of cavalry actions in which the German and Turkish rearguards were either overrun or harried into surrender. On 30 September the 4th and 12th Light Horse Regiments carried out a small reprise of their Beersheba exploits by drawing swords and successfully charging an enemy delaying position with fire support from horse artillery at Kaukab, south-west of Damascus. On the same day the 5th Cavalry Division turned eastwards to intercept and destroy the remnants of the Turkish Fourth Army just before it reached Damascus, and the 5th Light Horse Brigade cut off and decimated a Turkish–German column trying to escape Damascus via the Barada Gorge.[105]

Early the following morning the 10th Light Horse Regiment became the first troops into Damascus when they passed through the city, effectively taking its surrender on the way, followed shortly thereafter by the advance guard of the 14th Cavalry Brigade, then T.E. Lawrence and the forces of the Arab uprising. Following a number of smaller actions north of the city on 2 September, the Australian Mounted Division was then kept around Damascus. Tripoli having also fallen to the EEF, a new supply route from the coast into northern Syria was open, and the 5th Cavalry

Division, supported by the 4th and assisted by Hejaz forces advancing on a parallel route, was soon sent northwards to Aleppo. This town was the rail junction on the Anatolian frontier on which the Turks relied to support their territory in both Palestine and Mesopotamia but, after some skirmishes with the advancing Arab and British forces, the Turks abandoned it, leaving it to the 5th Cavalry Division, which occupied it on 26 October.[106] The 4th Cavalry Division had been so reduced by malaria that it had to stop. The Australian Mounted Division was similarly afflicted, as was the whole EEF, but was despatched to take its place.

The Ottoman Empire was in dire straits. It had been focused on exploiting a power vacuum in the Caucasus for much of 1918, then been undone by the collapse of Bulgaria, which left its Balkan frontier (and hence Constantinople) open, a situation that a British force was preparing to exploit by coming through Bulgaria from the old Salonika front. This situation was only made worse by the British advances in Syria and Mesopotamia, and in mid-October Constantinople began seeking an armistice. The Australian Mounted Division, on its way to Aleppo, had got as far as Homs where, on 30 October, it stopped upon receiving the news that the Ottoman Empire was out of the war.[107]

Disease was now the greatest threat, and all the formations of the Desert Mounted Corps were afflicted. Malaria, contracted largely in the territory occupied by the Turks before 19 September, had, by the time the Desert Mounted Corps reached Damascus, gone through its incubation period and its effects were beginning to be felt.[108] Men who had contracted it in the Jordan Valley and who were now tired and worn down after the long advance to Damascus were also brought down. The Anzac Mounted Division had similarly been struck soon after its capture of Amman.[109] For all its operations in the jungles of the South-West Pacific and South-East Asia after 1941, the Australian Army has never again suffered malaria rates as high as it did in Palestine and Syria in 1918–19. In early October, too, the worldwide influenza epidemic began to make its way through the ranks. In the week ending 5 October more than 1200 men of the corps were admitted to hospital; the following week another 3100 were similarly treated.[110]

MEGIDDO AND THE LIGHT HORSE

Tactically, the last phase of the Palestine campaign had strongly justified Hodgson's faith in swords and determination to get them, and this marked a change in light horse history. Light-horsemen had drawn their new weapons and used them numerous times to great effect. The attacks at Semakh and Kaukab have been mentioned, but there were numerous other examples. The light-horsemen and the French cavalry of the 5th Light Horse Brigade had undertaken numerous charges during the advance, particularly on the first day of the Megiddo offensive. One charge by B Squadron of the 15th Light Horse Regiment on 19 September, with excellent fire support from machine-guns, took five Turkish machine-guns, a field gun and 170–200 prisoners for the loss of one killed and three wounded.[111] The 3rd Light Horse Brigade had also charged at Jenin, then made more charges during operations around Damascus.

There were numerous instances throughout the advance of bold mounted action bringing about a speedy conclusion to what might have otherwise developed into a more difficult firefight.[112] Reflecting again how the sword bestowed flexibility, the 3rd Light Horse Brigade, faced repeatedly during the advance with enemy delaying positions that would fight with machine-guns before retiring at the last possible moment, often leaving their guns behind, the brigade quickly developed a practice in which a mounted flanking attack with swords drawn was launched in conjunction with a dismounted attack in front.[113] A mounted attack against delaying positions was frequently the best and fastest course open. The 4th Light Horse Brigade recorded its experience doing so against the enemy delaying force at Kaukab on 30 September:

> 'A' Squadron took the right flank of the 4th [LHR] line & 'C' Squadron to the left, with 'B' Squadron in reserve behind the low ridge. Both Squadrons had ground scouts out in front, as they advanced at the trot, this proved very fortunate as just before the final assault 'C' Squadron ground scouts gave the signal to take ground to the left, and the whole squadron as one man swung to the left thus avoiding disaster in an impassable ravine. After passing this obstacle 'C' Squadron again swung to the right and both squadrons locked in one strong line charged the position; 12th Regiment charging their sector on the right at the same moment. Covering fire was given by the artillery [the Notts Battery RHA] until the charging line was very close to its objective, with the result that the enemy was unable to work his machine guns, and at the near approach of steel fled, leaving his guns and prisoners.[114]

British and Indian regiments made at least six notable charges during the same period, only one of which, by the Indian 2nd Lancers at Irbid on 26 September, was a failure. It reinforced lessons about adequate reconnaissance and fire support.[115] Two weeks after the Armistice, the 'Official Correspondent with the AIF' Henry Gullett wrote in the troop newspaper *Kia Ora Coo-ee*:

> This great cavalry triumph vindicated the continued use of the sword and lance, and will probably lead to the sword being added permanently to the arms of Australian Light Horsemen. Had the Australian Mounted Division been armed only with rifles as in previous fights, its performance would not nearly have been so remarkable. Again and again Australian Regiments were able, because they possessed a mounted weapon, to gallop down the Turks and cause them to surrender. Without the swords they would have been compelled to dismount and go in on foot with their rifles, and it is certain that in many instances when thousands of Turks put up their hands the galloping advance of the horse and the sight of the sword, there would have been stout and perhaps successful resistance to our men approaching on foot... Before this campaign many experienced Light Horse officers were strongly opposed to the sword, but since they have seen the remarkable saving it has made in hard fighting and in casualties they have entirely changed their opinion.[116]

There seems little doubt that the disintegrating state of the Ottoman army made mounted actions easier to make but, as was demonstrated at Semakh, Irbid and even at Kaukab, not all the Turks who faced the EEF's cavalry in September and October 1918 could be treated as defeated rabble. Moreover, the value of mounted action had been realised as far back as 1916, and the Ottoman army was not a disintegrating force then. There was clearly a feeling that the sword gave the light-horsemen a tool with which to better exploit Turkish weaknesses during a pursuit in the open. Reflecting on the events in those two months the Australian Mounted Division concluded: '[O]ur force had its force practically doubled by the issue of the sword. They retained all their old value as mounted rifles with exactly the same firepower, and added to this was the power of shock action – a power [the lack of which] had keenly been felt on previous occasions...'[117] As the soon to be official historian Henry Gullett noted in 1918, the 'Light Horseman has become a cavalryman'.[118]

After the armistice

With the cessation of hostilities the light horse began a process of securing the gains. Sickness remained an issue for some time, but by late 1918 the light horse units had generally been moved to healthier climes. Although some regiments were detached for duties in other places, the Australian Mounted Division went to Tripoli on the Syrian coast and the Anzac Mounted Division was located in southern Palestine, both moving on to Egypt in March 1919. In camp they maintained a gentle training regime, ran sporting competitions and undertook educational courses aimed at giving light-horsemen useful civilian skills.[119] Although there were sometimes local patrolling jobs or a reconnaissance to be done, most of the occupation work was left to the Indian formations, apart from the 7th Light Horse Regiment, which briefly went to the Dardanelles to assist the occupation forces in December 1918 before returning to Rafah in early 1919.[120]

The post-war period was marred in early December 1918 following the death of a New Zealand soldier at the hands of an Arab thief one night near the camps of the Anzac Mounted Division. In response to the death, and perhaps a longer-running general sentiment that Arab banditry should be dealt with, soldiers from the division, mostly New Zealanders, surrounded the nearby village of Surafend where the alleged perpetrator had fled and awaited the official intervention of military legal authority. When such an intervention did not become apparent, the men took things into their own hands, and soldiers, again mostly New Zealanders (although a few Australian and British troops were almost certainly involved) raided the village on the night of 10 December. Separating the women and children, they then burned the village and attacked the men, killing more than 20 and injuring many more (there is considerable variation in the figures proffered). After also burning the nearby Bedouin camp, the men returned to their lines. It was impossible to identify the attackers, and Allenby, understandably incensed at the riot and mass killing, with his characteristic explosiveness, gave the entire division a dressing-down in person (which did little but further offend the men before him). Punishment was impossible in the face of a collective silence from the division, but the bestowal of honours and awards to members of the division was noticeably absent in the coming months, as was any general recognition of the formation by Allenby.[121] The murders at Surafend were, and remain, a stain on the reputation of the Anzac Mounted Division.

Aside from this, to the obvious disappointment of many men it was decided that the horses they had been riding were not to be returned to

Australia, the expense and quarantine risks being considered too great.[122] After some consideration the horses were classified according to age and fitness, with the better horses being passed to the imperial authorities in Egypt and Syria and those thought too old or sick for further service being destroyed. About 6000 horses were passed to the imperial authorities and about half that number were destroyed by the Australian or imperial military. Despite the persistence of the commonly asserted claim that many light-horsemen slipped away from camp with their horses and shot them so that they might be spared being sold to the Arab population, there is no substantive evidence to suggest that this ever took place. As financial adjustments between the Australian and British governments were at stake, the process of transfers and destruction was carefully managed and the horses were carefully accounted for.[123]

The general process of horse disposal was thrown into some confusion in 1919 when a civil uprising in Egypt required the hurried reissuing of horses to the light horse so that it could assist in restoring order.[124] The first disturbances began in March not long before the bulk of the light horse was to depart for Australia (the 1st Light Horse Brigade and 4th Light Horse Regiment had already left). Initially telegraph and telephone lines were cut, railway lines were destroyed and riots were common. Being virtually the only troops available, the light horse was remounted and reissued with equipment to help put down the uprising. There followed several months of active patrolling and a number of brief violent incidents. The light horse, perhaps reflecting long war service and the troops' undoubted racial antipathy towards the Arab population, acted harshly at times, and there were incidents that resulted in Arab deaths. Patrols of the 3rd Light Horse Brigade, for example, used their machine-guns several times on 22 March to disperse riotous crowds, killing or wounding about 60 Egyptians. The casualties were not all one way, however, and a few light-horsemen were also killed during the uprising.[125]

The attitude and apparent harshness of the light-horsemen to the local population has come in for understandable criticism over the years. The use of mounted troops to suppress a rebellion in a British colonial territory was hardly new, however, and with no specific training or equipment (if indeed any such thing existed) it is not surprising that the results were as bloody as in other parts of the empire at various times. Although a few, apparently genuine, enquiries were made into a number of the more violent or destructive episodes and some steps taken to minimise Egyptian casualties, the British authorities seem to have expressed little concern about how the situations were handled, and Allenby, now British High Commissioner in Egypt, thanked the light horse for what it had done. There was some international press grumbling about the British response, particularly in the United States where the brutalities of the British Empire often found a ready audience,[126] but the light horse role in the uprising was not an exceptional one by contemporary standards, even if this role was fulfilled at a substantial cost in Egyptian lives.

The uprising was effectively over by June, and soon thereafter the remaining regiments embarked for Australia, then, after perhaps enduring a brief period of influenza quarantine in their home port, they were disbanded.[127]

The First World War had provided the greatest test for the light horse. Despatched to war in 1914, the mounted formations of the AIF drew on the officers and men of the militia regiments but soon had little in common with their forebears. Formed and trained as completely new entities and put into battle, they achieved a remarkable standard of efficiency. Basic training in Egypt was tested and built on at Gallipoli before a return to the desert and an eventual commitment against Turkey in Palestine. Throughout the ensuing campaign, but most prominently in the early Sinai operations, the light horse had been a crucial element of the Egyptian Expeditionary Force. It has become habitual in Australia to pay little heed to the infantry forces of the British Army in this campaign and it should be borne in mind that they did much of the fighting, especially from late 1917, but throughout the entire period of operations the mounted troops played a crucial role. The light horse was pivotal to that role and provided much of the strength of first the Desert Column, then its successor the Desert Mounted Corps. As the war progressed yeomanry and later Indian cavalry became an increasingly significant part of this corps, but the experienced light horse and New Zealand Mounted Rifles remained important. The contrast with the sometimes indifferent performance of Australia's mounted troops in South Africa could not have been greater.

Of great significance also were the many lessons learned. Gullett's assertion that the light-horseman had 'become a cavalryman' by the end of 1918 was only partly true. The light horse, as mounted rifles, had always been a type of abbreviated cavalry. The difference between them and Britain's other imperial cavalrymen, be they regulars, yeomanry or Indian army, had always been one of degree rather than kind. After a few years of war whatever differences there may have been in efficiency or battlefield presence had all but disappeared, and the only remaining divergence remained the matter of the *arme blanche*. Light-horsemen, imbued with pre-war theories about firepower, had initially viewed the sword with suspicion. But in a theatre where the enemy's defensive schemes were rarely as tough as those on the Western Front the possibilities of mounted action seemed to open up. The light horse officers who made use of the sword in this last phase of the war clearly became converts because the *arme blanche* gave them a degree of tactical flexibility that the more simple mounted rifle model lacked and which had been a limitation earlier in the campaign. This marked a substantive change in the evolution of the light horse. It was not just the tactical matters that would reverberate, however, and after the war the campaign in Palestine would often be examined for whatever lessons it might offer on modern war. The apparently mobile and less costly nature of the war in the Middle East led to its being viewed by some as possibly providing lessons for the future; as a way to avoid repeating the costly experiences of the Western Front. The campaign would certainly leave its legacy on the light horse after the war, particularly as Harry Chauvel would return to Australia to become the senior Australian army officer of the 1920s. His views and the broader cavalry lessons of 1918 were to have a significant influence.

CHAPTER 8

THE LIGHT-HORSEMEN 2
The light-horseman at war

The light-horseman of the AIF is a figure to which a long-established set of written and visual images has been attached. Henry Gullett wrote a chapter in his official history of the AIF in Sinai and Palestine on the men and their horses that has done much to set the precedent. To him the light-horsemen was 'in body and spirit the true product of the wide Australian countryside'; 'the very flower of their race'; 97 'out of every hundred came from pure British stock'; all were 'men of resource, initiative and resolution'; and all were 'horsemen of various degrees of excellence'. From the bush, fighting 'under conditions closely resembling those to which he had been accustomed to all his life', they found 'rigid discipline irksome', but applied 'strong common sense' to their war and fought it 'with all [their] will as a task which interested [them] or which had to be done', and when they went on leave engaged in nothing more than a whole-hearted 'joyous demonstration'.[1] Reflecting some of the same thinking, the *Kia Ora Coo-ee* had provided a similar sketch in June 1918:

> Tall, brown, broad shouldered, deep-chested, clean shaven, with a lazy slouching gait like that of a sleepy tiger, and calculating eyes; there is the Light Horseman as I know him. Easy going mostly he is full of surprises when aroused... The daily patrols that leave in the old grey dawn to probe the enemy's line are part of the Light Horsemen's life... he sallies forth to joust with 'Jacko's' outposts. His sense of direction is true... he sees all tracks, spots any

movement and knows how to bluff when in a tight corner. His training in scouting he does not need to remember; it is all second nature with him now. He could not give you the reasons, but he seldom fails to do anything but the right thing when carrying out his private daily fight of his own... he obeys orders without question, and when no orders are forthcoming, he acts instinctively. With bayonet fixed, and galvanized into a rushing charge he is invincible.[2]

Such sentiment has repeatedly been grist for the mill for authors with a bent for boosting the Anzac legend. John Laffin's portrait of the light-horseman for popular history audiences, for example, is simply a touched-up paraphrasing of Gullett's pages.[3] Even as esteemed an historian as Bill Gammage, although pointing to some of the light-horseman's foibles in an altogether more sophisticated analysis, drew to a noticeable extent on the model of the mounted soldiers used in the official history, and the 'Last Crusaders' chapter of his landmark *Broken Years* treats the events in Palestine as something of a romantic alternative to the grimness of the Western Front: 'this was often a gay war'.[4]

Allusions to bush heritage, the similarities of the natural conditions of the Palestine theatre to those in Australia, and the light-horsemen's laconic ways and indifference to army discipline mean that the mounted branch of the AIF has found a place in broader Anzac legend, which draws on many of the same elements.[5] Notions of the bushman-soldier were not new when Gullett's official history was published in 1923, however, nor were they new in 1918 when the *Kia Ora Coo-ee* was printed. As we saw in chapter 5, they had been part of Australia's military heritage since the middle of the nineteenth century and been particularly popular in the 1890s before the sobering experiences of South Africa. There was little difference between Gullett's assertion that the light-horseman 'needed only to learn discipline, and become skilled in the effective use of modern destructive weapons, to be a formidable soldier', and what had been written in the pre-Federation *Bushman's Military Guide*, or Edward O'Sullivan's *Power of Mounted Riflemen*.[6] After the First World War the idea that the bushman was already half a soldier (and that the light-horseman was perhaps the clearest example) was given new impetus, but this idea obscures the fact that the light-horsemen of the AIF, whatever the traits they brought from home, were largely a product of the military institution in which they trained and fought and, as a collection of individuals, reacted to their environment and experiences in many and varied

Photo 28 David Barker's rendering of a typical (if somewhat elderly) light-horseman for the *Kia Ora Coo-ee*. It reflected a self-image of an assured, competent, worldly wise soldier (even if only temporarily in the ranks) who took all in his stride and fought with chivalrous aplomb. (AWM RC08397)

ways. The idea that there was a typical light-horsemen is one that should be approached with scepticism, as should the notion that the Sinai and Palestine was somehow a pleasant sideshow.

THE LIGHT-HORSEMEN

The assertion that the light-horsemen (or any other Australian soldier) were already well prepared for a military campaign by their pre-war life in the bush is perhaps the idea most in need of qualification. After the war

Harry Chauvel, who had reputation as an officer with a strong interest in training, observed of the light-horseman that the bush 'had developed to an extraordinary degree his individuality, self-reliance and power of observation' and that the mobile style of warfare in Palestine 'brought out his special qualities far more than any trench fighting would have done'.[7] The idea that bush life gave men an ability to shift for themselves, improvise or keenly observe the ground in front of them seems reasonable, and it is indeed likely that many light-horsemen did actually bring qualities of this sort with them to the military.

Such skills, however, do not make a soldier and, whatever their worth, constituted but a fraction of the knowledge needed of the light-horsemen. To them needed to be added such abilities as to shoot, control fire, take horses in and out of action, treat wounded comrades, indicate targets, provide covering fire, operate a Hotchkiss gun and apply its fire, provide a useful report on enemy movements, brief a sentry, know the duties of a piquet, and tend to a horse on campaign. The list goes on, and for officers another set of skills was required. For soldier-specialists could be added things like knowledge about operation of a heliograph, wireless or a Vickers machine-gun, or even how to fill in the plethora of returns that headquarters constantly demanded and which was the basis of so much administration. These things, in all their myriad forms, had not just to be learned by each individual but also applied at the troop, squadron, regimental, brigade and higher levels.

In short, light-horsemen, as soldiers, regardless of their origins, were largely created by training in an army that taught them their military duty, then had those skills honed by practical experience in war. Perhaps only certain specialists, like farriers, had a military job that drew extensively on their civilian skills.[8]

Of Gullett's claims, the idea that the mounted soldiers were almost entirely countrymen is perhaps the most accurate, although here too some qualification is required. The effort to recruit as many men as possible from the militia in 1914 and 1915 notwithstanding, the general call for recruits meant that the men who enlisted in the light horse of the AIF were not necessarily the same sort of men who served in pre-war militia regiments. One study, based on the 7th Light Horse Regiment (raised in New South Wales), reveals that although country men undoubtedly predominated in the ranks, nearly 20 per cent of the men who passed through this unit during the war were from the city. Similarly in the 1st Light Horse Regiment about 26 per cent of the men came from Sydney.[9] Whether these overall percentages can be extrapolated to units raised in less urbanised states is doubtful, but clearly the idea that the men were more or less all bushmen was not accurate. Moreover, in the 7th Regiment at least, more than half the city men came from white-collar or skilled labourer backgrounds. Of the 1664 men who served in the regiment, and who came from rural backgrounds, 892 were unskilled rural labourers and only 392 called themselves farmers or graziers.[10] Thus the pre-war social make-up of the rural light horse units in which farmers and landowners had made up, in most cases, well over half the strength of units, and labourers had been a distinct minority, was effectively inverted in the AIF. There were undoubtedly constitutional differences between units, however, and Bert Delpratt, who served in both the Queensland-raised 2nd and 5th Light Horse Regiments, after moving to the latter in 1916 following a failed attempt at getting an infantry commission, noted that although the units were similar in many ways, in his new regiment the men 'are better riders being mostly western [Queensland] men'.[11] As highlighted by the problems experienced in Egypt after 1916 with recruits not being able to ride (see chapter 6), not every light-horseman was as effortlessly at home on horseback as is often written, and city men were not uncommon.

Given the overall proportions of labourers to landowners, it therefore appears that pre-war militia experience was not as common in the light horse as Gullett suggests, especially in the rank and file later in the war.[12] The greatest carry-over of the militia or pre-war permanent forces was to be found in the officer ranks, especially in the more senior appointments. Every man who commanded a light horse brigade during the war had pre-war militia experience as an officer (except Chauvel and Anthill, who were permanent officers, and Jack Royston, whose experiences were in Africa), and much the same could be said for most men who commanded a squadron. Charles Cox, for example, commanding the 1st Light Horse Brigade for much of the war, had served in New South Wales mounted units since the 1890s, as had Granville Ryrie. Lachlan Wilson, arguably the most impressive senior light horse commander of the war, and who had left Australia as a major before rising to brigade command in 1917, had served in Queensland militia regiments after being a ranker in South Africa.

Although higher officer ranks were far from being a 'closed shop' given the importance of performance during the war, the links and knowledge of other men that stemmed from militia service were probably important. William Grant, for example, who became commander of the 4th Light Horse Brigade in 1917, had had most of his militia courses as a captain and major before the war in Queensland overseen by Harry Chauvel when he was permanent staff officer there.[13] Given that Grant had received high pass marks on those courses, it seems likely that Chauvel's appraisal of him was not based simply on his performance during the war but also on an impression of him gained before 1914. If nothing else, the indications are that militia service proved the crucial first step to a successful officer career in the light horse of the AIF.

The connection between the militia and the AIF did not end with the war, and this should be borne in mind in the history of the mounted branch. Many officers who fought in Palestine would go on to hold militia command in the interwar years. Granville Ryrie commanded a cavalry division in the 1920s; Lachlan Wilson commanded a Queensland infantry brigade before similarly becoming commander of the 1st Cavalry Division in 1929. Murray Bourchier went from regimental command in the AIF to brigade command and then divisional command in the militia in the 1930s. Similarly at lower levels during the interwar years many militia squadron and regimental commanders had seen service in the AIF. Younger permanent officers also got their start in the AIF light horse, and Robert Nimmo, who was graduated early from Duntroon at the beginning of the war, spent much of it serving in the 5th Light Horse Regiment and on brigade staffs. After brigade command and staff appointments during the Second World War, he went to Kashmir in 1950 and became the longest serving commander of a United Nations peacekeeping mission to date. Horace Robertson was similarly graduated early from Duntroon and served with the 10th Light Horse Regiment, leading it at Magdhaba, before commanding the 19th Brigade in North Africa, the 1st Armoured Division in Australia and the 6th Division in New Guinea during the Second World War, then the Australian occupation forces in Japan from 1946.[14] The Chief of the General Staff of 1950–53, Lieutenant-General Sir Sydney Rowell, served with the light horse at Gallipoli before being invalided home, and one of the key officers involved with the development of armour in the Australian Army, the later Major-General R.N.L. Hopkins, also served with the light horse during the war.

While militia service and links were important for junior officers getting their appointments with the first contingents of the AIF, this link became less important as the war went on. After early 1915 the only way to join the AIF was as a private, although throughout the war men deemed suitable for commissions would be separated out as recruits and put through officer training establishments. This appears to have been more the case for the elements in France than Palestine, however, and until early 1918 when an officer cadet training school for the EEF was established at Zeitoun in Egypt, new light horse officers were largely commissioned from the ranks in the field. Even with the establishment of the school the officer candidates came there from the EEF. This was not a uniquely Australian process, and the British Army, despite its supposed officer elitism, followed much the same policies about promotion from the ranks as the AIF, both in Palestine and on the Western Front.[15] Men who received light horse commissions had therefore generally proven themselves on campaign, although the common description of second lieutenants as 'war babies' does not suggest that they were universally honoured for it.[16]

Generally speaking, however, it appears that men promoted from the ranks held only lowly officer positions in the light horse in Palestine. Although the casualties of Gallipoli heralded the more democratic approach to handing out commissions,[17] the relatively low casualty rates in the Middle East meant that the men who held squadron commands or higher after 1916 had usually been pre-war militia officers who might have been lieutenants or captains at Gallipoli. Similarly regimental commanders had usually started the war as majors appointed from the militia. Murray Bourchier's rise was perhaps the most dramatic: he joined the AIF as a lieutenant and ended it as a lieutenant-colonel commanding a quasi-brigade, Bourchier's Force, in late 1918 during the advance to Damascus.

RELATIONSHIPS

How much officers shared the backgrounds of their men is difficult to discern. Given the men in the ranks were often from rural labourer backgrounds, it seems likely that they did not always have a lot in common with the officers who were, even with the more democratic officer selection policies that came after 1915, more probably from the educated landowner or commercial classes.[18] The stories of well-born and educated rankers and working-class officers are so common, however, that there was a noticeable overlap. Pelham Jackson, a rather proper-minded Old Collegian of Scotch College, Melbourne, who served as a ranker in the 11th Light Horse Regiment, approvingly wrote home of the following exchange in his squadron: 'An officer who in private life is a carpenter joiner told one of our fellows the other day that he had a good job getting 5/ per day and tucker. The reply was picturesque and to the point, as the trooper addressed has a splendid sheep property not very far from Kyunna and holds a letter of credit in Egypt for several hundreds.'[19]

As Jackson's attitude to the officer in this case suggests, the relationship between officers and men was not automatically happy, and in reality it varied greatly depending on the circumstances and the personalities involved. Jackson, who asked to be reverted to the ranks after being a lance corporal for a time and who found the pandering to officers required for promotion distasteful, was scornful of 'war babies' after seeing 'too many swanking about Cairo [and having] observed their mental weaknesses & other peculiar traits of character'.[20] In his memoir of the campaign, *Morale*, George Berrie, who fought as a trooper, NCO and junior officer in the 6th Light Horse Regiment, recalled one officer who had 'a reputation as an uncompromising disciplinarian, and was probably the best hated man in the regiment'.[21] Henry Sullivan, a soldier in the 5th Light Horse Regiment, seemed unimpressed on hearing that this commanding officer, Lachlan Wilson, had just got his CMG and derisively noted in a letter that it must have stood for 'Commander of Midnight Gork Acts'.[22] Arthur Rouget, serving with the 13th Light Horse Regiment in France, felt after the first serious action of his squadron on the Somme that the officers took too much credit for themselves and recounted that, after one them had crawled under a log when exhorting his men to fire on a German aircraft attacking them, 'this was the first inkling that we got as regards the sort of officers we had [and] as a result... the men would hardly take any notice of them'.[23] Similarly Edward Dengate wondered about officers whose sense of example was 'getting drunk and singing the vilest of vile songs in Arabic'. What, he asked his wife in a letter, 'do you think of an officer who would walk into the Mess room wearing only spurs, Sam Browne belt and identification discs?'[24]

Although officers and men campaigned alongside each other and accounts such as Gullett's like to accentuate how similar they were and how well they got on together, there were distinct differences between them. When he was commissioned in 1918 after serving as a soldier and NCO for most of the war, Bert Delpratt found 'being an officer alright so far and much more comfortable than being an NCO'. When he received his first troop-leading appointment, he wrote home that he had 'quite a good batman & groom the former washes my clothes & makes bed and does it all willingly'.[25] To soldiers who spent almost all their time in uniform labouring in the form of tending to their horses, maintaining equipment, doing piquets and undertaking the multitude of work parties required to keep their part of the military working, the small privileges and relief from toil that came with a commission were likely very evident. In such circumstances their treatment at the hands of officers who sometimes seemed self-serving or inconsiderate of the men's outlook could become a source of grievance. Pelham Jackson complained that the 'officers treat us as if we were a bunch of mercenaries'.[26] Ion Idriess, in the 5th Light Horse Regiment, bemoaned 'some wretchedly petty rules and orders' that threatened to bring them to the level of the 'poor devil Tommies', who, in his opinion, led an altogether more servile life than the light-horsemen. This situation was all the more galling as at the next battle 'those same generals will be expecting us to win them KCMG's and DSO's'.[27] A lot of this was just soldier griping; we 'abuse our heads [i.e. officers] a lot, which is just as it should be',[28] but sometimes things escalated. Edward Dengate recorded one instance during the Egyptian Uprising in 1919 when, with the war over and repatriation delayed, tempers might have been more prone to fraying:

> [The] squadron went on strike, in other words mutinied, Bolshied, they all got put under open arrest, the officers brought it on themselves, they are to blame, the men were getting guard duty every night and horse piquet in between, in the afternoon they would have to exercise the horses through clouds of blinding dust then when they came back do half an hour of grooming... and if a man went into Minia to get away from the dust he was crimed for being absent from stable parade or some such trumpery charge. [A]nyhow the men refused to stick it, refused to do guards exercise horses in fact everything they thought was unnecessary, the old fool of an OC tried to make them do it and they promptly counted him out, after the word nine they shouted as one man... 'you rotten B____!'[29]

In this case it took the arrival and intervention 'of our old colonel' to settle things down by listening to the men's complaints and ensuring that the potential charges of mutiny were quietly put away.

This is not to say that officers were universally despised, and men who combined what seemed like the right combination of competence, fairness and empathy with their men could, and did, enjoy warm relations with their soldiers. Gullett thought that in the light horse there was 'more hero worship than in the infantry' and, given the nature of mounted warfare, there was probably some truth to this. Light horse officers in action, particularly at the regimental level, were perhaps more often required to lead than command, and were required to make quick decisions on the move sometimes at crucial moments. A gallop in the wrong direction could soon lead to disaster. In his memoir *The Desert Column*, Ion Idriess regarded one of his regimental commanders, Lachlan Wilson, highly and, in the early days of the Sinai Campaign, noted that 'our canny colonel will never let us be taken by surprise'.[30] Even when it came to Berrie's 'best hated man in the regiment' it had to be noted that 'no one ever doubted his cool nerve' in battle. Reflecting on the death of a troop leader in southern Palestine in 1917, he wrote that the 'troop lost more than its officer – it lost a friend, a soldier who played the game to the last'.[31] The liking or hating of an officer depended very much on his qualities in the eye of the beholder, and in early 1916 Idriess thought that some of his brigade's officers 'are pigs', but 'all the officers of our own regiment are liked. I detest two of them; but I suppose other men think they are all right.'[32] Serving in the same regiment Bert Delpratt thought that his squadron commander 'is very popular with all the men and seems a really good sort'.[33] Even if a soldier felt an officer's wrath they could still respect and like him. When one trooper was found playing cards instead of being on horse piquet by the orderly officer in 1918, he received a stern lecture from his squadron commander, but still had to admit he 'is a bonza old chap, sticks up for his men like a brick'.[34]

The officers' view of the men they commanded is often harder to fathom than the view upwards from the ranks, where particular likes and dislikes could be focused on one or two people. Officers, without any hint of them seeing their men as indistinguishable from each other, tended to reflect on them collectively. Having been given command of a troop in 1918, one new troop leader reviewed his command for his sister, simply stating he had a 'nice lot of chaps in my troop... and a very good [Sergeant] which is a very great help'.[35] Even an officer like Granville Ryrie, who was well known for the warmth he showed to the men of his brigade and his ability to get on with them, rarely made comments more precise than 'all the horses and men are in good condition' when writing home.[36] This cut both ways, and condemnations could also be made against groups in which individuals might not have deserved it. Lachlan Wilson thought that regimental drivers 'may be efficient, but are often lazy [and are] the dirtiest and most undisciplined part of a unit'.[37] Undoubtedly individuals came to the attention of officers for both good and bad reasons (there would be no need for medals or courts martial otherwise), but ruminating on the positive contributions or evil doings of one or two of them when there was an entire command to attend to (no matter how big) does not seem to have been a priority for most officers, at least when writing in diaries or to home.

Troopers too were not always the most expressive when outlining their views of their comrades. Even insights into that most basic and intimate of light horse organisations, the four-man section, are elusive, although Ion Idriess gives us an excellent summary of its essentials and the trooper's perspective of life in a regiment:

> We are all concentrated in sections. A section is four men. A section eats together, sleeps together, and when a shell lands on it, dies together. A full troop of men has eight sections. There are four troops to a squadron, three squadrons to a regiment. Our big world is the regiment and even then most of us don't know intimately the men outside our own squadron. Our life is just concentrated in the 'section'. We growl together, we swear together, we take one another's blasted horses to water, we conspire against the damned troop-sergeant together, we growl against the war and we damn the officers up hill and down dale together; we do everything together...[38]

The composition of sections was far from permanent, and casualties, illness and organisational reshuffles meant that these small groups were all more or less temporary in composition.[39] Bert Delpratt wrote to his sister providing a sketch of one such association:

> I have still the same section Lawless, Mackay, & Macfarlane... Of the three I like Mackay the best, nothing I think could disturb him not even a high explosive shell he is always in good spirits & never in a bad temper... Lawless is just the opposite as far as temperament goes but is a good sort of heart & smart at most things especially at shooting... Macfarlane is a very nice chap and is always glad to do anything for you & is a good chap in a dug out in the way of cooking etc. They are all very young & I feel quite a veteran beside them.[40]

The section, troop or squadron was a military organisation before it was a social entity and, having been thrown together by circumstance, the bonds within them were as variable as can be imagined. Men made both friends and enemies; in the words of one trooper, in the 'constant association & fellowship with the same men & sharing the same dangers & discomforts & chances, one picks up lasting friendships (as well as very many lasting dislikes)'.[41] In his memoir *Red Dust*, John Gray (using the pseudonym Donald Black) wrote of the section that what 'one has, we all have; we are as four brothers'.[42] Conversely Pelham Jackson's heightened sensibilities seem to have been eventually wearied by the 'general tone & thought of a military camp composed for the main part of men of very little erudition, and a paucity of ideas on any subject... with the exception of beer, prize fighting & women'.[43]

Beyond the section lay a series of concentric circles of association in which the sense of bond grew weaker the further out one looked. If the section was the most intimate grouping, the troop and squadron seem to have been only slightly less so. The regiment was perhaps the real mental boundary; a 'big world' (as Idriess described it) presided over by a commanding officer in whom the powers of military use and discipline were entrusted, and in which the officers and NCOs had the greatest influence on the lives of their men. George Berrie, in a common wartime analogy, likened it to a home and did not warmly anticipate its break up in 1919.[44] Like all organisations, squadrons and regiments had their own culture, and the differences between them could be quite marked, at least to the inhabitants. Bert Delpratt wrote to his sister that the 5th Light Horse Regiment's C Squadron was the 'society squadron' because its members were bank clerks or jackeroos, although his letter suggests this might have been an ironic assessment.[45]

The mental territoriality that existed between regiments is maybe best highlighted by the arguments in 1915 over who could and could not wear what is now widely thought to be the essential and ubiquitous light horse adornment, emu plumes. The first Queensland regiment, the 2nd Light Horse Regiment (followed by the 5th, also from Queensland) had secured a prime ministerial endorsement of their right to wear the plumes at a pre-embarkation parade in 1914. This, they felt, perpetuated the traditional Queensland mounted unit honour of wearing the plumes, which dated back to their service in the Shearers' Strike of the 1890s. When the 3rd Light Horse Brigade arrived in Egypt wearing them as a good conduct badge (which reflected the fact that Western Australians, Tasmanians and South Australian light horse had also been wearing emu plumes for many years after Federation) there was uproar from the Queenslanders. The matter eventually made it all the way to the Minister for Defence, Senator George Pearce, who decreed that all light horse could wear them provided the Commonwealth did not foot the bill. Despite this, not every unit took them up (the 4th, 6th and 7th Regiments never did – the 6th wore a distinctive wallaby fur pugaree), and the Queenslanders felt that the right was still theirs. Although Gallipoli is usually painted as the time when Australia's colony/state-centric views went by the wayside, it was not until after the battle of Romani and the other trials of the Sinai that the opinion of the Queenslanders softened enough for Chauvel to approach the minister again and obtain another decision encouraging a wider adoption of the plumes, which was duly provided and which enabled them to be taken up by most units.[46]

Beyond the regiment lay the entities of brigade, division, corps and army, all of which seem to have mattered little for most in the ranks. Alongside were the other elements of the EEF, which also seem to have been little contemplated except when they directly affected the light-horsemen. The English and Scot gunners of the horse batteries that were part of the mounted divisions were regularly praised for their work in battle, but otherwise the interactions were few. Much the same applied to the British infantry, who bore the brunt of much of the fighting once the EEF reached the frontiers of Palestine. The yeomanry was viewed more askance, partly because of its sometimes indifferent performance early in the campaign. Of the large numbers of Indian cavalry and other troops little comment was recorded.[47]

The everyday life of the light-horsemen, when not fighting, was, as mentioned above, one that involved a great deal of labour. Much of this stemmed from their horses, which required a daily routine of feeding, watering, grooming and piqueting. The stories of the bonds between man and horse are legion and have been enshrined as part of light horse lore.[48] There is little doubt that this was often the case, but there would appear to also be a degree of post-war romanticising involved. When reading letters and diaries of light-horsemen it is striking how little men made mention of their horses, and when they do it often reflected a utilitarian view rather than a sentimental one. In an age when the horse was most often a working animal and working animals were expected to earn their keep, it seems probable that many men looked upon their mounts more prosaically than some writers have suggested since. In March 1919 Edward Dengate wrote home that at 'last we are without horses, we handed them over yesterday. I don't think there is a man sorry either.'[49] Dengate's sense of liberation might have reflected the prospect of returning to Australia, but it also probably reflected the relief at release from long hours, day after day, of tending to a horse on campaign, always with an NCO or officer ensuring that the duty was carried out.

If the ordinary trooper had enough to do, certain specialists often had more. John Fowler, of the 12th Light Horse Regiment, recalled that being in a Hotchkiss section meant there were six instead of four horses for the section to care for. When a corporal was posted to the section he was glad to move on because, as a trooper doing the duties of a corporal, he had not been exempt from the normal work of the troop, despite the extra responsibilities that had come with the Hotchkiss.[50] In contrast one trooper admired the apparent ability of signallers to have a ready excuse for avoiding the piquets that might come their way.[51]

THE LIGHT-HORSEMEN'S ENVIRONMENT

The Middle East was a far from pleasant place to campaign, and the hardships experienced by troops were considerable. If the soldiers on the Western Front had to contend with mud, rain and cold, the light-horsemen had to deal variously with the extereme heat of the Sinai and the deep cold of the Palestine hills and the Moab east of the Jordan. The desert was a draining place in which to campaign, and most soldiers were grateful to leave it in early 1917 when they crossed over into Palestine. Yet their elation was short-lived, and the sand was soon regarded nostalgically compared to the dust churned up by the frequent movements of the EEF in southern Palestine. Water was a constant problem both in the desert and in Palestine, and EEF soldiers frequently had to operate with little more than a single waterbottle of water (which in the desert was often brackish). Existing at the end of a long supply line also meant that the rations were frequently monotonous in the extreme, and eating just tinned meat and biscuits for long periods was common, especially during an advance. Moreover there was little escape from the frontline, and the regular rotation, rest and relative relaxation experienced by Western Front soldiers was not – indeed could not be – replicated in the EEF. Units typically spent long periods operating opposite the enemy, and there were usually no comfortable villages where troops could be billeted. Unit rest periods often involved simply transferring the regimental environment from the front to a rest camp.

Relief from regimental life for the light-horsemen was strictly limited by their location and circumstances. Amusements within the unit were few and included sports, which ranged from betting on fights between spiders and scorpions to the more traditional football or other games.[52] Outside the regiment, sports or other occasional days were common, and race days arranged at brigade or higher levels, as the demands of campaign allowed, were popular. Further afield there might be the opportunity to take part in something like the Port Said Rest Camp aquatic carnival or attend the Ismailia horse show, both of which were held in June 1918.[53] During periods when the divisions were being spelled they might be encamped near the coast, where the men could be afforded the opportunity for a

Photo 29 Campaigning in the Sinai and Palestine meant long periods away from civilisation, and much entertainment, like race meetings such as this one held by the 4th Light Horse Brigade in 1918, had to be self-generated. Otherwise, amusements ranged from the wholesomeness of the nearest YMCA tent to all the vices that Middle Eastern cities and towns could generate. (AWM J05997)

daily swim, or drink might make its way to a unit. On one such occasion Edward Dengate wrote to his wife that the 'boys are very merry tonight [as a] result of a wagon load of beer for the Regiment[,] their songs are not what one would call decent, there seems to be more noise in the sergeant's mess than anywhere else'.[54] More wholesome was the respite offered by the Australian Comforts Fund, the canteens run by philanthropists like Mrs Alice Chisholm, the AIF Canteens and the facilities established by the Young Men's Christian Association (YMCA).[55] Of the latter, one trooper described one of their tents: 'it is well lit up with hanging lamps, and tables with plenty of writing paper handy, stools to sit on... there is a piano here too, it is like old time in Menagle...'[56]

Apart from a lucky few who got to England or home (virtually all of them officers) the only places where men could take their leave was Egypt or, usually more briefly, the towns they found themselves located near in Palestine. The *Kia Ora Coo-ee* suggested that in Egypt the lighthorsemen's rounds consisted of 'motor trips to the Pyramids, Heliopolis, Helouan and San Giovani Café on the banks of the Nile', apart from which he 'sticks chiefly to Cairo' where he revelled in hot baths, ate the best food 'with studied zeal', and attended the city's 'inferior vaudevilles'.[57] Another edition of the same newspaper includes a cartoon in which, despite its light-hearted depiction, the activities seem less innocent, and where a 24-hour leave to Cairo involves drinking, apprehension and jailing by the Assistant Provost Marshal (i.e. the military police), and eventually the imposition of disciplinary sanction back in the unit.[58]

Australian soldiers in Egypt have an often well-deserved reputation for getting out of hand, although this status was largely established by the masses of raw soldiers who were packed into Egypt in 1914–15 and again in 1916. Years after the war Major-General Sir Arthur Lynden-Bell, the EEF's Chief of the General Staff for much of 1916–17, recalled that the 'misbehaviour of the Australians in Cairo will never be forgotten' and had several anecdotes ready as supporting evidence, which included a recollection of Australians firing from the windows of a house.[59] With the departure of the infantry to France and the dispatch of the light horse and cameleers to the Sinai matters never were so bad again, but the light-horsemen on leave were still capable of vexing their superiors. Major-General Sir Henry Hodgson, the British officer who commanded the Australian Mounted Division, offered the following reflections on the character of his command to his brother: 'My Australians are in great heart. Not too particular about their behaviour in Jerusalem and Bethlehem, but that can only be expected. They are a rough old crowd, but first rate fellows to fight, and really splendid chaps to deal with. We have our troubles with discipline etc, but I get on with them very well...'[60]

An officer did not have to be British to make the same observations about behaviour on leave. The recently commissioned Bert Delpratt took a small leave party into Jerusalem in June 1918 and 'had a rotten time[,] 5 out of 14 got drunk & I had a very bad time getting them home'. Not everyone was so inclined, of course. In the same letter Delpratt told his sister of taking leave in Alexandria where he had a 'very nice time playing tennis, bathing and having a good lie in bed'.[61] Pelham Jackson, who spent a good deal of time in Cairo in early 1916, engaged the services of a French woman to teach him the language.[62]

Not surprisingly the light-horsemen's proclivities on leave included carnal matters. John Gray wrote that the soldier 'has an instinctive sense for feminine companionship' and describes how the presence of prostitutes when on leave in Jaffa was marked by a grouping of 'some khaki-clad figures outside a house'. Gray expressed revulsion at the women within and thankfulness that 'the urge is not strong within me', especially as there was little doubt in his mind that they were diseased.[63] Posted to a guard in Damascus, another trooper remembered that a drunk and injured Australian 'said he wouldn't go to any hospital and all he wanted was to go to a brothel'.[64]

Inevitably there were problems with venereal disease. Between June 1917 and May 1918, for example, the Venereal Section of No. 2 Australian Stationary Hospital in Moascar had 1256 men admitted for treatment. Infection rates in 1917 were generally low when the light horse and cameleers were engaged in operations on the Gaza–Beersheba front, but during periods when greater leave was allowed there were noticeable spikes in infection rates, as there were throughout 1918 when Australian units occupied, passed near or visited the cities and towns of Palestine.[65] The light-horsemen were by no means alone in these matters, nor was it confined to the Middle East. Even in wartime military camps in Australia, where brothels were quickly found established nearby, there were high rates of venereal disease. In the three months between the end of June 1916 and the end of October the same year, for example, 2004 men were admitted to hospital from camps in Australia for the same reason.[66] The military looked on the matter seriously and, viewing it as essentially a self-inflicted wound, decreed that while undergoing treatment, which could be extended (and to modern readers painfully primitive), soldiers were in forfeit of their pay.[67]

The interactions between the light-horsemen and other soldiers of the AIF with the inhabitants of Egypt and Palestine were generally uneasy. There is no escaping the conclusion that most Australian soldiers, reflecting the society from which they came, exhibited a deep racism that pervaded the way they viewed the local inhabitants and consequently treated them. One trooper's recollection of his arrival in Egypt was being 'greatly impressed with the niggers, they seem to be very lazy and have to be driven to work also being knocked about by the water police'. One of his first acts was, with his comrades, to buy some 'water melons from the natives and pelt the skins back at them'.[68] With many starting from such a viewpoint life in Egypt usually confirmed their first impressions. In mid-1915 Pelham Jackson was initially taken with the beauty of Cairo and the colour of life in its streets, but also noted the 'squalor, filth and general unsavoriness of the slums of Cairo'. By early the following year, however, he had, after observing the 'decay . . . indolence . . . lack of ambition, and complete lack of moral cause in nine-tenths of Egyptians', become 'completely disenchanted'.[69] The dirtiness of the cities and villages of the Middle East were a recurrent theme and taken to signify the inferior status of the inhabitants. George Berrie wrote that the centre of Ludd made the worst of 'Old Cairo' seem like a sanatorium by comparison. That the light-horsemen had to regularly deal with beggars or traders who seemed to be out to fleece them did not improve their outlook. In his memoir Berrie has one character exclaim that 'if a man robbed these thieving bastards for the rest of his life he wouldn't get square with 'em'.[70] Edward Dengate's view was typical of many, writing to his wife that the 'Arabs are about the most miserable race of people I have ever seen, dirty, sore eyed, lazy, whining creatures without any morals, they are everlasting crying for "Backsheesh" [charity or alms]...[T]hey make a fellow feel sick.'[71] These views were perhaps softened only for the thousands of Egyptians who served in the Egyptian Labour Corps, which helped keep the EEF supplied, as they, having shared some of the difficulties of the campaign, had earned a degree of condescending respect.

If the Egyptian or Palestine Arabs were looked down upon, then the Bedouin nomads of the Sinai and Palestine were even less well regarded, being generally thought of as treacherous and suspected of spying for the Turks. The fact that they killed lone soldiers or downed airmen so as to steal their possessions, stole from Australian dead or, as Ion Idriess noted in his diaries, dug up the dead to steal from them, meant that the passions against them were often strong. Retaliation against them was strictly forbidden and the higher command appeared to take the Bedouin accusations of soldier impropriety seriously, which led to further anger.[72] Edward Dengate wrote of the Bedouin that the men 'don't mention him without a curse, they are rotten mongrels'. Perhaps perversely the Arab and Bedouin could go up in the light-horsemen's estimation if they were wearing a Turkish uniform (and as subjects of the Ottoman Empire they were conscripted). Soon after joining his regiment in 1917 Dengate noted that the men 'speak of the Turks without the least sign of anger, in fact they respect him as a fighter'.[73] Reflecting on the final advance on Amman in October 1918, Bert Delpratt noted that none 'of the troops here have any time for the Germans but always treat the Turks well'.[74] Apart from whatever respect was shown to Turkish soldiers, the only inhabitants of Palestine who were generally regarded warmly by the light-horsemen were the white European Jewish settlers who had established themselves in central Palestine; they were considered clean, orderly and industrious.

In these circumstances the poor relations between the white soldiers of the EEF (and the view of British and New Zealand soldiers seemed to have differed little from the Australians) and the majority of people they were campaigning among led to bloody incidents. The events at Surafend in 1919 where New Zealand, Australian and perhaps some British troops surrounded a village, murdered many of its male inhabitants and burned it down in revenge for the death of a New Zealander has already been mentioned (see chapter 7), but there was also a noticeably hard edge to the light-horsemen's activities helping to put down the Egyptian Uprising in 1919. Brigadier Lachlan Wilson, commanding most of the light horse regiments involved in quelling the uprising, later wrote:

> As the natives apparently did not understand anything except force, what they required was some of the German frightfulness which our Teutonic friends exhibited towards the civil populations under their control. We certainly never descended to these methods, but we found it necessary to adopt stern measures to convince the natives we intended to restore order. Like other Eastern races, including the Arabs in Palestine, they could not understand kindness or courtesy. If you treated them with those qualities they thought you were afraid of them...[75]

The light-horsemen's ultimate purpose was of course to fight. Compared to the awful conditions endured and high casualties incurred on the Western Front, the costs incurred by the Australians in the Sinai and Palestine will always seem light. The figures speak for themselves, and on the Western Front more than 45 000 Australians died in battle, of wounds or of illness; another 130 000 were wounded and nearly 4000 were declared missing. In the Sinai and Palestine there were 1282 deaths, of which 574 were killed and another 288 died of wounds, with disease taking the rest; in total there were just over 4000 Australian casualties among those who served in the EEF.[76] In part the figures reflect the nature of the Australian contribution. Although there were numerous and obvious exceptions, the mounted troops for much of the campaign were involved in the sort of skirmishing and mobile warfare for which they were intended. This type of activity, although it could have costly moments, was less dangerous than the sort of deliberate attacks against well-prepared enemy defences that often fell to the infantry of the First World War. In considering the Palestine campaign the nearly 5000 casualties the British infantry suffered at Second Gaza, or the 1100 lost taking even the relatively thin trenches west of Beersheba, should be remembered; and they are not the only instances of their taking substantial casualties. If less terrible than the experience of the soldiers who fought in France and Belgium, or even Gallipoli, it is misleading to consider that the light-horsemen's war in the Middle East was, as has been mentioned above, 'often a gay war'.

Invidious comparisons of the men in the Sinai and Palestine to those fighting in France and Belgium were apparently part of the light-horsemen's experience. In *The Desert Column*, Ion Idriess recounted how one light-horseman had received a comfort package addressed to 'a lonely soldier', in which he found a letter expressing the hope that it had gone to a brave soldier in France and 'not a cold-footed squib' in Egypt. The recipient reportedly responded by sending back some photos of some of the desert graves in which his comrades were lying.[77] The story is plausible, and no doubt reflected common sentiment, but it has the air of an apocryphal tale that did the rounds. More authentic is one of Edward Dengate's letters to his wife. After taking part in the charge at Beersheba with the 12th Light Horse Regiment, he had written to his wife outlining his experience. She appears to have offered some objection to what she thought was his colouring of the event. He responded:

> [B]ut it's a fact, the bullets were that thick one could not spit through them. 'Cold-footed Light Horse', they call us, if they could only see the graves... scattered about the desert from the Canal to the Jordan they would (or might) change their views, or if they could have seen the Battlefield after the 19th of April last year [second Gaza]... they would have seen the bones of 'cold-footed Light Horsemen' slowly bleaching in the hot summer sun...[78]

Casualties were usually highest as a result of deliberate attacks, such as that at Second Gaza. Sent to deal with redoubts to the south of the town at that battle, the Imperial Mounted Division suffered nearly 550 casualties in a fruitless attack. The 4th Light Horse Brigade alone suffered more than 180 casualties.[79] Given that a dismounted mounted brigade amounted to little more than 800–900 men in the firing line, the figure of nearly 200 casualties represents a considerable loss. John Fowler recalled after that battle that his troop of the 12th Light Horse Regiment was only about a third of its strength at the beginning of the day.[80] Similarly at Amman in March 1918 the light horse regiments were required to attack well-prepared Turkish and German defences and suffered for it. The 6th Light Horse Regiment was particularly hard hit, losing nearly a hundred men, nearly a quarter of the unit's full strength and perhaps a third of the men available for the firing line.[81] George Berrie, who wrote the regiment's history, expressed the sense of loss in the unit following the battle and at the same time bitterly reflected on wartime recruiting methods: '[A] very striking spectacle were noticed during the [next two days]. Horseholders, sole survivors in many sections, leading the saddled

Photo 30 The human cost of Australia's involvement in the Sinai and Palestine will always seem light compared to that on the Western Front, but the light-horsemen did not escape the horrors of war. These men of the 11th Light Horse Regiment were killed at Semakh, in northern Palestine, in September 1918. (AWM P01474.006)

horses of their missing mates, silently echoed the "empty" saddle appeal of Sydney recruiting picnics. No women here leading saddled-up horses though, and no recruits heartened by Dutch courage, bribed by insurance policies or conscripted by white feathers, to fill the empty saddles.'[82] Perhaps the saving grace was that in Palestine, unlike on the Western Front, attacks such as these rarely lasted more than a day or two and the casualties did not accumulate.

Other types of operations came with their costs, too. It is impossible to read Ion Idriess's account of the fighting in the Sinai before and after the battle of Romani in 1916 and be anything but made aware of its deadliness. Pursuing Turkish forces who left snipers and strong rearguards with artillery support was not for the faint-hearted, and wounding or death was as real a possibility as it was elsewhere in the war. Wounded by a glancing hit in the head by a bullet at Romani, Pelham Jackson thought it was 'terribly painful at the time just like a kick from a horse'.[83] In the pursuit after the battle one of the men in Idriess's section was killed by a bullet. Unable to push him away or use him as a sandbag in case it attracted more attention from snipers, they dug a hole in the sand, pushed him into it, 'but left his face uncovered. Then we lay in partial safety across him and went on firing.'[84]

During the fighting in which the Turks pushed back the 4th Light Horse Brigade from their positions around Red Hill during the Es Salt operations in April 1918, Edward Dengate was moving back when he came across an abandoned Hotchkiss gun. Moving on and getting into a better position, he got it into action by himself and 'had a duel with a Turkish Machine Gun at about 1400 yards'. Writing home (and reflecting one of the few times light-horsemen went into action wearing steel helmets), he did not 'know if I hit him or not, he sent a darn lot of bullets at me, I kept my head down, the old tin hat didn't feel half big enough'.[85]

Even in what appeared to be relatively quiet periods of the campaign when the armies were mostly stationary, the mounted troops were constantly involved in reconnaissance work, probing and patrol skirmishes. Confirming the location of the Turkish lines each morning (in case they had occupied new positions) required riding out and, as often as not, being shot at. Doing such work on the Gaza–Beersheba line in 1917 Ion Idriess thought that to lose one's life in a skirmish was 'pretty miserable' compared to fighting a big battle when something was at stake.[86] In *Morale* George Berrie described the tension for a war-weary soldier riding out on a half-section daily clearing patrol in the Jordan Valley in 1918 for which the Turks' standard response was a few salvoes from their guns;

a simple operation that perhaps made him the 'windiest' thing on earth (to be 'windy' was to be scared).[87]

Living a far from bloodless existence in the Sinai and Palestine, the light-horsemen's world was one of considerable flux. Battle casualties and the grim reality of war were part of that and should not be forgotten or glossed over. Similarly his experiences and world had many facets that should similarly be recognised rather than being buried under the vague notions of what a light-horseman was, which often come to us through the prisms of legend and myth. Inside every uniform was an individual, and those individuals reacted to their environment in different ways. They were not, as one historian has stressed, 'khaki-clad robots', but a collection of individuals in which loyalty, friendship and even enmity were part of their social existence;[88] factors, it should be recognised, that are not uniquely Australian and which are experienced, broadly speaking, by all combatants in warfare – mateship has its international equivalents.

Moreover, leaving aside the supposedly common traits such as indifference to conventional authority or larrikinism, the light-horsemen's military character was not shaped much, if at all, by the skills the men possessed before their enlistment. To a much larger extent they were created by their experiences once they had donned that uniform. Bush skills, which were certainly not ubiquitous for all light-horsemen, were not without value, but in a modern war these skills counted for a lot less than the multitude of abilities in which the light-horsemen were trained by the army of which they were part. This was certainly no less the case in the Sinai and Palestine than it was in France or Belgium.

CHAPTER | 9

THE FINAL YEARS
The light horse at home, 1921–44

The light horse units sent overseas as part of the AIF had earned themselves tremendous experience and great laurels, but with the end of the war the focus of military efforts had, once again, to become the militia at home. When the time for the necessary home force reorganisation finally came it was these strained and beleaguered units that were to form the basis of the Australian Military Forces during the austere and difficult interwar years. These years would see the role of the light horse change to reflect the lessons of the war and a failure, due to constrained resources and an apparent unwillingness to address mounted troop modernisation, to prepare the light horse adequately for the next war.

THE 1920S

As highlighted in chapter 4 the militia light horse was in poor shape by the end of the First World War, and it was also clear that the militia as a whole was going to require significant reform if it were to make a useful contribution to the nation's post-war defence. The Military Board had considered the matter as early as January 1919 when it suggested to the government that a 300 000-man citizen force – which included 26 light horse regiments in two divisions and another 12 squadrons of divisional cavalry – was a suitable goal.[1] For a government that had just spent a great deal of the nation's coin on the war (and would continue to do so for some time yet to pay its loans) this was too much, and instead it commissioned the Victorian politician George Swinburne to chair a committee of enquiry into the matter. He proposed a force of 180 000 in which the mounted branch would again have two divisions.² Yet Swinburne's report did not find favour either, and it was another committee, this one of senior officers, formed in 1920 under the chairmanship of Lieutenant-General Sir Harry Chauvel, that would attempt to set the tone for the interwar years.

Chauvel echoed Swinburne's ideas on the size of the force, but the financial situation was still tight and it was accepted that the militia would have to be smaller than might otherwise be hoped for (180 000 was still considered the acceptable minimum). Chauvel proposed that during peacetime only 130 000 men should be enlisted at any one time. There was a certain hollowness to this figure as it did not take into account the multitude of support and service troops that would be required to keep the force in the field, nor the replacements needed to replenish losses during a war. For the light horse the recommendation was for the establishment of two divisions (alongside four infantry divisions) plus three regiments as part of the mixed brigades to be raised in the smaller states (Queensland, Western Australia and Tasmania) and an additional two regiments allocated as corps troops. During peace the strength of the light horse was to be 11 000 men, which was an ambitious target given that before the war the branch had not been able to recruit anywhere near that number. On the outbreak of war it was to expand to 22 000 men.³

Chauvel's template, adopted as the basis of planning, was brought into effect in mid-1921. Each regiment was again reorganised and its framework structure expanded to reflect wartime experiences. To the three-squadron system introduced in 1912 was added a headquarters squadron, which in turn included a command group, an administration troop, a signals troop, a transport troop and a machine-gun troop. Squadrons also had increased command establishments and, for the first time at home, this was specifically described as a squadron headquarters. Squadrons were to consist of four troops, one of which was a Hotchkiss gun troop. As in the years just after Federation, the restricted peacetime establishment meant that a near-full number of officers and senior NCOs would be kept on strength but the number of men they would command would be restricted. Still, the plans set out in 1921 had a light horse regiment at full peacetime strength numbering 400 men and 29 officers, which was a considerable improvement on the manning levels maintained for much of the pre-war period.⁴

Perhaps the greatest change for the light horse to come out of this period was a modification in its role and equipment. No doubt as a result of the lessons of Palestine in 1917–18, and the mobile warfare that had taken place periodically on the Western Front, it was decided that all the light horse would 'be trained as Cavalry in future'.[5] It was an explicit affirmation of the experience of the Australian Mounted Division in 1918 and a general recognition that cavalry, trained in modern fire tactics but also trained and equipped for the judicious use of the *arme blanche*, was a tactically flexible and still useful arm. The change brought to an end the simplified mounted rifle template that had been in use since before Federation, which Hutton had made universal at Federation, and which had seen the light horse through most of the war. The sword, as used by the light horse in Palestine, was the chosen weapon, although the somewhat strange decision was taken to continue with *Yeomanry and Mounted Rifle Training, 1912*, last given a small update in 1915, and which contained no sections on sword training, as the training manual. The change to cavalry was to be gradual and, although a definitive date is elusive, it appears that the first swords were not issued to regiments until 1926.[6] In contrast to the conversions from the sword and lance under Hutton, there appears to have been no objection to the change – or at least none have survived.

This reform in combination with the organisational changes resulted in the light horse brigades being renamed cavalry brigades, and the two new divisions were similarly titled the 1st and 2nd Cavalry Divisions (headquartered in Sydney and Melbourne respectively). To make up these divisions six brigades, each of three regiments, were to be raised. Queensland and South Australia supported one apiece, New South Wales and Victoria two each. Queensland maintained a fourth regiment above the brigade requirement as part of the mixed brigade also raised in its Military District. Tasmania and Western Australia's solitary regiments were similarly allocated to mixed formations based on their military districts. South Australia and Victoria were also to maintain one additional regiment each, allotted as corps cavalry in support of the infantry.[7]

The changes brought into effect in 1921 were, however, quickly undermined by massive cuts to defence spending the following year. The limitations put on naval construction by the Washington Naval Conference of 1921 provided the Hughes Nationalist government, already a reluctant defence spender, with a pretext for making deep cuts to a defence force already working towards what was regarded as the bare minimum, a trend that would be further reinforced in 1923 when the succeeding Bruce ministry subscribed itself to the imperial guarantees of the Singapore Strategy. The cuts of 1922 saw the militia reduced from 3256 to

2332 officers and from 86 586 to 35 228 other ranks.[8] The net effect was that the military forces were reduced to what the government described as a 'cadre formation of practically 25% of war strength'. Given that neither the military nor the government tumult had yet set the war establishments, any firm claims about proportional strengths should be taken as being of the somewhat arbitrary political variety rather than something to set too much store by.[9] Universal training was to be maintained but was scaled back to just two years in the ranks, and encompassed only the cities and large towns, thereby forcing the light horse to rely still more heavily on voluntary enlistment.

Perhaps more disturbing was a drastic reduction of the time allocated to training to just six days in camp and another four days of home training.[10] This was not only contrary to all the advice on the matter over the previous years (as were many decisions during this period) but also, for the light horse, completely disregarded the lessons of the pre-war years when the even eight-day camps had proven too short and efforts had been made to increase the length to more than 20 days. Given that one day could effectively be taken off both ends of any training program owing to the administrative requirements of marching in and out of camp,[11] the introduction of six-day camps was nearly a regression to the pre-Federation habit of four-day Easter camps.

The divisional and brigade structure set out by Chauvel's committee was maintained, but regiments would now be much smaller than planned the year before, reduced to a smaller headquarters squadron and just two 'sabre' squadrons (expanding to three in war).[12] Each squadron was similarly reduced from four to three smaller troops – Hotchkiss gun troops being maintained. The permanent forces, recently reformed from the old Administrative and Instructional Staff into the Australian Instructional Corps (AIC), made up mostly of the NCO instructors, and the new Australian Staff Corps, consisting of permanent arms corps officers, were also drastically reduced. In 1921 the Central Training Depot, which included a Cavalry Wing, had been established to provide badly needed regularised and consistent training to the permanent instructors, but it also fell victim of the 1922 cuts.[13] The demands of reorganisation meant that no camps were again held during 1922.[14]

After the ambivalence of the war and immediate post-war years, followed by a period of organisational tumult, it is no surprise to find that the condition of some regiments at this time was far from rosy.[15] The mid-1920s thus became the period in which regiments, and the new formations above them, spent much of their time trying to establish themselves and find a degree of stability. For many units getting their manning up was a key priority. Tasmania's lone regiment, for example, in a state that had long had trouble raising mounted troops, exhorted its members to be active in their community recruiting as the unit was much below strength.[16] This was all the more important as the roll-back of universal training meant that the only compelled trainees finding their way into some regiments were the occasional infantryman with a horse, no doubt sick of walking, who transferred from a nearby battalion.[17]

Attempts were made to make service more attractive, and in 1923 the leather leggings that had been on issue to the light horse just before the war and in the AIF, and which seem to have been both a practical and a cherished item of uniform for mounted troops, were authorised for general use. Similarly emu plumes, which had been allowed for the light horse of the AIF and for regiments in some states before the universal training, were also approved for general light horse adoption in 1923, provided, of course, no expense was incurred by the Commonwealth.[18] Granville Ryrie, now commanding a cavalry division, had been behind these changes so that 'the uniform should be made smarter and more distinctive [and] the result will be an appreciable increase in esprit de corps'.[19] Reflecting the change in role from mounted rifles, and formalising the honorific tradition, the rank of the most junior soldiers was altered from private to the traditional cavalry title of trooper in late 1924.[20] In 1926, in a partial reversal of the wartime decisions about unit identification, territorial titles were again introduced.[21]

At a time when there were few material resources to make use of, small trappings like these, aimed at boosting morale and spirit, were about all the military authorities could hand out to their soldiers. In the same vein much effort was directed at trying to ensure that the honour and *élan* of the AIF was carried over into the citizen forces. Battle honours earned by units of the AIF had been handed out to the regiments that now carried their unit number, and from 1926 they could be emblazoned on the newly authorised guidons.[22] Highlighting the whole rationale behind the unit renumbering that had taken place in 1918, units were told that the history of their AIF forebears 'should be studied and lectures given on its experiences, sacrifices, and victories'. The example was not just to be moral but also practical, and history was also to provide the basis of tactical training. Leaders with war experience were to 'recall incidents in the field upon which to base' their exercises and in doing so 'bring to the minds of the younger men the brave deeds of the past'.[23] In these ideas there was a strong echo of what Hutton and others had hoped of the returned officers from South Africa some 20 years earlier. This time, however, so that men with war experience could have the most influence on their units it became policy that men with war service became preferred for command appointments over those who had served only in the militia.[24] Although a sensible policy, it must have disappointed militia officers, many of whom had served under difficult circumstances at home and legitimately been unable to render war service, who might otherwise have expected promotion and command. It did, however, have its limitations.

As after Federation, the pool of officers with war experience proved to be a diminishing resource. Of the 32 officers who served in the 1st Light Horse Regiment between 1921 and 1924, for example, 20 had served in the AIF, and of these three had also served in South Africa. Yet, by the end of 1924, only 12 of them were still active members of the regiment.[25] Similarly, of the 43 officers who served in the 6th Light Horse Regiment during the same period, 30 had been in the AIF and, again, three of these had also been to the war in South Africa. By the end of 1924, however, the number still serving was down to 13.[26] These figures for 1924 were still quite respectable and in each case would have represented about half the regiment's officer establishment, but the attrition rate was of concern. By the mid-1920s Sir Harry Chauvel, now in the combined appointment of Chief of the General Staff and Inspector-General, was increasingly worried that the difficulties of militia service were discouraging and noted the smaller number of war experienced officers to be found in uniform each year.[27] Many of these men had merely transferred to the reserve list, but it was well understood that once these men had been out of touch for a few years they rapidly lost their usefulness.[28] The loss of experience might well have been greater the further down the ranks one looked. By 1925 the forces were 40 per cent under establishment for NCOs.[29]

Chauvel's warnings about the loss of ex-AIF officers had been accompanied by entreaties to improve the quality and amount of training of the citizen officers who had to take their place. The restricted peacetime establishments and the accompanying cadre system meant that interwar training was largely about training officers and NCOs so that in the event of war the expanded army could be adequately led.[30] Cavalry schools of instruction, in replacement of the old light horse schools of instruction, were a regular part of the training cycle and were supplemented by a new range of courses through the 1920s and 1930s. The pre-war staff rides that Hutton instituted appear to have gone by the wayside after 1914, but much the same thing continued under the new guise of 'tactical exercises without troops' (or TEWTs).³¹ The various United Service Institutions, which had long been semi-formal places of officer education and discussion, became increasingly important, and they hosted lectures on a wide range of military topics aimed at assisting NCOs looking for commissions or officers seeking promotion.³² How helpful they would have been to light-horsemen in rural areas is open to question.

Unit training was also meant to be a significant part of officers and NCOs learning their trade but, although things gradually improved through the 1920s, it was never established on a genuinely satisfactory basis. The limitation to six-day camps introduced in 1922 did not, fortunately, last long, and from mid-1924 units could again hold eight-day affairs together with another four days home training, which Chauvel noted brought improved results and 'justified the extra expenditure'.³³ The conversion to cavalry and the necessary sword training also brought problems, and it was soon pointed out that it was difficult to reach a suitable standard with the weapon during the small amount of home training available.³⁴ Chauvel soon had to admonish regiments over a tendency to ignore rifles, machine-guns and the balance between fire and shock action while trying to perfect their handling of the *arme blanche*.³⁵ According to Chauvel, matters did improve, but if anyone remembered the thinking about it being easier to train citizen horse soldiers as mounted rifles rather than as cavalry proper, then equip them with the *arme blanche* only in wartime, there is no record of it. Using old doctrine cannot have helped and, on Chauvel's recommendation, and after some camp trials, the updated *Cavalry Training* at last replaced the pre-war *Yeomanry and Mounted Rifle Training* in 1928.³⁶

British example was also being observed in organisational matters, although with mixed results. Despite the successes of cavalry in Palestine in 1918, it had been clear that continued organisational and doctrinal changes would be required to maintain it as a useful arm for the future. At the end of the war there had been an effort to adopt an empire-wide organisational template for the British and dominion army's units.³⁷ Budgetary circumstances in Australia were not conducive, however, and the proposed new cavalry divisional organisation, with its greatly increased firepower in the form of extra artillery and a divisional machine-gun regiment, was not adopted locally.³⁸ Later, in 1923, the Military Board approved the adoption of a new cavalry war establishment based on a new British 'Small Wars' (i.e. colonial wars) template, which lacked much of the firepower thought necessary at the end of the First World War.³⁹ This was followed by another attempt, in 1926, to follow recent British

Photo 31 An interwar light-horseman tent-pegging with the 1908 pattern cavalry sword issued to militia light horse regiments in the 1920s. Skill-at-arms competitions were prolific at this time, but their pervasiveness often detracted from more useful tactical training. (State Library of Victoria H98.105/3698)

practice and boost the firepower and tactical flexibility at regimental level by disbanding the squadron Hotchkiss gun troops and distributing one such weapon to each of the sabre troops instead. This was a curious reform as the Australian Mounted Division had done the exact opposite to boost its tactical flexibility in 1918. Nevertheless, to carry out this relatively small change required increasing the peace establishment of each regiment by 16 men and, despite Military Board support, it was knocked back by the government on grounds of cost.

It was not until the late 1920s that Chauvel managed to arrange a substantial reform aimed at improving the firepower and flexibility at regimental level. Again following the British example, regiments were reorganised, from mid-1928, to include a regimental headquarters, a headquarters wing, which included all the ancillary services, a new machine-gun squadron and just one sabre squadron (expanded to two in the event of war), which consolidated much of the available manpower to raise four reasonably manned sabre troops that proved more useful for training purposes.[40]

Any sense of progress that might have accompanied the small changes in the second half of the 1920s probably dissipated with further drastic cuts to defence spending that came in 1929. Labor's long-standing support for compulsory military training had waned through the 1920s following its schism over conscription during the war, and one of its first acts on gaining government in October 1929 was to suspend the universal training scheme and replace it with a voluntary service system. Building on reductions already made by the outgoing conservative government, and coinciding with the onset of the Great Depression, the changes of the new Scullin Labor government were accompanied by swingeing cuts to defence expenditure that meant the militia was reduced from 46 176 personnel in February 1929 to 25 785 by April the following year.[41] Universal training was suspended in November 1929 and, as the new system did not start until the next January, for two months the largely volunteer enlistment regiments of light horse were effectively the only formed units the nation had.[42]

The number of mounted regiments was also reduced, but these cuts had been decided on well before the change of government and were therefore the result of the austerities of the old conservative Bruce ministry rather than a decision by the new government.[43] The Military Board, in an usually consultative step, had circulated a memo in July 1929 to some of the military districts asking which regiments, in their view, were the most suitable for 'non-maintenance'. South Australia's 4th Military District suggested the 3rd or 18th Light Horse Regiments were suitable candidates, and in Queensland they offered up the 2nd Light Horse Regiment, just north of Brisbane.[44] They were spared, however, and the 19th Light Horse Regiment in Victoria – remote, understrength and devoid of inherited battle honours – was selected for disbandment (it was eventually linked to the 17th Light Horse Regiment). In New South Wales the 1st

(New South Wales Lancers) and 21st Light Horse Regiments, both under-strength and unsatisfactory, were amalgamated to form the amalgamated 1st/21st Light Horse Regiment.[45]

Despite the long-standing principle that the mounted arm be raised and maintained mainly in country areas, it is clear that some units had, through the 1920s, generously availed themselves of the men in urban areas who were compelled to serve by universal training. With the scheme's suspension in late 1929 there came a sudden and urgent need to reorganise and adjust in the units that had taken advantage of this resource, particularly for support troops such as signallers and machine-gunners, and had encroached on urban areas. How much of a general problem this was is not clear, but in South Australia's 6th Cavalry Brigade more than 50 per cent (368 of 711 men) of the other ranks were trainees living in or near the metropolitan area. This constituted the 'whole of the 18th LH Regiment, the Regimental signallers and two Machine Guns Troops of each of the 3rd, 9th, and 23rd LH Regiments'.[46] Reorganisation, largely back into country districts, followed, and a much smaller percentage of men were drawn from Adelaide, although the whole episode must have been very disruptive.

Such changes also brought to the surface an increasing problem that was now affecting almost all light horse units – the quality and quantity of horseflesh. The 6th Cavalry Brigade's troubles stemmed not just from the suspension of universal training but also from a growing difficulty in finding men who owned suitable horses. The 2nd Light Horse Regiment had been put forward for disbandment in mid-1929 because it was raised in districts that did not 'produce the proper stamp of either men or horses', the men being employed either on small dairy or banana farms, or being drawn from close to Brisbane and Sandgate where good horses were now scarce. Their brigade commander reported that at the last camp numerous men had, in a step once inconceivable in a light horse regiment, brought hired horses to camp.[47] If nothing else this was evidence that the requirement for light-horsemen to possess their own suitable mount was now either being liberally interpreted or had been watered down considerably. Similarly South Australia's 18th Light Horse Regiment had been offered up for disbandment because its men were largely drawn from Adelaide, and there too men were attending camp on hired horses or even dismounted.[48] This was, in part, a continuation of an old difficulty of raising mounted units in urban areas where horse-owners were relatively uncommon, but the spread of the major urban centres and a decline in the levels of horse ownership, exacerbated by indifferent horse-breeding standards, in a rapidly industrialising society were beginning to have their effect.

Despite all that has been written praising Australian horses at war, the reality was that finding sufficient good-quality horseflesh for the light horse and other arms had been a continuous problem since at least Federation. Hutton had complained about horse quality from the earliest days of his period in command, and his comments had been frequently echoed in the years leading up to the war.[49] A key cause was the requirement for men to provide their own horses for light horse service. Men generally bought horses with their civilian needs and budgets in mind, not the requirements of the government, and therefore to some extent the military had to make do with what was offered. In Queensland after the Russo-Japanese War, for example, there had been a notable drop in the quality of horses brought into camp. This proved to be the result of a significant rise in the local horse price due to Japanese horse-buyers taking the best of what was on offer to replenish their stocks.[50] What was left was of poorer quality and more expensive owing to increased demand and, although the authorities could issue reproofs about what light-horsemen bought, there was, in the end, little that could be done about it.

Over the years various schemes had been proposed to encourage the horse-breeding industry to improve the stock it produced. These efforts were often meant to contribute to the existing and successful horse trade to the Indian Army, as well as enhance the standing Australian requirement also to have suitable horses for the field artillery. In 1902 Colonel James Mackay had suggested to the government that it appoint a suitable person to be an overseer of the imperial remount trade. His justifications for the post were that it would ensure Australia's fair share of the imperial remount market, encourage good horse-breeding in Australia and underpin local military needs. Hutton, probably correctly, divined that this was one of Mackay's typical efforts to blend his own and the military's interests and, while supporting the creation of the appointment, he just as typically believed it should be filled by a suitable imperial officer with an understanding of imperial requirements.[51] The scheme evidently came to nothing, but other efforts followed over the years, including proposals for government horse-breeding stations or breeder subsidisation and export bans.[52]

Despite the various plans and proposals, little was done. In 1911–12 the government did establish a small remount system to ensure that the largely urban-based field artillery and the permanent forces had an adequate supply of suitable horses, but the light horse was left to its own devices.[53] There was almost certainly a degree of contentment that in a country like Australia there was little to be worried about when it came to horses. One journalist and veteran of the Boer War wrote in 1913 of the many excellent light horse mounts that militiamen brought to camp. They were, he noted, 'the property of their riders, and this fact, in such a horse-loving country as Australia, is alone guarantee of their quality'.[54] The sudden requirement to find plenty of good-quality horses with the outbreak of war proved this view unduly sanguine. In 1927 the Military Board, reviewing the horse-breeding situation, summed up the unpleasant wartime surprise the authorities had faced:

> In 1913 the number of horses in Australia was approximately 2,521,000, of which it was estimated that 20% were suitable for Military purposes. This was considered to be absurdly low, but on being put to the test in 1914 when the Australian Army Remount Department began purchasing operations, it very soon became apparent that not more than 6% would comply with the standard required for the army. This estimate ultimately proved much nearer the mark, as during the period of the War, the number purchased represented approximately 5%.[55]

The Quartermaster-General had told the government much the same thing during the war and warned that the performance of the light horse's mounts overseas, although a cause for pride, had to be kept in some perspective as 'these regiments were mounted on carefully selected horses'. Moreover, 'the pity [was] that so many of them were mares which will be lost for breeding purposes'.[56] Australian wartime shipments to Egypt had ceased in 1916 (although sales to India continued throughout the war) mostly due to shipping constraints, but even then complaints about the quality of Australian horses were beginning to be heard.[57] In general the problem was not the number of horses being bred but their quality. During the war the Quartermaster-General had complained of the 'haphazard manner' of local horse production in which 'unfits are allowed to reproduce themselves'.[58] Wartime efforts to correct this state of affairs appear to have become bogged down by inter-governmental inertia (horses being an agricultural matter and hence within the purview of the states) and came to nothing by 1918, when the concern evaporated.[59]

A report written by a British Army remount officer on the Australian horse-breeding industry in 1922 reiterated this and recounted how the local industry largely bred under 'perfectly natural conditions', whereby mares were turned out into large paddocks with a stallion to breed at will, annual musters being held to collect the resultant issue. Not surprisingly this lack of supervision, the genetic contributions of indifferent mares and stallions that evaded muster, and the injuries that equines received in these circumstances produced what this officer described, frankly, as mostly 'useless horses'. Droughts destroyed much stock, and an oversupply of horses in India at the end of the war compounded the situation by depressing the market and forcing many horse-breeders to turn their land over to more lucrative cattle-rearing.[60] Thus by the early 1920s the horse-breeding industry in Australia, already far from being the military powerhouse that is popularly remembered, was in rapid and serious decline. In 1927 the worried Military Board concluded that of the estimated 2.1 million horses then in Australia, only 3 per cent could be expected to meet the army's standards – a proportion considered 'dangerously low'.[61]

Chauvel and the Military Board repeatedly drew the situation to the government's attention in the late 1920s, but political indifference, in combination with a rapidly mechanising civilian economy and the closure of some horse-breeding farms owing to urban expansion, meant that by the late 1920s the standard and number of horses in light horse regiments, particularly those near larger urban areas, was becoming a serious problem.[62] During the 1930s it would prove to be the diminution of horseflesh, as much as a desire to modernise, that would drive the slow mechanisation of the light horse.

The 1930s

Mechanisation had been an important topic of discussion since the end of the First World War, although for many years transportation and the requirements of the artillery had been of the greatest concern. By the early 1930s it was also clear that a degree of cavalry mechanisation was required. In 1930 Chauvel, following recent British reforms, had canvassed the possibility of changing the cavalry organisation by replacing one brigade in each division with two armoured car regiments, which would, when combined with enhanced mechanisation in other parts of the division, increase both its mobility and its striking power. Reflecting the thinking then in vogue about combining the action of mechanised and horsed cavalry, the idea was that a cavalry division could deploy in a series of echelons with the armoured cars arriving at the scene of action first, to be followed up by mechanised (truck-transported) machine-guns, then finally the slower but more flexible horsed cavalrymen.[63]

The idea was suggested as the depression worsened and the military was being cut, so it is no surprise that it went nowhere, but in 1933 a conference was held at Army Headquarters to give the matter further consideration. It concluded that in order to adopt the British cavalry divisional organisation and give Australian cavalry greater mobility, and because of the worsening situation with horses, it was necessary to begin an experimental armoured car cavalry regiment.[64] Where such a unit could be raised was significant, but after some deliberation it was decided that a light horse country area would be most suitable as it would perpetuate the 'value of the cavalry spirit' and because in country districts there were likely to be found more drivers 'with an eye for ground and experience in handling [motor transport] over rough tracks'.[65] Thus the martial skills of the bush horseman were transposed to the mechanical age and the bush lorry-driver.

There was a strong desire to keep the experimental unit close to Melbourne from where it could be observed easily, but it was decided not to disturb an existing unit and instead resuscitate the 19th Light Horse Regiment.[66] Although the authorities hoped that the Australian prototypes then in development would soon lead to something, there were as yet no armoured cars to form this unit, so for the foreseeable future it had to improvise with hired trucks.[67] Accordingly the regiment was raised in 1933–34 and, with its title changed to the 1st Armoured Car Regiment in 1935, it was allocated to the 2nd Cavalry Division.[68]

Raising armoured car units was geared, not surprisingly, to the eventual replacement of at least some of the horsed cavalry rather than just augmentation. The Chief of the General Staff, Major-General Julius Bruche, recommended adopting the general policy of raising two cavalry armoured car regiments per cavalry division over a period of three to four years,[69] which clearly implied that the aim was to adopt at least some of the British divisional organisation that had been behind Chauvel's efforts in 1930. There were limits to all this, however, and while armoured cars would have represented a significant step forward, they were only part of the picture. By 1930 the only things not mechanised in a British cavalry division, on paper at least, were the sabre squadrons of the horsed brigades themselves. Everything else, from the headquarters to the artillery, machine-gun squadrons and support services, was truck-, car- or motorcycle-borne. By comparison Australia's cavalry was almost entirely mounted on, or drawn by, horses.[70] Should the 1st Armoured Car Regiment have been called on, it would soon have found itself devoid of the motorised artillery and logistic support it would quickly need in action. The plan was a half measure compared to Chauvel's deeper 1930 proposal and, although laudable, it proved overly optimistic. This first regiment would remain the only such unit until 1939 when the 2nd Armoured Car Regiment was raised in New South Wales.[71]

During the deliberations about armoured cars Bruche had pointed to a requirement for the army to be seen to be modernising and for it thus to 'increase the interest both of the public and the Militia personnel'.[72] The heightening of interest for potential recruits was also a significant factor when, in 1936, the 2nd Cavalry Division proposed to the Military Board that it be allowed to raise 'light car' troops in its regiments. Its commander, Brigadier Sir Murray Bourchier, commanding officer of the 4th Light Horse Regiment during its charge at Beersheba in 1917, requested in early 1936 that consideration be given to the creation of such elements 'for experimental purposes'. Bourchier contended that, apart from providing useful experience on their tactical employment and organisation, it would 'provide an added interest in militia training'. His comments also reflected the deeper problems with light horse recruitment, noting that in 'every regimental area certain of the larger country towns are unsuitable for the location of cavalry subunits owing mainly to lack of riding horses'. Light cars would thus 'tap a source of... excellent recruits' hitherto excluded from consideration.[73]

Soon the possibility of raising more light car troops was being discussed in other areas. In 1937 four regiments were allowed them and the following year another six were given the same opportunity.[74] The prospect of such an organisation in Queensland was eased by the happy coincidence of the commander of the 1st Cavalry Brigade also being on the committee of the Royal Automobile Club of Queensland.[75] As with the armoured cars, the authorities wanted to keep an eye on how things progressed, and in Queensland the new light car troop was made part of the near metropolitan 2nd/14th Light Horse Regiment.[76] In northern New South Wales the troop of the 12th Light Horse Regiment was raised where the permanent brigade major could oversee things.

At first 'light car' was interpreted literally and owners of light roadsters were the main recruiting targets but, as was soon pointed out by country-based cavalry units, vehicles of this type were not always suited to work on country roads, and light utility trucks were far more common in the bush. The commander of the 1st Cavalry Division, perhaps because he had no armoured car regiment at his disposal, thought the role of these utility-equipped light car troops might be 'extended to one of reconnaissance in lieu of or as a link with Armoured Cars'. This would have meant that, if so

Photo 32 Men of the 1st Light Horse (Machine Gun) Regiment dismount from their hired civilian trucks during training in 1937. Poorly attended to during the 1930s, mechanisation was in large part driven by declining horse quality and numbers. (Mitchell Library, State Library of NSW, Hood_16345)

required, light car troops might have been called on to conduct offensive action in order to win information,[77] but the Military Board was not so inclined and, following the British example, made it clear that they should only be 'devoted to a study of the roles of intercommunication and of such reconnaissance as can be carried out without offensive action'.[78] This realistic restriction both reflected the utility that light cars had provided in the last war and the limitations of their having no (or very little) firepower or armoured protection. As *Cavalry Training* made clear, the 'light car troop in a cavalry regiment is intended to save time and horseflesh, it has no offensive value and only slight powers of resistance'.[79]

Light car troops were intended only as a supplement to the training and operational efficiency of light horse regiments and, while they were useful to mechanisation, they did not represent a significant change to the conception or organisation of the mounted branch in the 1930s. What did represent such a change was the conversion of a number of units to machine-gun regiments. These changes commenced from 1936, and four units were initially chosen for conversion in order to provide each of the two cavalry divisions with two light horse (machine-gun) regiments apiece. Not surprisingly, the units chosen were those in or near urban centres that were now finding it almost impossible to find enough horsemen to fill their ranks.[80] The regimental history of the now Royal New South Wales Lancers, continued at this time with the title of the 1st/21st Light Horse Regiment, records that it was probably inevitable that it would be included among those first converted, as horse ownership in the unit's area was an acute problem. Despite the reality, the conversions were undoubtedly met with regret in the units.[81] One NCO, in a common step for the time, took up his pen:

> So good-bye my four footed cobber,
> Good-bye to your welcoming neigh,
> Good-bye to the scampering gallop
> And, what will the Number Threes say?
> But it's no use regretting and pining,
> When the folks up above have decreed
> That the Royal New South Wales Lancers,
> Have got to be blanky M.G.-ed.[82]

Such grassroots sentiment not withstanding, there appears to have been no organisational objection to the change. Units retained their light horse traditions, uniforms and titles, but the regiments themselves were reorganised to accommodate a regimental headquarters and three machine-gun squadrons, each equipped with suitable privately owned trucks (which the government hired) and 12 Vickers machine-guns.[83] Units were allowed to retain four sets of saddlery and swords per troop for the purpose of participating in mounted sports but, as one history notes, they were soon little used.[84] The changes, as usual, were more technical than real at first, and it was to be early 1939 before the Royal New South Wales Lancers, at least, went into a brigade camp mounted on trucks carrying their new weapons.[85] The lack of horseflesh proved a key imperative, and there is no doubt that the cavalry was badly in need of the increased firepower that had been advocated as far back as 1919, and it was probably this combination of factors rather than a systematic effort to mechanise the cavalry that drove the conversions. By 1939 a total of six light horse regiments had been converted to machine-gun regiments, and this, alongside the creation of the armoured car regiments, the establishment of light car troops and the mechanisation of light horse first-line transport in 1938, was largely the extent of efforts during the 1930s to modernise the light horse.[86]

For those units for which resources did not allow mechanisation the situation was much the same as it had been at the turn of the last decade. The cuts of 1929 had been followed by continued economies through the early 1930s as the depression worsened. Camps again fell foul of the need to save money, and some units had to make do with the occasional short troop or squadron camps as their only opportunity for collective training.[87] Equipment shortages could not be overcome, and the demands of staying afloat during the depression meant that many officers and men did not have the time to participate fully in part-time soldiering. A concurrent shortage of permanent officers did little to help. When camps were held they were often again reduced to a six-day event, which was still an insufficient period and brought the usual complaints.[88] In an effort to counter this, many units (using a new term for camps) began to hold non-compulsory, unpaid 'bivouacs' of three or four days at the end of their camps. In an extension of the principle it was common to see regiments holding pre-camp training weekends for the officers and NCOs so that their military memories were refreshed before they saw their men.[89]

As the British Army had discovered, the adoption of the regimental machine-gun squadrons in the late 1920s had proven a poor decision as the reduction in the number of sabre squadrons had reduced tactical flexibility.[90] In a telling indication of the uncertainties of mechanisation during these years British cavalry had also found its truck-mounted machine-gun squadrons unable to keep within supporting distance of the sabre squadrons when operating cross-country.[91] Britain abandoned the idea in the early 1930s and returned the regimental machine-guns to pack horses – and in 1932 Australia followed suit. Units returned to the old structure of a headquarters squadron, including the machine-gun and signals troops, alongside two sabre squadrons (expanding to three in the event of war).

The regimental establishments remained restricted at just 225 men all ranks, in 1932.[92] As had always been the case, constrained establishments continued to make it difficult for units to train effectively, and the 3rd Light Horse Regiment, for example, grumbled in 1933 that in its machine-gun troop, in particular, if one or two of the men were absent 'the organisation is very much upset'.[93] Perhaps owing to the low targets set it, light horse strengths in the early to mid-1930s were fairly close to the establishments. In 1932 there were 3899 men on the roll books against an

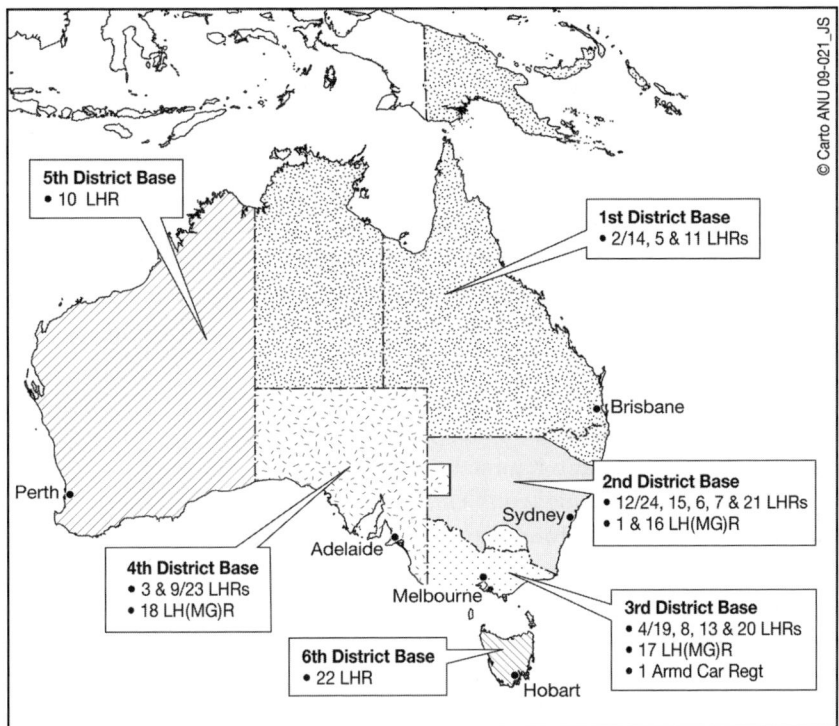

Map 6 Distribution of light horse regiments, late 1930s

establishment of 4174, and similarly the strength of the cavalry arm was only 237 men short of the desired establishment in 1934.[94] Conditions of service remained uninspiring, however, and men still received only the four shillings per day introduced in 1912 and the same horse allowance (now called horse hire) introduced in 1913. In an effort to maintain horse standards any light-horseman who brought to camp a mount valued at less than six pounds now received no horse allowance.[95]

From 1936, with the international situation deteriorating and war being spoken of again, things began to improve for the light horse, in some respects at least. Apart from the limited efforts aimed at mechanisation, 1936 finally saw improvements in service conditions and a trooper's pay was doubled to eight shillings per day, the same rate that had been introduced in 1903. Horse allowance was also nudged upwards to five shillings a day. Perhaps more significantly the men now received their pay every six months rather than annually, as had been done formerly. In late 1936 the restrictions on establishments were at last wound back, and regiments were finally expanded to include three sabre squadrons.[96] For the first time in nearly 20 years the authorised peacetime establishment of 428 men meant that regiments were organised with enough strength to do effective training.[97] Units suddenly had to train enough officers and NCOs to cater for the expansion, and much time was otherwise spent training large numbers of new recruits, although one regimental history recalls that the expansion and the worsening international circumstances drew quite a few ex-AIF men back into uniform. As war approached training tempos increased and, by the late 1930s, light-horsemen were supposed to attend eight days home training per year and spend another 12 days in camp.[98]

The slow return of funds and extra training time meant that tactical training could again take up much of the time in camp. By 1939 it was possible for the machine-gun regiments to take to the training field with their horsed brethren. Teething troubles were to be expected, and the 1st Light Horse (MG) Regiment found when it went into camp in 1939 that the differences between the speeds of trucks and horses caused 'great difficulty ... in keeping touch'.[99] Militarily there was nothing new in this. Cavalry had been outpacing their fire support, in the form of horse artillery, for centuries, but now the roles were reversed and adjustments had to be made. Cross-country, the truck-mounted machine-gunners would, as the British Army had found in the late 1920s, have again found themselves left behind.

THE SECOND WORLD WAR

The revived emphasis on tactical training was in many ways too late for the light horse. The modernisation efforts were necessary and welcome, but it was clear that by now the military authorities were simply trying to make the best of what they had at their disposal. Whereas once the role, place and organisational requirements of the light horse had been a frequent and necessary part of military deliberations, the records of the mid- to late 1930s indicate that its importance had waned considerably. In a period when the place and utility of horse-mounted cavalry was increasingly being questioned, or even dismissed completely, this might have been the result of the rest of the military not understanding the mounted arm as much as anything else. In 1937 one divisional commander complained of how the other arms of the service were in 'total darkness' with regard to understanding the cavalry's role and work.[100]

That the light horse was in many ways now considered almost irrelevant was perhaps best illustrated by the 1938 production of the first annual report written since Sir Harry Chauvel's of 1930. Lieutenant-General E.K. Squires, a British officer appointed to the revived job of Inspector-General, wrote that year of the enthusiasm of the militiamen in the Australian Military Forces but, as General Sir Ian Hamilton had done nearly a quarter of a century earlier, worried about the generally low levels of training. Yet, contrary to Hamilton's report, there were no polite and encouraging words for the mounted branch – there were no words at all – and the report contained no mention of light horse or cavalry. Squires suggested to the government the raising of a number of permanent combat units as a method of boosting defence readiness but, although the proposed force included infantrymen, gunners, engineers and support troops, it did not propose any place for cavalry, horsed or mechanised.[101]

By now the light horse had to be managed and given some encouragement, because it was effectively the only mobile element the forces possessed, but clearly the military authorities foresaw limited utility for the horsed arm. When war broke out in September 1939 it proved necessary to assess quickly what real value the arm offered. In February 1940 the Military Board circulated a discussion paper in which grave concerns were expressed about the suitability of the tactics used as the training basis of the mounted branch, particularly those for use against enemy armour.[102] The paper outlined a number of deficiencies, including a lack of both small arms (mostly machine-gun) and anti-tank firepower, the use of a tactical doctrine 'presupposing... a repetition of the conditions prevailing in Palestine in 1918', inadequate mobility compared to motorised or mechanised troops, and a shortage of engineer and artillery support. In a statement that was probably as close as the military authorities were going to come to admitting they had virtually ignored the light horse for some years, the paper noted that in light of recent military developments 'the evolution of our doctrine for the employment of light horse may have lagged behind'.[103]

The Military Board took a dim view of a training film then in use, which, it believed, exemplified a number of the problems, and argued that the most likely role of the light horse was the defence of Australia, rather being part of any expeditionary force. Hence it proposed that its employment and training should reflect local and modern conditions. The contemplated roles were to block routes from the coast, to watch possible landing places, to cooperate with fortress forces and, if the enemy should

Photo 33 Sights like this Queensland light horse unit patrolling in 1941–42 quickly disappeared with the outbreak of the Pacific War as the process of mechanisation that had started in 1940 gathered pace through 1942 and into 1943. (State Library of Victoria, H98.105/5162)

gain a foothold, to execute raids on the enemy's lines of communications ashore. Because of the threat from armoured vehicles and the new roles it was proposing, the Military Board suggested that the light horse should now be trained to operate in smaller groups (squadron or smaller) rather than in the traditional cavalry masses, that it operate in 'enclosed country' inaccessible to armour, that troopers improve their skills with small arms and demolitions and that, finally, the sword be dispensed with as a weapon.[104] Perhaps because the military problem was similar, these roles bore a remarkable resemblance to those that had been advocated as suitable for the mounted soldiers of Australia's colonies in the nineteenth century.

The responses the Military Board received reflected just about every possible viewpoint it was possible to have on the place of horse-mounted troops in modern warfare. The then General Officer Commanding of Eastern Command, and later twice appointed Chief of the General Staff, Lieutenant-General Vernon Sturdee, thought that much of the problem stemmed from the continued use of the term 'cavalry' and proposed that abolition of it 'would eradicate the cavalry complex and would enable us to concentrate on the fact that we are or should be dealing with Mounted Infantry'.[105] Without elaborating on what the 'cavalry complex' actually was, he then went on to recommend that all the mounted formations, with substantial augmentation of firepower and mechanisation, drop 'cavalry' from their titles and again become 'Light Horse', focused on using their horses for mobility. Supping from the same table the Commandant of the Royal Military College, Duntroon, advocated much the same in regard to terminology and added to it a detailed proposal for the creation of new mounted infantry divisions similar in outline to what Sturdee had proposed.[106]

Their interest in mounted infantry was a curious throwback to the pre-war, even pre-Federation, years but seems somewhat misguided. The ideas reflected not so much the creation of infantry battalions given mobility but a change from the cavalry model adopted in the 1920s to an updated form of the mounted rifleman ideal that had seen the light horse through much of its history; nor did they reveal a deep appreciation of the performance and role of cavalry during the First World War. Conversely, Colonel Horace Robertson, who as acting commanding officer had ordered the mounted attacks of the 10th Light Horse Regiment at Magdhaba in 1916, and who was now Commandant of the 7th Military District, railed against any effort to maintain a horse-mounted arm and advocated its abolition in favour of armoured formations, although how such a change was to be accommodated within the existing resources was not explained.[107]

Most of the remaining responses were broadly in agreement with the Military Board. It was generally acknowledged that the light horse, in the age of reliable and capable motor or armoured vehicles, no longer had the relative mobility advantages it once enjoyed. Clearly the arm was also lacking in sufficient firepower to take the field against a well-equipped and modern foe in open country. Accordingly almost all the respondents believed that, although horse-mounted troops still had a useful role to play, it would largely be restricted to the close terrain along Australia's eastern seaboard where, it was thought, both friendly and enemy vehicles would be limited in their movements. What was once considered good cavalry country now belonged to the tanks. The general view was that training had to be geared to halting and hindering enemy landings, defending routes inland, general patrolling tasks and possible raids on the enemy's land-based lines of communication. Greater machine-gun and anti-tank firepower was advocated, as was greater mobility in the form of motorised or mechanised troops to be made part of each cavalry division. It was generally held that trying to combine vehicle and horse-mounted troops below divisional level would not work. Most tactical employment would, it was thought, be at the squadron level, although there was no agreement about this.

Opinions on the continued use of the sword were, surprisingly, almost evenly split. Of the thirteen responses that voiced some opinion of its value, seven were opposed to continuing with the weapon, only one more than those who supported it. Those who favoured continuing with it were under no illusions, however, that another Beersheba awaited the light horse. The general view among those who supported the *arme blanche* was that since it was little extra weight, gave horsemen a useful mounted weapon that did much for morale, and might prove useful in brief patrol encounters, it was worth maintaining.[108] It would seem that in the end the use of the sword remained a discretionary matter and photographic evidence of the period shows units both equipped with it and without it.

While this high-level debate about the role and place of the light horse was taking place there was other activity elsewhere. Upon the outbreak of war in August 1939 the 17 horse-mounted regiments, along with the rest of the militia, were authorised to be brought up to war establishment. This required significant expansion, and in 1940–41 about 10 000 light-horsemen were serving in the militia.[109] Despite this, mobilisation remained limited to short periods on duty conducting local patrolling tasks or collective training. The Scullin government's suspension of compulsory military training was cancelled on 1 January 1940, but the requirements of horse ownership were extant and the light horse largely continued to recruit its men on a voluntary basis.[110] In another gauge of the diminishing value of the mounted arm no steps were taken to organise a methodical nationwide remount system, and units were left to a program of horse self-help. One New South Wales brigade commander, touring his formation in October 1940, told his troop leaders to scour their local area so as to establish a register of suitable mounts for when the moment of crisis came.[111]

Otherwise equipment shortages were a problem, as was the loss of men to the 2nd AIF after it was allowed to recruit from the militia.[112] In those areas where maintaining citizen mounted units had long been a challenging proposition the circumstances meant that some units were soon unable to do what was required of them. In Tasmania the effects of the confluence of unsuitable horses, occupational changes and enlistments of militiamen in the AIF soon made itself felt, and the commander of the military district requested in late 1940 that the 22nd Light Horse Regiment be reprieved through mechanisation as soon as possible.[113]

Light cars proved, not surprisingly, to be little more than a peacetime fancy and, despite some complaints, by the end of 1940 their lack of armour and armament had seen them struck from light horse war establishments.[114]

No light horse units were raised as part of the 2nd AIF for service overseas. In an act that is periodically used by historians to highlight the poor state of the Australian forces on the outbreak of war the government enquired of London in early 1940 whether 'horsed cavalry [should] be in any additional part of the 2nd AIF that may be raised and despatched'.[115] Despite the harsh light usually cast on such statements, this query was not completely detached from the military reality. The final mechanisation of British regular cavalry was only then taking place and, for those regiments not part of the British Expeditionary Force sent to France in 1939, the conversion was, for some time to come, more technical than real. One regiment of the Household Cavalry was not motorised until 1940. Much of the surviving yeomanry was still horse-mounted and, as the 1st Cavalry Division, was mobilised on horseback in 1939. Sent to Palestine, it served on policing and military operations in Palestine and western Iraq, including fighting the Vichy French in Syria, until it was finally mechanised in late 1941 as the 10th Armoured Division. It was not until late 1940 that the last Indian Army regiments were converted.[116]

These facts do serve, admittedly, to highlight Britain's poor preparedness for war as much as anything but, given that in 1939–40 almost all major armies still maintained some horsed cavalry, the idea that the question should be asked is not as ridiculous as has sometimes been made out. It was still early in the war and, as Lieutenant-General Vernon Sturdee rightly pointed out in May 1940, 'At the present time there are mounted troops in Palestine and it is too early to state definitely that Australia may not be asked to supply Light Horse for this War.'[117] Britain was, nevertheless, meeting her mounted troop requirements from her own resources and Australia's query remained just that.

Expediency meant that a few small Australian horsed units did, however, briefly come into war service in both the Syrian and New Guinea campaigns. In Syria the mechanised 6th Division Cavalry Regiment (AIF) briefly mounted a group of 40 men, made up largely of former lighthorsemen, to carry out local protection and patrolling duties in terrain unsuited to the employment of armoured vehicles. In New Guinea during 1942 selected horses from ex-racing stock of the Koitaki Estate were used to create the 1st Independent Light Horse Troop. Used for patrolling and searching for missing aircraft, they also performed supply transportation duties in the early days of the Kokoda campaign. At home improvisation and the threat posed by the advancing Japanese resulted in the creation, in 1942, of the North Australia Observer Unit, and it used horses, among other things, to patrol and observe potential invasion places in the Northern Territory and the north of Western Australia well into 1943 when the tide of war removed much of the threat and it was disbanded. Similarly the 1st Independent Light Horse Squadron, raised from the 2nd Australian Cavalry Regiment (AIF), itself created out of the militia 2nd/14th Light Horse Regiment, operated as part of York Force, in Cape York, from mid-1943 until its disbandment at the end of March 1944.[118]

At home mechanisation gradually affected more and more regiments. As resources allowed units found themselves recast as motor regiments, reconnaissance battalions, machine-gun regiments or armoured regiments. As the conversions took place regimental numbers were typically retained, but the designation of light horse regiment was removed. Units were retitled, given new roles or completely disbanded in a series of bewildering bureaucratic decisions that reflected the confusion of trying to maintain two military forces, the 2nd AIF and the militia, alongside each other while also allowing militia units to transfer to the AIF if enough men in the unit were willing to volunteer. By 1942 the cavalry divisions had become motor divisions, and by the middle of that year the government, having been advised that the horsed units were 'no longer effective under present conditions', was considering ways to complete

Photo 34 One of the last: a member of Western Australia's 10th Light Horse Regiment (AIF) strikes a dramatic pose for the camera in 1943. Dismounted and disbanded the next year, his regiment was the last horse-mounted cavalry unit in the Australian Army. (State Library of Victoria H98.201/2819)

the final mechanisation of all remaining cavalry units.[119] As the number of armoured fighting vehicles available from Britain and the United States was gradually increasing, it was now clear that full mechanisation was the best course open.[120] The Treasury, although admitting itself unqualified to comment on operational requirements, had its eyes on the coffers and wondered whether the generals were being sufficiently prudent. Pointing to the continued use of Cossack cavalry by the Red Army, it questioned whether 'it might be pertinent for corroborative evidence to be sought from other authorities as to the desirability of converting Australian Light Horse units'.[121] This had little effect, and through 1942 and into 1943 light horse regiments continued to lose their horses; by the end of 1943 only one traditional light horse regiment remained. Some converted units found their way to war as part of the 2nd AIF, but most found it to be only a temporary reprieve as the invasion threat receded and the fighting in the South-West Pacific required relatively little in the way of armoured or otherwise motorised troops. Most of these converted regiments were themselves disbanded through 1943 and into 1944, the men finding their way into more useful units. The last mounted regiment, Western Australia's 10th Light Horse Regiment, now part of the 2nd AIF, went into its last mounted camp in April 1944 and was disbanded soon afterwards.[122]

The rapid changes and conversions that were made to the light horse and its cavalry organisation during the Second World War were the result of the government and military authorities having rapidly to catch up with recent military developments. The light horse, like all the nation's forces, had to contend through the interwar years with numerous and prolonged austerities that made even the most basic training regimes difficult and which effectively precluded many efforts at modernisation. The attempts to introduce increased mechanisation to the light horse through the 1930s were laudable but fundamentally flawed because of the limited basis on which it could be done. Such restrictions notwithstanding, it is difficult to escape the conclusion that the military authorities had, by the late 1930s, abrogated their responsibilities in regard to the development of the mounted arm. Nor was there a compensating push for change from the light horse units or formations themselves. The sudden clamour in 1940 to try to figure out how best to use, organise and equip the light horse was the inevitable result of little *thought* being given to the mounted branch in the preceding years. What had once been considered the most valuable and useful arm of the entire military establishment had become, in its last years, little more than a military afterthought. The light horse had been converted from mounted riflemen to cavalry in the 1920s as a direct result of the lessons of British Empire mounted troops during 1914–18, which had clearly established that modern cavalry, thoroughly trained in modern fire tactics as well as the astute use of the *arme blanche*, was more tactically flexible than the simpler mounted rifleman model. Through much of the 1920s, while the tank and other armoured vehicles were still far from perfected, horse-mounted soldiers still had a useful military role to play. At some indefinable point during the interwar years that usefulness began rapidly to disappear. During the 1930s the pace of change began to increase, but little or no effort was made to keep the light horse up to date. Despite the resource constraints there should have been a concerted effort to establish how best to make use of the mounted troops it did have at its disposal. When in late 1939 and early 1940 the Military Board was forced suddenly to think about the two cavalry divisions it maintained, the inevitable result was the tumultuous discussion brought about by the Military Board's discussion paper. The various ideas advanced were all sensible and useful, but it was a discussion that should have already happened, or at least been well underway, even if the resources were scarce.

Conclusion

The light horse's last years were unfortunate ones. The now perfected internal combustion engine, along with armoured protection and heavy armament, had finally been combined to produce machines that could do almost everything that cavalry had been doing for centuries. Military horsemen continued to exist, but it now became a niche role, generally utilised as a supplement to motorised or mechanised forces, or in those places where terrain made the use of vehicles impossible, or at least impracticable. The light horse, like so many other cavalry forces, was completely overtaken by these events and disappeared. That the interwar period had seen it starved of resources and few efforts made to adjust its doctrine or organisation did little to help.

The eclipse of cavalry had been long coming and, as this book has shown, had been predicted as long ago as the middle of the nineteenth century. That challenge brought on various responses from a whole range of would-be reformers. Most reformers believed that cavalry had to embrace firepower and modify its operational action in order to survive. How firepower should be embraced, and whether that embrace should also see the rejection of the *arme blanche*, proved to be the crux of the debate. In that debate there were more than a few protagonists, but one of them, George Denison, is particularly noteworthy for anyone with an interest in Australian mounted troops because he won a number of adherents, most notably Edward Hutton, who went on to have a profound influence on Australia's mounted arm.

During the nineteenth century some of Australia's mounted troops had established themselves as cavalry, but trying to make citizen soldiers into effective cavalry was difficult. Cavalry required much training and expertise to be successful, and part-time soldiers could rarely afford the time to become truly proficient. Generally understood was that citizen mounted soldiers were more easily created if raised as mounted riflemen; that is, they used firepower and dismounted action, but were generally raised with a view to their fulfilling all the roles of cavalry except the charge with the *arme blanche*. There were colonial variations on this idea, and Queensland's military authorities went out of their way more than once to quash any cavalry pretensions their mounted troops might have been developing, reminding them that they were no more than mobile infantrymen. The other colonies, particularly New South Wales after Edward Hutton commanded the local forces in the mid-1890s, were more orthodox, and in those colonies where there were enough citizens willing to act as mounted soldiers it was mounted riflemen who generally found favour. Helping this military model was a growing mythology, by no means restricted to Australia, that hardy men from the country who could already ride and shoot were excellent natural material for spirited, if unconventional, military use.

Such ideas were tried in South Africa and found to be somewhat short of the truth. Undertrained and poorly led colonial contingents had provided the raw numbers that the British Army required during the Boer War but had otherwise proved a mixed blessing. They sometimes performed well but, being generally poor horsemasters and unsteady in battle until they gained enough on-the-job experience, and otherwise troublesome, the ideal of the citizen-cum-*ad hoc* soldier proved to have its limitations. The evolution of almost all the mounted troops in South Africa into mounted riflemen, however, provided enough evidence for those already so inclined to reassert their view that traditional cavalry was an anachronism. In Australia the new General Officer Commanding of the Commonwealth Military Forces, the apparently ubiquitous Edward Hutton, ensured that this argument largely prevailed.

Hutton's tenure in Australia was fraught with numerous difficulties, but among his successes was his reformation of the various colonial mounted units into the new Australian Light Horse. The changes were not without their challenges. Cavalrymen were not happy at the loss of their *arme blanche* weapons, units objected to the changes being forced on them and many men disliked the new conditions of service. Aside from the organisational changes Hutton wrought, he also established a model that would see the light horse through to late in the First World War. Drawing on his well-established ideas on mounted soldiering, he raised the new light horse firmly as mounted riflemen, not the mounted infantry as they are so often, but incorrectly, described. As such the light horse was established along traditional cavalry organisational guidelines as a form of abbreviated cavalry, designed to carry out all the traditional cavalry duties except the *arme blanche* charge, and Hutton did in fact refer to the light horse as cavalry on occasion. Hutton also created mounted infantry in Australia, but these units were to be drawn from the infantry regiments of his Field Force, and he made it quite clear that for them the horse was merely a form of locomotion, not the basis of all their tactical action. When at the place of battle they were to dismount and engage the enemy as traditional infantry. The infantry was never pleased with the role, and it was quickly abandoned when Hutton returned to Britain. Only in the ranks of the Imperial Camel Corps of the First World War would Australia again supply mounted infantrymen.

Hutton did not eschew the mounted charge completely, and it is now forgotten that he foresaw that on war breaking out at least part of the light horse should be equipped with the lance for mounted work. This idea, like many others, does not seem to have survived past his tenure. His placement of the light horse and the mounted infantry at the centre of his all-arms Field Force brigades was too out of step with imperial thinking to last long, and in the years between his departure and the First World War the light horse role was further redefined, although the essential mounted rifleman model remained largely unchallenged. Despite some effort, unique to the mounted branch, to try to maintain an Australian direction for the light horse, this was perhaps too ambitious for a young and inexperienced army, and these efforts were not overly successful. The importation of new training and organisational templates from Britain just a few years before the war was undoubtedly a positive step, and they better integrated the light horse into the broader national and imperial military structures.

During this period also the light horse suffered from a number of organisational weaknesses that made its existence difficult at times. Some of these were specifically the result of what Hutton or his successors had introduced to defence planning, and aspects of the introduction of universal training in 1912 proved to be a serious challenge for the mounted branch. Other problems were simply the continuing manifestations of long-existing problems that had beset Australia's mounted troops from the beginning. The introduction of new and thorough federal schemes of defence were not enough to escape the limits that part-time citizen soldiers self-imposed on their military commitments. These limitations resulted in many organisational problems, and it is perhaps remarkable that the light horse and its antecedent citizen soldier formations were as successful and resilient as they were in the face of them. The social characteristics that mounted units thus took on as a result of the men who filled its officer and soldier ranks undoubtedly gave Australia's mounted units their own flavour, although the differences between units could be marked.

The social experiences of the light-horsemen at war deserve consideration too. The stereotyped image of the light-horsemen at war is one that often prevails. Despite the dominance of the image of the bushman as soldier, the reality is that many light-horsemen were from the city and more than a few were not born riders. Once in uniform their ability as soldiers was shaped far more by their training than by their experiences at home before the war. Within their units their experiences and relationships were many and as varied as the circumstances in which they found themselves.

Evident in both the militia and wartime light horse was that Australia's mounted units were also heavily influenced by the thoughts and actions of many men who had ideas and experiences gained in other parts of the British Empire. Indeed in a broader sense the light horse was but a local example of a type of mounted soldier who could be found around the empire. In Britain and every major colony or dominion there were similar part-time units. Australia's peacetime militiamen probably had a great deal in common with their counterparts in, for example, Britain's yeomanry. With ranks made up primarily of farmers and other local men of some means there are obvious comparisons to be made. After the Boer War in particular the similarities became more than simply social. Both the yeomanry and light horse were organised along similar lines and trained to much the same template as mounted riflemen. That the two organisations fought alongside each other in the Middle East brings to mind further comparisons and, although this book has made some efforts to this end, a full investigation of the similarities and differences is beyond its scope and awaits another historian.

As a local example of an empire-wide conception of dominion mounted troops it is no surprise, then, that the light horse should face its greatest military test as part of the empire's forces during the First World War. After a period of training in Egypt, then a dismounted diversion to Gallipoli, the light horse was given the task of taking part in a campaign in which cavalry was to play a prominent role. In a theatre where the terrain allowed open manoeuvring, and where the enemy never developed the defensive tactical competence of his German allies, the potential of mounted troops could be realised. During the early Sinai operations the light horse, New Zealand Mounted Rifles and, to a lesser extent, the available yeomanry proved to be the most important formations at the disposal of the British forces employed there. Largely responsible for the defeat of the Turks at Romani, then their expulsion from the Sinai, the light horse brought competence and mobility to operations that proved invaluable. As the campaign progressed the arrival of other mounted troops and more infantry meant that the light horse might no longer have been the dominant element of the Egyptian Expeditionary Force, but its experience and value ensured that it remained important. The Desert Mounted Corps, essentially built around the light horse as time progressed, proved to be one of Allenby's greatest assets as the campaign continued.

As it progressed the light horse learned a series of tactical lessons that would eventually result in a fundamental change to its method of tactical action. Dismounted action had been at the centre of light horse thinking since Hutton's days as General Officer Commanding, and it continued to be so for most of the war in Palestine. What was gradually discovered was that mounted manoeuvring under fire was not as foolhardy as had hitherto been believed. From that discovery it was but a small step to the realisation that, despite what was occurring on the Western Front, perhaps mounted attack might also prove to be a useful tactic in Palestine. Throughout 1916 and 1917 these ideas became increasingly common, and in a number of light horse actions during this period such manoeuvring was tried. That such things were possible had long been the belief of many British cavalry officers who were an ever-increasing element in the Middle East. When one of them, Sir Henry Hodgson, assumed the command of the Imperial Mounted Division (later the Australian Mounted Division) he began to advocate that his light-horsemen should be issued with swords. He was unsuccessful at first but, following the success of his 4th Light Horse Brigade in charging Beersheba, then further mounted charges in the following weeks by yeomanry and other light-horsemen, he seemed to have an improving case. Through 1918 there were continuing examples of successful mounted actions by mounted troops in Palestine, and eventually Chauvel acceded to Hodgson's agitation to get swords. Thus equipped, the Australian Mounted Division took part in the final cavalry operations of the campaign and used its swords to great effect. This confirmed that cavalry trained to use both firearms and charge tactics with the *arme blanche* in a tactically sensible fashion were a more flexible form of mounted soldier than the simpler mounted rifle model that the light horse had been using since Federation.

Although the Australian and New Zealand Mounted Division stuck with the mounted rifles models until the armistice, the lesson had been learned, and after the war Australia's militia light horse regiments were recast as cavalry. This change reflected the lessons of the war in Palestine and, while horsemen still had a place on the battlefield, it was an entirely suitable decision. As the interwar period continued, it became increasingly clear that cavalry modernisation was required. But with extremely limited resources any such efforts were severely handicapped. Resource constraints in combination with many of the long-existing limitations of citizen forces made the militia light horse a shadow of even its troubled pre-war former self. Under strength, structured in a way that was increasingly irrelevant, and virtually ignored in the 1930s by the military authorities who should have been doing more, the light horse was becoming a nearly ignored military legacy of former years. When another war came it was found to be largely outdated, and the result was a long-overdue scramble to make some use of the only large-scale mobile force the government had at its disposal. Yet it was too late and, after a period of making do, they were turned over in favour of mechanised and motorised formations. Although mounted soldiers had been a significant part of the pre-Federation military landscape, the light horse had not even existed fifty years before it was removed from the military establishment. In that time, however, it made a remarkable and lasting impression on Australia's military history.

Epilogue

Although the last horse-mounted units were disbanded in 1944, Australia continues to maintain units that carry the title of light horse regiments. Like the cavalry units of so many armies around the world, they are now organised as units of the nation's armoured forces. With the re-establishment of a peacetime army in 1948 nine units of the Australian Armoured Corps (later granted a Royal prefix; the RAAC) were created in the part-time (militia) Citizen Military Forces that drew on a pre-war light horse or motor regiment heritage. By blending new roles with old numbers and titles, new units such as the 1st Armoured Regiment (New South Wales Lancers) and the 3rd/19th Armoured Car Regiment (South Australian Mounted Rifles) were raised. Reforms, renamings and reorganisations, and inevitably periodic army reductions, have resulted in numerous changes over the years. In the late 1950s, for example, the 2nd/14th Queensland Mounted Infantry was organised as an anti-tank regiment, and during the same period the 8th/13th Victorian Mounted Rifles was a medium tank regiment. By the 1960s most units that had survived were organised as cavalry or armoured personnel carrier regiments. In the twenty-first century most have again been reorganised and lost their armoured vehicles in favour of specially equipped four-wheel-drive Land Rovers to fulfil a new 'light cavalry' role.

Of the armoured units raised as part of the Australian Regular Army after the Second World War none were created that overtly drew on pre-war light horse traditions or titles, although periodic efforts have been made to link these regiments more clearly to the old light horse; the general adoption of light horse colour patches and emu plumes by the RAAC in the 1990s being some of the more recent examples.

Several unit titles have disappeared. The modern army's order of battle no longer has units using the titles of the Victorian Mounted Rifles, the New South Wales Mounted Rifles or the Australian Horse. Other changes have been more subtle, and in 2005 the 2nd/14th Light Horse Regiment,

an integrated regular and reservist regiment since the mid-1980s, was converted, abruptly and without ceremony, to an all-regular unit. Without any attempt at due recognition it brought to an end a more than century-old record of militia cavalry service in Queensland. The regiment itself continues and, alone among these descendant units, it has seen active service in recent years in East Timor (Timor Leste), Iraq and Afghanistan. The light horse regimental identities still in existence in 2009 are:
- 1st/15th Royal New South Wales Lancers
- 2nd/14th Light Horse Regiment (Queensland Mounted Infantry)
- 3rd/9th Light Horse (South Australian Mounted Rifles)
- 4th/19th Prince of Wales's Light Horse
- 10th Light Horse Regiment
- 12th/16th Hunter River Lancers.

APPENDIX

The 'Beersheba charge photo'

The battle of Beersheba is perhaps the best-known light horse action of the Palestine campaign, having caught the public's attention more than any other single event of Australia's war in the Middle East. The attention stems, in large part, from a fascination with the remarkable charge by the 4th Light Horse Brigade, which captured the town of Beersheba and its wells at the end of a day-long fight on the last day of October 1917. This fascination is reflected in one of the enduring controversies surrounding the light horse, which relates to a photo held by the Australian War Memorial showing light-horsemen charging. The controversy arises because it has been claimed to be a photo of the 4th Light Horse Regiment taken during its charge on Beersheba, a claim that has been championed by the light horse historian Ian Jones, and to which he first gave new impetus in an article in 1983. His argument, made repeatedly and as one of the few detailed examinations of the photograph to have been made, met with a degree of acceptance through the 1980s and 1990s and has been repeated in serious history books several times; to such a point, indeed, that his claims have to some extent become established as part of light horse history. There are significant doubts about his claim, however, and whether it can be supported is hotly disputed. Since the photo first came to light in Australia some 90 years ago there has been a vigorous argument about what the photo actually depicts. Is it a picture of the charge, is it picture of a re-enactment of the charge, or is it something else altogether?

Photo 35 A contentious photograph – often presented as being a picture of the charge of the 4th Light Horse Regiment at Beersheba in 1917, it was more probably taken during a re-enactment or training in 1918. (AWM A02684)

The background

The early years of this photograph's history are now obscured, but it seems to have been circulating among troops in Palestine in 1918.[1] It made its first known public appearance in 1920 when, presented as being a genuine picture of the charge, it was part of an exhibition of war photographs that travelled around Australia under the directorship of Donovan Joynt. Its inclusion, noted Ian Jones, who has been the most fervent advocate of the photo's authenticity, meant it was the subject of much discussion even then, and Brigadier William Grant, who commanded the 4th Light Horse Brigade during the charge, was moved to make statements (although they were less than emphatic) that supported its authenticity.[2] The other main theories advanced then or during the 1920s were that the picture was taken by an Ottoman army soldier who, with his camera, was later captured, or that the photo was taken by the official photographer Frank Hurley at a re-enactment of the charge done some months later at a place called Belah. The Turkish soldier theory has long been dismissed as rather absurd and will not be examined here.[3]

The matter then largely rested until the late 1960s when Donovan Joynt sought a copy of the photograph for R.J. Hall's forthcoming book, *The Australian Light Horse*. At this point the Director of the Australian War Memorial, W.R. Lancaster, wrote to Joynt outlining the view that the photo was not genuine. The reasons given were, first, that the formation evident in the photo differed from that in the accounts of the battle; second, that the dust and vegetation evident in the photo did not match the descriptions of the charge; third, that the shadows of the horsemen in the photo should be behind them, not to their right; fourth, that the charge was made downhill, not uphill as the photo showed; and finally, that it was improbable that such a photo could have been taken at all.[4]

Apparently undeterred, Joynt subsequently found Eric George Elliott, an ex-soldier of the 4th Machine Gun Squadron, who signed a declaration that he had in fact taken the photo at Beersheba. The essence of his claim was that as a member of the machine-gun squadron he was working on range charts south-east of Beersheba on the day of the battle when he noticed the charge approaching, and he removed his camera from his haversack, took a photo, mounted his horse and got out of the way. The roll of film was reportedly given to a man returning to Australia in January 1918; Elliott asked him to develop it and pass the results to his parents. The photo he was then given when he returned to Australia, he claimed, was identical to the one in Joynt's possession and used in Hall's book.[5]

There followed another quiet spell before Ian Jones, a journalist, scriptwriter, television producer and director, and historian, who had extensively researched the light horse in Palestine, published an article in the *Journal of the Australian War Memorial* in 1983 which argued that the photo was 'undoubtedly genuine'. He produced a lengthened version of Elliott's declaration as well as a detailed rebuttal of the argument that the Memorial's director had outlined in 1967. Its key elements were:

1. that the formation in the photo was in fact accurate (even though this would seem to contradict Jones's own conclusions on the formation in an article on the charge, which was accompanied by his analysis of the photograph)
2. that the accounts of the dust raised were exaggerated by men looking into the sun: that the reddish sunlight at the end of the day, combined with the reddish dust, when looking from the photographer's perspective, would actually minimise the dust's appearance in the photo
3. that the evident vegetation was the remains of a Bedouin crop
4. that the location of the shadows were correct given the direction of the charge and where the sun was setting on that day
5. that the uphill effect of the photo was created by a tilted camera, and
6. finally, that the Elliott statement removed all suggestion that the photo was taken by a Turk.[6]

When, in 1987, Jones produced a book, also titled *The Australian Light Horse*, he did not revisit his polemic on the image, but somewhat inconsistently contended in a photo caption that Elliott was not a member of the machine-gun squadron working on range charts but, rather incredibly, an advance scout who stopped during the charge to take the photo.[7] Jones's argument, passionately made as it was, and being virtually the only recent analysis available, met with some acceptance, and through the 1990s a number of books appeared that accepted his version to a greater or lesser extent.[8]

But Jones had not convinced everyone, and in 1997, in the first edition of the Australian War Memorial's new magazine, *Wartime*, Matthew Woodhead, a curator of photographs at the Memorial, and Jacqui Lobach, a visiting 'summer scholar', took issue with several of Jones's points, dismissing his arguments as to why the dust was not evident, his assertions about the vegetation and his contention that a tilted camera caused the uphill effect. Moreover they questioned how a relatively high-resolution photo of moving objects was made as the day's light was fading (when the charge took place) using the very slow-speed film available in 1917. Drawing on various sources they, echoing the Memorial's view in the 1920s, concluded that the photo was probably the result of a recreation of the charge made for the official cine-photographer, Frank Hurley, in 1918.[9]

In 2007 Ian Jones retorted in a revision of his 1987 book, published as *A Thousand Miles of Battles*. Here he did not address the concerns of the *Wartime* article; rather he briefly reiterated most of his arguments from 1983 and added to them a claim that at least two individuals have been picked out of the photo. Also included is a frame purportedly taken from Hurley's lost footage of the light horse galloping for him at the re-enactment, which Jones used to dispute the claim that the photo could have been taken at Belah. Finally, he included a facsimile copy of a statement made by Eric Elliott which, although it outlines essentially the same story, is not the same statement that was reproduced either in Hall's 1967 book or Jones's 1983 article.[10]

This is by no means a comprehensive review of the arguments put forward over the years, and in late 2008 and early 2009 there was another exchange (involving Ian Jones, through Neil McDonald, and myself) on the pages of the polemical magazine *Quadrant*.[11] It should also be noted that underneath these printed exchanges has been a less public one that has probably always existed but recently progressed to full flight owing to the internet, where the debate over the photo's authenticity is sometimes carried on with gusto in discussion forums and the like.[12] It is clear from a survey of the internet discussions, as it is from the survey of the published literature outlined above, that no consensus exists. It is necessary, therefore, to consider the evidence in detail.

THE EVIDENCE

The starting point for any such consideration must be the statement by Eric Elliott that he was the person who took the photo and that it was taken of the 4th Light Horse Brigade during the charge in 1917. This is a potentially persuasive piece of evidence in that it appears to demonstrate the authenticity of the photo. It is certainly capable of generating powerful emotions, but not all of these are happy ones, and people can and do take issue with one or more elements of his declaration. How do we know he was telling the truth? Was he where he said he was? If so, why was he there when his squadron was doing X? Why do no accounts (either by participants or the numerous bystanders) recall a man riding out of the charge's path? How did he know the photo is the one he took, given that he never saw the negative? These are all good questions, but Elliott, and the men he served alongside, are not here to answer to them. Conversely, there are those who are inclined to approach Elliott's statements, as those of a soldier who was there, with a high degree of reverence and readily accept them. Ian Jones has perhaps best exemplified this by strongly asserting that 'Elliott... was no liar'.[13] These approaches are guaranteed eventually to produce a good deal of heat, especially if they come into contact, but not a lot of light.

The protests of Elliott's defenders notwithstanding, there is no doubt that his claim must be treated with caution by anyone making a serious examination of the photograph. All historical evidence must be approached with scepticism, especially oral or testimonial evidence not committed to paper until 40 years after the event as Elliott's was. This is not to say that he was lying (although the possibility cannot be discounted either), but as all historians – and indeed police and court officials – know, memory is a very fallible thing: it can readily mislead us, and its quality diminishes at an alarming rate. In the historian's rough guide of evidential reliability anything relying on memory will generally rate well down the list.

Furthermore, Elliott's memory is not the only one with which we must contend. Other men who were there have differing accounts, and in 1997 Woodhouse and Lobach drew on one who was adamant that the photo was of the re-enactment at Belah.[14] Similarly another trooper in the 4th Light Horse Regiment, C.A. Schimmelbusch, who charged at Beersheba, put a copy of the picture in his photo album after the war and captioned it as 'Light Horse Charge (Drilling) Belah'.[15] Another photo album compiled by a light-horseman, which was put up for sale by an antique dealer in 2008, has the disputed photo captioned as being a charge by the 9th Light Horse Regiment![16] Where, when and for what purpose – who knows? Those who believe Elliott will no doubt object that he was supported by the statements made by Grant in 1920 or Elliott's comrades, but evidentiary problems of time and memory exist here, too, and this really reduces us to a sort of returned soldier poker: I will see your veteran and raise you two of my own.

Elliott's testimony is not convincing by itself because of the time that elapsed between the charge and his claim coming to light, but it cannot be dismissed out of hand. It must therefore be treated as a piece of the puzzle and tested against the other evidence available to us. For corroboration or otherwise we are left with the photo itself and the accounts of the battle, both contemporary and historical.

The print in the Memorial's collection is made from a glass plate negative (about 15 cm by 9 cm in size), which in turn was made from a print loaned to the Memorial – this is important; it is a copy of a print so the resolution is not good. The Memorial has subsequently come to own other copies of the print, but the original negative has never been found.[17] Larger prints also exist but, as far as can be ascertained, they were all created by enlargement of the existing small print (or someone's equivalent copy), and the resolution of these images is even poorer. People often wonder about the existence of larger prints taken from the original negative, but no such print has ever been presented for examination by the Memorial or, it seems, by anyone who has seriously looked into the photo. That they exist is merely speculation. The photo also defies the promise of modern technology in that attempts to enlarge and digitally enhance it do not produce markedly better results. Unlike in spy and police television dramas, pixels cannot be created where they do not exist – an enhanced black blob is still a black blob.

With this in mind the elements in the photo can be examined. An early point of conflict was the formation of the horsemen depicted. The Memorial contended in 1967 that it was incorrect, and Jones responded that, according to Grant and other veterans, the three extended lines of horsemen did accurately portray the formation. The sources conflict quite a lot on the formation used during the charge, and coming to a definitive answer is probably impossible, but it could be that in a sense both might be right. Two regiments charged side by side at Beersheba, the 4th on the right and the 12th on the left. The very earliest reports by the two regiments, written within days of the event, indicate that the 4th Light Horse Regiment deployed with its three squadrons in successive extended lines and charged that same way. The 12th appears to have deployed with its two leading squadrons extended, but with the third in troop columns (there is no reason why the two regiments cannot have deployed with slightly differing formations, although most analysts try to reconcile the formation one way or the other).[18] The photo is claimed to be of the 4th Regiment, however, and not the 12th, so, while significant doubts will remain, the formation can be taken as being correct for our purposes.

Jones's 2007 assertion that individuals can be identified from the photograph can be quickly discounted. The photo is too small and of too poor a resolution for any facial detail to be picked out (and the faces are in the shadow of the hats anyway); and the idea that because some veterans

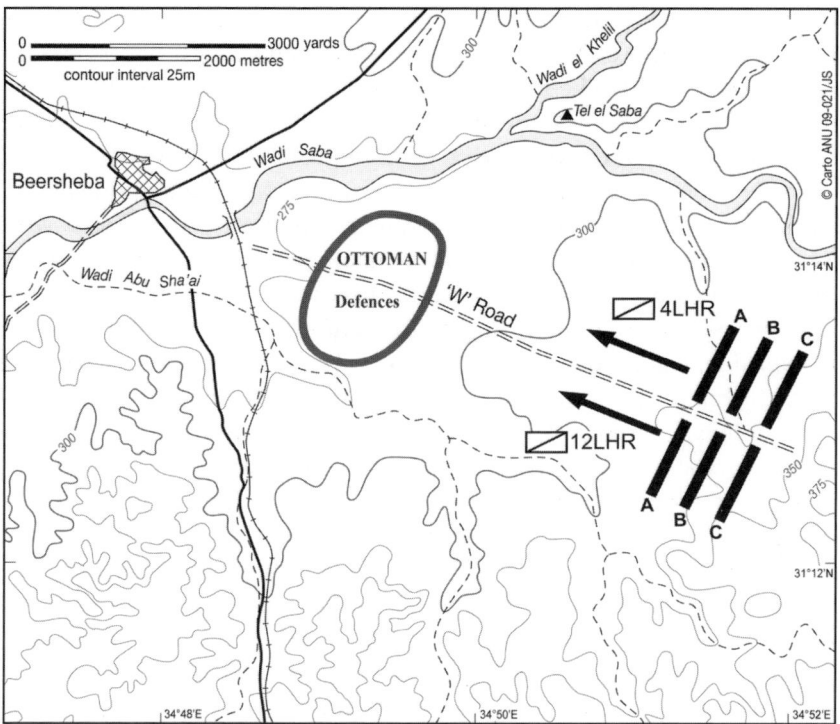

Map 7 The charge at Beersheba, 31 October 1917. This map gives the essentials of the charge and the ground over which it took place. The Turkish positions south-east of town were made up of a series of trenches and pits supported by posts along Wadi Abu Sha'ai but, crucially, were unwired. The formation of two C Squadrons in the mounted attack is subject to some dispute as to whether they were in extended order or troop columns, or both. C Squadron, 12th Light Horse Regiment, also seems to have made its advance in conformation with Wadi Abu Sha'ai rather than following the two lead squadrons along the 'W' road.

recalled in 1937 that some men had formed an impromptu bodyguard around their commanding officer, so therefore that cluster of men on the right must be them, as Jones does, relies on a logic that is faulty in the extreme.[19] All psychologists know that people often see what they want – or simply expect – to see, and this is just wishful thinking. By uncritically repeating a returned soldier's similar process of identifying another person Jones is simply being misleading.

Other elements within the photo can also be of interest, and in 1997 Woodhead and Lobach questioned why, if the photo was taken at Beersheba, the men did not seem to be appropriately equipped, there being no evidence of 'grain bags, overcoats, saddlebags, haversacks or bandoliers'.[20] The soldiers certainly would have been carrying this equipment, and the regiments undoubtedly went to Beersheba in full marching order carrying all they were meant to, and probably a bit besides. There is no mention in any account of the brigade off-loading equipment to conduct the charge, and the two regiments seem to have charged with everything aboard, which is typical for mounted actions. The quality of the photo presents difficulties in that details cannot be picked out, but the accumulation of equipment attached to saddlery and men would certainly make a significant alteration to their appearance in terms of outline and apparent bulk. The quality of the photo and the Memorial's negative is high enough to show this and is enhanced by the way the light falls on several horses and riders in the centre of the front rank, giving the viewer a relatively good look at them. We are therefore able to distinguish that the men in the photo appear to be travelling 'light' and certainly do not seem to be in marching order, which does not tally with their being on operations on the first day of a great offensive for which it was intended that they ride deep into Palestine.[21]

With a similar aim of finding something useful in the photograph is the 2008 analysis by an avid researcher and blogger on the light horse, Bill Woerlee, who has enlarged and examined parts of the picture. He has concluded that there is a group of bystanders observing the second rank of chargers and that the second rank is in fact stationary. The problem with image resolution is difficult to resolve, however, and his results are, I think, only partially successful. I replicated his experiment using a 1200 dpi scan of the photo, and his claim that there are dismounted bystanders at the end of the second line is quite plausible, but the results of the enlargement are ambiguous and opponents will no doubt readily dismiss them. The assertion that the horses in the second and probably third rank are stationary has considerably more credence, and it seems that this is indeed the case, which serves to cast further doubt on the possibility that Eric Elliott took the photograph at Beersheba once the charge was well underway or, given the attitude of the horses in the second rank, even while the charge was forming up.

Examinations of these elements of the photo are helpful, but suffer a fundamental limitation caused by the quality of the print. The resolution is simply not good enough to get us very far, and the conclusions drawn are all contestable to a degree. But there are still significant elements in the photo that can assist us.

Also to be considered is the dust in the photo, or rather the lack of it. Jones has contended that the dust is not evident because its supposed density had been exaggerated by men watching the charge from behind and because the 'combination of reddish brown dust and reddish sunlight [at the end of the day from the photographer's perspective] minimised the effect of the dust'.[22] It is possible that men viewing the charge from behind might have thought there would be more dust than there actually was but, regardless, all accounts agree that there was quite a lot of it. The Australian official historian, H.S. Gullett, drawing on various sources, wrote that the chargers were 'swallowed up in their own dust and the gathering twilight'.[23] The New Zealand official history noted that 'the plain was covered in a fine dust' and that the sight of it enveloping the charge and trailing away into the air 'was a magnificent sight'.[24] R.M.P. Preston, a British artilleryman who witnessed the charge, recalled in *The Desert Mounted Corps*, that it was 'half obscured in clouds of reddish dust'.[25] Reviewing the charge in December 1917, the commander of the 4th Light Horse Regiment, Murray Bourchier, thought the dust 'was of great assistance to us, the enemy being unable to estimate the number of troops attacking'.[26] John Fowler, who charged in the second line of the 12th Light Horse Regiment, recalled that 'we could see only a few yards, our eyes almost filled with dust, and caked around our mouths'.[27]

That the reddish light with the coming sunset would minimise the reddish dust is possible, but is also contestable, and responses to my enquiries with astronomers, who deal with light dust as a matter of professional necessity, indicated that red light shining on red dust might easily accentuate the dust rather than minimise it. Dust is certainly visible in the photo around the horses' hooves, so why it would be visible here and not elsewhere if there was a lot of it is unclear. Still, even in the event that the light did manage to suppress the dust's appearance, it would not render it transparent, and in this photo the successive lines of horsemen can be clearly seen, which does not accord with reliable accounts of the charge.[28]

The matter of light brings us to another aspect of Woodhead and Lobach's critique, namely, whether it was technically possible for the photo to have been taken on the day in the circumstances that existed. They pointed out that the action has been well 'frozen' in the photo, meaning a high shutter speed was employed, and that its 'depth of field' indicates the photo was made using a narrow aperture, a combination that can be achieved only in good light, particularly given the film stock available in 1917.[29] This is an important consideration because these technical issues are immutable. Depth of field – that is, the amount of the photo (depth wise) that is in focus – is related to several factors but is contingent on the lens aperture selected. A long depth of field can be achieved only by using a narrow aperture, which lets in less light, and a wide aperture will produce photos with only a shallow depth of field. The photo has a quite long depth of field, stretching from just in front of the photographer to virtually the horizon, which indicates that a narrow aperture was used. If the light was poor a narrow aperture could have been used, but only with a slow shutter speed. The fact that moving bayonets and the horses' hooves have been 'frozen' indicates, however, that a high shutter speed was used. To this must be added the film's speed, which in 1917 cannot have been greater than 10 to 12 ASA. A film's speed rating reflects its sensitivity to light. A slow film will requires a longer exposure, and a high-speed film requires shorter exposure. Ten ASA is a very slow film speed. Modern professional photographers, for example, shooting action or sports subjects before the widespread adoption of digital cameras would typically use 400, 800 or higher ASA (now called ISO) speed film.[30]

These technical considerations indicate quite clearly that for this photo to have been taken the light must have been good, but we know that the charge took place as the day was ending (it moved off at about 4.30 p.m. or soon thereafter, and sunset was at about 4.55 p.m.), and several sources indicate that the light was not good. Ion Idriess's often quoted account – 'galloping through the red haze – knee to knee and horse to horse – the dying sun glinting on bayonet points' – is likely a literary fabrication to enhance his 1932 book, *The Desert Column*. Deployed with the 5th Light Horse Regiment in the area around the Hebron Road, some distance from the location of the charge, it is doubtful that he saw any of the charge, and he certainly made no mention of it in his diary, on which most of his book is based.[31] More credibly the 4th Light Horse Brigade's divisional commander, Major-General Sir Henry Hodgson, wrote home in February 1918 that 'the light was going so I decided to gallop it'.[32] R.M.P. Preston recalled, 'It was growing dark, and the enemy trenches were outlined in fire by the flashes of their rifles. Beyond and a little above them, blazed the bigger deeper flashes of their field guns, and our own shells burst like a row of red stars over the Turkish positions.'[33]

The coming into action of the Notts Battery during the charge and its silencing of machine-gun fire from a Turkish redoubt, which was raking the 12th Light Horse Regiment, with their second shot has long been lauded as a fortunate piece of gunnery. Its reputation is only further enhanced by recognising that, as the 4th Light Horse Brigade's war diary points out, it 'was then practically dark and impossible to take distances with the [optical] range finder'.[34] When the 11th Light Horse Regiment received a message to redeploy in support of the charge at around 4.40 p.m., about the time the charge was taking place, it found it was too dark to issue the necessary orders to its squadrons by signal (whether by heliograph or other means is not clear, but it matters little) and had to send gallopers instead.[35] If it was dark enough, therefore, for Turkish muzzle flashes and shell bursts to be evident, for optical range finders to be unusable and for a regimental headquarters to be unable to send signals to its squadrons visually, then it seems nigh on impossible that a hand-held camera using slow film could take a well-lit photo with considerable depth of field and no blurring of the subject.

Photographic impossibility leads to the final evidentiary matter, topography. The entire charge at Beersheba took place down a long, very shallow slope. This was more the case for the 4th Light Horse Regiment, which attacked north of the 'W' Road, than for the 12th Light Horse Regiment, which charged south of it and alongside Wadi Abu Sha'ai, and which had to contend with numerous wash-outs and smaller wadis that emptied into it (although the 4th faced these, too). The photo shows the horsemen charging uphill, however. Jones contended that this is an effect brought about by a tilted camera and that with 'true verticals restored, the formation is heading down a very slight slope'.[36] A tilt of the camera by the photographer either up or down would have done nothing in this regard, serving only to increase or decrease the amount of sky to be seen. A sideways tilt by the photographer would readily be corrected by tilting and reframing (or cropping) the print, but a tilt to the right only serves to increase the apparent slope. A tilt to the left helps the horsemen on the left by giving them an apparent slope to run down (sort of), but is not helpful to those on the right who are coming on more directly, and it gives them an unhealthy, and physically improbable, lean to their right. It also introduces to the horizon a rise in ground to the right, which places an inconvenient mountain range in what is now called the Negev Desert. Moreover, tilting the photo also appears to produce unlikely attitudes among the horsemen, particularly in the second rank.

More recently Jones has apparently abandoned this tilting thesis, and he now contends that the uphill effect was created by the copying process in combination with the haze of dust, which creates an 'effect similar to that of a modern telephoto lens slightly altering the perspectives'.[37] There are several problems with this theory. First, it assumes that all the prints in circulation have come from the same copying source some time after the original prints were made (the implication is that this is the Memorial). But given the way copies show up in ex-soldiers' photo albums, this is a risky assumption; the photo was in circulation well before the Memorial got a copy and made more. Second, it assumes that the Memorial's copy was made with a gross indifference to an original thought interesting enough to be brought into the Memorial's collection. This might be so, but it seems unlikely and there is no evidence of such gross negligence from the 1920s elsewhere in the Memorial's photographic holdings. Third, it is improbable that a two-dimensional copying process would introduce such a distortion to the picture. Finally, if it did introduce a distortion, it is even more improbable that it would be so uniformly neat as affect the ground only in such an imperceptible way, without causing changes to the horsemen, whose attitude seems perfectly correct given the terrain they are evidently on.

This simply confirms what our eyes have already told us, which is that the photo is level or at least so close to level as not to make any perceptible difference. Thus the horsemen are galloping up what is a noticeable slope out of what is a substantial depression behind them. There is no point on the route of the charge that corresponds with this topographical feature, especially on the path taken by the 4th Light Horse Regiment. An examination of contemporary topographical maps prepared by Royal Engineer surveyors readily shows that the entire charge route was downhill. There were wadis to contend with, for sure, and perhaps very slight undulations, but the map indicates no significant depressions nor any crests large enough to register on the map's contour markings (and these reflect elevation changes of just 30 feet – 9.1 metres). Indeed to the casual observer the striking thing might be the relative flatness of the ground. This was certainly my impression when I visited the battlefield in 2007, and Sloan Bolton, who charged with the 4th Light Horse Regiment, recalled that on forming up Beersheba could be seen over 'what seemed to be perfectly level plain'. Along the 'W' Road, which formed the axis of the attack, the ground falls only about 120 feet (36.5 metres) over 5000 yards (4572 metres) – there are no noticeable elevations to be found here (which is easily verified today by using such tools as Google Earth).[38]

Alternative explanations

The possibility that the photo was taken at Belah in 1918 during a re-enactment of the charge for Frank Hurley has been the most often mentioned alternative explanation of the photo's origins. Hurley visited the AIF in Egypt and Palestine in 1918 and was with the Australian Mounted Division in early February where it was then resting on the Palestine coast. On 6 February he met up with the 4th Light Horse Brigade at Belah and immediately got to work taking photographs and filming moving sequences. His diary noted on that day: 'I had two squadrons sent up to Gaza to participate in my pictures', a role that we know through the war diaries was fulfilled by the 11th Light Horse Regiment.[39] The following day he wrote: 'Photographed various stunts... Afternoon two regiments turned out and re-enacted their famous charge at Bersheba [sic] The scene was filled with excitement, and I well imagine the demoralising effect on the enemy, of two regiments with bayonets drawn sweeping down on to them. In some small degree I sensed the excitement myself, for the charge was directed at the position I occupied.'[40] Which regiments did this is not immediately clear as the war diaries are not forthcoming, but Hurley implies that it was the 4th and 12th; other evidence seems to support this, and neither Jones nor anyone else has demurred.[41]

What happened to the film (still or moving) Hurley took on that day is unknown. A motion picture credited to Hurley in the Memorial's collection, *With the Australian Forces in Palestine*, contains a tantalising brief sequence captioned 'Australian Light Horse advancing across open country ready to charge', but while the ground bears some resemblance to the terrain in the photo, the direction of the galloping horsemen, their formation and the camera angle do not match the contentious picture, so no direct comparison is possible.[42] In *A Thousand Miles of Battles* Ian Jones reproduced a still taken from a film that he asserts is from the Hurley footage. If this is the case this is a noteworthy discovery, but the provenance of this film is obscure at best. Although Jones presents his assertion about the origins of this film as something of a *fait accompli* in his book, when I questioned him it became apparent that he had taken it from Charles Chauvel's 1940 feature film *Forty Thousand Horsemen*, where it seems to be an out-of-place shot in the film's climactic charge scene. He has concluded that this is a segment of Hurley's film that was used in the 1940 feature – and this is possible as footage from the First World War sometimes shows up in unusual places – but the evidential trail is non-existent and numerous questions remain.[43] In the first instance: how do we know it is the Hurley film? Is it really the supposed re-enactment, or is it something else? Even if it was accepted that it is footage of the Hurley re-enactment, this *might* prove that the charge photo was not taken at Belah, but it does not prove it was taken at Beersheba.

The possibility that a few frames of Hurley's film found its way into *Forty Thousand Horsemen* aside, his work from Belah is considered lost, and the evidence that the charge photo was taken by him is somewhat circumstantial. We have a documented case of a photographer taking a photo of a re-enactment of the charge, but Hurley never claimed to have taken the picture being discussed here, and the results of his work on that day is lost to us. We do not know where the re-enactment exactly took place. The Belah encampment was on the coast and somewhat sandy with plenty of dunes, but the re-enactment could easily have taken place inland nearby over more fertile ground, so the opportunity to compare the terrain in the photo and the topography of Belah is not available to us.[44] Ian Jones has contended that the Hurley re-enactment took place at a grassy spot near Gaza nicknamed St James's Park,[45] but another person who looked into the photograph in the 1980s, Pat Gallagher, drawing on the recollections of his father who charged with the 12th Light Horse Regiment, believes that the re-enactment took place over old Turkish trenches near Gaza. (He has also pointed to the similarity between the terrain in the charge photo and terrain evident in photos of the old Turkish trenches at Gaza.)[46] That the photo is the result of Hurley at Belah is a possibility in which only probabilities rather than certainties can be argued.

Other explanations can also be considered, the most promising being that in early 1918 the units of the Australian Mounted Division, in the light of events at Beersheba and elsewhere, were going through a period of learning and executing mounted attacks with the bayonet in lieu of the sword.[47] It is possible that the photograph was taken during the training exercises that accompanied this development, although who might have taken it is unknown, and it has to be acknowledged that there is no obvious evidence to support this possibility.

Conclusion

There is little doubt that the photo is not of the charge at Beersheba. Elliott's testimony, satisfying as it might be for some, cannot be taken at face value, and it lacks corroborating evidence. Elliott might have been where he said he was and taken a photo, but this picture is not the result. While the photo *might* depict the charge formation correctly, there is no way to identify anyone in the charge, it is evident that the horsemen are not equipped as they most likely were during the charge and, as Bill Woerlee has argued, the second line is likely stationary. More tellingly, no large amounts of dust are evident in the photo and, despite Ian Jones's debatable reasons why this was so, the contemporary accounts and the likely light conditions mean that some of the voluminous dust produced would be visible or at least obscure elements in the photo. Moreover, it is clear that a hand-held camera containing slow-speed film could not take a picture in which the action is frozen while also giving the photo a considerable depth of field in poor light, which was certainly the prevailing light at Beersheba. The technical problems with this are insurmountable, as are the topographical ones. Contemporary maps make it certain that, minor undulations aside, the entire charge took place down a long, shallow slope, yet the photo clearly shows horsemen galloping uphill out of a considerable depression. What the photo might be of instead is less obvious. That it is the result of Frank Hurley's work in February 1918 is by no means certain as the evidence is sketchy and debatable, but as the only verified case of a photographer taking a photo of the light horse charging it must, based on the available evidence, still be considered a probable explanation. That it might be a shot taken during the Australian Mounted Division's mounted tactical training is possible, and an attractive idea (to which I personally incline), but without substantive evidence it remains just a theory. Unless new evidence comes to light, the reality is that we will probably never know the full story of this photograph.

Notes

Author's note
1. Although I have modified them for my own use, these definitions are based on Stephen Badsey's; see Badsey, 'Fire and the sword'.
2. 'The disastrous defeat inflicted on the Turkish arms at Romani, and the pursuit which followed... demonstrated the inestimable value of the horsemen of Australasia as cavalrymen...' (Chauvel, Preface, in Gullett and Barrett (eds), *Australia in Palestine*, p. ix).

Introduction
1. Hammond, 'Civilians give history a gallop', *Courier-Mail*, 29 June 2005, p. 19.
2. Australian Light Horse Association, www.lighthorse.org.au/light.htm.
3. 'Bean, Charles', in *The Oxford Companion to Australian Military History* (1st edn), p. 89.
4. Gullett, *The AIF in Sinai and Palestine*, p. 29.
5. See for example Jones, *A Thousand Miles of Battles*, p. 14.
6. For an excellent examination of the way cavalry and cavalrymen have been treated in historiography see Phillips, 'The scapegoat arm'.
7. For more see Badsey, *Doctrine and Reform in the British Cavalry*; Badsey, 'Fire and the sword'; Phillips, 'The scapegoat arm'; Badsey, 'The Boer War (1899–1902) and British cavalry doctrine'; Bou, 'Cavalry, firepower and swords'; and Kenyon, 'British cavalry on the Western Front'.
8. Luvaas, *The Military Legacy of the Civil War*, pp. 21–46; Denison, *Modern Cavalry*, passim; Badsey, 'Fire and the sword', pp. 112–13; Badsey, *Doctrine and Reform in the British Cavalry*, pp. 65–7.
9. See for example Boguslawski, *Tactical Deductions from the War of 1870–71*.
10. Denison, *Modern Cavalry*, pp. v–11, 72, 162–3, passim; Denison, *A History of Cavalry*, pp. 413–40.
11. Strachan, *From Waterloo to Balaclava*, p. 88.
12. Stanley, *The Remote Garrison*, p. 32; Lucas, *Camp Life and Sport in South Africa*, pp. 49–50.
13. Strachan, *From Waterloo to Balaclava*, pp. 88–9.
14. Hutton, 'Mounted infantry', p. 696.
15. Badsey, *Doctrine and Reform in the British Cavalry*, pp. 62–3.

16 Luvaas, *The Military Legacy of the Civil War*, p. 50. The schools were at Aldershot and Curragh.
17 Douglas Haig, 1890, cited in Badsey, 'Fire and the sword', p. 107.
18 Phillips, 'The scapegoat arm', passim.
19 Badsey, 'Fire and the sword', pp. 116–19.
20 Army Order 39, March 1903, cited in Anglesey, *A History of the British Cavalry*, vol. 4, p. 392.
21 Badsey, 'Fire and the sword', pp. 48–9, 104.
22 See Childers, *German Influence on British Cavalry*, and *War and the Arme Blanche*; French, Preface, in von Bernhardi, *Cavalry in War and Peace*.
23 Badsey, 'Fire and the sword', pp. 252–4.
24 Holmes, *The Little Field Marshal*, p. 162.
25 Anglesey, *A History of the British Cavalry*, vol. 4, p. 421.
26 Badsey, 'Fire and the sword', p. 270; *Cavalry Training, 1912*, passim.
27 *Cavalry Training, 1912*, p. 230.
28 Badsey, 'Fire and the sword', p. 273.

1 Ancestors

1 Stanley, *The Remote Garrison*, pp. 21–2, 32, 38–9, 50–1, 58.
2 Connor, *The Australian Frontier Wars*, passim.
3 Stanley, *The Remote Garrison*, p. 50; Vazenry, *Military Forces of Victoria 1854–1967*, chapter 1, p. 6.
4 Anon., 'Reedbeds to regiment', *Cavalry in SA: To Commemorate the 150th Anniversary of the First Cavalry Squadron in South Australia*, A Sqn, 3rd/9th South Australian Mounted Rifles and Army Museum of South Australia, undated; Return for militia, 1842, SRSA, GRG 24/51/2; Burness, 'Australian colonial forces', pp. 1–11. This last unit is sometimes also called the South Australian Mounted Rifles, but this is a title more accurately applied to a later colonial unit.
5 Burness, 'New South Wales Cavalry 1854–1935', p. 246.
6 Millar, 'The history of the defence forces of the Port Phillip District', pp. 78–9.
7 Ibid., p. 90; Holloway, *Hooves, Wheels and Tracks*, pp. 7–8; Wyatt, *A Lion in the Colony*, pp. 4–5; Weick, *The Volunteer Movement in Western Australia*, p. 30.
8 Johnson, *Volunteers at Heart*, p. 30.
9 Wyatt, *A Lion in the Colony*, p. 18.
10 Johnson, *Volunteers at Heart*, p. 24.
11 Vazenry, *Military Forces of Victoria*, chapter 4, p. 27.
12 Weick, *The Volunteer Movement in Western Australia*, pp. 31–2.
13 Templeton, *The Consolidation of the British Empire*, pp. 26–7 (publication of a lecture given at the Melbourne Town Hall, 29 July 1900).
14 Evidence by Captain Pitt, Royal Artillery, to Queensland Joint Select Committee on the Defence of the Colony, 1866, cited in Johnson, *Volunteers at Heart*, p. 48.
15 *Advertiser*, 9 August 1861, cited in Vazenry, *Military Forces of Victoria*, chapter 4, p. 25.

16 *Moreton Bay Courier*, 12 March 1862, cited in Johnson, *Volunteers at Heart*, p. 31.
17 Weick, *The Volunteer Movement in Western Australia*, pp. 30–2.
18 Holloway, *Hooves, Wheels and Tracks*, pp. 5, 7.
19 Hon. Mr Baker, South Australia, *Parliamentary Debates*, 21 September 1858, column 175.
20 Ibid., column 176. Mr Baker's complete statement to the house would indicate that he himself was the member of a new, unnamed mounted corps that had recently failed to gain government approval.
21 South Australia, *Report of Commission Appointed by the Governor-in-Chief to Report on Colonial Defences*, 1865, SRSA, GRG 24/90/413.
22 South Australia, *Report of Commission Appointed to Inquire into the Whole Question of the Defences of the Province*, 1876, p. vii, SRSA, GRG 24/90/232.
23 New South Wales Legislative Assembly, *Military Defences Inquiry Commission*, 1881, pp. 24, 67. There were also a number of minority opinions in favour of establishing a body of cavalry or mounted rifles in New South Wales, but no agreement could be reached on this proposal.
24 Burness, 'New South Wales cavalry', p. 247.
25 Johnson, *Volunteers at Heart*, p. 128.
26 Calder, *Heroes and Gentlemen*, p. 26.
27 Ibid., p. 20.
28 Vernon, *The Royal New South Wales Lancers*, pp. 4–7.
29 Burness, 'New South Wales cavalry', pp. 247–8; Vernon, *The Royal New South Wales Lancers*, p. 11; see also, Anon., *A Short History of the New South Wales Mounted Rifles, 1888–1913*, pp. 7–8.
30 The change to the partially paid establishment took place on 1 January 1890, Vernon, *The Royal New South Wales Lancers*, p. 14.
31 Johnson, *Volunteers at Heart*, pp. 128, 132.
32 Hill, *Chauvel of the Light Horse*, p. 7.
33 Zwillenberg, 'Citizens and soldiers', p. 147.
34 According to one source, there is evidence that a number of Western Australia's infantry corps may have unofficially established their own small mounted infantry detachments in order to maintain some mounted capability during the 1890s. No official body was again sanctioned until 1900 (Weick, *The Volunteer Movement in Western Australia*, p. 58).
35 Johnson, *Volunteers at Heart*, pp. 19, 115–22.
36 Zwillenberg, 'Citizens and soldiers', p. 138.
37 Ibid., p. 146; and the Hon. A. Catt, South Australia, *Parliamentary Debates*, 4 September 1889, column 796. Catt thought that this Adelaide force should be raised as the current mounted rifles, being based in country districts, were too far from Adelaide to be effective if required.
38 Zwillenberg, 'Citizens and soldiers', p. 148.
39 Howard, 'Men against fire', *passim*.
40 Holloway, *Hooves, Wheels and Tracks*, p. 17. In colonial services bodies of this type would often be termed 'irregular cavalry' or 'auxiliaries'.

41 Lord Knutsford to the Governors of the Australian Colonies, 17 June 1889, *Correspondence Relating to the Inspection of the Military Forces of the Australasian Colonies by Major-General J. Bevan Edwards*, Great Britain, Parliamentary Papers, 1890, vol. 49, p. 6.
42 Maj-Gen J. Bevan Edwards, Memorandum on the Proposed Organisation of the Military Forces of the Australian Colonies, Serial 11, in ibid., p. 22.
43 Ibid.
44 Ibid., pp. 8–27.
45 Remarks by the Colonial Defence Committee to the Proposed Organisation of the Military forces of the Australasian Colonies, Enclosure to Serial 12, ibid., p. 31.
46 These imperial manuals were either brought out from Great Britain or reproduced without modification locally. The relevant cavalry manual during this period was the various permutations of *Cavalry Drill*.
47 The correct title of the 1888 manual is unclear. The original cover and title page of the State Library of South Australia's copy is missing, and the work is simply titled *Mounted Rifles, 1888* for catalogue purposes. This may be the original title but it is unlikely. The manual clearly outlines as the role of mounted rifles the sort of roles that are traditionally light cavalry duties, essentially outpost and screening; see also South Australia, *Regulations and Field Service Manual for Mounted Infantry*, p. 5.
48 Queensland Defence Force, *Drill Regulations and Field Exercises for Mounted Infantry*, issued with General Orders, 16 April 1892, p. 5.
49 Notes on W. Okeden's memo, QSA, PRE/20. This item is undated and its author unknown, but it probably dates from late 1893 or early 1894.
50 He arrived in Sydney by train from Melbourne on Sunday, 28 May 1893, and took up his appointment the following day (Perry, 'Military reforms of General Sir Edward Hutton', p. 67).
51 Hutton, 'The evolution of mounted infantry', p. 374. Hutton had served in the Zulu War of 1879, South African War 1880–81, Egyptian War 1882 and the Sudan War.
52 Hutton, 'Mounted infantry', pp. 695–738.
53 Hutton, 'Tactical and strategical power of mounted troops in war', *The Defence and Defensive Power of Australia*, p. 8. This chapter of this 1902 publication was originally given as a lecture at the United Service Institution of New South Wales on 28 August 1894.
54 Hutton, 'Our comrades of Greater Britain', in ibid., p. 47 (a lecture he originally gave at Aldershot on 24 November 1896).
55 Vernon, *The Royal New South Wales Lancers*, p. 18.
56 Maj-Gen Hutton to the Principal Undersecretary, 28 June 1893, SRNSW, CSC, box 5/6139, item 93/8407.
57 The imperial appointment was intended to be for only three years during which time a local officer could be prepared to take over (ibid.; New South Wales, Military Forces of the Colony: Report for the Year 1894 by Major-General E.T.H. Hutton, *New South Wales Legislative Council Journal*, 1895, part 2, pp. 10–11). Although parliament voted funds for the appointment to be filled by an imperial officer for a number of years, no

British officer ever took up the position. In 1896 the government decided that the appointment should be filled by a local officer (SRNSW, CSC, box 5/6351, item 96/18506). Hutton had tried to get an officer from India, Captain Marling VC (probably the later Colonel Sir Percival Scope Marling, who had won his VC as a lieutenant in the King's Royal Rifles – Hutton's regiment – in the Sudan), to fill the job with the local rank of lieutenant-colonel in 1894, but Marling declined (SRNSW, CSC, box 5/6225, items 15258 and 94/2182).

58 Maj-Gen Hutton to the Principal Undersecretary, 28 June 1893, SRNSW, CSC, box 5/6139, item 93/8407.
59 Hutton, 'The mounted infantry question in its relation to the volunteer force of Great Britain', p. 787.
60 New South Wales, Military Forces of the Colony: Report for the Year 1893 by Major-General E.T.H. Hutton, *New South Wales Legislative Council Journal*, 1894–95, part 3, p. 10.
61 Hutton, 'Mounted infantry', pp. 698–701.
62 New South Wales, Military Forces of the Colony: Report for Year 1895 by Major-General E.T.H. Hutton, SRNSW, CSC, box 5/6257, item 95/4827.
63 Emphasis in original; Col Joseph Gordon to Chief Secretary, 19 June 1894, SRSA, GRG 24/6/657/1894.
64 Maj-Gen Alex Tulloch to Victorian Secretary of Defence, 4 June 1894, copy held in QSA, COL/A 785.
65 Queensland's commandant had contemplated sending Major Percy Ricardo, but the Queensland Government had not felt disposed to do so, probably for reasons of economy (note attached to telegram, J. Brinker, Chief Secretary of New South Wales, to Premier of Queensland, QSA, COL/A 785).
66 New South Wales, Military Forces of the Colony: Report for Year 1895 by Major-General E.T.H. Hutton, SRNSW, CSC, box 5/6257, item 95/4827. Once the conference report was approved by the New South Wales Government it was circulated among the other colonies.
67 Hutton, Preface, in *Manual of Drill for the Mounted Troops of Australia, 1895*, p. iii. Parts of this preface were taken directly from a lecture Hutton delivered to the New South Wales United Service Institution in 1894 on the 'Tactical and strategical power of mounted troops in war'.
68 In the preface Hutton even went so far as to use the same basic premise that Denison had in his works and point out Napoleon's belief 'that the value of troops in war . . . is in inverse ratio to their rapidity of movement. This axiom is more especially true of mounted troops' (Hutton, Preface, in *Manual of Drill for the Mounted Troops of Australia, 1895*, p. vi–viii).
69 O'Sullivan was particularly interested in the battle of the Five Forks near the end of the American Civil War when Union troops had played an important part against Lee's fast-fading Confederate army. Denison had written of the actions of Union cavalry under General Sheridan at Five Forks in his *History of Cavalry*, pp. 390–1, and it seems likely that this was the source for O'Sullivan's interest in this example of American mounted troops using mounted rifle-style tactics with great success (O'Sullivan, *The Power of Mounted Riflemen*, p. 3, passim).

70 Ibid., pp. 7, 19.
71 Ibid., pp. 2–3.
72 *Adelaide Observer*, 25 January 1896, p. 12.
73 New South Wales, Military Forces of the Colony, Report for the Year ending 30th June, 1897, by Major-General G.A. French, RA, CMG, Commanding Military Forces, p. 5, SRNSW, CSC, box 5/6395, item 97/15032, emphasis in original.
74 Ibid., pp. 5–6.
75 Sutton, 'French, Sir George Arthur', *Australian Dictionary of Biography*, www.adb.online.anu.edu.au.
76 Lord Brassey was Governor of Victoria 1895–1900 (B.R. Penny, 'Brassey, Thomas, first Earl Brassey', *Australian Dictionary of Biography*, www.adb.online.anu.edu.au).
77 Penny, 'Brassey, Thomas, first Earl Brassey', *Australian Dictionary of Biography*, www.adb.online.anu.edu.au; Lord Brassey to Joseph Chamberlain, 23 August 1897, Appendix to Memorandum by the Colonial Defence Committee, Secret No. 126M, Mounted Rifles for Imperial Service in War, 5 February 1898, TNA (UK), CAB 8/2.
78 Clarke, 'Marching to their own drum', pp. 263–4.
79 Lord Brassey to Joseph Chamberlain, 23 August 1897, Appendix to Memorandum by the Colonial Defence Committee, Secret No. 126M, Mounted Rifles for Imperial Service in War, 5 February 1898, TNA (UK), CAB 8/2.
80 Ibid.
81 Memorandum by the Colonial Defence Committee, Secret No. 126M, Mounted Rifles for Imperial Service in War, 5 February 1898, TNA (UK), CAB 8/2.
82 Sir Henry Loch, Governor of Victoria, to Earl of Derby, 30 March 1885, Correspondence Respecting Offers by the Colonies of Troops for Service in the Soudan, Great Britain, *Parliamentary Papers*, 1884–85, vol. 52, item 14; see also telegram sent to Adjutant-General, 17 February 1885, NAA B3756, 1885/1395.
83 Unsigned notes 10 December 1890 attached to letter, Victorian AAG to E.J. Dye, 24 November 1890, NAA B3756/0, 1890/3749. The notes also outlined an objection to having a volunteer unit established in what was now largely a militia system. The note also mentioned that the 'opinion of the highest authorities at home as well as those in command here are strongly against Cavalry'.
84 Cited in Vernon, *The Royal New South Wales Lancers*, p. 18
85 *Sydney Morning Herald*, 3 January 1902, p. 6.
86 New South Wales, Military Forces of the Colony, Report for the Year 1893 by Major-General E.T.H. Hutton, *New South Wales Legislative Council Journal*, 1894–95, part 3, p. 10.
87 French cited in *Sydney Morning Herald*, 3 January 1902, p. 6.
88 Vernon, *The Royal New South Wales Lancers*, pp. 18–20, 25–30.
89 Bridges, 'The New South Wales Lancers and the Anglo-Boer War', pp. 27–8.

90 The regiment's historian, P.V. Vernon, has followed the lead of the journalist Frank Wilkinson, who wrote a small book on New South Wales cavalry in 1901, in which he claimed that Burns only wished to 'make his regiment efficient – efficient in the only true meaning of the term, through knowledge of the rigours and realities of active service' (ibid. and Wilkinson, *Australian Cavalry*, passim). The more scornful interpretation is made by Barry John Bridges in 'The New South Wales Lancers and the Anglo-Boer War', pp. 28–9. It should be noted that Bridges makes these comments in light of this offer and the way efforts were made to get lancers to South Africa in 1899, which is covered in a later chapter.
91 Clarke, 'Marching to their own drum', p. 264.
92 Cited in Vernon, *The Royal New South Wales Lancers*, p. 31.
93 Lt-Col Mackay to Governor of New South Wales, Earl Beauchamp, 18 July 1899, NSW, no. 24346, Colonial Office 201/629, PRO–AJCP.
94 Peter Burness, 'Mackay, James Alexander Kenneth', *Australian Dictionary of Biography*, www.adb.online.anu.edu.au. When he began recruiting for this unit Mackay was still only a captain in the NSW forces. He was promoted to lieutenant-colonel in 1898.
95 Clarke, 'Marching to their own drum', pp. 275, 276.
96 Earl Beauchamp to the Secretary of State for the Colonies, Joseph Chamberlain, 9 August 1899, NSW, no. 24346, Colonial Office 201/629, PRO–AJCP.
97 Clarke, 'Marching to their own drum', pp. 275–6.
98 Minute by E.H.M, 14 September 1899; and Maj W. Nathan to Sir E. Wingfield, 21 February 1900, both in NSW, No. 24346, Colonial Office 201/629, PRO–AJCP.

2 Tough lessons

1 The war is known by a number of titles, and 'Boer War' is still the most commonly used description in Australia. 'South African War' is frequently used nowadays, as is 'Second Anglo-Boer War', which better situates the war for those not from the Commonwealth.
2 Chamberlain, *Australians in the South African War*, p. 88. A primary source provides other figures: NSW 4756, Vic. 2445, Qld 2056, SA 1038, WA 923 and Tas. 555, for a total of 11 773 men sent overseas (Return of all Military Contingents to South Africa, NAA B168, 1901/3438). Another return in another file gives slightly different figures (NAA B168, 1901/4678).
3 Wilcox, *Australia's Boer War*, p. xiii.
4 Bridges, 'The New South Wales Lancers and the Anglo-Boer War', pp. 30–6.
5 Ibid., pp. 46, 89–90.
6 Tpr Bert Barclay cited in ibid., p. 73.
7 Clarke, 'Manufacturing spontaneity', pp. 133–44.
8 Despatch by Colonial Secretary to Canada, South Australia, New South Wales and Victoria, 3 October 1899, cited in *Report of His Majesty's Commissioners Appointed to Inquire into the Military Preparations and Other Matters Connected with the War in South Africa* (London:

HMSO, 1903), p. 77. Hereafter referred to as the Elgin Commission Report.
9 Elgin Commission Report, pp. 76–8.
10 Bridges, 'The New South Wales Lancers and the Anglo-Boer War', p. 389.
11 Wilcox, *Australia's Boer War*, pp. 389–413; Chamberlain, *Australians in the South African War*, pp. 30–2.
12 Wilcox, *Australia's Boer War*, p. 22. As with so much else relating to contingents to this war, this is also subject to dispute. One source claims that the New South Wales Mounted Rifles could not find a full quota and had resort to public enlistments (see Bridges, 'The New South Wales Lancers and the Anglo-Boer War', pp. 157–8).
13 Report by Maj P. Ricardo cited in Clark, *First Queensland Mounted Infantry Contingent in the South African War*, p. 8.
14 Bridges, 'The New South Wales Lancers and the Anglo-Boer War', pp. 159–60.
15 Wilcox, *Australia's Boer War*, pp. 25–30.
16 Ibid., p. 31; Chamberlain, *Australians in the South African War*, pp. 32–3.
17 Wilcox, *Australia's Boer War*, pp. 33–5.
18 Chamberlain, *Australians in the South African War*, pp. 33–6.
19 Ibid., pp. 7–11, 13–26; Wilcox, *Australia's Boer War*, p. 162.
20 Wilcox, *Australia's Boer War*, pp. 58, 63–4.
21 Chamberlain, *Australians in the South African War*, pp. 47–50.
22 Edward Hutton to wife, 2 April 1900, Hutton, Edward T.H., Letters and Press Cuttings, 1900–04, NLA MS 1215.
23 Chamberlain, *Australians in the South African War*, pp. 47–50.
24 Wilcox, *Australia's Boer War*, pp. 119–27.
25 Tylden, *The Armed Forces of South Africa*, p. 19.
26 Van der Waag, 'An overview of the nature, origin and development of the commando system in South Africa, c. 1715–1899', p. 6. Hereafter 'An overview of the commando system'.
27 Tylden, *The Armed Forces of South Africa*, p. 17.
28 Van der Waag, 'An overview of the commando system', p. 8.
29 Wilcox, *Australia's Boer War*, p. 12.
30 Capt John Antill, OC NSWMR to AAG NSW Forces, 7 January 1900, AWM 1, 4/8.
31 Beckett, 'The South African War and the late Victorian army', p. 36.
32 Ibid.; Badsey, 'Mounted combat in the Second Boer War', p. 15.
33 Van der Waag, 'An overview of the commando system', p. 8; Wilcox, *Australia's Boer War*, p. 125.
34 Maj Percy Ricardo to brother, 14 and 19 May 1900, Ricardo Papers, 1900–27, NLA MS 1928.
35 Badsey, 'Mounted combat in the Second Boer War', p. 15.
36 Spence, 'To shoot and ride', p. 119.
37 Badsey, 'Mounted combat in the Second Boer War', p. 16.
38 Ibid., pp. 16–17.
39 Ibid., p. 18.
40 Elgin Commission Report, p. 49.

41 Wilcox, 'Citizen mounted riflemen and the South African War of 1899–1902', pp. 15, 11–12.
42 Badsey, 'Mounted combat in the Second Boer War', pp. 17–19.
43 L.S. Amery cited in ibid.
44 Badsey, 'Mounted combat in the Second Boer War', p. 17.
45 Bridges, 'The New South Wales Lancers and the Anglo-Boer War', p. 162.
46 Anon., *A Veterinary History of the War in South Africa 1899–1902*, p. 230. Later published as F. Smith, *A Veterinary History of the War in South Africa 1899–1902*; hereafter Smith, *A Veterinary History*, meaning the 1910 edition.
47 Ibid., p. 239.
48 Maj G. Lee, OC NSWL, diary entry, 8 December 1899, AWM 1, 4/6. The NSWL had disembarked on 2–3 December 1899 and received their first operational tasking, and enemy fire, on 8 December.
49 Maj G. Lee, OC NSWL, diary entry, 23 December 1899, AWM 1, 4/6.
50 Badsey, 'Mounted combat in the Second Boer War', p. 16.
51 Capt J. Antill, OC NSWMR to AAG NSW, 8 February 1900, AWM 1, 4/8. 'Mealies' is a common term in South Africa for maize (or corn), and a waler is a horse bred in New South Wales, originally for the British Indian Army in the nineteenth century.
52 Capt J. Antill, OC NSWMR to AAG NSW, 12 March 1900, AWM 1, 4/8.
53 Badsey, 'Mounted combat in the Second Boer War', p. 15; Wilcox, *Australia's Boer War*, p. 133.
54 Spence, 'To shoot and ride', pp. 125–6.
55 Badsey, 'Mounted combat in the Second Boer War', p. 18.
56 Beckett, 'The South African War and the late Victorian army', p. 36.
57 Lt Granville Ryrie to wife, 13 August 1900, Sir Granville Ryrie, Letters, NLA MS986.
58 Green, *The Story of the Australian Bushmen*, p. 168.
59 'African horse sickness', in *Foreign Animal Diseases* ('The Gray Book'), www.vet.uga.edu; Parsonson, *Vets at War*, pp. 23–4.
60 Green, *The Story of the Australian Bushmen*, p. 24.
61 Parsonson, *Vets at War*, p. 20.
62 Badsey, 'Mounted combat in the Second Boer War', p. 15.
63 Badsey, 'Fire and the sword', p. 233.
64 Smith, *A Veterinary History*, pp. 186, 226; Spence, 'To shoot and ride', p. 121.
65 Smith, *A Veterinary History*, p. 227.
66 Badsey, 'Mounted combat in the Second Boer War', p. 18.
67 Smith, *A Veterinary History*, p. 186.
68 Assistant IG of Remounts, to IG of Remounts, War Office, 8 February 1900, cited in ibid., p. 143.
69 Marquis of Tullibardine, evidence, Elgin Commission Report: *Minutes of Evidence*, vol. 2, p. 451.
70 Col Douglas Haig, evidence, in ibid., p. 403.
71 Lt-Gen Sir John French, evidence, in ibid., p. 301.
72 Green, *The Story of the Australian Bushmen*, p. 128.

73 Spence, 'To shoot and ride', p. 123.
74 Chamberlain, 'The Wilmansrust affair', pp. 49–50.
75 Orders Books, 5th Queensland Imperial Bushmen, 15, 22 and 23 April 1901, and other various dates, NAA MP744/14/05.
76 Capt J. Antill, OC NSWMR to AAG NSW, 16 January 1900, AWM 1, 4/8.
77 Maj G. Lee, OC NSWL to CSO NSW, 8 July 1900, AWM 1, 4/6.
78 Maj Percy Ricardo to son, 29 September 1900, Ricardo Papers, 1900–27, NLA MS 1928.
79 Anglesey, *A History of the British Cavalry 1816–1919*, vol. 4, 1899 to 1913, p. 316; Smith, A *Veterinary History*, pp. 230–2.
80 Capt J. Antill, OC NSWMR, to AAG NSW, 16 January 1900, AWM 1, 4/8.
81 Capt J. Antill, OC NSWMR, cited in Wallace, *The Australians at the Boer War*, p. 64.
82 Col J.C. Lyster, 'Commonwealth military forces in New South Wales: The standard of efficiency of the Commonwealth military forces', lecture delivered at the United Service Institution, Sydney, 12 May 1905, NAA B168, 1906/1604 (hereafter Lyster, 'Commonwealth military forces in New South Wales').
83 Elgin Commission Report, p. 79.
84 Badsey, 'Fire and the sword', p. 138.
85 Elgin Commission Report, p. 80.
86 Wilcox, *Australia's Boer War*, pp. 375–6.
87 Lt Granville Ryrie to wife, 30 August 1900, Sir Granville Ryrie, Letters, NLA MS986.
88 Elgin Commission Report, p. 80.
89 Lt Granville Ryrie to wife, 22 May 1900, Sir Granville Ryrie, Letters, NLA MS986.
90 Elgin Commission Report, p. 80.
91 Green, *The Story of the Australian Bushmen*, p. 62.
92 Wilcox, *Australia's Boer War*, p. 191.
93 Wilcox, 'Citizen mounted riflemen and the South African War of 1899–1902', p. 18; Wilcox, *Australia's Boer War*, p. 191.
94 Wilcox, *Australia's Boer War*, pp. 109–11, 204–9.
95 Orders Book, 5th Queensland Imperial Bushmen, 3 August 1901, NAA MP744/14/6.
96 Orders Book, 5th Queensland Imperial Bushmen, 31 January 1901, NAA MP744/14/6.
97 Wilcox, *Australia's Boer War*, pp. 325–7.
98 Maj J. Antill cited in Bridges, 'New South Wales and the Anglo-Boer War', p. 603. Antill was often called a martinet after his controversial role at the Nek in 1915.

3 The Hutton era

1 Perry, 'Military reforms of General Sir Edward Hutton in the Commonwealth of Australia, 1902–04', pp. 36–7.
2 Hutton, *Minute Upon the Defence of Australia*, 7 April 1902, pp. 1–2, NAA B168, 1902/2688. Herafter, Hutton, *Minute Upon the Defence of Australia*.

3 Ibid., pp. 1–6.
4 Defence Scheme for the Commonwealth of Australia, July 1904, NAA B168, 1904/185.
5 Hutton, *Minute Upon the Defence of Australia*, p. 4.
6 Ibid., pp. 3–4; Hutton, *The Defence and Defensive Power of Australia*, pp. 15, 19; Hutton to Minister of Defence, 8 July 1903, NAA B168, 1902/2688, pt 6.
7 Defence Scheme for the Commonwealth of Australia, July 1904, NAA B168, 1904/18; Militia and Volunteer Peace and War Establishments, pp. 6–7, NAA B168, 1902/2688. A light horse regiment of four squadrons would have to find 6 officers, 3 staff sergeants, 16 sergeants, 12 artificers, and 250 rank and file in order to bring itself up to war establishment. For the financial motivations see Palazzo, *The Australian Army*, p. 23.
8 Bingham, 'The Australian soldier', p. 1169.
9 Palazzo, *The Australian Army*, pp. 22, 32.
10 Wilcox, 'Australia's citizen army', p. 157.
11 Aside from his experiences in South Africa, Hutton had maintained other connections with Australia's mounted troops and had been, since 1896, honorary colonel of the New South Wales Mounted Rifles (anon., *A Short History of the New South Wales Mounted Rifles, 1888–1913*, pp. 34–5).
12 Wilcox, 'Australia's citizen army', pp. 105–10.
13 Weick, *The Volunteer Movement in Western Australia*, p. 58.
14 Col G.H. Chippindall, Report of the Commandant of the Local Forces of West Australia for the Twelve Months ending 30th June 1901, NAA B168, 02/5748. Western Australia had briefly considered a cavalry officer to command their forces in 1898 owing to his possible value in creating a local mounted force but did not pursue the matter (Governor G. Smith to Sir John Forrest, 26 March 1898, PRO-WA: WAS 527, 1505/1895).
15 Wyatt, *A Lion in the Colony*, p. 51; Wyatt, *With the Volunteers*, p. 65.
16 Establishments and Strength of 12th LHR, NAA B168, 1903/1489 pt 8.
17 Wyatt, *With the Volunteers*, p. 68.
18 Return of Establishment of Military Forces (Militia), 1898–1902, AWM 3, 02/673. New South Wales infantry establishments for the period stayed at about 2500 men, Victoria at about 1900 men and Queensland between 1200 and 1300 men.
19 Ibid.
20 Agent-General for Queensland to Under-Secretary of State, Colonial Office, 12 December 1899, QLD 34638, Colonial Office 234/69, PRO-AJCP.
21 Minute regarding VMR enrolments, 2 July 1900, NAA B3756, 1900/6576.
22 Victorian Commandant, date unknown, 1900, NAA B3756, 1900/6576. This seems to have been an attempt to combine the traditional quasi-military endeavour of military-sponsored rifle clubs, in which some basic drill instruction was common and for which the government provided rifles, with some form of mounted activity.
23 Minutes of Meeting between Victorian Minister of Defence, Colonial Commandant and Deputation for Metropolitan Cavalry Corps, 28 February 1901, AWM 3, 02/479.

24 Hutton to Secretary of Defence, 17 March 1902, AWM 3, 02/479.
25 Lt-Col Onslow, CO NSWMR, to AAG Sydney, 24 October 1902, AWM 3, 02/2809.
26 Return of Establishment of Military Forces (Militia), 1898–1902, AWM 3, 02/673.
27 Chief Secretary's Office to the Governor and Executive Council, 13 June 1900; SRNSW: box 5/6550, item 00/11902; Haken, 'Lineage and development of NSW military forces', section 117.
28 Information on the NSW Border Scouts, Brig-Gen Finn, NSW Commandant, to Lt-Col W.T. Bridges, AQMG, 23 June 1903, AWM 3, 03/677 pt 2.
29 Rates of pay for NSW Lancers Regiment, NAA B168, 1901/3425.
30 Extract of QDF Regulations attached to, Commandant QDF to Minister of Defence, 8 November 1901, NAA B168, 1901/4387; Wilcox, 'Australia's citizen army', p. 209.
31 Rates of pay for Victorian forces, 1901, NAA B168, 1901/3425.
32 Federal Military Committee, 1901, NAA B168, 1901/4532.
33 Figures derived from: Strength of the Commonwealth Forces, 1 July 1901, Federal Military Committee, 1901, NAA B168, 1901/4532; Costs of defence, year ending 30 June 1901, NAA B168, 1901/3716.
34 Strength of the Commonwealth Forces, 1 July 1901, Federal Military Committee, 1901, NAA B168, 1901/4532.
35 Wilkinson, 'Australian army reorganisation', pp. 77–8; Wilkinson, *Australian Cavalry*, p. 45.
36 Minister for Defence to Hutton, 18 December 1901, NAA A2657, vol. 1.
37 Wilcox, 'Citizen mounted riflemen', p. 19.
38 Denison, *Modern Cavalry*, p. 13.
39 Hutton, 'The evolution of mounted infantry', p. 373.
40 Sir George Chesney quoted in ibid., p. 377. Hutton ultimately maintained a sensible and diplomatic position in the cavalry and mounted rifle/infantry debates. In a 1906 article he attacked 'some enthusiasts' who believed that well-trained regular cavalry could be completely replaced by mounted infantry. Dominion-provided mounted rifle units could, however, be used as a valuable support to regular cavalry. It was a neat way to combine two of his long-standing hobby horses: imperial defence cooperation and dominion mounted rifles organisations, which he had had such a hand in fostering (Hutton, 'The cavalry of Greater Britain', p. 24).
41 Hutton, 'The evolution of mounted infantry', pp. 376–8.
42 Hutton, *The Defence and Defensive Power of Australia*, pp. 16–17.
43 Hutton, 'The cavalry of Greater Britain', p. 24.
44 Hutton to Field Marshal Lord Roberts, 19 August 1903, Hutton Papers, 50085; see also Badsey, *Doctrine and Reform in the British Cavalry*, pp. 170–4.
45 *Mounted Service Manual for Mounted Troops of the Australian Commonwealth*, p. 15; Australian Regulations and Orders for the Military Forces of the Commonwealth, Provisional Edition, 1904, sect 14, NAA A2657, vol. 1.
46 Hutton to Secretary of Defence, 24 March 1902, NAA A6443, 281.
47 Carmen, *Light Horse Volunteers and Mounted Rifle Volunteers*, passim.

48 White, 'Light horse of Australia', p. 80.
49 Hutton, *Minute Upon the Defence of Australia*; Hutton, 'The cavalry of Greater Britain', p. 24.
50 Militia and Volunteer Peace and War Establishments, pp. 7, 19, NAA B168, 1902/2688. A light horse regiment of four squadrons had a war establishment of 581 personnel all ranks, an infantry regiment 1010 all ranks. Neither figure includes the prescribed attachments.
51 Ibid., pp. 5, 8–9. A light horse squadron at peace establishment would total 72 personnel, with 16 in each troop and another 8 fulfilling squadron command or integral support functions (trumpeters, farriers, armourers etc). The war establishment would expand the squadron to 135 personnel with 31 in each troop and 11 in squadron command or support appointments. In neither establishment was a specific permanent squadron headquarters allowed for, and the distribution of command and support appointments was discretionary in order to 'best meet local conditions'. The half-squadrons allocated to the Garrison Forces would remain on the peace establishment upon mobilisation.
52 Australian Regulations and Orders for the Military Forces of the Commonwealth, Provisional Edition, 1904, part 8, sections 8, 10, NAA A2657, vol. 1.
53 Militia and Volunteer Peace and War Establishments, pp. 6–7, NAA B168, 1902/2688.
54 Australian Regulations and Orders for the Military Forces of the Commonwealth, Provisional Edition, 1904, part 8, section 11, NAA A2657, vol. 1.
55 Hutton, *Minute Upon the Defence of Australia*, p. 5.
56 Ibid.; Australian Regulations and Orders for the Military Forces of the Commonwealth, Provisional Edition, 1904, part 8, section 37, NAA A2657, vol. 1.
57 Hutton, *Minute Upon the Defence of Australia*, p. 5.
58 Hutton to DQMG, 6 September 1902, NAA B168, 1902/6660.
59 Hutton to Lt-Gen T. Kelly Kenny, 4 August 1902, Hutton Papers, 50097.
60 Hutton, Preface, *Mounted Service Manual for Mounted Troops of the Australian Commonwealth*, pp. x–xiv.
61 Wilcox, 'Australia's citizen army', pp. 164, 199.
62 Secretary of Defence to the authorising officer, Military Forces, Sydney, 6 September 1904, NAA B168, 1902/6660.
63 Wilcox, 'Australia's citizen army', p. 199.
64 Hutton, Preface, *Mounted Service Manual for Mounted Troops of the Australian Commonwealth*, pp. xii–xiii. Emphasis in the original.
65 Hutton, *Minute Upon the Defence of Australia*, p. 4.
66 Frank Wilkinson, 'Australian army reorganisation', p. 77; Bingham, 'The Australian soldier', p. 1169.
67 Senator Lt-Col J.C. Neild, 'The naval defence of Australia', NAA B168, 1902/2688, pt 7.
68 Victoria would not initially have to support two complete brigades as one of the regiments of the 4th ALH Brigade, the 12th LHR, would be raised in

Tasmania. Only later in the decade would Victoria's establishment be increased to two full brigades. New South Wales would support a full six regiments from the start.
69 Wilcox, 'Australia's citizen army', p. 159.
70 Ibid., pp. 200–2.
71 Extract from *Kerang Times*, 22 September 1903, in NAA B168, 02/2688.
72 Wilcox, 'Australia's citizen army', p. 203; Hutton to Secretary of Defence, 19 September 1903, NAA B168, 02/2688 pt 4.
73 Wilcox, 'Australia's citizen army', pp. 203–8.
74 Brig-Gen H. Finn, Commandant NSW, to DAG Melbourne, 28 October 1903, AWM 3, 1710.
75 Wilcox, 'Australia's citizen army', pp. 208–9.
76 Extract from *Age*, 19 June 1903, NAA B168, 02/1631.
77 Brig-Gen J. Gordon, Commandant Victoria, to Col J. Hoad, DAG and CSO, 20 June 1903, NAA B168, 02/1631; Hutton to Secretary of Defence, 3 July 1903, NAA B168, 02/1631.
78 Lt A. Rushall to District Headquarters, Victoria, 17 July 1903, NAA B168, 02/1631.
79 Secretary of Defence to Hutton, 27 July 1903, NAA B168, 02/1631.
80 Brig-Gen. Gordon to DAG and CSO, 10 August 1903, NAA B168, 02/1631.
81 Hutton to Secretary of Defence, 20 October 1903, NAA B168, 02/1631.
82 Minister for Defence to Hutton, 6 November 1903, NAA B168, 02/1631.
83 The splitting of NSW units was not restricted to the Lancer Regiment. Both the NSW Mounted Rifles and 1st Australian Horse were also to be split. From the NSW Lancers would come the 1st and 4th LHRs, the NSW Mounted Rifles would provide the nuclei of the 2nd and 5th LHRs and the 1st Australian Horse that of the 3rd and 6th LHRs (Burness, 'New South Wales cavalry', pp. 249–50).
84 Col Burns to NSW Lancer officers, 1902, in Vernon, *The Royal New South Wales Lancers*, p. 66.
85 Hon. Sir John Forrest, 30 April 1902, *Commonwealth Parliamentary Debates*, vol. 11, p. 12099.
86 Wilkinson, *Australian Cavalry*, pp. 2, 41–4.
87 Hon. John Watson, 30 April 1902, *Commonwealth Parliamentary Debates*, vol. 11, p. 12099.
88 Vernon, *The Royal New South Wales Lancers*, pp. 66–7. For the envisaged use of the lance by certain units during wartime see correspondence between Hutton and Minster for Defence, A. Dawson, 1904, NAA B168, 1903/4892; *Mounted Service Manual for Mounted Troops of the Australian Commonwealth*, p. 15; Australian Regulations and Orders for the Military Forces of the Commonwealth, Provisional Edition, 1904, sect 14, NAA A2657, vol. 1.
89 Buckley, *Sword and Lance*, p. 202. According to the author, this mass resignation took place in March 1903.
90 Perry, 'Military reforms of General Sir Edward Hutton in the Commonwealth of Australia: 1902–04', pp. 44–5; Wilcox, 'Australia's citizen army', p. 189.

91 Wilcox, 'Australia's citizen army', pp. 189–90.
92 Extract from *Herald* (Melbourne), 18 March 1903, included in correspondence, NAA B168, 1903/849 pt 3.
93 DAG and CSO to Commandant Victoria, 20 March 1903, NAA B168, 1903/849 pt 3.
94 Hutton to Sir John Forrest, 25 March 1903, Hutton Papers, 50084/2E.
95 Sir John Forrest to Hutton, 26 March 1903, Hutton Papers, 50084/2E.
96 Sir Edmund Barton, Prime Minister, to Sir John Forrest, Minister of Defence, 31 March 1903, communicated to Hutton, 2 April 1903, AWM 3, 03/677 pt 2.
97 Wilcox, 'Australia's citizen army', p. 192.
98 Hutton, 'Our comrades of Greater Britain', pp. 27–8.
99 Parliament of the Commonwealth of Australia, *Second Annual Report upon the Military Forces of the Commonwealth of Australia by Major-General Sir Edward Hutton*, p. 13.
100 Wilcox, 'Australia's citizen army', p. 163.
101 *Narrative of Instructional Operations by a Cavalry Division ... and Remarks Thereon By Major-General Sir Edward Hutton*, pp. 6–7, NAA B168, 1902/618.
102 Ibid.
103 Ibid, p. 7.
104 Ibid.; italics in the original. The relevant order was paragraph 1 of GO no. 247 (subparagraph 4), 27 October 1903.
105 *Narrative of Instructional Operations by a Cavalry Division ... and Remarks Thereon By Major-General Sir Edward Hutton*, pp. 6–7, NAA B168, 1902/618.
106 Hutton to Minister for Defence, 15 February 1902, NAA MP84/1, 1930/1/12.
107 Hutton believed that the decision in 1903 by the Prince of Wales to accept the position of Honorary Colonel of the Australian Light Horse was recognition of the services performed by Australian mounted troops in South Africa (report of Hutton's speech at Melbourne Lord Mayor's Banquet, *Age*, 10 November 1903, NAA B168, 6238).
108 Confidential officer reports, 1–6 LHRs, 1904, NAA MP84/1, 430/2/44.
109 Hutton to Secretary of Defence, 22 November 1902, NAA MP84/1, 1930/1/12.
110 Ibid.
111 Parliament of the Commonwealth of Australia, *Second Annual Report upon the Military Forces of the Commonwealth of Australia by Major-General Sir Edward Hutton*, p. 13.
112 Hutton to Secretary of Defence, 22 November 1902, NAA MP84/1, 1930/1/12.
113 *Narrative of Instructional Operations by a Cavalry Division ... and Remarks Thereon By Major-General Sir Edward Hutton*, p. 6, NAA B168, 1902/618.

114 *Narrative of a Staff Ride by the Commonwealth Military Forces of Tasmania . . . 18 & 19 February 1904, and Remarks Thereon by Major-General Sir Edward Hutton*, p. 6, NAA A1194, 12.42/4796.
115 Hutton to Secretary of Defence, 29 June 1903, AWM 3, 03/624.
116 Secretary of Defence to Hutton, 1 June 1903, and Hutton to Secretary of Defence, 8 July 1903, AWM 3, 03/624.
117 Hutton to Secretary of Defence, 2 June 1903, AWM 3, 03/624.
118 Hutton to Minister for Defence, 8 April 1903, AWM 3, 03/624; *Mounted Service Manual for Mounted Troops of the Australian Commonwealth*, p. 15.
119 Correspondence between Hutton and the Minster for Defence, A. Dawson, 1904, NAA B168, 1903/4892; Hutton to Minister for Defence, 8 April 1903, AWM 3, 03/624.
120 Col H. Le Mesurier, Chief of Ordnance, to Secretary of Defence, 30 May 1905, NAA B168, 04/6604.
121 Commandant Qld to Secretary of Defence, 20 July 1905, NAA B168, 04/6604; comments by Maj N.J. Moore, CO 18th LHR, Western Australia: Meeting of Commanding Officers, 1 May 1905, NAA B168, 1905/1678.
122 Comments by Cols Lassetter and Carrington, NSW: Commanding Officer's Conference, 16 March 1905, NAA B168, 1905/1678.
123 *Herald* (Melbourne), 13 June 1903 cited in Wilcox, 'Australia's citizen army', p. 198.
124 Lt-Col D. McLeish, Commander 3rd LH Bde, to AAG&CSO, 23 August 1907, NAA MP84/1, 1977/2/25; *Herald* (Melbourne), 13 June 1903, cited in Wilcox, 'Australia's citizen army', p. 198. Requests to get rid of the white adornments was considered in 1908, but most brigade commanders and the Military Board though the change not worth the trouble (Military Board decision of 31 March 1908, minuted to Chief of Ordnance, 13 April 1908, NAA MP84/1, 1977/2/25).
125 Wilcox, 'Australia's citizen army', pp. 260–1.
126 Vernon, *The Royal New South Wales Lancers*, pp. 67, 72. It is not clear when this practice stopped, although it seems unlikely that it would have continued after the introduction of Universal Training in 1912.
127 Hutton to Secretary of the Army Council (Britain), Col Sir Edward Ward, 5 June 1904, Hutton Papers, 50098.
128 Hutton, 'The cavalry of Greater Britain', pp. 25–6.
129 Bou, 'Modern cavalry', p. 113.

4 Unfulfilled promise

1 Palazzo, *The Australian Army*, p. 34; Grey, *The Australian Army*, pp. 138, 162.
2 RO No 3, TMI, 29 January 1903, AWM 1, 19/1.
3 Comments by Maj N.J. Moore, CO 18th LHR, Western Australia: Meeting of Commanding Officers, 1 May 1905, NAA B168, 1905/1678.
4 RO No 19, 12th LHR (TMI), 28 July 1904, AWM 1, 19/1.

5   Lt-Col W.T. Bridges, AQMG, to Qld Commandant, 3 July 1903, AWM 3, 03/677 pt 1; Lt-Col W.T. Bridges, AQMG, to Secretary of Defence, 14 September 1904, AWM 3, 03/600.
6   Lt-Col W.T. Bridges, AQMG, to Tasmanian Commandant, 3 July 1903, AWM 3, 03/677 pt 1; HQ Melbourne to SA Commandant, 3 July 1903, AWM 3, 03/677 pt 2.
7   RO no. 3, 12th LHR, 31 January 1907, AWM 1, 19/2, pp. 111–12.
8   Annual Establishments of the Commonwealth Military Forces of NSW, 1906–07, AWM 1, 16/2.
9   Comments by an unnamed light horse officer, Victoria: Meeting of... Officers with the Minister of Defence, 23 February 1905, NAA B168, 1905/1678; Acting Commandant Qld, Lt-Col W. Plumer, to DAG & CSO Melbourne, 19 December 1903, AWM 3, 03/677 pt 22; comments by Lt-Col Granville Ryrie, CO 3rd LHR, New South Wales Commanding Officer's Conference, 16 March 1905, NAA B168, 1905/1678.
10 Annual Return of Military and Naval Resources, 31 December 1904, NAA B168, 1903/1489 pt 8.
11 Lt-Col Martin, CO 12th AIR, to Military Board, date unknown, NAA B168/0, 1903/1489 pt 8.
12 Lt-Col Reade, SA Acting Commandant, to DAG Melbourne, 1 July 1904, AWM 3, 03/677 pt 2.
13 NSW Commandant to DAG Melbourne, 13 July 1904, NAA B168, 02/2688 pt 4; see also Anon, 'Some Notes on the Regiments of New South Wales (continued)', p. 27, reprinted from *Evening News*, 23 November 1910.
14 Capt Little to Commander 4th LH Bde, 17 February 1905, NAA B168, 1905/9151 pt 2.
15 Return of parades by Casterton Detachment attached to correspondence, Victorian Headquarters to Captain Little, 6 February 1906, NAA B168, 1905/9151 pt 2.
16 Inspector-General's Report on his Visit to 1 Sqn, 17th LHR on 17 March 1906, NAA B168/0, 1906/5262.
17 Senator J.C. Neild in Parliament, 1 December 1904, cited in Wilcox, 'Australia's citizen army', p. 199.
18 Wilcox, 'Australia's citizen army', p. 251.
19 There were at least two proposals of this kind. The first was by James Kenneth Mackay, the invasion novelist and founder of the 1st Australian Horse, who in 1910 unsuccessfully advocated the recruitment of a volunteer force of mounted troops drawn from men ineligible to serve in the light horse for a variety of reasons, including age (Col Kenneth Mackay to AAG&CSO Sydney, 2 May 1910, forwarded to Secretary of Defence, NAA MP84/1, 1970/1/65). The second was from the periodic calls to expand the role of cyclist troops in infantry regiments. In 1905 the Secretary of the NSW League of Wheelmen had written to the Minister for Defence asking that he consider the creation of a regiment of cyclists a thousand strong in New South Wales, but the proposal foundered on costs (A. O'Brien, Secretary of the NSW League of Wheelmen, to Minister for Defence, 16 July

1905, NAA B168/0, 05/10849). Later the Military Board also proposed, without result, expanding the use of cyclists (Military Board Meeting, 19 July 1907, NAA A2653, 1907–08, vol. 2, p. 58). Although cyclists were used valuably in communications roles, their utility as mobile infantry never seems to have been of particular interest to the authorities until cyclist companies were formed as part of the 1st AIF.

20 Notes submitted with Report of the Committee of Officers on Organisation of Military Forces, 12 September 1906, p. 27, NAA B173, S06/60.
21 Lt-Col C. Cox, CO 1st LHR, to Col James Burns, Commander 1st LH Bde, 22 October 1906, NAA MP84/1, 1903/6/9.
22 Col James Burns, Commander 1st LH Bde, to AAG&CSO Victoria Barracks Sydney, 25 October 1906, NAA MP84/1, 1913/6/9.
23 NSW Commandant to DAG, 16 November 1906, NAA MP84/1, 1913/6/9.
24 *Light Horse Manual for the Drill Training and Exercise of the Light Horse Regiments of Australia*, 1907; Proceedings of a Board of Officers at Victoria Barracks Sydney for Compiling a Drill and Training Manual for the Australian Light Horse, 4 December 1906, NAA MP84/1, 1913/6/11.
25 White, 'Light horse of Australia', p. 83.
26 *Light Horse Manual*, 1907, passim.
27 Palazzo, *The Australian Army*, pp. 39–44.
28 Holloway, *Hooves, Wheels and Tracks*, p. 100; Anon., 'A Short History of the New South Wales Mounted Rifles 1888–1913', pp. 43–4; Vernon, *The Royal New South Wales Lancers*, p. 71.
29 Vernon, *The Royal New South Wales Lancers*, p. 71.
30 Notes submitted with Report of the Committee of Officers on Organisation of Military Forces, 12 September 1906, p. 27, NAA B173, S06/60.
31 Wilcox, 'Australia's citizen army', p. 238; comments by Maj N. Moore, CO 18th LHR, Western Australia: Meeting of Commanding Officers, 1 May 1905, NAA B168, 1905/1678.
32 Commonwealth Military Forces of Western Australia, Return of Easter Camp of Training, 1909, NAA MP84/1, 2002/6/82; Commonwealth Military Forces, Victoria, Report on Annual Continuous Training, 1911, NAA A1194, 12.30/4547.
33 Vernon, *The Royal New South Wales Lancers*, pp. 69–70, 74–5; Minister for Home Affairs to Minster for Defence, 24 December 1913; Minister for Defence to Minister for Home Affairs, 8 January 1913, NAA MP84/1, 202/4/439. By the time of the ceremonies the 1st LH Bde had been renamed the 3rd LH Bde.
34 Vernon, *The Royal New South Wales Lancers*, pp. 74–5.
35 Commonwealth Military Forces of Victoria, Return of Camps of Continuous Training, 1909, NAA MP84/1, 2002/6/82. Victorian attendances against strength for 1909 were poor across the board: 7th LHR – 75 per cent; 8th LHR – 62 per cent; 9th LHR – 64 per cent; 10th LHR – 80 per cent; 11th LHR – 66 per cent; 5 Sqn, 10th LHR (Garrison Force) – 69 per cent; 6 Sqn, 10th LHR (Garrison Force) – 82 per cent. Only the two brigade headquarters, with strengths of three men each, achieved 100 per cent attendance.

36 Commonwealth Military Forces of Western Australia, Return of Easter Camp of Training, 1909, NAA MP84/1, 2002/6/82.
37 Commonwealth Military Forces of Queensland, Return of Camps of Continuous Training, 1908–09, NAA MP84/1, 2002/6/82.
38 Lyster, 'Commonwealth military forces in New South Wales'; Commander 1st LH Bde, 3 July 1912, NAA MP84/1, 202/4/439.
39 White, 'Light Horse of Australia', pp. 82–3; Tasmanian Commandant to Secretary of Defence, 10 December 1909, NAA MP84/1 2002/1/47.
40 Lyster, 'Commonwealth military forces in New South Wales'.
41 Everett, 'The future use of cavalry and our light horse', p. 99.
42 Syllabus for Light Horse School of Instruction, attached to correspondence from Commandant Tasmania to Secretary of Defence, date unknown, NAA MP84/1, 1994/1/44. Schools of instruction were sometimes of much longer duration and light horse officers in Western Australia in 1903 took part in a three-week course to qualify for their ranks (Lt-Col P. Ricardo, Commandant WA, to DAG & CSO Melbourne, 23 December 1903, AWM 3, 03/677 pt 2).
43 Report on a Staff Ride held in South Australia under the direction of the Chief of Intelligence in November 1907, p. 6, NAA A1194, 12.42/4632; Report on a Staff Ride held in Queensland, under the direction of the Commandant, in September 1908, p. 11.
44 *Report of the Conference of Militia Officers, 1912*, pp. 9, 22–3.
45 CGS to Military Board, 13 March 1911, NAA MP84/1, 1930/2/30.
46 Crouch, 'The Australian militia', pp. 389–90.
47 Sen George Pearce, Minister for Defence, address by the minister in *Report of the Conference of Militia Officers, 1912*, p. 7.
48 Everett, 'The future use of cavalry and our light horse', pp. 99, 101.
49 Ibid., p. 100.
50 Comments by Col Vernon and others in ibid., p. 103.
51 Comments by Lt-Col George Lee in ibid., p. 102.
52 Secretary of Military Board to State Commandants, Composition of Committee for ALH Manual Revision, 23 June 1909, NAA MP84/1, 1913/6/40.
53 *Light Horse Manual for the Drill Training and Exercise of the Light Horse Regiments of Australia*, 1910, pp. 212, 257, 271.
54 Comments by Col W. Vernon regarding proof copy of light horse manual, undated but probably October–November 1909, NAA MP84/1, 1913/6/59; remarks by Maj F.A. Maxwell, Staff Officer 3rd LH Bde, attached to correspondence, DMT to State Commandants, 3 August 1910, NAA MP84/1, 1913/6/70.
55 Palazzo, *The Australian Army*, pp. 37–45.
56 *Memorandum on the Defence of Australia by Field Marshal Viscount of Khartoum*, passim, p. 6.
57 Palazzo, *The Australian Army*, pp. 43, 47–8.
58 War Establishments of the Australian Military Forces, 1912, NAA A1194, 22.14/6970.

59 Burness, 'New South Wales cavalry', p. 250; Numerical Order of Brigades and Regiments, Proceedings of Military Board, 1 August 1912, NAA MP84/1, 1937/1/252.
60 Wilcox, 'Australia's citizen army', pp. 304, 312; *General Scheme of Defence for Australia. Report of Committee of Officers Appointed by the Minister of Defence to Consider and Report Upon the General Scheme of Defence for Australia as Submitted by the Committee of Imperial Defence*, p. 7, NAA B173/0, 506/60.
61 RO No 1, 26th LHR (TMI), 21 February 1913, AWM 1, 19/3, pp. 139, 141. Under the new establishments a light horse squadron would have 118 men, all ranks, in peacetime and 154 in wartime. Annual Establishments of Personnel, 1912–13. AWM 27, 301/9; War Establishments of the Australian Military Forces, 1912, NAA A1194, 22.14/6970.
62 War Office, *Yeomanry and Mounted Rifles Training*, parts 1 & 2, 1912; Commonwealth Military Forces, military order 625, 1912.
63 War Office, *Field Service Regulations*, pt 1: *Operations, 1909* (reprinted with amendments, 1912), p. 15.
64 RO no. 4, 26th LHR (TMI), 12 April 1913, AWM 1, 19/3, pp. 156–7.
65 Palazzo, *The Australian Army*, p. 51; Wilcox, *For Hearths and Homes*, p. 59.
66 Howell-Price, *The Light Horse Pocket Book*, pp. 18–19; Wilcox, *For Hearths and Homes*, p. 65; Comments by Maj N.J. Moore, CO 18th LHR, Western Australia: Meeting of Commanding Officers, 1 May 1905, NAA B168, 1905/1678.
67 Despite the principle it was an imperfect system as expansion occurred. Some gaps were left in the numbering sequence to facilitate the later raising of regiments, which never occurred owing to the intervention of the First World War. Other units that were raised, regardless of where they may have been formed, took a number from the bottom of the stack. For example Victoria would support the 13th, 15th, 16th, 17th, 19th, 20th and 29th LHRs. See Hall, *The Australian Light Horse*, pp. 70–1, for a detailed light horse order of battle for the time.
68 Numerical Order of Brigades and Regiments, Proceedings of Military Board, 1 August 1912, NAA MP84/1, 1937/1/252.
69 Hall, *The Australian Light Horse*, pp. 70–1.
70 *Annual Report by Major-General G.M. Kirkpatrick, C.B. Inspector-General of the Military Forces of the Commonwealth of Australia, 30 May 1912*, p. 8, NAA D845/1 41/1912.
71 Remarks on 16th, 17th, 22nd, 23rd and 24th LHRs for commanding officers by Inspector-General, 28 June and 3 July 1913, NAA D845/1, 46/1912.
72 Conway, 'The Australian light horseman', pp. 520–1. The experiment in home training was made by Lt-Col Findlater, CO 16th LHR.
73 CO 25th LHR to Headquarters, 5th MD, 31 July 1913, NAA A2023/0, A75/4/99.
74 Conway, 'The Australian light horseman', p. 521.

75 *Annual Report by Major-General G.M. Kirkpatrick*, 1912, p. 8.
76 Commonwealth Military Forces, Victoria, Report on Annual Continuous Training, 1911, NAA A1194, 12.30/4547.
77 Instructions for Training, 1913–14, NAA MP84/1, 2002/1/133.
78 Ibid.; *Extracts of the Annual Report of Major-General G.M. Kirkpatrick*, pp. 8–9, NAA A1194, 20.15/6699.
79 *Extracts of the Annual Report of Major-General G.M. Kirkpatrick*, pp. 8, NAA A1194, 20.15/6699.
80 *Resolutions of a Conference of Militia Officers, 1913*, p. 19, NAA A1194, 05.44/3011.
81 Ibid., p. 15.
82 *Report of the Conference of Militia Officers, 1912*, pp. 15, 44, resolution 89.
83 Comments by Lt-Col J. Paton, 2nd MD, in ibid., p. 44.
84 Recommendation of the Military Board, 17 December 1912, NAA A2023/1, A229/1/1; Finance Member of the Military Board to Secretary of Defence, 13 January 1913, NAA A2023/1, A229/1/1; AG to Secretary of Defence, 2 September 1913, NAA A2023/1, A229/1/1.
85 *Resolutions of a Conference of Militia Officers, 1913*, p. 17, NAA A1194, 05.44/3011; RO no. 11, 26th LHR (TMI), 12 December 1913, AWM 1, 19/3, pp. 176–7.
86 *Extracts of the Annual Report of Major-General G.M. Kirkpatrick*, 1913, p. 15, NAA A1194.
87 *Report on an Inspection of the Military Forces of the Commonwealth by General Ian Hamilton*, p. 36.
88 Hamilton in correspondence, cited in Hill, *Chauvel of the Light Horse*, p. 43; see also Hill, Introduction, in Gullett, *The AIF in Sinai and Palestine*, pp. xxxiv–xxxv.
89 *Report on an Inspection of the Military Forces of the Commonwealth by General Ian Hamilton*, pp. 36–8.
90 Comments by Lt-Col George Lee following, Everett, 'The future use of cavalry and our light horse', p. 102.
91 Everett, 'The future use of cavalry and our light horse', p. 99.
92 Palazzo, *The Australian Army*, pp. 70–1.
93 RO no. 18, 26th LHR, 12 November 1914, AWM 1, 19/4.
94 Palazzo, *The Australian Army*, pp. 70–1; Wilcox, 'Defending Australia', p. 21.
95 Return of troops doing duty on home defence, 26 May 1917, NAA B543, W246T/1/2393.
96 Report by the Military Board, 1917, cited in Palazzo, *The Australian Army*, p. 76.
97 Military Board meeting, 5 September 1914, cited in Palazzo, *The Australian Army*, p. 71.
98 2nd Light Horse Brigade, *Standing Orders, Camp: West Maitland, June 15th to June 26th 1915*.
99 Correspondence register regarding light horse formation, NAA B536, A229/8.

100 Annual Return of Military and Naval Resources, 31 December 1914, NAA B197, 1972/3/137; Annual Return of Military and Naval Resources, 31 December 1916, NAA B197, 1972/3/166.
101 The exact proportions of volunteers and UT-obligated men in the light horse during the war is unknown. In 1912–13 about a sixth of light-horsemen were serving as universal trainees (1064 of 6401 men in mid-1913). Whether this proportion can be projected forward to the war years is debatable.
102 Annual Return of Military and Naval Resources, 31 December 1916, NAA B197, 1972/3/166; Hall, *The Australian Light Horse*, pp. 75–6.
103 Australian Military Forces, military order 364, 3 August 1918, military order 388, 17 August 1918.
104 Palazzo, *The Australian Army*, pp. 75–6.
105 Australian Military Forces, Tables of Peace Organisation and Establishments, 1915–16, NAA A1194, 21.20/6895.
106 War Establishments of the Australian Military Forces, 1912, pp. 23, 26, NAA A1194, 22.14/6970; Military Board Meeting, recommendation no. 15, 1 July 1914, NAA A2653, 1914; see also Bou, 'An aspirational army'.
107 Palazzo, *The Australian Army*, pp. 71, 75.
108 Details of command appointments, NAA A2023, A95/2/27 and A2023, 95/6/68. For example the command of the 2nd, 5th, 9th and 28th LHRs had all passed to captains by the end of March 1915 (Palazzo, *The Australian Army*, pp. 71–2).
109 2nd Light Horse Brigade, *Standing Orders, Camp: West Maitland, June 15th to June 26th 1915*, p. 3. For example the command of the 2nd LH Bde had passed to Major F. Thrift by mid-1915 (Military Board Agenda, 3–4 March 1915, NAA A2653/1, 1915). The minutes of these days give an example of the frequent decisions the Military Board had make regarding unit command for the forces at home during the war.
110 Grey, *The Australian Army*, p. 55.
111 Beaumont, *Australian Defence: Sources and Statistics*, p. 116. The breakdown of conjugal status of the 1st AIF was: 81.62 per cent single, 17.38 per cent married, 0.84 per cent widowed and 0.16 per cent unknown.
112 Grey, *The Australian Army*, p. 55.
113 RO nos 6 and 7, 26th LHR, 14, 26 July 1915 and RO no. 12, 26th LHR, 15 October 1915, AWM 1, 19/4.
114 Palazzo, *The Australian Army*, p. 74; RO no. 1, 26th ALH, 27 January 1916, AWM 1, 19/4.
115 RO no. 5, 26th LHR, 3 February 1917, AWM 1, 19/4; Palazzo, *The Australian Army*, p. 74.
116 Camp order no. 4, 26th LHR, [?] March 1917, AWM 1, 19/4.
117 Grey, *The Australian Army*, pp. 74–5.
118 Citizen Forces Amalgamation Proposal, NAA MP367/1, 549/3/5.
119 Defalcations of Light Horse Accounts, NAA A1831, 1922/6569; Andrews, *The Department of Defence*, pp. 50–60. The total fraud was £67 012.18.6 and the amount recovered £19 726.5.7, leaving a balance of

£47 286.12.11 to be written off. A number of public servants also lost their jobs or were demoted as a result of this crime.
120 RO no. 3, 26th LHR, 15 June 1920 and RO no. 9, 26th LHR, 17 September 1919, AWM 1, 19/4.
121 Review of Citizen Force Training, 1920–21, NAA A1194, 12.30/4477.

5 The light-horsemen 1

1. Mr J. McDougal to OC NSW Regiment of Cavalry, 6 March 1890, SRNSW: CSC, box 5/5982, item 90/5944.
2. Mr Hudson to Maj-Gen. Richardson, NSW Commandant, 5 November 1888, SRNSW: CSC, box 5/5982, item 90/5944.
3. Calder, *Heroes and Gentlemen*, p. 20.
4. Unsigned, undated note attached to list of applications 1886–89, SRNSW: CSC, box 5/5982, item 90/5944.
5. Col W. Spalding to Principal Under Secretary, 17 August 1891, SRNSW: CSC, box 5/6038, item 91/10862.
6. Correspondence relating Lismore Cavalry Troop application, 1890, SRNSW: CSC, box 5/5982, item 90/5944.
7. Eyland, 'The New South Wales military forces 1870–1890', p. 20.
8. Undated and unsigned memorandum to Chief Secretary of Queensland, QSA: PRE/20. This item probably dates from late 1893 or early 1894.
9. Brig-Gen H. Finn, NSW Commandant, to DAG, Melbourne, 30 December 1903, AWM 3, 03/677 pt 2.
10. 'Strength and organisation of 1 and 3 Sqns, 13th LHR', 12 March 1909, NAA MP84/1, 713/3/10.
11. Cavalry Brigade Muster Roll, Sydney Troop 1885–89, *Royal New South Wales Lancers, Records 1888–1956*.
12. Cavalry Brigade Muster Roll, Illawarra Troop 1885–89, *Royal New South Wales Lancers, Records 1888–1956*.
13. Bridges, 'The New South Wales Lancers and the Anglo-Boer War', pp. 16–19.
14. Everett, 'The future use of cavalry and our light horse', p. 100.
15. Eyland, 'The New South Wales military forces 1870–1890', p. 29.
16. Correspondence relating to Lismore cavalry troop application, 1890, SRNSW: CSC, box 5/5982, item 90/5944.
17. Figures derived from the Muster Roll of the 6th LHR, 1907–10, AWM 1, 17/3. Sample taken by recording the details of all men with surnames starting with the letters A, B, C and F, 99 in total. Of these, 52 (51.48 per cent) were farmers or graziers and 24 (23.76 per cent) were stockmen or labourers.
18. Col W. Legge to Parliament, cited in Wyatt, *With the Volunteers*, p. 65.
19. Hon. Mr Baker, South Australia, *Parliamentary Debates*, 2nd Session, 1st Parliament, 1858, p. 175.
20. F. Wright to J. Brunker, Chief Secretary, 1 March 1895, SRNSW: CSC, box 5/6254, item 95/4126.
21. Bridges, 'The New South Wales Lancers and the Anglo-Boer War', pp. 14–16.

22 Vernon, *The Royal New South Wales Lancers*, pp. 78–9.
23 Bridges, 'The New South Wales Lancers and the Anglo-Boer War', pp. 14, 15, 31.
24 Wilkinson, *Australian Cavalry*, p. 10.
25 Bridges, 'The New South Wales Lancers and the Anglo-Boer War', p. 19.
26 Vernon, *The Royal New South Wales Lancers*, p. 398. He enlisted as a trooper on 6 June 1891 and received his commission as a captain on 23 July 1891.
27 Wilkinson, *Australian Cavalry*, p. 18.
28 Eyland, 'The New South Wales Military Forces 1870–1890', p. 33.
29 Hill, *Chauvel of the Light Horse*, p. 7.
30 General Order for Victoria, no. 13, 22 January 1884, cited in Lt-Gen Sir Carl Jess, *Report of the Activities of the Australian Military Forces, 1929–1939*, AWM 1, 20/9, pt 3.
31 Everett, 'The future use of cavalry, and our light horse', p. 100.
32 Twining and Twining, *South Australian Military Volunteers for 1855*, p. 21.
33 Burness, 'Australian colonial forces: A sketch', pp. 8–9.
34 Bridges, 'The New South Wales Lancers and the Anglo-Boer War', p. 24; Dunn and Blundell (eds), *The Boys in Green*, p. 5.
35 Bridges, 'The New South Wales Lancers and the Anglo-Boer War', p. 20. For example the Murrumbidgee troop of the New South Wales Cavalry was disbanded in December 1892 when no suitable officer could be found (Vernon, *The Royal New South Wales Lancers*, p. 18).
36 Lt-Col Mackay to Governor of New South Wales, Earl Beauchamp, 18 July 1899, PRO-AJCP: NSW no. 24346, Colonial Office, 201/629.
37 Hutton to Secretary of Defence, 22 December 1902, AWM 3, 02/2846.
38 Hutton to Secretary of Defence, 28 May 1903, AWM 3, 03/677 pt 2.
39 Adjutant General to Secretary of Defence, 20 September 1909, NAA MP84/1, 1930/2/21.
40 Annual Report for the Year 1907, p. 16.
41 *Report of the Conference of Militia Officers*, pp. 15, 44.
42 Howell-Price, *The Light Horse Pocket Book*, p. 19.
43 Jess, *Report on the Activities of the Australian Military Forces*, p. 26.
44 Western Australia: Meeting of Commanding Officers, pp. 6–7, NAA B168, 1905/1678. Reginald Spencer Browne cited in Wilcox, 'Australia's citizen army', p. 31.
45 Schmitt, 'The Victorian Mounted Rifles in Gippsland', p. 12.
46 Brig H. Finn, NSW Commandant, to AQMG, Melbourne, 14 October 1903, AWM 3, 03/677 pt 2.
47 Calder, *Heroes and Gentlemen*, p. 54.
48 Details on prizes for North Gippsland Agricultural Show, 1896, NAA B3756, 1896/2689.
49 RO no. 29, 12th LHR (TMI), 20 October 1905, AWM 1, 19/2, p. 41.
50 Buckley, *The NSW Northern Rivers Lancers*, p. 10.
51 Unnamed newspaper cited in Holloway, *Hooves, Wheels and Tracks*, pp. 102–3.

52 Buckley, *The NSW Northern Rivers Lancers*, pp. 4–5.
53 Dunn & Blundell, *The Boys in Green*, p. 12.
54 Maj-Gen French, 1898, cited in Burness, 'The Australian horse', p. 38.
55 Letter to OC Northern District Reserves, 28 December 1888, SRNSW: CSC, box 5/5982, item 90/5944.
56 O'Sullivan, *The Power of Mounted Riflemen*, p. 20.
57 Col Tom Price cited in Calder, *Heroes and Gentlemen*, p. 46.
58 Templeton, *The Consolidation of the British Empire*, p. 28.
59 *Adelaide Observer*, 26 June 1896, pp. 45–6, cited in Wilcox, 'Australia's citizen army', p. 73.
60 Brig-Gen H. Finn, NSW Commandant to DAG, 13 July 1904, NAA B168, 02/2688, item 4.
61 Bridges, 'The New South Wales Lancers and the Anglo-Boer War', p. 24.
62 Calder, *Heroes and Gentlemen*, pp. 23, 26, 51.
63 Vernon, *The Royal New South Wales Lancers*, p. 18.
64 Calder, *Heroes and Gentlemen*, p. 51.
65 Return on VMR attendance, December 1897, NAA B3756, 1898/1463.
66 Wilkinson, 'Australian army reorganisation', p. 77.
67 Howell-Price, *The Light Horse Pocket Book*, pp. 6–7.
68 RO no. 8, 12th LHR (TMI), 6 Apr, 1905, AWM 1, 19/2, pp. 8–9; Comments by Maj Smith in *Report of the Conference of Militia Officers, 1912*, p. 46.
69 Hutton, *Second Annual Report upon the Military Forces of the Commonwealth of Australia*, p. 13.
70 Brig-Gen H. Finn, NSW Commandant, to DAG, Melbourne, 30 December 1903, AWM 3, 03/677 pt 2.
71 Conway, 'The Australian light horseman', pp. 519–21.
72 Training Schedule, 4th Sqn, 11th LHR, November 1906, AWM 1, 18/5, p. 44.
73 RO no. 19, 12th LHR (TMI), 28 July 1904, AWM 1, 19/1.
74 White, 'Light horse of Australia', p. 85.
75 Comments by Maj Smith and other officers in *Report of the Conference of Militia Officers, 1912*, pp. 16, 50.
76 James Burns to Charles Cox, 27 March 1899, in Cox, Charles Frederick 1863–1944, Papers on the South African War, 1897–1933, MS37.
77 Wilkins, 'The bated shining sword', p. 35.
78 Calder, *Heroes and Gentlemen*, p. 23.
79 Figures derived from Muster Roll of 6th LHR, 1907–10, AWM 1, 17/3. Sample taken by recording the details of all men with surnames starting with the letters A, B, C and F, 99 men in total. Of these, 43 (42.57 per cent) had left or been discharged as non-efficient by late 1910.
80 Correspondence relating to distribution of 13th LHR, 1908–12, NAA MP84/1, 713/3/2, 713/3/8, 713/3/12 and 713/3/18.
81 OC 4 Sqn, 13th LHR to HQ 13th LHR, precise date unknown but mid-1908, NAA MP84/1, 713/3/12.
82 Hutton to Principal Under-Secretary, 28 May 1895, SRNSW, CSC, box 5/6268, item 95/8136.

83 OC VMR to AAG Victoria, 26 May 1893, NAA B3756, 1893/1081; Calder, *Heroes and Gentlemen*, pp. 27–8; Vazenry, *Military Forces of Victoria*, ch. 2, p. 4.
84 Calder, *Heroes and Gentlemen*, pp. 27–8.
85 Correspondence regarding cuts to mounted troops, SRNSW, CSC, box unknown, item 93/471; Vernon, *The Royal New South Wales Lancers*, p. 21.
86 Notes on W. Okeden's memo attached to undated and unsigned memorandum to Chief Secretary of Queensland, QSA: PRE/20. This item probably dates from late 1893 or early 1894.
87 Millar, 'The history of the defence forces of the Port Phillip District', p. 87; Holloway, *Hooves, Wheels and Tracks*, p. 7.
88 Vernon, *The Royal New South Wales Lancers*, p. 14; Anon, *A Short History of the New South Wales Mounted Rifles 1888–1913*, p. 32.
89 Vazenry, *Military Forces of Victoria*, ch. 3, p. 37.
90 A reference to the event at St Peter's Fields, Manchester, on 16 August 1819 when yeomanry weighed into a crowd of about 60 000 people (the precise figure is unknown) assembled for a peaceful demonstration, killing 11 and injuring about 500. It was dubbed 'Peterloo' in an ironic reference to Waterloo.
91 Col G. French, Commandant QDF, cited in Starr & Sweeney, *Forward: The History of the 2nd/14th Light Horse*, pp. 6–8.
92 Johnson, *Volunteers at Heart*, p. 167.
93 Notes on W. Okeden's memo attached to an undated and unsigned memorandum to Chief Secretary of Queensland, QSA PRE/20. This item probably dates from late 1893 or early 1894.
94 Johnson, *Volunteers at Heart*, pp. 167–8.
95 'Law, military', in Dennis et al., *Oxford Companion to Australian Military History* (1st edn), p. 342.
96 O'Sullivan, *The Power of Mounted Riflemen*, pp. 2–3, 19.
97 *Adelaide Observer*, 25 January 1896, p. 12.
98 Hutton, 'Our comrades of Greater Britain', p. 47.
99 Hutton, Preface, in *The Manual of Drill for the Mounted Troops of Australia, 1895*, p. iii.
100 Hutton to Gen R. Buller, 19 January 1896, cited in Clarke, 'Marching to their own drum', p. 303.
101 Neil Moffat to Premier of NSW, G. Reid, 18 March 1896, SRNSW: CSC, box 5/6319, item 96/4514. The government's response to Moffat is not recorded.
102 Lord Brassey to unknown, 8 August 1898, TNA (UK): WO 32/6365.
103 Lt-Col Mackay to Governor of New South Wales, Earl Beauchamp, 18 July 1899, PRO-AJCP: NSW no. 24346, Colonial Office 201/629.
104 Mackay, *The Yellow Wave: A Romance of the Asiatic Invasion of Australia*, Enstice & Webb (eds), passim. Originally published as *The Yellow Wave*, 1895.

105 Adjutant 1st AH to regimental officers, 18 February 1898, cited in Dunn & Blundell (eds), *The Boys in Green*, p. 4.
106 Wilcox, *For Hearths and Homes*, p. 25; *Truth*, 1897, cited in Enstice & Webb, Introduction, to Mackay, *The Yellow Wave*, p. xxii. See also Ryan, 'The Bush Brigade: Being the remarkable story of the "First Australian Horse"', p. 52.
107 Mackay, Introduction, *The Bushman's Military Guide*, p. iii, NAA A1194, 11.00/4855; Burness, 'Australian colonial forces: A sketch', p. 7. The imperial cavalry manual was titled *Cavalry Drill* up to the 1898 edition. From 1904, when the next edition was issued, it carried the new title *Cavalry Training*.
108 Thompson, Preface, *The Bushman's Military Guide*, pp. v–vii, NAA A1194, 11.00/4855.
109 Abbott, 'The light horse regiments', p. 403.
110 Hutton, 'The cavalry of Greater Britain', p. 25.
111 Wilcox, 'Australia's citizen army', pp. 27–8; Wilcox, 'Citizen mounted riflemen and the South African War of 1899–1902', p. 4.
112 Queensland Military Forces, *Report of the Commandant for the Year 1891–92*, QSA: CRS/278.
113 O'Sullivan, *The Power of Mounted Riflemen*, p. 8.
114 Weick, *The Volunteer Movement in Western Australia*, pp. 30–1.
115 Vernon, *The Royal New South Wales Lancers*, pp. 4–5.
116 Burness, 'New South Wales cavalry', p. 248; Confidential Officer Reports, 1st, 2nd, 3rd, 4th, 5th and 6th LHRs, 1904, NAA MP84/1, 430/2/44.
117 Box, *Saddle and Spur*, p. 1.

6 Mounted rifles

1 Brig-Gen W.T. Bridges to Minister for Defence, 8 August 1914, NAA A2657, vol. 2.
2 Palazzo, *The Australian Army*, pp. 63, 65; Hall, *The Australian Light Horse*, p. 72.
3 There is, as far as this author knows, no extant document that reveals why the AIF numbering system was established as it was.
4 Brig-Gen W.T. Bridges to Minister for Defence, 8 August 1914, NAA A2657, vol. 2.
5 Instructions in regard to clothing of the expeditionary force, Australian Military Forces, 12 August 1914, AWM 25, 187/19.
6 Table of Equipment for Australian Light Horse, AIF, issued with AIF order no. 17, undated, AWM 25, 455/64. Unit establishments varied considerably as the war progressed. One establishment table, undated but probably from 1916, has a regiment holding 26 officers and 523 men, although it seems likely that this set-up was more for the militia at home than the regiments at war. The removal of machine-gun sections in 1916 altered the establishments again, and other minor changes would mean that there is not one set establishment figure that covers the entire war, although in general about 25 officers and between 450 and 460 men seems to be representative for 1916–18. Actual strengths were of course much

more variable. By 1918 each regiment was allowed, on paper at least, to maintain an in-unit pool of reinforcements above the establishment (but not use them in action), and this again skews the figures (Returns of 10th LHR, 1915–16; Returns of 10th LHR, 1918, AWM 25, 861/5; Establishments and Equipment for a Light Horse Regiment, undated, AWM 25, 905/16).

7 It seems unlikely that the use of the term 'trooper' spontaneously came into use in 1914, but it has not been possible to ascertain clearly whether this title was used in the AMF's pre-war militia. The extant records from this period, being largely official in nature, use the title of 'private' for pre-war light-horsemen. Unit routine orders indicate that 'trooper' was adopted in April 1915, although the decision may have been local rather than authorised by the AIF or Department of Defence (RO no. 188, 8th LHR, 7 April 1915, AWM 25, 707/5). I owe thanks to Bill Woerlee and Jeff Pickerd of the Australian Light Horse Association discussion forum for this reference.
8 Grey, *A Military History of Australia*, p. 86.
9 James, *The History of King Edward's Horse*, p. 89.
10 Transport A47, ship order no. 12, 10 February 1915, AWM 25, 455/59.
11 Hill, *Chauvel of the Light Horse*, pp. 45–6.
12 Holloway, *Hooves, Wheels and Tracks*, pp. 111–12.
13 3rd LH Bde, Syllabus of work for week commencing 22 March 1915, AWM 25, 941/1 pt 11; Memo on training 1st LH Bde to 1st and 2nd LHRs, 23 January 1915, AWM 25, 941/1 pt 1.
14 2nd LH Bde, Syllabus of work for week ending 3 April 1915, AWM 25, 941/1 pt 11.
15 Hill, *Chauvel of the Light Horse*, p. 49.
16 1st LH Bde to 1st and 2nd LHRs, 23 January 1915, AWM 25, 941/1 pt 1; 3rd LH Bde, Syllabus for training for week ending 10 April 1915, AWM 25, 941/1 pt 11.
17 Kent, 'The Australian remount unit in Egypt, 1915–19', pp. 10–11, 14.
18 Alterations to establishment A&NZMD, 31 July 1917, AWM 27, 302/97.
19 See for example Jones, *The Australian Light Horse*, p. 21.
20 Anglesey, *A History of the British Cavalry*, vol. 5, p. 189.
21 Bean, *The Story of Anzac*, vol. 1, pp. 599–600; Bean, *The Story of Anzac*, vol. 2, p. 116.
22 Nutting, *History of the Fourth Light Horse Brigade*, pp. 15–17.
23 Wilson & Wetherell, *History of the Fifth Light Horse Regiment*, p. 15.
24 Olden, *Westralian Cavalry in the War*, p. 24; Bourne, *'Nulli Secundus'*, p. 16.
25 Bean, *The Story of Anzac*, vol. 2, pp. 292–4.
26 Wilson & Wetherell, *History of the Fifth Light Horse Regiment*, pp. 21–3.
27 Burness, *The Nek*, passim; Hill, *Chauvel of the Light Horse*, pp. 52–61.
28 Bean, *Anzac to Amiens*, pp. 153–6; Wilson & Wetherell, *History of the Fifth Light Horse Regiment*, pp. 37–42.
29 Bean, *The Australian Imperial Force in France, 1916*, pp. 959–64; Becker, 'The history of the composite Australian Light Horse Regiment', passim; Foster, 'Operations of the mounted troops of the EEF', p. 7. The regiment

was authorised on 19 November 1915 and had its first parade the following day, and the last squadron was disbanded on 9 February 1916.
30 Returns of 10th LHR, 1915–16, AWM 25, 861/5.
31 Chief Medforce to Chief London, 21 January 1916, Murray papers, IWM; Grey, *The Australian Army*, p. 44; Mallett, 'The interplay between technology, tactics and organisation in the First AIF' (hereafter 'The interplay'), pp. 142–3.
32 Holloway, *Hooves, Wheels and Tracks*, p. 119.
33 ANZAC to 1st, 2nd, 3rd LH Bdes and NZMR Bde, 30 January 1916, AWM 25, 945/1 pt 2.
34 Maj-Gen J. Spens, Commanding Cairo District, to GOC ANZAC, 9 January 1916, AWM 22, 123/14/30.
35 ANZAC to OC AIF Intermediate Base, Cairo, 10 January 1916, AWM 25, 455/66.
36 Hill, *Chauvel of the Light Horse*, p. 66.
37 Ibid.
38 Australian and New Zealand Forces, circular memorandum, no. 38, 11 March 1916, AWM 27, 302/92.
39 Foster, 'Operations of the mounted troops of the EEF', p. 8.
40 Chauvel, 'The Australian Light Horse in the Great War', NAA A1194, 33.68/15152, p. 1 (hereafter, Chauvel, 'The Australian Light Horse').
41 Holloway, *Hooves, Wheels and Tracks*, p. 147; Nutting, *History of the Fourth Light Horse Brigade*, pp. 17–18.
42 War Office to Department of Defence, Melbourne, 15 May 1916, NAA B539, AIF264/1/233; General Staff circular no. 6, I Anzac Corps, 9 May 1916, AWM 27, 303/30.
43 Hunter, *My Corps Cavalry*, pp. 28–37.
44 Holloway, *Hooves, Wheels and Tracks*, pp. 147, 242; Hall, *The Australian Light Horse*, p. 41; Nutting, *History of the Fourth Light Horse Brigade*, pp. 17–18.
45 Hunter, *My Corps Cavalry*, pp. 100–3.
46 Holloway, *Hooves, Wheels and Tracks*, pp. 247–63, 278–9.
47 1st Aust Div to GOC 1st Infantry Bde, 9 January 1916, AWM 25, 157/2.
48 Correspondence relating to raising of camel corps, January 1916, AWM 25, 157/2; Foster, 'Operations of the mounted troops of the EEF', p. 9; Chauvel, 'The Australian Light Horse', p. 1.
49 Extract from RO no. 5, by Maj-Gen H. Chauvel, 27 September 1916, AWM 25, 157/8; Chauvel to Maj-Gen Sir A. Lynden-Bell, CGS EEF, 6 June 1917, NAA MP367/1, 469/6/12.
50 Mallett, 'The interplay', p. 142.
51 Camel Corps (For Service in Egypt) War Establishment, 9 May 1916, AWM 25, 157/5.
52 Langley, *Sand, Sweat and Camels*, pp. 44, 57–73; Gullett, *The AIF in Sinai and Palestine*, p. 211. Eventually there would be 18 camel corps companies, but only four of the six British companies would serve within the brigade at any one time.

53 Report of 4th Aust. Camel Regiment, [November 1916?], AWM 25, 157/7; *Camel Corps Training (Provisional), 1913*, passim.
54 *Camel Corps Training (Provisional), 1913*, p. 59.
55 'The Employment of Camel Corps', issued by the Gen Staff, GHQ EEF, 11 January 1918, AWM 25, 157/5.
56 Foster, 'Operations of the mounted troops of the EEF', pp. 5–7; Hill, *Chauvel of the Light Horse*, pp. 64–9; Gullett, *The AIF in Sinai and Palestine*, pp. 203–5.
57 Foster, 'Operations of the mounted troops of the EEF', pp. 15–16. The mission included a squadron of the 9th LHR plus attachments from the 8th LHR, Camel Corps, Engineers and Camel Transport Corps.
58 Gullett, *The AIF in Sinai and Palestine*, p. 110; Foster, 'Operations of the mounted troops of the EEF', p. 18.
59 Hill, *Chauvel of the Light Horse*, p. 71.
60 Chauvel, 'The Australian Light Horse', p. 3; Hill, *Chauvel of the Light Horse*, pp. 80–1.
61 Maj-Gen Sir A. Lynden-Bell, CGS EEF, to Maj-Gen Frederick Maurice, DMO War Office, 17 August 1916, Lynden-Bell Papers, IWM; Tactical comments of the action at Romani [by Gen Sir A. Murray] passed to Lt-Gen H.A. Lawrence, undated [August 1916], Murray papers, IWM.
62 Chauvel, 'The Australian Light Horse', p. 5; Hill, *Chauvel of the Light Horse*, pp. 75–85; Gullettt, *The AIF in Sinai and Palestine*, pp. 142–93, 'Lessons from the Great War, Egypt and Palestine up to June 1917', Shea 4/7, Shea Papers, LHCMA; Maj-Gen Sir A. Lynden-Bell to Maj-Gen Sir F. Maurice, DMO, 17 August 1916, Lynden-Bell papers, IWM.
63 Special Order by Maj-Gen H.G. Chauvel, Commander A&NZ Mtd Div, 13 September 1916, AWM 22, 84/2/2001.
64 Chauvel, 'The Australian Light Horse', p. 7.
65 Ibid., p. 8; Hill, *Chauvel of the Light Horse*, pp. 87–9; Gullett, *The AIF in Sinai and Palestine*, pp. 214–28.
66 Chauvel, 'The Australian Light Horse', p. 9; Gullett, *The AIF in Sinai and Palestine*, pp. 229–43; Hill, *Chauvel of the Light Horse*, pp. 90–4.
67 Gullett, *The AIF in Sinai and Palestine*, p. 235.
68 Bou, 'Cavalry, firepower and swords', pp. 105–6; Wavell, *The Palestine Campaigns*, pp. 120, 125, 170; Gullett, *The AIF in Sinai and Palestine*, p. 235.
69 Chauvel, 'The Australian Light Horse', p. 11; Hill, *Chauvel of the Light Horse*, pp. 96–107; Grainger, *The Battle for Palestine*, pp. 17–36; Woodward, *Hell in the Holy Land*, p. 78.
70 Chauvel, 'The Australian Light Horse', pp. 11–12; Grainger, *The Battle for Palestine*, pp. 38–57; Gullett, *The AIF in Sinai and Palestine*, pp. 297–339.
71 Maj-Gen H. Hodgson, GOC IMD, to brother, 5 April 1917, Hodgson papers, IWM; Lt-Gen Sir P. Chetwode to Chauvel and Hodgson, 29 March 1917, Chetwode papers, IWM.
72 The division fought First Gaza without the 4th Light Horse Brigade as it was still in the process of formation.

73 Browne, 'Operations of the Mounted Troops of the EEF (continued)', p. 223.
74 Lt-Gen Sir C. Dobell, GOC Eastern Force, to Lt-Gen Sir P. Chetwode, GOC Desert Column, 17 January 1917, Chetwode papers, IWM; Maj-Gen Sir A. Lynden-Bell, CGS EEF, to Maj-Gen F. Maurice, DMO War Office, 17 January 1917, and Lynden-Bell to Chetwode, 22 January 1917, Lynden-Bell papers, IWM.
75 Chauvel, 'The Australian Light Horse', pp. 10–12; Browne, 'Operations of the Mounted Troops of the EEF (continued)', p. 223.
76 Maj-Gen Sir A. Lynden-Bell, CGS EEF, to Maj-Gen Sir F. Maurice, DMO War Office, 19 September 1916, Lynden-Bell papers, IWM; Lynden-Bell to Chetwode, 29 January 1917, Chetwode papers, IWM.
77 Hill, *Chauvel of the Light Horse*, pp. 96–7.
78 Maj-Gen Sir A. Lynden-Bell, CGS EEF, to Maj-Gen Sir F. Maurice, DMO War Office, 17 January 1917, Lynden-Bell papers, IWM.
79 Maj-Gen Sir A. Lynden-Bell, CGS EEF, to Chetwode, 22 January 1917, Chetwode papers, IWM.
80 Hill, *Chauvel of the Light Horse*, pp. 97, 110–11.
81 Brig-Gen R. Anderson, Commandant AIF HQ, to Lt-Gen W. Birdwood, GOC AIF, 27 April 1917; Lt-Gen W. Birdwood to Sen. G. Pearce, Minister for Defence, 23 April 1917, NAA MP367/1, 469/6/12; Brig-Gen R. Anderson to Lt-Gen W. Birdwood, 15 May 1917, Birdwood papers, British Library.
82 Hill, *Chauvel of the Light Horse*, p. 99.
83 Brig-Gen G. Ryrie to wife, 7 July 1918, in Vincent, *My Darling Mick*, pp. 173–4.
84 Chauvel quoted in Hill, *Chauvel of the Light Horse*, p. 97.
85 Brig-Gen R. Anderson to Lt-Gen W Birdwood, 15 May 1917, Birdwood papers, BL D686/77/108; Lt-Gen W. Birdwood, GOC AIF, to Sen G. Pearce, Minister for Defence, 23 April 1917, NAA MP367/1, 469/6/12.
86 Telegram, Secretary of Defence to Administrative HQ, AIF, 21 April 1917, AWM 22, 236/2/2000.
87 Hill, *Chauvel of the Light Horse*, p. 97; Cable, Admin HQ AIF to Department of Defence, 24 April 1917, AWM 22, 236/2/2000.
88 Chauvel to Secretary of Defence, cable, 22 May 1917, AWM 22, 236/2/2000.
89 Chauvel to Maj-Gen Sir A. Lynden Bell, CGS EEF, 6 June 1917, AWM 22, 236/2/2000.
90 Chauvel, 'The Australian Light Horse', pp. 13–14.
91 Gen Sir A. Murray, to Department of Defence, cable, 8 June 1917, AWM 22, 236/2/2000.
92 Force order no. 44, by Gen Sir A. Murray, C-in-C, EEF, 17 June 1917, AWM 22, 236/2/2000.
93 *A Brief Record of the Advance of the Egyptian Expeditionary Force*, p. 40, TNA(UK) CAB 44/12; Chauvel, 'The Australian Light Horse', p. 14.
94 'Machine gun battalions', in Dennis et al., *Oxford Companion to Australian Military History* (1st edn), p. 372; Mallett, 'The interplay', p. 147.

95 Pakenham-Walsh, *Elementary Tactics or the Art of War British School*, p. 26. I am indebted to two members of the H-War discussion list, Gervase Phillips and Gordon Angus Mackinlay, for valuable information regarding the selection of Hotchkiss guns for British mounted troops; Chappell, *British Cavalry Equipment*, p. 20. I am indebted to David Kenyon for this reference; Gullett, *The AIF in Sinai and Palestine*, p. 325; Returns of Rifles, MGs & Ammunition, 7th LHR, 27 December 1916 and 9 May 1917, AWM 25, 49/18; Kenyon, 'British cavalry on the Western Front', p. 35; Mallett, 'The interplay', p. 147.
96 Hill, *Chauvel of the Light Horse*, p. 114.
97 BM 2nd LH Bde to 5th, 6th and 7th LHRs, 19 September 1916, AWM 25, 941/1 pt 2.
98 Lt-Gen Sir P. Chetwode to Maj-Gen A. Lynden-Bell, CGS EEF, 22 July 1917, Chetwode papers, IWM.
99 HQ A&NZ MD to subordinate brigades, 30 July 1917, AWM 25, 941/1 pt 4.
100 Lt-Gen Sir P. Chetwode to Maj-Gen A. Lynden-Bell, CGS EEF, 28 May 1917, and Lynden-Bell to Chetwode, 30 May 1917, Chetwode papers, IWM.
101 General Staff, DMC to A&NZMD, 25 July 1917, AWM 25, 941/1 pt 6.
102 OC No. 1 Training Area to CO Isolation Camp, Moascar, 28 June 1917, AWM 22, 752/3/2.
103 Secretary of Defence to CO AIF HQ, Cairo, 18 June 1918, AWM 22, 752/3/2.
104 CO A&NZ Training Centre to HQ AIF, re Light Horse Training Regiment, 4 May 1916, AWM 25, 941/1 pt 2.
105 Report of OC 3rd Light Horse Training Regiment to GOC AIF in Egypt, 4 July 1917, AWM 25, 455/42; AIF, *Syllabus of Training for Light Horse, Infantry and Machine Gun Reinforcements*, pp. 2–5.

7 Cavalry

1 General Sir E. Allenby, GOC-in-C EEF, to CIGS, 12 July 1917, TNA(UK) WO106/716.
2 Cutlack, *The Australian Flying Corps*, pp. 74–7.
3 Grainger, *The Battle for Palestine*, pp. 81–101; Gullett, *The AIF in Sinai and Palestine*, pp. 354–67; Hill, *Chauvel of the Light Horse*, pp. 114–18; Hughes, *Allenby and British Strategy in the Middle East*, pp. 9–42; Sheffy, *British Military Intelligence in the Palestine Campaign*, pp. 267–92.
4 Lt-Gen Sir P. Chetwode, notes on Palestine operations, 21 June 1917, Chetwode papers, IWM.
5 Hill, *Chauvel of the Light Horse*, p. 115.
6 Chauvel, 'The Australian Light Horse', pp. 15–16; Sheffy, 'Origins of the British breakthrough into southern Palestine', p. 125.
7 Hill, *Chauvel of the Light Horse*, p. 125.
8 Grainger, *The Battle for Palestine*, p. 115.
9 Correspondence between Lt-Gen Sir P. Chetwode, GOC Eastern Force, and Maj-Gen Sir A. Lynden-Bell, CGS EEF, 30 April–11 May 1917,

Chetwode papers, IWM; Gullett, *The AIF in Sinai and Palestine*, pp. 389–92; Osbourne, 'Operations of the mounted troops of the EEF', pp. 346–51; Wavell, *The Palestine Campaigns*, p. 120; 'Egypt 1917: Composition of Force', Murray papers, IWM; Mallett, 'The interplay', p. 151. The 19th Brigade RHA, supporting the AMD, had swapped their 18-pounders for 13-pounders in September (Australian Mounted Division, divisional order no. 9, 12 September 1917, p. 2, AWM 4, 1/58/58/3, pt 1; Goold-Walker (ed.), *The Honourable Artillery Company in the Great War*, pp. 136, 140). I am indebted to Jeff Pickerd and Geoff Smith of the Australian Light Horse discussion forum for these two latter references.

10 Hill, *Chauvel of the Light Horse*, pp. 127–8; Gullett, *The AIF in Sinai and Palestine*, pp. 392–403.
11 Lt-Col M. Bourchier for commander 4th LH Bde to HQ AMD, 20 December 1917, AWM 25, 455/2.
12 Jones, 'The charge at Beersheba and the making of myths', p. 15; Hill, *Chauvel of the Light Horse*, p. 125.
13 Osbourne, 'Operations of the mounted troops of the EEF', p. 335.
14 Maj-Gen H. Hodgson to Barnard [brother?], 8 February 1918, Hodgson papers, IWM; Preston, *The Desert Mounted Corps*, pp. 95, 311–21.
15 Hill, *Chauvel of the Light Horse*, p. 136.
16 Chauvel, 'The Australian Light Horse', pp. 21–2; Gullett, *The AIF in Sinai and Palestine*, pp. 528–9.
17 Badsey, 'Fire and the sword', pp. 282–93.
18 Maj-Gen Sir A. Godley, GOC NZEF, to Senator G. Pearce, Minister for Defence, 16 April 1915, Godley correspondence, AWM 3 DRL/2233.
19 Ian Jones, *The Australian Light Horse*, pp. 24–5.
20 Untitled paper by Maj-Gen Phillip Chetwode, Commander 2nd Cavalry Division, [1916?], AWM 25, 941/1 pt 3.
21 Gullett, *The AIF in Sinai and Palestine*, p. 403.
22 Anon., 'Operations of the mounted troops of the EEF', p. 387.
23 Drill for Mounted Riflemen, Cape Colonial Forces, 1906, Appendix 3, Mounted Bayonet Practice, AWM 25, 941/1, pt 1. An article reprinted from the *Army Review* in the *Australian Military Journal* in early 1914 had referred to South African trials of using the bayonet when mounted. The article claimed that the trials had found it unsuitable for such use but does not mention whether the bayonet was held in the hand or fixed to the rifle as per the 1906 instructions. See 'GGA', 'The bayonet for mounted riflemen', p. 135.
24 Memo on Dismounted Attack, A&NZMD to 1st LH Bde, 9 October 1917, AWM 25, 941/1, pt 4.
25 Gullett, *The AIF in Sinai and Palestine*, pp. 171–2; Likeman, *From Law to War*, pp. 91–2.
26 Robertson, 'The Australian 10th Light Horse attack at Magdhaba', p. 230; Gullett, *The AIF in Sinai and Palestine*, p. 182.
27 Gullett, *The AIF in Sinai and Palestine*, pp. 219–24.
28 Robertson, 'The Australian 10th Light Horse attack at Magdhaba', p. 233.

29 'Notes on Recent Cavalry Fighting up to 7th April 1917', AWM 25, 923/27.
30 Maj Lord Hampton, Worcestershire Hussars, cited in Badsey, *Doctrine and Reform in the British Cavalry*, p. 285.
31 See for example Grainger, *The Battle for Palestine*, p. 118.
32 Preston, *The Desert Mounted Corps*, pp. 55–6; Badsey, *Doctrine and Reform in the British Cavalry*, p. 285.
33 Gullett, *The AIF in Sinai and Palestine*, p. 403.
34 Burness, 'The Australian horse', pp. 44–5; Osbourne, 'Operations of the mounted troops of the EEF', *Cavalry Journal* (1921), p. 351.
35 AMD, preliminary instructions no. 1, 26 October 1917, AWM 4, 1/58/4, pt 3.
36 Ibid.; Osbourne, 'Operations of the mounted troops of the EEF', *Cavalry Journal* (1921), p. 351.
37 'History of the 4th Light Horse Brigade, 1915–19' (anonymous typescript), pp. 10–11, AWM 25, 455/67. The charge was not at a defended locality but across the front of two separate ones in order to find the cover of a wadi.
38 Gullett, *The AIF in Sinai and Palestine*, pp. 432–3.
39 Anglesey, *A History of the British Cavalry*, vol. 5, p. 181; Osbourne, 'Operations of the mounted troops of the EEF', *Cavalry Journal* (1921), p. 364.
40 Maj-Gen Shea, GOC 60th Division, to Chauvel, cited in Anglesey, *A History of the British Cavalry*, vol. 5, p. 175.
41 Anglesey, *A History of the British Cavalry*, vol. 5, p. 198; Table of Mounted Actions of Des. Corps, Oct–Nov 1917, AWM 25, 923/27.
42 Osbourne, 'Operations of the mounted troops of the EEF', *Cavalry Journal* (1921), pp. 371–5; Anglesey, *A History of the British Cavalry*, vol. 5, p. 198.
43 Table of Mounted Actions of Des. Corps [DMC], October–November 1917, AWM 25, 923/27.
44 DMC to all subordinate formations, 24 January 1918, AWM 25, 923/27; Gullett, *The AIF in Sinai and Palestine*, pp. 437, 480–1.
45 Training notes regarding recent operations by A&NZMD, 16 December 1917, AWM 25, 941/1 pt 4.
46 Brig-Gen W. Grant cited in Osbourne, 'Operations of the mounted troops of the EEF', *Cavalry Journal* (1921), pp. 365–6.
47 Wilson, *Narrative of Operations of Third Light Horse Brigade*, pp. 53–4; Osbourne, 'Operations of the mounted troops of the EEF', *Cavalry Journal* (1921) 366; Likeman, *From Law to War*, pp. 119, passim.
48 Memorandum on recent operations attached to Gen. Staff DMC to A&NZMD, AMD, YMD and 7th Mounted Bde, 24 January 1918, AWM 25, 923/27.
49 Badsey, *Doctrine and Reform in the British Cavalry*, p. 231; Osbourne, 'Operations of the mounted troops of the EEF', *Cavalry Journal* (1921), p. 333.
50 Results of examinations, Imperial School of Instruction – Cavalry Wing, 28th course, 27 July 1917, AWM 27, 306/1; Imperial School of Instruction,

Zeitoun – Cavalry Course, Syllabus, May 1918, AWM 25, 877/11. The only distinction was a few extra lessons on use of the sword/lance for those who came from regiments equipped with it.
51 *The Palestine Campaign*, monograph of the United States Cavalry School, p. 66, cited in Badsey, 'Fire and the sword', p. 325.
52 For more see Bou, 'Cavalry, firepower and swords', pp. 116–17.
53 Assistant BM, 3rd LH Bde to 8th, 9th and 10th LHRs, 4 March 1918, AWM 25, 941/1 pt 7. The instruction in the use of the bayonet mounted was supervised by an Australian-born imperial officer, Col Rex Osbourne, who was CSO of AMD (Gullett, *The AIF in Sinai and Palestine*, p. 676).
54 Lt-Col J. Browne, A&NZMD to 1st, 2nd and 3rd LHRs, 28 February 1918, AWM 25, 941/1 pt 7.
55 Chauvel, 'The Australian Light Horse', p. 22.
56 A&NZMD order no. 121, 21 March 1918, A&NZMD war diary, AWM 4, 1/60/25, pt 2; Chauvel, 'The Australian Light Horse', p. 22; Hill, *Chauvel of the Light Horse*, p. 143.
57 Hill, *Chauvel of the Light Horse*, p. 143; Gullett, *The AIF in Sinai and Palestine*, pp. 561–83.
58 *A Brief Record of the Advance of the Egyptian Expeditionary Force*, pp. 21–2, copy in TNA(UK) CAB 44/12; Hill, *Chauvel of the Light Horse*, p. 144.
59 Badsey, 'Fire and the sword', pp. 333–5.
60 Chauvel, 'The Australian Light Horse', p. 28.
61 Gullett, *The AIF in Sinai and Palestine*, p. 594.
62 Hill, *Chauvel of the Light Horse*, p. 146.
63 Sir P. Chetwode to Archibald Wavell, 28 March 1939, Allenby papers, LHCMA: Allenby 6/IX/18.
64 Chauvel, 'The Australian Light Horse', p. 28.
65 Barron, 'Es Salt and the Jordan Valley', p. 21. Orders of the 3rd LH Bde were that they were to wear steel helmets (3rd LH Bde order no. 9, 29 April 1918, 3rd LH Bde war diary, AWM 4, 10/3/39). Thanks to Bill Woerlee for this order reference. How often the light horse wore steel helmets in 1918 is unclear. I know of no photographs showing light-horsemen in steel helmets, but the sources indicate that they were worn at Es Salt, at least at the beginning of the operation. A training syllabus of the 12th LHR from April 1918 also calls for two squadrons to turn out for training wearing them, so it seems clear that they did in fact do so at times (HQ 12th LHR to squadrons, 14 April 1918, AWM 25, 941/1 pt 8).
66 Chauvel, 'The Australian Light Horse', p. 28; Gullett, *The AIF in Sinai and Palestine*, p. 604.
67 Barron, 'Es Salt and the Jordan Valley', p. 21; Hill, *Chauvel of the Light Horse*, pp. 145–52; Gullett, *The AIF in Sinai and Palestine*, pp. 594–622.
68 Gullett, *The AIF in Sinai and Palestine*, p. 620.
69 Chauvel, 'The Australian Light Horse', pp. 24–5.
70 Falls, *Military Operations in Sinai and Palestine*, part 2, p. 415.
71 GHQ EEF to War Office, 6 July 1918, TNA(UK) WO106/14: HQ AIF to Secretary, Department of Defence, 5 September 1918, NAA MP367/1,

469/20/14; Imperial Camel Brigade reorganisation order no. 8, 25 July 1918, AWM 25, 157/1; Gullett, *The AIF in Sinai and Palestine*, pp. 640–1.
72 Chauvel, 'The Australian Light Horse', p. 27.
73 5th LH Bde, war diary, August 1918, AWM 4, 10/5/1. Macarthur-Onslow was not appointed to command until 28 August, but the brigade and the two LHRs appear to have become formally established on 1 August.
74 HQ AIF to Secretary, Department of Defence, 5 September 1918, NAA MP367/1, 469/20/14.
75 Hill, *Chauvel of the Light Horse*, p. 154.
76 AMD Tactical narrative, operations east of Jordan – Es Salt area, AWM 25, 455/8.
77 Hill, *Chauvel of the Light Horse*, p. 160.
78 Anglesey, *A History of the British Cavalry*, vol. 5, pp. 239–40; Falls, *Armageddon, 1918*, pp. 31–2.
79 Notes on enemy attack on Desert Mounted Corps, 14 July 1918, by Brig-Gen Godwin, Gen Staff DMC, AWM 25, 941/1 pt 8.
80 Maj-Gen Hodgson to DMC, 27 July 1918, AWM 25, 941/1 pt 8. It is clear that once authorised to use the sword the AMD effectively abandoned *Yeomanry and Mounted Rifle Training*, which did not include sections on sword use, in favour of *Cavalry Training*, which included drill specifically designed for use with the *arme blanche* (Lt-Col R. Osbourne, Gen Staff, AMD to 3rd, 4th and 5th LH Bdes, 14 July 1918, AWM 25, 941/1, pt 8).
81 Lt-Col R. Osbourne, Gen Staff AMD, to 3rd, 4th and 5th LH Bdes, 14 July 1918, AWM 25, 941/1, pt 8; For more see also, Bou, 'Cavalry, firepower and swords', pp. 118–19.
82 Hill, *Chauvel of the Light Horse*, p. 154; Anglesey, *A History of British Cavalry*, vol. 5, p. 223.
83 Table of marching order AMD, 10 September 1918, AWM 25, 941/1 pt 9.
84 Darley, *With the Ninth Light Horse*, p. 143; History of the 4th LH Bde, AWM 25, 455/67.
85 Wilson, *Narrative of Operations of Third Light Horse Brigade*, p. 53.
86 HQ 12th LHR to Squadrons, 14 April 1918, AWM 25, 941/1 pt 8. Machine-guns were useful during mounted actions only if sent to places where they could be concentrated and give effective fire support, something that any effective attack, mounted or otherwise, required. To take them along on the charge was to squander the advantages they offered. In his post-Beersheba report Bourchier noted that at that action, where at least some of the guns had accompanied the charge, 'The Hotchkiss guns were useless, the fast pace affording no time to get them into action' (Lt-Col M. Bourchier for Commander 4th LH Bde to HQ AMD, 20 December 1917, AWM 25, 455/2).
87 Brig Gen W. Meldrum, 11 January 1918, Archives New Zealand: WA 40/3, box 7; Lt-Col W. Meldrum, 'Handling of mounted rifles independently and in brigade', 14 November 1914, Archives of New Zealand: WA 42. I am indebted to Terry Kinloch for this information and these references.

88 Osbourne, 'Operations of the mounted troops of the EEF', *Cavalry Journal* (1921), p. 350. Gullett offers a similar assessment in *The AIF in Sinai and Palestine*, p. 676.
89 Erickson, *Ordered to Die*, pp. 195, 198.
90 Force order no. 68 by Gen Sir E. Allenby, 9 September 1918, and Instructions to General Officer Commanding, Desert Mounted Corps, from GHQ EEF, 9 September 1918, Chetwode papers, IWM; Chauvel, 'The Australian Light Horse', p. 33.
91 Hill, *Chauvel of the Light Horse*, p. 161.
92 Badsey, *Doctrine and Reform in the British Cavalry*, p. 251.
93 Chauvel, 'The Australian Light Horse', p. 33.
94 Osbourne, 'Operations of the Mounted Troops of the EEF (continued)', *Cavalry Journal* (1923), pp. 150–1.
95 Ibid., p. 151; Chauvel, 'The Australian Light Horse', p. 34.
96 Wavell, *The Palestine Campaigns*, pp. 205–6.
97 'History of M.T. of the Desert Mounted Corps during operations in Palestine and Syria 1918', passim; Mordike, *General Sir Edmund Allenby's Joint Operations in Palestine, 1917–18*, pp. 20–7.
98 Gullett, *The AIF in Sinai and Palestine*, p. 697.
99 Chauvel to his wife, 20 September 1918, Chauvel papers, AWM PR00535.
100 Gen Sir E. Allenby to Adelaide Allenby, 3 October 1918, Allenby papers, LHCMA: Allenby 1/9/12.
101 11th LHR war diary, September 1918, AWM 4: 10/16/36; 12th LHR war diary, September 1918, AWM 4, 10/17/18; Appendix A, attack on Semakh, AWM 25, 455/15; Gullett, *The AIF in Sinai and Palestine*, pp. 730–4.
102 Gen Sir E. Allenby to Adelaide Allenby, 24 September 1918, Allenby papers, LHCMA: Allenby 1/9/6.
103 Chauvel, 'The Australian Light Horse', pp. 36–8.
104 Ibid., pp. 39–41; Gullett, *The AIF in Sinai and Palestine*, pp. 713–27.
105 Lt-Col M Bourchier, OC Bourchier's Force, to HQ AMD, 4 October 1918, AWM 25, 455/15; Gullett, *The AIF in Sinai and Palestine*, pp. 738–60; Chauvel, 'The Australian Light Horse', pp. 40–4.
106 Bowman-Manifold, *An Outline of the Egyptian and Palestine Campaigns*, p. 89; GHQ EEF to War Office, 26 October 1918, TNA(UK) WO 106/14.
107 Stevenson, *1914–1918*, pp. 483–4; Erickson, *Ordered to Die*, pp. 179–92; Chauvel, 'The Australian Light Horse', p. 49.
108 Lt-Col R. Fowler, ADMS AMD to DMC, 12 December 1918, AWM 27, 376/150.
109 Gullett, *The AIF in Sinai and Palestine*, p. 780.
110 Hill, *Chauvel of the Light Horse*, p. 183.
111 Narrative of 5th LH Bde, 17 September–3 October 1918, AWM 25, 455/7.
112 Chauvel, 'The Australian Light Horse', pp. 36–44.
113 AMD, tactical narrative, operations resulting in capture of Damascus, AWM 25, 455/9.
114 History of the 4th LH Bde, AWM 25, 455/67.

115 Anglesey, *A History of the British Cavalry*, vol. 5, passim; see p. 319 for the 2nd Lancers.
116 H.S. Gullett, cited in 'A retrospect', *Kia Ora Coo-ee*, 15 November 1918, p. 1. (*Kia Ora Coo-ee* was the troop newspaper published for Australian and New Zealand troops in Egypt and Palestine in 1918.)
117 AMD, Tactical narrative – operations resulting in the capture of Damascus, 2 October 1918, AWM 25, 455/9.
118 H.S. Gullett, cited in 'A retrospect', *Kia Ora Coo-ee*, November 1918, p. 1.
119 Agricultural and mechanical courses, AMD GHQ, war diary, January 1919, AWM 4, 1/60/35, appendix 6; 4th LH Bde, syllabus of training, week ending 18 January 1919, AWM 25, 941/1 pt 10.
120 7th LHR, war diaries, December 1918–January 1919, AWM 4, 10/12/39 and 10/12/40.
121 Coleman, 'A proper soldiers' vengeance?', pp. 62–3; Gullett, *The AIF in Sinai and Palestine*, pp. 782–90; Hill, *Chauvel of the Light Horse*, pp. 192–3.
122 Gullett, 'The horses stay behind', *Kia Ora Coo-ee*, November 1918, p. 10.
123 The AIF had 9751 horses on charge upon the armistice; 3059 were destroyed in February 1919 as part of this process. Finance Secretary to Secretary of Defence (for the Minister), 15 March 1932, NAA B1535, 799/3/99; Extensive horse returns in AWM 25, 29/61 pt 1 and pt 2; 4th LH Bde war diary, February 1919, AWM 4, 10/4/26. For more see also Bou, 'They shot the horses – didn't they?'; Bou, 'Sold or shot'.
124 W. Birkbeck, appointment unknown, to Kemble, appointment unknown, 1 August 1919, AWM 25, 29/1.
125 Wilson, 'The 3rd Light Horse Brigade, Australian Imperial Force in the Egyptian Rebellion 1919', pp. 6–8, 12–13; Brugger, *Australians and Egypt*, passim.
126 Brugger, *Australians and Egypt*, pp. 132, 138–41; Wilson, 'The 3rd Light Horse Brigade, Australian Imperial Force in the Egyptian Rebellion 1919', p. 24.
127 Bourne, *'Nulli Secundus'*, p. 86.

8 The light-horsemen 2

1 Gullett, *The AIF in Sinai and Palestine*, pp. 29–39.
2 'Surcingle', 'The Light Horseman', *Kia Ora Coo-ee*, June 1918, p. 15.
3 Laffin, *Anzacs at War*, pp. 50–6.
4 Gammage, *The Broken Years*, pp. 154–61.
5 Beaumont, 'Australia's war', in Beaumont, *Australia's War, 1914–18*, p. 27.
6 Gullett, *The AIF in Sinai and Palestine*, p. 32; *The Bushman's Military Guide*, pp. v–vii; O'Sullivan, *The Power of Mounted Riflemen*, pp. 2–3, passim.
7 Gen Sir H. Chauvel, Foreword, in Idriess, *The Desert Column*, p. v.
8 Stanley, 'Our big world', p. 9.
9 J. Davies to Sir W. Birkwood, 4 August 1930, Birdwood papers, British Library.

10 Gullett, *The AIF in Sinai and Palestine*, p. 33; Walk, 'Rural Australia and the Great War', pp. 11, 55–8; J. Davies to Sir W. Birdwood, 4 August 1930, Birdwood papers, British Library.
11 LCpl B. Delpratt to sister, 17 April 1916, Depratt papers, AWM 3 DRL/3741.
12 Gullett, *The AIF in Sinai and Palestine*, p. 33.
13 Certificates for School of Instruction for Light Horse, 1906, and School of Instruction for Tactical Fitness for Command, 1911, Grant papers, AWM PR01850.
14 Vincent, *My Darling Mick*, passim; Likeman, *From Law to War*, p. 159; Grey, 'Robertson, Sir Horace Clement Hugh', James & Londey, 'Nimmo, Robert Harold', Hill, 'Cox, Charles Frederick', Hill, 'Ryrie, Sir Granville de Laune', *Australian Dictionary of Biography*, www.adb.online.anu.edu.au; Gullett, *The AIF in Sinai and Palestine*, passim.
15 Robson, 'The origin and character of the First AIF', p. 747. The school at Zeitoun was for all officer candidates in the EEF (Gullett, *The AIF in Sinai and Palestine*, p. 533). In Britain the 1916 establishment of officer cadet battalions saw many tens of thousands of men commissioned who had previously served in the ranks (Griffith, *British Fighting Methods in the Great War*, p. 61).
16 Tpr P. Jackson to mother, [?] April 1916, Jackson papers, AWM 1 DRL/0380; Berrie, *Morale*, passim.
17 Stanley, 'Our big world', pp. 7–8.
18 Gullett, *The AIF in Sinai and Palestine*, p. 533; Robson, 'The origin and character of the First AIF', pp. 747–8.
19 Tpr P. Jackson to mother, 8 November 1916, Jackson papers, AWM 1 DRL/0380.
20 Tpr P. Jackson to mother, 9 February and 8 November 1916, Jackson papers, AWM 1 DRL/0380.
21 Berrie, *Morale*, p. 193.
22 'Gork' is an alternative spelling for 'gawk', which is to look at something. CMG: Companion of the Order of Michael and St George. Diary of Tpr H. Sullivan, 4 June 1916, AWM PR01058.
23 Account of Pte (Tpr) A. Rouget, Rouget papers, AWM PR02084.
24 Tpr E. Dengate to wife, 3 March 1918, Dengate papers, AWM 3 DRL/7678.
25 Gullett, *The AIF in Sinai and Palestine*, p. 533; Lt B. Delpratt to sister, 26 March and 9 April 1918, Delpratt papers, AWM 3 DRL/3741.
26 Tpr P. Jackson to mother, 8 November 1916, Jackson papers, AWM 1 DRL/0380.
27 Tpr I. Idriess, 19 March 1917, Idriess diary, AWM 1 DRL/373.
28 Idriess, *The Desert Column*, p. 162.
29 Tpr E. Dengate to wife, 25 May 1919, Dengate papers, AWM 3 DRL/7678.
30 Idriess, *The Desert Column*, p. 85.
31 Berrie, *Morale*, pp. 193, 164.
32 Idriess, *The Desert Column*, p. 67.
33 Tpr B. Delpratt to sister, 17 April 1916, Delpratt papers, AWM 3 DRL/3741.

34 Tpr E Dengate to wife, 11 April 1918, Dengate papers, AWM 3 DRL/7678.
35 Lt B. Delpratt to sister, 9 April 1918, Delpratt papers, AWM 3 DRL/3741.
36 Brig-Gen G. Ryrie to wife, 23 December 1916, in Vincent, *My Darling Mick*, p. 128.
37 Brig-Gen L. Wilson, 'Military law as applied to members of the AIF', memo, reproduced in Likeman, *From Law to War*, p. 174.
38 Idriess, *The Desert Column*, p. 83.
39 Stanley, 'Our big world', p. 11.
40 Tpr B. Delpratt to sister, 4 December 1916, Delpratt papers, AWM 3 DRL/3741.
41 Tpr P. Jackson to mother, 3 January 1916, Jackson papers, AWM 1 DRL/0380.
42 Black [Gray], *Red Dust*, p. 15.
43 Tpr P. Jackson to uncle, 29 December 1916, Jackson papers, AWM 1 DRL/0380.
44 Berrie, *Morale*, p. 219.
45 Lt B. Delpratt to sister, 13 August 1918, Delpratt papers, AWM 3 DRL/3741; Stanley, 'Our big world', p. 7.
46 Correspondence in NAA MP367/1, 584/15/473 and MP84/1, 2011/8/25. In 1915 Chauvel had defended the primacy of the Queensland troops in this matter. See also Thomas, 'The history of the emu plume and the Australian Light Horse', for the origins of the plume; 'Emu plumes', *Oxford Companion to Australian Military History* (2nd edn), pp. 198–9.
47 Gullett, *The AIF in Sinai and Palestine*, pp. 534–5; Idriess, *The Desert Column*, passim; Jones, *The Australian Light Horse*, p. 119.
48 The examples are too many to list, but for an example see 'The Light Horseman', *Kia Ora Coo-ee*, June 1918, p. 15.
49 Tpr E. Dengate to wife, 12 March 1919, Dengate papers, AWM 3 DRL/7678.
50 Fowler, *Looking Backward*, pp. 15, 19.
51 'Aram', 'Solely about "sigs"', *Kia Ora Coo-ee*, July 1918, p. 16; Stanley, 'Our big world', pp. 9–10.
52 Berrie, *Morale*, pp. 153–5, describes the finding and husbanding of a champion spider; see p. 139 for a football match.
53 *Kia Ora Coo-ee*, July 1918, p. 14.
54 Tpr E. Dengate to wife, 22 March 1918, Dengate papers, AWM 3 DRL/7678.
55 Gullett, *The AIF in Sinai and Palestine*, pp. 649–50.
56 Tpr E. Dengate to wife, 27 August 1917, Dengate papers, AWM 3 DRL/7678.
57 'Surcingle', 'The Light Horseman', *Kia Ora Coo-ee*, June 1918, p. 15.
58 'Twenty-four hours leave', *Kia-Ora Coo-ee*, April 1918, p. 17. The term 'military police' is from a later war, and the APM were the police of concern to light-horsemen.
59 Account by Maj-Gen Sir A. Lynden-Bell, 1975, Lynden-Bell papers, IWM.
60 Maj-Gen H Hodgson to brother, [undated letter fragment, but 1918], Hodgson papers, IWM.

61 Lt B. Delpratt to sister, 11 July 1918, Delpratt papers, AWM 3 DRL/3741.
62 Tpr P. Jackson to mother, 9 February 1916, Jackson papers, AWM 1 DRL/0380.
63 Black [Gray], *Red Dust*, pp. 68–9.
64 Unidentified solder, quoted in Hollis, *Thunder of the Hooves*, p. 88.
65 Report of the Venereal Section... June 1st 1917 to May 31st 1918, AWM 25, 267/52; Graph of weekly admission for venereal disease, AIF in Egypt, 1918–19, AWM 27, 376/164.
66 Figures in hospital admissions for venereal disease in Australia, AWM 27, 376/166.
67 Staff paymaster to AAG, AIF in Egypt, 3 July 1917, AWM 25, 743/14.
68 Account of Pte (Tpr) A. Rouget, Rouget papers, AWM PR02084.
69 Tpr P. Jackson to mother, 31 July 1915 and 19 February 1916, Jackson papers, AWM 1 DRL/0380.
70 Berrie, *Morale*, p. 174.
71 Tpr E. Dengate to wife, 11 April 1918, Dengate papers, AWM 3 DRL/7678.
72 Tpr I. Idriess, various diary entries, January to March 1917, Idriess diary, AWM 1 DRL/373; Pte H. Sullivan, 5 April 1916, Sullivan papers, AWM PR01058; Berrie, *Morale*, p. 110; Grainger, *The Battle for Palestine*, p. 101. There seems little doubt the Bedouin did pass information to the Turks, but as nomads living a precarious existence in the desert it is likely, and perhaps understandable, that they took their opportunities as they were presented.
73 Tpr E Dengate to wife, 27 July 1917, Dengate papers, AWM 3 DRL/7678.
74 Lt B. Delpratt to sister, 14 October 1918, Delpratt papers, AWM 3 DRL/3741.
75 Wilson, 'The Third Light Horse Brigade... in the Egyptian Rebellion', p. 24.
76 Beaumont, *Australian Defence: Sources and Statistics*, pp. 274–7. Like all such figures, there are disputes about them, and different figures are sometimes proffered.
77 Idriess, *The Desert Column*, pp. 295–6.
78 Tpr E. Dengate to wife, 30 March 1918, Dengate papers, AWM 3 DRL/7678.
79 Gullett, *The AIF in Sinai and Palestine*, p. 334; 'History of the 4th Light Horse Brigade, 1915–19' (anonymous typescript), p. 10, AWM 25, 455/67.
80 Fowler, *Looking Backward*, p. 17.
81 Bou, 'To Amman with the 6th Regiment', pp. 53–5; Gullett, *The AIF in Sinai and Palestine*, pp. 565–84.
82 Berrie, *Under Furred Hats*, p. 128. In his work Berrie often expressed deep bitterness at the failures of the conscription referenda, essentially calling them betrayal of the men at the front.
83 Tpr P. Jackson to mother, 30 August 1917, Jackson papers, AWM 1 DRL/0380.
84 Idriess, *The Desert Column*, p. 142.
85 Tpr E. Dengate to wife, 5 June 1918, Dengate papers, AWM 3 DRL/7678.
86 Tpr I. Idriess, dairy entry, undated but early 1917, Idriess diary, AWM 1 DRL/373.

87 Berrie, *Morale*, pp. 206–7.
88 Stanley, 'Our big world', p. 14.

9 The final years

1 Military Board Agenda, 21 January 1919, NAA A2653/1, p. 12.
2 Palazzo, *The Australian Army*, pp. 86–8. Swinburne was assisted in his deliberations by Lt-Gen C.B.B. White, Maj-Gen J.W. McCay and Maj-Gen J.G. Legge. Swinburne delivered his report to the government in June 1919.
3 Palazzo, *The Australian Army*, pp. 90–1.
4 Annual Training Establishments (Provisional), 1921–22, NAA A1194, 22.34/6984; RO, 1st Cavalry Division, 8 November 1921, AWM 1, 17/18.
5 Correspondence regarding Divisional Organisation, NAA MP367/1, 549/1/6.
6 Ibid.; Inspection Report, Annual Camp 1926, 11th LHR, p. 7; Military Board Agenda 165/1926, 13 October 1926, NAA A2653/1, 1926, vol. 1.
7 Annual Training Establishments (Provisional), 1921–22, NAA A1194, 22.34/6984.
8 Grey, *The Australian Army*, pp. 78–9.
9 Military Board Agenda 111/1922, 7 June 1922, NAA A2653/1, 1922, vol. 2; War Establishments for Units of a Cavalry Division, Military Board Agenda 160/1923, 10 October 1923, NAA A2653/1, 1923, vol. 2. The board noted that since 'the recent war, no Commonwealth War Establishments have been issued and in case of necessity, improvisation must be resorted to'.
10 War Establishments for Units of a Cavalry Division, Military Board Agenda 160/1923, 10 October 1923, NAA A2653/1, 1923, vol. 2.
11 Review of Citizen Force Training, 1920–21, NAA A1194, 12.30/4477.
12 Tables of Composition, Organisation and Distribution of the Australian Military Forces, 1922–23, NAA A1194, 21.20/6900; RO, 1st Cavalry Division, 2 August 1922, AWM 1, 17/18.
13 Grey, *The Australian Army*, p. 78; Central Training Depot, Instructions and Syllabus of Training (Provisional), July 1921, Military Order no. 338/1921, NAA A1194, 12.30/4479.
14 'History of Cavalry in New South Wales, Notes on History of NSWMR, 2nd LHR and 6th LHR, 1888–1940' (anonymous document), p. 29, AWM 1, 17/1.
15 See for example notes by Maj Couchman, Adjutant and QM, 6th ALH Regiment, 30 June 1923, in ibid., p. 30.
16 RO, part I, para. 16, 22nd LHR, 30 November 1923, AWM 1, 19/5.
17 RO no. 7, 22nd LHR, 27 March 1923, AWM 1, 19/4; Annual Training Establishments (Provisional), 1921–22, p. 4, NAA A1194, 22.34/6984.
18 RO no. 121, 1st Cavalry Division, 28 August 1923, AWM 1, 17/18.
19 Submission to Military Board by Maj-Gen G. Ryrie, Military Board Agenda 97/1923, 25 July 1923, NAA A2653, 1923, vol. 1.
20 RO no. 48–51, 22nd LHR, 4 November 1924, AWM 1, 19/4; Australian Military Forces, Military Order 503, 24 November 1923.
21 Military Board Agenda, 185/1926, 18 November 1926, NAA A2653, 1926, vol. 2.

22 Military Board Agenda 176/1926, 2 October 1926, NAA A2653, 1926, vol. 2.
23 Australian Military Forces, Instructions for Training, part 1 and 2, July 1924, p. 7, NAA A1194, 12.30/13378.
24 Military Board Agenda 227/20, 25 August 1920, NAA A2653/1, 1920, vol. 1.
25 Service Records of Officers of 1st LHR, 1921–24, AWM 1, 17/2.
26 Service Records of Officers of 6th LHR, 1921–24, AWM 1, 17/2.
27 AMF, *Report for the Inspector-General of the Australian Military Forces by Lt-Gen. Sir H.G. Chauvel, CGS*, 31 May 1924, NAA D845/1, 22/1924; AMF, *Report for the Inspector-General of the Australian Military Forces by Lt-Gen. Sir H.G. Chauvel, CGS*, 31 May 1926, p. 7, AWM 1, 20/8.
28 AG to CGS, 11 June 1926, NAA MP367/1, 549/1/34.
29 AMF, *Report for the Inspector-General of the Australian Military Forces by Lt-Gen. Sir H.G. Chauvel, CGS*, 31 May 1925, p. 10, NAA A1194, 20.15/14731.
30 Grey, *The Australian Army*, pp. 79–80.
31 Holloway, *Hooves, Wheels and Tracks*, p. 302.
32 For example nearly every routine order promulgated by the 2nd Cavalry Division between 1924 and 1930 included a list of lectures to be given at the United Service Institution (AWM 1, 17/5).
33 RO 48–51, 22nd LHR, 4 November 1924, AWM 1, 19/4; AMF, *Report for the Inspector-General of the Australian Military Forces by Lt-Gen. Sir H.G. Chauvel, CGS*, 31 May 1925, p. 5, NAA A1194, 20.15/14731.
34 AMF, *Report for the Inspector-General of the Australian Military Forces by Lt-Gen. Sir H.G. Chauvel, CGS*, 1927, p. 12, NAA A1194, 20.15/15926.
35 AMF, *Report for the Inspector-General of the Australian Military Forces by Lt-Gen. Sir H.G. Chauvel, CGS*, 1928, p. 11, NAA A1194, 20.15/16596.
36 AMF, *Report for the Inspector-General of the Australian Military Forces by Lt-Gen. Sir H.G. Chauvel, CGS*, 1929, p. 13, NAA A1194, 20.15/17139.
37 B.B. Cubitt, War Office, to Undersecretary of State, Colonial Office, 5 November 1919, NAA MP367/1, 549/1/6.
38 Proposed Cavalry Division Organisation, NAA MP 367/1, 549/1/6.
39 Military Board Agenda 160/1923, 10 October 1923, NAA A2653/1, 1923.
40 AMF, *Report for the Inspector-General of the Australian Military Forces by Lt-Gen. Sir H.G. Chauvel, CGS*, 1929, p. 13, NAA A1194, 20.15/17139; Vernon, *The Royal New South Wales Lancers*, p. 185.
41 Grey, *The Australian Army*, pp. 86–7.
42 Lt-Gen Sir Carl Jess, *Report on the Activities of the Australian Military Forces, 1929–1939*, pp. 12–13, AWM 1, 20/9, part 2.
43 The cuts to the mounted branch are still sometimes blamed on Scullin. See for example the history of the NSW Lancers, which attributes them to the Scullin government (Vernon, *The Royal New South Wales Lancers*, pp. 185–7).
44 Brig-Gen Phillips, Commanding Field Troops, 4th MD to Secretary of Military Board, 6 July 1929; Commander 11th Mixed Brigade to Secretary of Military Board, 5 July 1929, NAA B1535, 849/3/35.

45 Military Board Agenda 49/1929, 17 July 1929, NAA A2653/1, 1929, vols 1–2.
46 Commander 6th Cavalry Bde to HQ 4th District Base, 12 December 1929, NAA B1535, 849/3/100.
47 Commander 11th Mixed Bde to Secretary of Military Board, 5 July 1929, NAA B1535, 849/3/35.
48 Brig-Gen Phillips, Commanding Field Troops, 4th MD, to Secretary of Military Board, 6 July 1929, NAA B1535, 849/3/35.
49 *Narrative of Instructional Operations by a Cavalry Division... and Remarks Thereon By Major-General Sir Edward Hutton.* p. 6, NAA B168/0, 1902/618. For example in 1912 one report noted of a Victorian camp that 'privately owned horses were not a uniformly serviceable lot'. Commonwealth Military Forces – 3rd MD, Report on Annual Continuous Training, 1912, NAA A1194, 12.30/4547.
50 *Annual Report for the Year 1905, by the Inspector-General of the Commonwealth Military Forces, Maj-Gen. H. Finn,* 1 January 1906, p. 12, NAA A1194, 20.15/6697. This development caused alarm all the way from Australia to Whitehall, from where queries into the state of the Australian horse stock were made. See correspondence in NAA B168, 1904/32 pt 1.
51 Correspondence regarding appointment of remount officer, NAA B168, 1902/795.
52 Maj-Gen J.C. Hoad to Secretary of Defence, 23 December 1910, NAA MP84/1, 1893/1/176; *Report of the Conference of Militia Officers, 1912,* pp. 17, 51.
53 Kent, 'The Australian remount unit in Egypt', p. 9.
54 Abbott, 'The light horse regiments', pp. 405–6.
55 Military Board Agenda 154/1927, 21 December 1927, NAA A2653/1, 1927, vol. 2.
56 Report on Horse Breeding in Australia, by QMG, undated but probably late 1916, p. 3, NAA MP367/1, box 59, 499/9/428.
57 Scott, *Australia During the War,* p. 543.
58 Report on Horse Breeding in Australia, by QMG, undated but probably late 1916, p. 2, NAA MP367/1, box 59, 499/9/428.
59 Correspondence regarding horse breeding, NAA MP367/1, box 59, 499/9/428.
60 Maj Scott, Army Remount Department, Report on a visit to Australia during 1922, NAA A1194, 29.24/6515.
61 Military Board Agenda 154/1927, 21 December 1927, NAA A2653/1, 1927, vol. 2.
62 See for example AMF, *Report for the Inspector-General of the Australian Military Forces by Lt-Gen. Sir H.G. Chauvel, CGS,* 31 May 1926, p. 21, AWM 1, 20/8 part 1, 1926; Whitfield, 'Horse breeding in Australia', p. 445.
63 Chauvel to AG&QMG, 19 March 1930, NAA B197, 1937/1/23.
64 Draft report on Organization of AC Regiments in Australia, NAA B1535, 849/3/400.
65 Maj-Gen Bruche, CGS, to AG & QMG, 21 March 1933, NAA B1535, 849/3/400. Armoured car regiments already existed on the war

establishments but had not been raised during peacetime; see *War Establishments*, vol. 1: *Units of a Cavalry Division*, 1933, NAA A1194, 22.14/190/17.
66 General Staff Proposal, Organisation of Militia Armoured Car Regiments, undated, NAA B1535, 849/3/400; Minutes of AHQ Meeting Regarding Formation of Cavalry Armoured Car Regiments, 8 May 1933, NAA B1535, 849/3/400.
67 Jess, *Report on the Activities of the Australian Military Forces, 1929–1939*, p. 24, AWM 1, 20/9, pt 2.
68 Holloway, *Hooves, Wheels and Tracks*, p. 300.
69 Copy of Military Board Agenda 64/1933, 21 June 1933, NAA B1535, 778/2/51.
70 War Organisation: Cavalry Division, NAA B197, 1937/1/23.
71 Hall, *The Australian Light Horse*, pp. 60–1.
72 Ibid.
73 Commander 2nd Cavalry Division, Brig Sir M. Bourchier, to Secretary, Military Board, 9 January 1936, NAA B1535, 849/3/898.
74 Those authorised to raise a troop in 1937 were the 2nd/14th (Qld), 9th/23rd (SA), 12th/24th (NSW) and 20th (Vic) LHRs. Units were allowed to take on up to nine cars to constitute the troop, and it was part of the Headquarters Squadron (see Establishments for Light Horse Regiments, 30 April 1937, NAA A5954/69, 191/28). Those authorised in 1938 were the 4th/19th (Vic), 5th (Qld), 6th (NSW), 7th (NSW), 10th (WA) and 22nd (Tas) LHRs; see CGS to AG, 6 May 1938, NAA B1535, 849/3/898.
75 Commander 11th Mixed Bde to Secretary, Military Board, 24 March 1936, NAA B1535, 849/3/898.
76 DMT to HQ Field Troops, 1st MD, 23 April 1936, NAA B1535, 849/3/898.
77 Commander 1st Cavalry Division to Secretary, Military Board, 20 April 1936, NAA B1535, 849/3/898.
78 QMG to CGS, 27 May 1936, NAA B1535, 849/3/898; Secretary, Military Board to HQ 1st Cavalry Division, 2 June 1936, NAA B1535, 849/3/898.
79 Amendment 4 January 1933, section 20A, *Cavalry Training*, vol. 2: *War, 1929*, p. 33.
80 Hall, *The Australian Light Horse*, p. 49.
81 Vernon, *The Royal New South Wales Lancers*, pp. 199–200. The 'Royal' designation had been granted in 1935.
82 Part of poem by Cpl W. Molineux, 'Mechanised', *Citizen Soldier of Australia* 1:5 (October 1937), p. 32. 'Number Three' refers to the horse-holder in each section.
83 Establishments for Light Horse (Machine Gun) Regiments, 30 April 1937, NAA A5954/69, 191/28.
84 Vernon, *The Royal New South Wales Lancers*, p. 201.
85 *The Lancer: The Regimental Journal of the NSW Lancers, 1st Light Horse (Machine Gun) Regiment*, 1:1 (Aug 1939) 5.
86 Morrison, 'The politics of change', p. 55.
87 Vernon, *The Royal New South Wales Lancers*, pp. 190, 193.

88 RO no. 9, Part 1, 2nd Cavalry Division, 29 July 1930, AWM 1, 17/5; Jess, *Report on the Activities of the Australian Military Forces, 1929–1939*, p. 17, AWM 1, 20/9, part 2; Training Report, 4th LHR, 17 May 1933, AWM 49, 11.
89 Report on Camp, 3rd LHR, 1933, NAA B1535, 808/16/9; RO no. 12, part 1, 2nd Cavalry Division, 17 December 1931, AWM 49, 4.
90 Chauvel to AG&QMG, 31 March 1930, NAA B 197, 1937/1/23.
91 Anglesey, *A History of British Cavalry*, vol. 8, p. 329.
92 RO, 2nd Cavalry Division, 14 September 1932, AWM 49, 5.
93 Report on Camp, 3rd LHR, 1933, NAA B1535, 808/16/9.
94 Annual Return of Military and Air Resources, 1932, NAA B197, 1972/3/314; Annual Return of Military and Resources, 31 December 1934, NAA B197, 1972/3/319. These figures do not include the six cavalry brigade bands.
95 RO, 5th LHR, 21 March 1935, AWM 1, 19/10. The valuations were done a veterinary officer.
96 Grey, *The Australian Army*, p. 93. Of the new pay rate three shillings was an efficiency allowance paid to men who attended all their prescribed parades; see Neumann, 'Australia's citizen soldiers, 1919–1939' p. 131; Holloway, *Hooves, Wheels and Tracks*, p. 302; Jess, *Report on the Activities of the Australian Military Forces, 1929–1939*, p. 32, AWM 1, 20/9, part 2; 'History of Cavalry in New South Wales, Notes on History of NSWMR, 2nd LHR and 6th LHR, 1888–1940' (anonymous document), p. 151, AWM 1, 17/1.
97 Establishments for Light Horse Regiments, 30 April 1937, NAA A5954/69, 191/28. During the mid-1930s the war establishment of a light horse regiment was 26 officers and 624 other ranks; see Neumann, 'Australia's citizen soldiers, 1919–1939', p. 101.
98 Jess, *Report on the Activities of the Australian Military Forces, 1929–1939*, p. 37, AWM 1, 20/9, part 2; Holloway, *Hooves, Wheels and Tracks*, pp. 296, 302–3.
99 *Lancer: The Regimental Journal of the NSW Lancers, 1st Light Horse (Machine Gun) Regiment*, 1:1 (August 1939) 5.
100 Commander 1st Cavalry Division in Anon., '1st Light Horse (Machine Gun) Regiment: Royal New South Wales Lancers', *Citizen Soldier of Australia*, 1:1 (June 1937) 29.
101 *First Report by Lt-Gen E.K. Squires, Inspector-General of the Australian Military Forces, 1938*, and *Revised Military Board Report* (Secret), pp. 6, 11, AWM 1, 20/11.
102 Morrison, 'The politics of change', p. 58.
103 Organisation and Tactical Training of Australian Light Horse, circulated 15 February 1940, NAA MP729/6, 37/401/759.
104 Ibid.
105 GOC Eastern Command, Lt-Gen V. Sturdee to Secretary, Military Board, 3 May 1940, NAA MP729/6, 37/401/759.
106 Commandant RMC to Secretary, Military Board, 28 February 1940, NAA MP729/6, 37/401/759.

107 Commandant 7th MD, Col H. Robertson, to Secretary, Military Board, 11 March 1940, NAA MP729/6, 37/401/759.
108 Various responses to Military Board paper, 'Organization and Tactical Training of Australian Light Horse', 1940, NAA MP729/6, 37/401/759. Of the 13 responses, six expressed support for the sword to some degree and five expressly opposed it. The remaining two respondents make no clear statement, but since they were Col H. Robertson, who was vehemently in favour in abolishing the light horse, and the Commandant of RMC, who advocated a mounted infantry model, I have included them as among those opposed to it.
109 Secretary, Military Board to Secretary, Department of the Army, 13 February 1940, NAA MP729, 50/401/113.
110 Grey, *A Military History of Australia*, p. 142; Wilcox, *For Hearths and Homes*, p. 117.
111 Commander 4th Cavalry Brigade to brigade officers, 23 October 1940, AWM 1, 17/1.
112 Ibid.; Wilcox, *For Hearths and Homes*, p. 117.
113 Commander 6th Military District to HQ Southern Command, 19 December 1940, NAA MP 385/3, 106/8/31.
114 Director of Staff Duties to Eastern Command, 8 November 1940, NAA MP729/6, 37/401/759.
115 PM Cable to Dominions Office, 5 March 1940, NAA A5954, 361/9, cited in Morrison, 'The politics of change', p. 57. See also 'Light horse' in *Oxford Companion to Australian Military History* (1st edn), p. 351, for similar views in regard to a proposal to raise a mounted squadron as part of the 6th Division, 2nd AIF.
116 Anglesey, *A History of British Cavalry*, vol. 8, pp. 315, 331, 342, 350.
117 GOC Eastern Command, Lt-Gen V. Sturdee to Secretary, Military Board, 3 May 1940, NAA MP729/6, 37/401/759.
118 Hall, *The Australian Light Horse*, pp. 51–2, 54; Vane, *North Australia Observer Unit*, pp. ix, 54, passim; war diary, 1 Independent LH Sqn, March 1944, AWM 52, 2/2/18.
119 Appendix A to War Cabinet agendum 166/1942, NAA A571/141, 192/1483. Also of concern was the situation with horses and the requirements to deploy cavalry units well forward along the coast, thus reducing their flexibility.
120 Minister for the Army, 15 June 1942, War Cabinet agendum 166/1942, NAA A571/141, 192/1483.
121 Treasury Representative, 26 March 1942, War Cabinet agendum 166/1942, NAA A571/141, 192/1483.
122 Hall, *The Australian Light Horse*, p. 64; 10th Australian Light Horse Regiment (AIF), *Scrap Book, 1944* (self-published, 1944).

Appendix

1 The Australian War Memorial file that relates to the photo, AWM 93, 17/3/144, has been missing since the 1980s. Any inclination to see nefarious intent behind the loss of this file should be resisted. The fact that

archives misfile, misplace or lose files, or even that files can be stolen, is a regrettable but unavoidable fact of life.
2 Jones, 'Is this the charge at Beersheba?', p. 32. Jones writes that the photo was in circulation in Palestine in 1918. One contributor to the Australian Light Horse Association discussion forums and blogger on the light horse, Bill Woerlee, has asserted that there are connections between the photo and the 9th LHR, although nothing definitive has been produced.
3 G. Lambert to J. Treloar, 24 October 1928, AWM 1DRL/405; Woodhead & Lobach, 'The Australian charge at Beersheba', p. 30.
4 W.R. Lancaster, Director AWM, letter, to Lt Col D. Joynt, in Jones, 'Is this the charge at Beersheba?', p. 32.
5 Statement by Eric George Elliott in Hall, *The Australian Light Horse*, p. 99.
6 Jones, 'Is this the charge at Beersheba?', pp. 32–3; Jones, 'Beersheba: The light horse charge and the making of myths', p. 31.
7 Jones, *The Australian Light Horse*, pp. 100–1.
8 Coulthard-Clark, *Where Australians Fought*, p. 135; Anglesey, *A History of British Cavalry*, vol. 5, pp. 349–52; Smith, *Men of Beersheba*, p. 138; Holloway, *Hooves, Wheels and Tracks*, pp. 165, opposite p. 178.
9 Woodhead & Lobach, 'The Australian charge at Beersheba', pp. 30–2. Summer scholars are history students who are typically about to undertake, or have just finished, an honours program in history at university. It is designed to offer a work experience stepping-stone to would-be historians. During the scholarship they are typically given one substantial project or matter to examine in detail.
10 Jones, *A Thousand Miles of Battles*, pp. 116–17. It differs in its precise wording and in some of the details.
11 McDonald, 'The photograph of the charge at Beersheba'; Bou, 'The Beersheba photograph'; McDonald, 'The Beersheba photograph'. The exchange resulted from press reports of a lecture I gave on the photograph at the Australian War Memorial on 31 October 2008. The lecture is the Memorial's sound collection at PASU0258.
12 The periodic debates and discussions on the Australian Light Horse Association forums come to mind readily. Indeed these debates have informed this appendix and thereby made a contribution to this book. See also Woerlee, '9th Light Horse on Manoeuvres', 19 July 2008, Australian Light Horse Studies Centre (blog), accessed 24 July 2008, <alh-research.tripod.com/>.
13 Jones, *A Thousand Miles of Battles*, p. 116.
14 Woodhead & Lobach, 'The Australian charge at Beersheba', p. 30.
15 Photo album of Tpr Charles Alexander Schimmelbusch, owned by Warwick Cary, copy provided to author by Dick Adams and in author's possession.
16 The album came up for sale on Ebay by Philicia Antiques and Collectibles of South Australia. The compiler of the album, according to the dealer, was Thomas O'Brien, who had served with the 3rd LHR. I have copies of the sale advertisement and examples of the photographs with their captions. The existence of the album was brought to notice by a contributor to the Australian Light Horse Association discussion forum.

17 Extant sources indicate that the print was originally loaned by Pte A.L. Johnston, who served with the 6th LHR – this was perhaps Pte Alexander Law Johnston. The whole negative is somewhat larger, but this is the area covered by the photo image.
18 Report of operations and attack on Beersheba on evening of 31st October 1917, Lt Col M. Bourchier, CO 4th LHR, 1 November 1917, AWM 25, 455/2; Report on the assault on Beersheba, 31.10.17, Lt Col D. Cameron, CO 12th LHR, undated but probably early November 1917, 12 LHR war diary, October 1917, 10/17/9, copy in AWM 25, 455/2. A hand-drawn map in the brigade's war dairy, which was apparently based on one made by the adjutant of the 12th LHR, Lt F.R. Massie, shows that the C Squadrons of both regiments charged in troop columns (see Map of Beersheba charge, 4th Bde war diary, March 1918, appendix 208, AWM 4, 10/4/15); sketch map by Lt F.R. Massie, Adjutant 12th LHR, State Library of NSW, MB 2, 414/1917/1.
19 Jones, *A Thousand Miles of Battles*, p. 116.
20 Woodhead & Lobach, 'The Australian charge at Beersheba', p. 32.
21 Woodhead and Lobach also wondered about the apparent lack of signs of battle, namely casualties or evidence of shellfire. As they point out, the charge came under fire almost as soon as it began, and it is reasonable to expect to see some evidence of that. Still battle photos are often disappointing in what they show us, and we should not expect that signs of battle will always be evident.
22 Jones, 'Is this the charge at Beersheba?', p. 33.
23 Gullett, *The AIF in Sinai and Palestine*, p. 402.
24 Powles, *The New Zealanders in Sinai and Palestine*, p. 139.
25 Preston, *The Desert Mounted Corps*, p. 29.
26 Lt Col M. Bourchier, 'Attack on Beersheba Trenches by 4th LH Regiment on 31/10/17', repeated in report compiled by Bourchier for commander 4th LH Bde, AWM 25, 455/2.
27 Fowler, *Looking Backward*, p. 23.
28 I am indebted to Bill Roberts and the astronomers at the ANU's Research School of Astronomy and Astrophysics for their help with regard to the likely interaction between red light and red dust, as well as looking into the time of sunset for me.
29 Woodhead & Lobach, 'The Australian charge at Beersheba', pp. 31–2.
30 Ibid. I would like to thank Ian Affleck, the AWM's recently retired senior curator of photographs, for his guidance on historical film stock. I would also like to thank the photographic section of the *Canberra Times* for information on what modern film speeds would be applied to action and sports photography.
31 Idriess, *The Desert Column*; Idriess, diary, entries around late October–early November 1917, AWM 1 DRL/373.
32 Maj-Gen Sir H. Hodgson to Barnard [brother], 8 February 1918, Hodgson Papers, IWM.
33 Preston, *The Desert Mounted Corps*, p. 29.

34 Brig W. Grant, Report on Operations (attack on Beersheba) by 4th ALH Brigade, 31.10.07, 2 November 1917, 4th LH Bde war diary, October 1917, appendix 188, AWM 4, 10/4/10.
35 CO 11th LHR to GOC 4th LH Bde, Operations carried out by 11th LH Regt against Beersheba on 31st Oct and 1st November 1917, 3 November 1917, 11th LHR war diary, October 1917, appendix XV, AWM 4, 10/16/25. The time of the charge's commencement cannot be confirmed with complete certainty, although most sources give the time as 16.30. Jones himself suggests that this is perhaps a bit generous and that it may have started anything up to ten minutes later (Jones, 'Beersheba, the light horse charge and the making of myths', p. 30). Sunset has been calculated by Bill Roberts of the ANU's Research School of Astronomy and Astrophysics as being at 16.54.
36 Jones, 'Is this the charge at Beersheba?', p. 33.
37 McDonald, 'The Beersheba photograph', p. 85.
38 Bolton, *Dream of the Past*, p. 16; Beersheba (Y.3) 1:40 000, secret, 1st edn, 26 January 1919, AWM G7500.s40; and Beersheba (B.6.) 1:20 000, secret, 2nd edn (provisional), 22 October 1917, AWM G7500.s20. The fall of the land can easily be confirmed in this era making use of readily available satellite data, such as that to be found with Google Earth.
39 Hurley diary, 6 February 1918, Frank Hurley papers, series 1, item 5, NLA MSS883; 4th LH Bde war diary, February 1918, AWM 4, 10/4/14; 11th LHR war diary, February 1918, AWM 4, 10/16/29.
40 Hurley diary, 7 February 1918, Frank Hurley papers, series 1, item 5, NLA MSS883. Woodhead and Lobach make an error in their work here and suggest that the diary entries of the 11th LHR for 6 February and Hurley's entry of 7 February refer to the same event, which they do not.
41 12th LHR war diary, February 1918, AWM 4, 10/17/13; 4th LHR war diary, February 1918, AWM 4, 10/9/38. Both war diaries have only general entries referring to training being undertaken, although they do state that mounted training was part of their activities. Jones comments that the men hated turning out to re-enact their charge in which mates had died (Jones, *A Thousand Miles of Battles*, p. 116), implying that it was the 4th and/or 12th LHR. A survey of the war diaries makes it clear that only regiments from the 4th LH Bde could have taken part as the rest were located elsewhere or were otherwise occupied.
42 The film's title is *With the Australian Forces in Palestine*, but it is catalogued as Hurley, *With the Australian Light Horse in Sinai and Palestine*, AWM, F00042. The scene is located approximately 43 minutes 10 seconds into the film. The vegetation bears some resemblance to that in the charge photo, and the horsemen are moving in a depression that is not dissimilar, but any comparison ends there. The film used in the feature ranges across much of the Palestine campaign, including parts of it for which Hurley was not present, so he cannot have filmed it all.
43 Jones, *A Thousand Miles of Battles*, p. 116; Ian Jones, telephone discussion with author, 30 July 2008; Chauvel, *Forty Thousand Horsemen*. The scene

is found at approximately 1 hour 20 minutes 50 seconds into the feature. In 1983 Jones speculated that an out-of-place shot in the charge scene of *Forty Thousand Horsemen* might offer an answer to the riddles about the controversial photo. If the film is as he declares it to be, it is a remarkable find, but many questions remain until his assertion can be fleshed out (Jones, 'Is this the charge at Beersheba?', p. 33).

44 The AWM's collection contains plenty of photos taken at Belah, and many show the sandy nature of the terrain next to the coast, although firmer ground and vegetation existed not far inland.

45 Jones, *A Thousand Miles of Battles*, p. 116.

46 Pat Gallagher, correspondence with author, 11 November 2008. Mr Gallagher had undertaken this work on the photo when working as a volunteer in the photographic section of the AWM. He points to the similarity between the terrain evident in the charge photo and that in photos taken near the old Turkish trenches near Gaza; see for example photo AWM A1958B.

47 See the war diaries for the 3rd and 4th LH Bdes and their constituent units for February 1918. For example, 11th LHR war diary, 6 February 1918, AWM 4, 10/16/29.

Bibliography

Archival sources
Australian War Memorial

AWM 1	Pre-Federation and Commonwealth records	1850–1943
AWM 3	Records of the Department of Defence, central registry	no dates
AWM 4	Australian Imperial Force unit war diaries, 1914–18 War	1914–20
AWM 22	Australian Imperial Force Headquarters (Egypt), Central Registry Files	1915–19
AWM 25	Written Records, 1914–18 War	1913–20
AWM 27	Records arranged according to AWM Library classification	1864–1970
AWM 49	Interwar army records	1920–42
AWM 51	AWM security classification records	1914–57
AWM 52	2nd AIF (Australian Imperial Force) and CMF (Citizen Military Forces) unit war diaries	1939–55

National Archives of Australia
Auditor-General's Office

A1831	Correspondence files, annual single-number series	1909–69

Department of Defence

A1194	Library material, single accession number series with decimal classification	1860–
A2023	Correspondence files, multiple-number series with A, B, C or E prefix	1907–17
A2653	Volumes of Military Board proceedings	1905–76
A2657	Volumes of papers of historical interest	1901–19
A5954	Shedden Collection	1901–71
B168	Correspondence files, annual single number	1901–06
B173	Secret correspondence files, annual single-number series with S (Secret) prefix	1905–09

331

B197	Secret and confidential correspondence files, multiple-number series	1894–1938
B536	Registration booklets for correspondence files, multiple-number series with A, B, D or E prefix	1913–17
B539	Correspondence files, multiple-number series with AIF (Australian Imperial Force) prefix	1914–17
B543	Correspondence files, multiple-number series with W (War) prefix	1914–17
B3756	Correspondence files, annual single-number series	1872–1901
D845	Security classified files, annual single-number series	1905–42
MP84/1	Correspondence files, multiple-number series	1894–1953
MP367/1	General correspondence files	1917–29
MP744/1	General correspondence	1901–03

Department of the Treasury

A571	Correspondence files, annual single-number series	1901–78

National Archives (United Kingdom)

CAB44	Committee of Imperial Defence, Historical Branch and Cabinet Office, Historical Section: War Histories: Draft Chapters and Narratives, Military	1914–65
CAB45	Committee of Imperial Defence, Historical Branch and Cabinet Office, Historical Section: Official War Histories Correspondence and Papers	1904–57
WO32	War Office and successors: Registered Files (General Series)	1845–1985
WO33	War Office: Reports, Memoranda and Papers (O and A Series)	1853–1969
WO106	War Office: Directorate of Military Operations and Military Intelligence, and predecessors: Correspondence and Papers	1837–1962
WO157	War Office: Intelligence Summaries, First World War	1914–1923
WO158	War Office: Military Headquarters: Correspondence and Papers, First World War	1909–1929
WO208	War Office: Directorate of Military Operations and Intelligence, and Directorate of Military Intelligence; Ministry of Defence, Defence Intelligence Staff: Files	1917–1974

Queensland State Archives

CRS/278	Papers relating to the despatch of the Queensland Defence Force to Barcaldine – 1891 Shearers Strike	1891
GOV/21	Governor's Secret Papers in connection with military matters	1895–1902
GOV/89	Defence forces: Reports of Defence 1889–90, with copies of various related secret and confidential communications	1885–1905
PRE/19	Defence (Land & Naval): Correspondence and associated papers related to the Queensland Defence Forces	1892–1901

State Records New South Wales

CGS 905	Colonial Secretary/Chief Secretary – main series of letters received	1826–1982

State Records of South Australia

GRG24/6	Correspondence files (Chief Secretary's Office files)	1842–1984
GRG24/51	Correspondence, returns and other papers relating to volunteer military forces and imperial troops	c. 1842–70
GRG24/90	Miscellaneous records of historical interest	1837–1963

PERSONAL PAPERS AND ORGANISATIONAL RECORDS

Australian Defence Force Academy Library
Hutton, Edward T.H. (microfilm copy of originals held in British Library)

Australian War Memorial
Brown, E.A., 2 DRL/1285
Chauvel, Sir Henry G., 2 DRL/0793 and PR00535.004
Delpratt, B.B., 3 DRL/3741
Dengate, E.C., 3 DRL/7678
Godley, Sir A., 3 DRL/2233
Grant, William, PR01850
Horder, L.S., 3 DRL/6595
Idriess, I.L., 1 DRL/373
Jackson, P.S., 1 DRL/380
Johnston, Alfred, PR91/111
Rouget, Arthur James, PR02084
Sullivan, Henry Ernest, PR01058

Imperial War Museum
Chetwode, Field Marshal Lord Phillip
Hodgson, Major-General Sir Henry West
Lynden-Bell, Major-General Sir Arthur
Murray, General Sir Archibald Murray

Liddell Hart Centre for Military Archives, King's College, London
Allenby, Field Marshal Edmund (Henry Hynman), 1st Viscount Allenby of Megiddo and of Felixstowe
Kirke, General Sir Walter Mervyn St George
Shea, General Sir John Stuart Mackenzie

National Library of Australia
Cameron, Sir Donald Charles (1879–1960), papers, 1917–23, MS3932
Cox, Charles Frederick, Papers on the South African War 1897–1933, MS37
Hurley, Frank, papers, MS883
Hutton, Edward T.H., Letters and Press Cuttings 1900–14, MS1215
Ricardo, Percy Ralph, MS1928
Royal New South Wales Lancers, records 1888–1956, Mfm G24577
Ryrie, Granville Sir, Letters, MS986

TRAINING MANUALS, REGULATIONS AND ORDERS – AUSTRALIA

2nd Light Horse Brigade, *Standing Orders, Camp: West Maitland, June 15th to June 26th 1915*, Sydney, Kingston Press, 1915

Australian Light Horse, *Orders and Duties*, Moascar, Ismailia (Egypt), Commandant Australian and New Zealand Training Centre, 1917

Bushman's Military Guide, The, arranged by Lt R.R. Thompson, Adjutant 1st Australian Horse, Sydney, William Appelgate Gullick, Government Printer, 1898

Light Horse Manual for the Drill Training and Exercise of the Light Horse Regiments of Australia, 1 January 1907, Melbourne, J. Kemp, Government Printer, 1907

Light Horse Manual for the Drill Training and Exercise of the Light Horse Regiments of Australia, 1 January 1910, Melbourne, J. Kemp, Government Printer, 1910

Manual of Drill and Field Service for Mounted Rifles, Adelaide, C.E. Bristow, Government Printer, 1891

Manual of Drill for the Mounted Troops of Australia, 1895, Sydney, F. Cunningham & Co., 1895

Mounted Rifles [?], Adelaide, 1888

Mounted Service Manual for Mounted Troops of the Australian Commonwealth, Sydney, F. Cunningham & Co., Government Printer, 1902; also produced under the title *Mounted Service Manual for Australian Light Horse and Mounted Infantry* (publication details unchanged)

Queensland Defence Force, *Drill Regulations and Field Exercises for Mounted Infantry*, Brisbane, James C. Beal, Government Printer, 1892, issued with general orders, 16 April 1892
Regulations and Field Service Manual for Mounted Infantry, Adelaide, H.F. Leader, Government Printer, 1889, copied from Army Order of 1 January 1889
Regulations for Mounted Infantry of Volunteer Militia Reserve Force, Adelaide, C.E. Bristow, Government Printer, 1891

Training manuals – Great Britain
Camel Corps Training (Provisional), London, HMSO, 1913
Cavalry Drill, London, HMSO, 1898
Cavalry Training (provisional), London, HMSO, 1904
Cavalry Training, London, HMSO, 1907
Cavalry Training, London, HMSO, 1912
Cavalry Training, vol. 1: *Training*, London, HMSO, 1921
Cavalry Training, vol. 2: *War*, London, HMSO, 1929
Cavalry Training, vol. 1: *Training*, reprinted with permission of HMSO, Melbourne, H. Green, 1931
Cavalry Training (Horsed), reprinted with permission of HMSO, Melbourne, McCarron, Bird & Co., 1937
Cavalry Training (Mechanised), pamphlet no. 1: *Armoured Cars*, reprinted with permission of HMSO, Melbourne, McCarron, Bird & Co., 1937; reprinted with amendments, 1939
Field Service Regulations, part 1: *Operations*, London, HMSO, 1909
Field Service Regulations, part 2: *Organisation and Administration*, London, HMSO, 1909
Field Service Regulations, part 1: *Operations*, London, HMSO, 1909; reprinted with amendments, 1912
Field Service Regulations, part 1: *Operations*, London, HMSO, 1909; reprinted with amendments, 1914
Field Service Regulations, vol. 2: *Operations, 1920 (provisional)*, London, HMSO, 1920
Field Service Regulations, vol. 2: *Operations – General*, London, HMSO, 1935
Infantry Drill, London, HMSO, 1896
Infantry Training, London, HMSO, 1905; reprinted with amendments, 1908
Mounted Infantry Training (provisional), London, HMSO, 1904
Mounted Infantry Training, London, HMSO, 1906
Mounted Infantry Training, London, HMSO, 1909
Yeomanry and Mounted Rifle Training, parts 1 & 2, London, HMSO, 1912
Yeomanry and Mounted Rifle Training, parts 1 & 2, London, HMSO, 1912; reprinted with amendments, 1915

Reports, memoranda and speeches
Annual Report for the Year 1905 by the Inspector-General of the Commonwealth Military Forces, Major-General H. Finn, 1 January 1906, Melbourne, Robert Brian, Government Printer, 1906

Annual Report for the Year 1907, by the Inspector-General of the Military Forces of the Commonwealth, 28 February 1908, Melbourne, 1908

Annual Report by Major-General G.M. Kirkpatrick, CB, Inspector-General of the Military Forces of the Commonwealth of Australia, 30 May 1911, Melbourne, Albert J. Mullet, Government Printer, 1911

Annual Report by Major-General G.M. Kirkpatrick, CB, Inspector-General of the Military Forces of the Commonwealth of Australia, 30 May 1913, Melbourne, Albert J. Mullet, Government Printer, 1913

Department of Defence, *Report of Committee on the Proposed Scheme of the Defence Department for the Ownership of Horses Etc, for Military Purposes*, 22 May 1909

Department of Defence, *Report of the Conference of Militia Officers Assembled at Headquarters, Victoria Barracks, Melbourne on the 22nd, 23rd, 24th & 25th October 1912*, Melbourne, Albert J. Mullet, 1912

Edwards, Maj-Gen J. Bevan, *Correspondence Relating to the Inspection of the Military Forces of the Australasian Colonies*, Presented to both Houses of Parliament by Command of Her Majesty, August 1890

Hamilton, Gen Sir Ian, *Report of the Inspection of the Military Forces of the Commonwealth of Australia by General Sir Ian Hamilton, GOC Commanding in Chief Mediterranean, and Inspector General of the Overseas Forces*, Melbourne, Albert J. Mullet, Government Printer, 1914

Hutton, Maj-Gen Sir Edward, *Minute Upon the Defence of Australia*, Melbourne, 1902

Lang, John, *How to Defend the Colony, being the substance of a speech in, the Legislative Assembly of NSW, on Tuesday, 20 December 1859*, Sydney, John L. Sherrif & F. Mason, 1860

Legislative Assembly of New South Wales, *Military Defences Inquiry Commission*, Sydney, Thomas Richards, 1881

Memorandum on the Defence of Australia by Field Marshal Viscount Kitchener of Khartoum, GCB, OM, GCSI, GCMG, GCIE, etc, Melbourne, J. Kemp, Government Printer, 1910

Report by the Inspector-General of the Commonwealth Military Forces, Major-General H. Finn, 1st September 1906, Melbourne, 1906

Report for the Inspector-General of the Australian Military Forces by Lieutenant-General Sir H.G. Chauvel, CGS, 31 May, 1924, Melbourne, 1924

Report for the Inspector-General of the Australian Military Forces by Lieutenant-General Sir H.G. Chauvel, CGS, 31 May 1925, part 1, Melbourne, 1925

Report for the Inspector-General of the Australian Military Forces by Lieutenant-General Sir H.G. Chauvel, CGS, 31 May 1926, part 1, Melbourne, 1926

Report for the Inspector-General of the Australian Military Forces by Lieutenant-General Sir H.G. Chauvel, CGS, 31 May 1927, part 1, Melbourne, 1927

Report for the Inspector-General of the Australian Military Forces by Lieutenant-General Sir H.G. Chauvel, CGS, 31 May 1928, part 1, Melbourne, 1928

Report for the Inspector-General of the Australian Military Forces by Lieutenant-General Sir H.G. Chauvel, CGS, 31 May 1929, part 1, Melbourne, 1929

Report for the Inspector-General of the Australian Military Forces by Lieutenant-General Sir H.G. Chauvel, CGS, 15 April 1930, part 1, Melbourne, 1930

Report of the Inter-colonial Committee for Framing a Manual of Drill etc for Mounted Troops in Australia, 2 November 1894

Report of His Majesty's Commissioners Appointed to Inquire into the Military Preparations and Other Matters Connected with the War in South Africa, London, HMSO, 1903

Report on a Staff Ride held in Queensland under the direction of the Chief of Intelligence in July 1907, and a Lecture on Military Science by the Director of Military Science Sydney University, Melbourne, J. Kemp, acting Government Printer, 1907

Report on a Staff Ride held in Queensland, under the direction of the Commandant, in September 1908, Brisbane, Anthony James Cumming, Government Printer, 1909

NEWSPAPERS, PERIODICALS AND UNIT PRODUCTIONS

10th Australian Light Horse, *Scrap Book, 1942–43*, self-published, 1943

10th Australian Light Horse Regiment (AIF), *Scrap Book, 1944*, self-published, 1944

Adelaide Observer

Cavalry in SA: To Commemorate the 150th Anniversary of the First Cavalry Squadron in South Australia, A Sqn, 3rd/9th South Australian Mounted Rifles & Army Museum of South Australia, undated information pamphlet provided to author by the Army Museum of South Australia

Courier-Mail

Kia-Ora Coo-ee

Lancer: The Regimental Journal of the Royal NSW Lancers, 1st Light Horse (Machine Gun) Regiment

Reveille

Senior Motor Transport Officer, the Desert Mounted Corps, *History of MT of the Desert Mounted Corps during operations in Palestine and Syria 1918*, printed by Palestine News, 1919

THESES, MONOGRAPHS AND UNPUBLISHED MANUSCRIPTS

Badsey, Stephen, 'Fire and the sword: The British army and the *arme blanche* controversy, 1871–1921', DPhil. thesis, University of Cambridge, 1981

Becker, Steve, 'The history of the composite Australian Light Horse Regiment', unpublished article provided to author

Bridges, Barry John, 'The New South Wales Lancers and the Anglo-Boer War, 1899–1902', MA thesis, University of South Africa, 1975

Clarke, Stephen J., 'Marching to their own drum: British officers as military commandants in the Australian colonies and New Zealand 1870–1901', PhD thesis, University College, Australian Defence Force Academy, University of New South Wales, 1999

Eyland, David William, 'The New South Wales military forces 1870–1890: Social composition and status', BA honours thesis, University College, Australian Defence Force Academy, University of New South Wales, 1992

Haken, J.K., 'Lineage and development of NSW military forces', unpublished manuscript, Australian War Memorial, AWM PR MF 43
Kennedy, Edwin L. 'The Australian Light Horse: A study of the evolution of tactical and operational maneuver', Master of Military Art and Science thesis, US Army Command and General Staff College, 1991
Kenyon, David, 'British cavalry on the Western Front, 1916–1918', PhD thesis, Cranfield University, 2007
Mallett, Ross, 'The interplay between technology, tactics and organisation in the First AIF', MA (hons) thesis, Australian Defence Force Academy, University of New South Wales, 1999
Millar, T.B., 'The history of the defence forces of the Port Phillip district and colony of Victoria 1836–1900', MA thesis, University of Melbourne, 1957
Morrison, James C., 'The politics of change: Army mechanisation policy and the conversion of the light horse 1920–1943', BA honours thesis, University College, University of New South Wales, Australian Defence Force Academy, 2003
US Cavalry Association, *Cavalry Combat*, Washington, Cavalry School, 1937
US Cavalry School, *The Palestine Campaign*, Fort Riley, Kansas, US Cavalry School Department of General Instruction, 1922
Van der Waag, Lt-Col Ian, 'An overview of the nature, origin and development of the commando system in South Africa, c. 1715–1899', unpublished notes provided to author
Walk, Jason, 'Rural Australia and the Great War: Some social and economic aspects', BA honours thesis, University College, University of New South Wales, Australian Defence Force Academy, 1993
Wilcox, Craig, 'Australia's citizen army, 1889–1914', PhD thesis, Australian National University, 1993
—— 'Citizen mounted riflemen and the South African War of 1899–1902', unpublished paper, given at the Sir Robert Menzies Centre for Australian Studies, London, 26 January 1999
Wilkins, Len, 'The bated shining sword: The colonial defence force as a mirror of colonial society in South Australia, 1836–1901', BA honours thesis, University of Adelaide, 1983
Wilson, L. C., 'The Third Light Horse Brigade, Australian Imperial Force, in the Egyptian Rebellion', narrative of Brig. L. C. Wilson, typescript, ADFA Library, Canberra.
Zwillenberg, H.J., 'Citizens and soldiers: The defence of South Australia 1836–1901', MA thesis, University of Adelaide, 1970

Articles

Abbot, J.H.M., 'The light horse regiments', *Lone Hand*, 12(71), 1 March 1913
Anon., 'Mounted rifles and mounted infantry', *Cavalry Journal*, 1, 1906
Anon., 'Operations of the mounted troops of the Egyptian Expeditionary Force', *Cavalry Journal*, 10, October 1920
Anon., 'The Australian light horse', *Cavalry Journal*, 19(74), October 1929
Anon., '1st Light Horse (Machine Gun) Regiment, Royal New South Wales Lancers', *Citizen Soldier of Australia*, 1(1), June 1937

Anon., *8/31 Victorian Mounted Rifles*, Victorian Mounted Rifles, 1962[?]
Badsey, Stephen, 'Mounted combat in the Second Boer War', *Sandhurst Journal of Military Studies*, 2, 1991
—— 'The Boer War (1899–1902) and British cavalry doctrine', *Journal of Military History*, 71(1), January 1997
Barrow, Gen Sir G., 'Two cavalry episodes in the Palestine Campaign, 1917–1918', *Cavalry Journal*, October 1936
Bingham, Col E.G.H., 'The Australian soldier', *Journal of the Royal United Service Institution*, 15(284), October 1901
Bou, Jean, 'Cavalry, firepower and swords: The Australian light horse and the tactical lessons of cavalry operations in Palestine, 1916–1918', *Journal of Military History*, 71(1), January 1997
—— 'To Amman with the 6th Regiment', *Wartime*, 37, 2007
—— 'An aspirational army: Australian planning for an citizen forces divisional structure before 1920', *Sabretache*, 49(1), 2008
—— 'They shot the horses – didn't they?', *Wartime*, 44, 2008
—— 'The Beersheba photograph: 1', *Quadrant*, March 2009
—— 'Sold or shot? The fate of the light horse's mounts – 1919', *Sabretache*, 50(3), September 2009
Brassey, T.A., 'Recent progress in Victoria: With observations on the defence forces', *Proceedings of the Royal Colonial Institute*, vol. unknown, 1901
Brennan, Godfrey, 'The light horse and mounted rifle volunteer corps', *Journal of the Society for Army Historical Research*, 21(81), Spring 1942
Brown, Lt-Col J.G., 'Operations of the mounted troops of the Egyptian Expeditionary Force (continued)', *Cavalry Journal*, 12(41), 1921
Burness, Peter, 'New South Wales cavalry 1854–1935', *Sabretache*, 16(4), February 1975
—— 'Australian colonial forces: A sketch', *Australian Military History Conference*, 11–13 February 1982, Australian War Memorial
—— 'The Australian horse: A cavalry squadron in the South African War', *Journal of the Australian War Memorial*, 6, April 1985
—— 'Mackay, James Alexander Kenneth', *Australian Dictionary of Biography*, vol. 10: 1891–1939, Melbourne, Melbourne University Press, 1986
Chamberlain, Max, 'The Australian Commonwealth Horse', *Sabretache*, 25(3), July–September 1984
—— 'The Australian Commonwealth Horse (continued)', *Sabretache*, 25(4), October–December 1984
—— 'The Wilmansrust Affair', *Journal of the Australian War Memorial*, 6, April 1985
Clarke, Rex, 'Lieutenant John Wasson, DCM: NSWMR and 2nd Light Horse Regt AIF', *Despatch*, 4(1), January 1962
Coleman, Lachlan, 'A proper soldier's vengeance?', *Wartime*, 39, 2007
Collyer, Lt-Col J.J., 'Mounted rifle tactics', *Australian Military Journal*, 6, April 1915
Conway, Lt T.P., 'The Australian light horseman', *Commonwealth Military Journal*, 2, June 1912
Cooke, Lt D.F., 'NSW Mounted Rifles 6th Light Horse Regiment', *Citizen Soldier of Australia*, 1(2), July 1937

Crouch, Maj the Hon. R.A., 'The Australian militia', *Lone Hand*, 12(71), 1 March 1913
de Lisle, Brig-Gen H. de B., 'The strategical action of cavalry', *Commonwealth Military Journal*, 3, September 1912
Dove, Maj F.A., 'Light horse duties in the field, scouting; A criticism of the article by Major P.H. Priestly... in the March issue of this journal', *Commonwealth Military Journal*, 2, May 1912
'Durbar', 'The functions of cavalry', *Commonwealth Military Journal*, 2, June 1912, reprinted from *United Service Magazine*, March 1912
Everett, Maj W.F., 'The future use of cavalry and our light horse', *Journal and Proceedings of the United Service Institution of New South Wales*, 21, lecture 38, 1909
Finn, Maj-Gen H., 'With the cavalry in Afghanistan and in Egypt', *Journal and Proceedings of the United Service Institution of New South Wales*, 17, lecture 59, 1905
Foster, Lt-Col W.J., 'Operations of the mounted troops of the Egyptian Expeditionary Force', *Cavalry Journal*, 12(39), January 1921
G.G.A., 'The bayonet for mounted riflemen', *Australian Military Journal*, 5, January 1914; reprinted from *Army Review*
Gray, Robert, 'Regiments raised in South Australia,1840–1937', *Journal of the Society for Army Historical Research*, 35, 1957
—— 'Reedbeds Mounted Volunteers (Reedbeds Cavalry)', *Despatch*, 4(11), November 1969
Hutton, Maj E.T.H., 'Mounted infantry', *Journal of the Royal United Service Institution*, 30(135), 1886
—— 'The mounted infantry question in its relation to the volunteer force of Great Britain', *Journal of the Royal United Service Institution*, 35(160), June 1891
—— 'The evolution of mounted infantry', *Empire Review*, 1(4), May 1901
—— 'The cavalry of Greater Britain', *Cavalry Journal*, 1, 1906
Immanuel, Maj, Infantry Regiment No. 158.,'The importance of fighting dismounted for cavalry, and the place to be assigned to it in action and instruction', *Commonwealth Military Journal*, 2, January 1912; German article reprinted from *International Review*
J.W.N., 'Sir Edward Hutton, an appreciation', *Lone Hand*, 12(71), 1 March 1913
Jones, Ian, 'The charge at Beersheba and the making of myths', *Australian War Memorial Conference*, 8–12 February 1983
——'Is this the charge at Beersheba?', *Journal of the Australian War Memorial*, October 1983
—— 'The case of the vanishing regiment: The Fourth Light Horse in France and Belgium 1916–18', *Sabretache*, 26, April–June 1985
Kent, David A., 'The Australian remount unit in Egypt, 1915–19: A footnote to history', *Journal of the Australian War Memorial*, 1, October 1982
Loir, Captaine, 'A study of patrol work', *Australian Military Journal*, 5, October 1914
Maxwell, Maj F.A., 'Notes on squadron training for light horse', *Commonwealth Military Journal*, 1, June 1911

McDonald, Neil, 'The Beersheba photograph', *Quadrant*, April 2009
—— 'The photograph of the charge at Beersheba', *Quadrant*, December 2008
Mitchell, Elyne, 'The Australian Light Horse legend', *This Australia*, 1(4), 1982
Osbourne, Lt-Col Rex, 'Operations of the mounted troops of the Egyptian Expeditionary Force', *Cavalry Journal*, 12(42), 1921
—— 'Operations of the mounted troops of the Egyptian Expeditionary Force (continued)', *Cavalry Journal*, 13, serialised over three issues (pp. 21–41, 138–56, 276–85), 1923
Penny, B.R., 'Brassey, Thomas, First Earl Brassey', *Australian Dictionary of Biography*, vol. 7: 1891–1939, Melbourne, Melbourne University Press, 1986
Perry, Warren, 'General Sir Edward Hutton', *Stand-To*, 4(4), July–August 1954
—— 'Military reforms of General Sir Edward Hutton in the Commonwealth of Australia: 1902–04', *Victorian Historical Magazine*, 29(1), February 1959
—— 'Military reforms of General Sir Edward Hutton in New South Wales,1893–96', *Australian Quarterly*, 28(4), December 1956
—— 'Australia's immediate post-Federation military forces', *Army Journal*, 328, September 1976
Phillips, Gervase, 'The scapegoat arm', *Journal of Military History*, 71(1), January 1997
Preston, A.W., 'British military thought, 1856–90', *Army Quarterly and Defence Journal*, 80(1), 1964
Priestly, Maj P.H., 'Light horse duties in the field', *Commonwealth Military Journal*, 2, March 1912
Purdy, Maj J.S., 'With the New Zealanders and Australians in the South African War', *Australian Military Journal*, 5, April 1914
Renny-Tailour, Col. H.W., 'The land forces of Australasia and their dispositions for war', *Journal and Proceedings of the Royal United Service Institution of New South Wales*, 4, 1892
Richardson, Brig J.D., 'Long overdue', *Citizen Soldier of Australia*, 1(1), June 1937
Robertson, Maj H.C.H., 'The 10th Australian Light Horse Attack at Magdhaba, 23rd December 1916', *Cavalry Journal*, 25(96), 1935
Robson, L.L., 'The origin and character of the First AIF,1914–18: Some statistical evidence', *Historical Studies*, 15(61), 1973
Ryan, J. Tighe, 'The Bush Brigade: Being the remarkable story of the First Australian Horse', *Review of Reviews*, 15 July 1898
Schmitt, David, 'The Victorian Mounted Rifles in Gippsland', *Gippsland Heritage Journal*, 2(1), 1987
Shaw, P.A., 'A brief history of the 10th Light Horse', *Sabretache*, October 1966
Sheffy, Yigal, 'Origins of the British breakthrough into southern Palestine: The Anzac raid on the Ottoman railway, 1917', *Journal of Strategic Studies*, 22(1), 1999
Stanley, Peter, '"Our big world": The social history of the Light Horse Regiment, 1916–18', *Sabretache*, 39, March 1998
Strange, Maj-Gen, 'The maxim gun', *Journal and Proceedings of the Royal United Service Institution of New South Wales*, 1, 1889

Sutton, R., 'French, Sir George Arthur', *Australian Dictionary of Biography*, vol. 8: 1891–1939, Melbourne, Melbourne University Press, 1986
Talbot, Phillip, 'The English yeomanry in the nineteenth century and the great Boer War', *Journal of the Society for Army Historical Research*, 79(317), Spring 2001
Vazenry, Sgt G.R., 'Reorganisation: The Australian Military Force 1800–1962', *Australian Army Journal*, 165, February 1963
White, Capt C.B.B., 'Light horse of Australia: Their organisation and training', *Cavalry Journal*, 4, 1909
Whitfield, Maj L.C., 'Horse breeding in Australia', *Cavalry Journal*, 20(77), July 1930
Williams, Jeff, 'The First AIF Overseas: 1914–16', *Australian War Memorial History Conference*, 8–12 February 1983
Woodhead, Matthew & Lobach, Jaqui, 'The Australian Charge at Beersheba', *Wartime*, 1, 1997

Books and book chapters

'An ex-C.M.R.', *With the Cape Mounted Rifles: Four Years Service in South Africa*, London, Richard Bentley & Son, 1881
Andrews, Eric, *The Department of Defence*, vol. 5, *The Australian Centenary History of Australian Defence*, Melbourne, Oxford University Press, 2001
Anglesey, Marquess of, *A History of the British Cavalry 1816 to 1919*, vol. 4, 1899 to 1913, London, Leo Cooper and Secker & Warburg, 1986
—— *A History of the British Cavalry 1816 to 1919*, vol. 5, *Egypt, Palestine and Syria 1914–1919*, London, Leo Cooper, 1986
—— *A History of the British Cavalry 1816 to 1919*, vol. 8, *The Western Front, 1915–1918; Epilogue, 1919–1939*, London, Leo Cooper, 1997
Anon., *12th Light Horse Regiment*, Sydney, W.A. Shearon, 1914[?]
Anon., *A Short History of the New South Wales Mounted Rifles, 1888–1913*, Sydney, Marchant & Co. Ltd, 1913
'Asiaticus', *Reconnaissance in the Russo-Japanese War*, trans. J. Montgomery, London, Hugh Rees Ltd, 1908
Austin, M., *The Army in Australia: Prelude to the Golden Years*, Canberra, AGPS, 1979
Badsey, Stephen, *Doctrine and Reform in the British Cavalry*, Farnham, Ashgate, 2008
Bates, I.B., *Commanders Queensland Mounted Units 1860–1940*, Brisbane, Victoria Barracks Museum and Historical Society, 1990
Bean, C.E.W., *Official History of Australia in the War of 1914–1918*, vol. 3, *The Australian Imperial Force in France 1916*, Sydney, Angus & Robertson, 1929
—— *Official History of Australia in the War of 1914–1918*, vol. 1, *The Story of Anzac: From the Outbreak of War to the End of the First Phase of the Gallipoli Campaign, 4 May 1915*, Brisbane, University of Queensland Press with Australian War Memorial, 1981; first published 1921
—— *Official History of Australia in the War of 1914–1918*, vol. 2, *The Story of Anzac From 4 May 1915, to the Evacuation of the Gallipoli Peninsula*,

Brisbane, University of Queensland Press with the Australian War Memorial, 1981; first published 1924
——— *Anzac to Amiens*, Canberra, Australian War Memorial, 1983; first published 1946
Beaumont, Joan (ed.), *Australia's War, 1914–18*, Sydney, Allen & Unwin, 1995
——— *Australian Defence: Sources and Statistics*, vol. 6, *The Australian Centenary History of Defence*, Melbourne, Oxford University Press, 2001
Beckett, Ian, *The Amateur Military Tradition*, Manchester, Manchester University Press, 1991
——— 'The South African War and the late Victorian army', P. Dennis & J. Grey (eds), *The Boer War: Army, Nation and Empire: The 1999 Chief of Army/Australian War Memorial Military History Conference*, Canberra, Army History Unit, 2000
Bennet, Will, *Absent-minded Beggars: Volunteers in the Boer War*, Barnsley, Leo Cooper, 1999
Berrie, George L., *Under Furred Hats (6th ALH Regt)*, Sydney, W.C. Penfold & Co. Ltd, 1919
——— *Morale: A Story of Australian Light Horsemen*, Sydney, Holland & Stephensen, 1949
Black, John [Gray, John], *Red Dust: An Australian Trooper in Palestine*, London, Jonathan Cape, 1931
Boguslawski, A.V., *Tactical Deductions from the War of 1870–71*, trans. Col. Lumley Graham, London, Henry S. King & Co., 1872
Bolton, Trooper Sloan, *Dream of the Past*, Geelong, Ken Jenkin Print, undated
Bou, Jean, 'Modern cavalry: Mounted rifles, the Boer War, and the doctrinal debates', P. Dennis & J. Grey (eds), *The Boer War: Army, Nation and Empire: The 1999 Chief of Army/Australian War Memorial Military History Conference*, Canberra, Army History Unit, 2000
Bourne, Lt-Col G.H., *Nulli Secundus: The History of the 2nd Australian Light Horse Regiment, Australian Imperial Force, August 1914–April 1919*, Swanbourne, WA, John Burridge Military Antiques, 1994; originally published 1926
Bowman-Manifold, Maj-Gen Sir M.G.E., *An Outline of the Egyptian and Palestine Campaigns, 1914 to 1918*, [London?], Institution of Royal Engineers, 1923
Box, Allan, *Saddle and Spur: A Photographic Record of Gippsland's Mounted Regiments 1885–1945*, Churchill, Vic., Centre for Gippsland Studies, 1989
Brugger, Suzanne, *Australians and Egypt 1914–1919*, Melbourne, Melbourne University Press, 1980
Buckley, Martin J., *Sword and Lance: The Story of the Richmond River Horsemen*, Lismore, NSW, M.J. Buckley, 1988
——— *The NSW Northern Rivers Lancers: Light Horse and Motor Regiments 1903–1944*, Lismore, NSW, M.J. Buckley, 1991
Burness, Peter, *The Nek: The Tragic Charge of the Light Horse at Gallipoli*, Kenthurst, NSW, Kangaroo Press, 1996
Calder, Winty, *Glimpses of Colonel Tom: A Collection of Addresses and Letters by Colonel Tom Price*, Melbourne, Jimaringle Publications, 1985

―――― *Heroes and Gentlemen: Colonel Tom Price and the Victorian Mounted Rifles*, Melbourne, Jimaringle Publications, 1985
Carmen, William Y., *Light Horse Volunteers and Mounted Rifle Volunteers, 1860–1901*, Farnham, Surrey, Arrow Press, 1995
Chamberlain, Denis J., *History of the Bathurst Contingents 1868–1987*, Bathurst, NSW, the author, 1987
Chamberlain, Max, *To Shoot and Ride: The Australians in the South African War, 1899–1902*, Ormond East, Vic., Military Historical Society of Australia, 1967
―――― *Australians in the South African War, 1899–1902: A Map History*, Canberra, author & Army History Unit, 1999
Chappell, M., *British Cavalry Equipment 1800–1941*, London, Osprey, 1983
Childers, Erskine, *War and the Arme Blanche*, London, Edward Arnold, 1910
―――― *German Influence on British Cavalry*, London, Edward Arnold, 1911
Clarke, Rex, *The First Queensland Mounted Infantry Contingent in the South African War*, Canberra, Military Historical Society of Australia, 1971
Clarke, Stephen, 'Manufacturing spontaneity? The role of the commandants in the colonial offers of troops to the South African War', P. Dennis & J. Grey (eds), *The Boer War: Army, Nation and Empire: The 1999 Chief of Army/Australian War Memorial Military History Conference*, Canberra, Army History Unit, 2000
Connor, John, *The Australian Frontier Wars, 1788–1838*, Sydney, University of New South Wales Press, 2002
Crum, F.M., *The Question of Mounted Infantry, by a Rifleman*, London, Hugh Rees Ltd, 1909
Cutlack, F.M. *The Official History of Australian in the War of 1914–1918*, vol. 8, *The Australian Flying Corps*, Brisbane, University of Queensland Press, 1984; first published 1923
Darley, Maj T.H., *With the Ninth Light Horse in the Great War*, Adelaide, Hassell Press, 1924
De Groot, Gerard, *Douglas Haig, 1861–1928*, London, Unwin Hyman, 1988
Delbruck, Hans, *The Dawn of Modern Warfare: History of the Art of War*, vol. 4, trans. Renfroe, Walter Jr. Lincoln, Nebraska, University of Nebraska Press, 1985; first published in German 1920
Denison, Lt-Col George T., *A History of Cavalry from the Earliest Times: With Lessons for the Future*, Westport, Conn., Greenwood Press, 1977 (reprint of 2nd edn, 1913); originally published 1877
―――― *Modern Cavalry: Its Organization, Armament and Employment in War*, London, Thomas Bosworth, 1868
Dennis, Peter, Grey, Jeffrey, Morris, Ewan, Prior, Robin with Bou, Jean (eds), *The Oxford Companion to Australian Military History* (2nd edn), Melbourne, Oxford University Press, 2008
Dennis, Peter, Grey, Jeffrey, Morris, Ewan, Prior, Robin with Connor, John (eds), *The Oxford Companion to Australian Military History*, Melbourne, Oxford University Press, 1995
Dunn, Brian & Blundell, Peter (eds), *The Boys in Green: A Centenary History of the 1st Australian Horse and the Light Horse Units of Harden and Murrumbarrah, New South Wales*, Binalong, NSW, Clarion Editions, 1997

Erickson, Edward, *Ordered to Die: A History of the Ottoman Army in the First World War*, Westport, Conn., Greenwood Press, 2001
Falls, Cyril, *Military Operations: Egypt and Palestine from June 1917 to the End of the War*, London, HMSO, 1930
────── *Armageddon 1918*, London, Weidenfeld & Nicolson, 1964
Fowler, John Ernest ('Chook'), *Looking Backward*, Canberra, Roebuck Society, 1979
Gammage, Bill, *The Broken Years: Australian Soldiers in the Great War*, Melbourne, Penguin Books, 1990; first published 1974
Garcia, Clive, *A Key to Victory: A Study in War Planning*, London, Eyre & Spottiswood, 1940
Goold-Walker, G. (ed.), *The Honourable Artillery Company in the Great War 1914–1919*, London, Seeley, Service & Co., 1930
Grainger, John D., *The Battle for Palestine 1917*, Woodbridge, Boydell Press, 2006
Green, James, *The Story of the Australian Bushmen: Being Notes of a Chaplain*, Sydney, William Brooks & Co. Ltd, 1903
Grey, Jeffrey, *A Military History of Australia*, 2nd edn, Melbourne, Cambridge University Press, 1999; originally published 1990
────── *The Australian Centenary History of Defence*, vol. 1: *The Australian Army*, Melbourne, Oxford University Press, 2001
Griffith, Paddy, *Military Thought in the French Army, 1815–51*, Manchester, Manchester University Press, 1989
Griffith, Paddy (ed.), *British Fighting Methods in the Great War*, London, Frank Cass, 1996
Gullett, H.S., *The Official History of Australia in the War of 1914–1918*, vol. 7, *The Australian Imperial Force in Sinai and Palestine, 1914–1918*, Brisbane, University of Queensland Press, 1984; first published 1923
Gullet, H.S. & Barrett, C. (eds), *Australia in Palestine*, Sydney, Angus & Robertson, 1919
Haig, Maj-Gen Douglas, *Cavalry Studies: Strategical and Tactical*, London, Hugh Rees Ltd, 1907
Hall, Major R.J.G., *The Australian Light Horse*, Blackburn, Vic., W.D. Joynt & Co., 1968
Hamilton, Lt-Gen Sir Ian, *A Staff Officer's Scrap Book: During the Russo-Japanese War*, London, Edward Arnold, 1905
Hannah, W.H., *Bobs, Kipling's General: The Life of Field Marshal Earl Roberts of Kandahar, VC*, London, Leo Cooper, 1972
Hill, A.J., *Chauvel of the Light Horse: A Biography of General Sir Harry Chauvel, GCMG, KCB*, Melbourne, Melbourne University Press, 1978
Hollis, Kenneth, *Thunder of the Hooves: A History of 12 Light Horse Regiment 1915–1919*, Loftus, NSW, Australian Military History Publications, 2008
Holloway, David, *Hooves, Wheels and Tracks: A History of the 4th/19th Prince of Wales's Light Horse Regiment and its Predecessors*, Fitzroy, Vic., Regimental Trustees, 4th/19th Prince of Wales's Light Horse Regiment, 1990
Holmes, Richard, *The Little Field Marshal: Sir John French*, London, Jonathan Cape, 1981

―――― *Riding the Retreat: Mons to the Marne 1914 Revisited*, London, Pimlico, 1995
Howard, Michael, *The Franco-Prussian War: The German Invasion of France, 1870–1871*, London, Rupert Hart-Davis, 1968
―――― *War in European History*, Oxford, Oxford University Press, 1976
―――― 'Men against fire: The doctrine of the offensive in 1914', in Peter Paret, Gordon A. Craig & Felix Gilbert (eds), *Makers of Modern Strategy: From Machiavelli to the Nuclear Age*, Princeton, NJ, Princeton University Press, 1986
Howell-Price, Lt D.C., *The Light Horse Pocket Book*, Sydney, Angus & Robertson, 2nd edn, 1914
Hughes, Matthew, *Allenby and British Strategy in the Middle East*, London, Frank Cass, 1999
Hunter, Doug, *My Corps Cavalry: A History of the 13th Australian Light Horse Regiment 1915–1918*, Rosebud, Vic., Slouch Hat Publications, 1999
Hutton, Maj-Gen Sir Edward T.H., *The Defence and Defensive Power of Australia*, Melbourne, Angus & Robertson, 1902
Idriess, Ion, *The Desert Column: Leaves from the Diary of an Australian Trooper in Gallipoli, Sinai and Palestine*, Sydney, Angus & Robertson, 1933
James, David, *Lord Roberts*, London, Hollis & Carter, 1954
James, Lt-Col Lionel, *The History of King Edward's Horse (the King's Oversea Dominion Regiment)*, London, Sifton Praed & Co., 1921
Jeal, Tim, *The Boy-Man: The Life of Lord Baden-Powell*, New York, William Morrow & Company, 1990
Johnson, D.H., *Volunteers at Heart: The Queensland Defence Forces 1860–1901*, Brisbane, University of Queensland Press, 1975
Jones, Ian, *The Australian Light Horse: Australians at War*, North Sydney, Time-Life Books, 1987
―――― *A Thousand Miles of Battles: The Saga of the Australian Light Horse in WWI*, Aspley, Qld, Anzac Day Commemoration Committee, 2007
Keogh, Col E.G., *Suez to Aleppo*, Melbourne, Directorate of Military Training, 1955
Kinloch, Terry, *Devils on Horses: In the Words of the Anzacs in the Middle East*, Auckland, Exisle Publishing, 2007
Laffin, John, *Anzacs at War: The Story of Australian and New Zealand Battles*, London, Abelard-Schuman, 1965
Langley, George F. & Edmee M., *Sand, Sweat and Camels*, Adelaide, Seal Books, 1980; first published 1976
Likeman, Robert, *From Law to War: The Life of Brigadier-General Lachlan Wilson of the Light Horse*, Rosebud, Vic., Slouch Hat Publications, 2004
Lucas, T.J., *Camp Life and Sport in South Africa: Experiences of Kaffir Warfare with the Cape Mounted Rifles*, Johannesburg, Africana Book Society, reprint of 1878 edn; 1975
Luvaas, Jay, *The Military Legacy of the Civil War: The European Inheritance*, Chicago, University of Chicago Press, 1959
Mackay, Kenneth, *The Yellow Wave: A Romance of the Asiatic Invasion of Australia*, Andrew Enstice & Janeen Webb (eds), Middletown, Conn., Wesleyan

University Press, 2003, reprint of *The Yellow Wave*, 1897, Australian edn, originally published London, 1895

MacMunn, George & Falls, Cyril, *Military Operations: Egypt and Palestine from the Outbreak of War with Germany to June 1917*, London, HMSO, 1928

Maude, Lt-Col F.N., *Cavalry its Past and Future*, London, William Clowes & Sons, 1903

Mordike, John, *General Sir Edmund Allenby's Joint Operations in Palestine, 1917–18*, Canberra, Aerospace Centre Paper No. 6, 2002

Moyse-Bartlett, H., *Louis Edward Nolan and his Influence on the British Cavalry*, London, Leo Cooper, 1971

Nutting, Lt G.W., *History of the Fourth Light Horse Brigade Australian Imperial Forces, War 1914–1918, and Egyptian Rebellion, 1919*, Brisbane, W.R. Smith & Paterson, 1953

Olden, Lt-Col. A.C.N., *Westralian Cavalry in the War: The Story of the Tenth Light Horse Regiment, AIF, In the Great War, 1914–1918*, Sydney, Bennet, 1985; first published 1921

O'Sullivan, E.W., *The Power of Mounted Riflemen: Illustrated by the Performances of the Boers in the Transvaal War and Sheridan's Mounted Regiments in the Great Civil War in the United States*, Queanbeyan, NSW, Age Office, 1894

Pakenham-Walsh, R.P., *Elementary Tactics or the Art of War British School*, London, publisher unknown, 1926

Palazzo, Albert, *The Australian Army: A History of its Organisation 1901–2001*, Melbourne, Oxford University Press, 2001

Parsonson, Ian M., *Vets at War: A History of the Australian Veterinary Corps 1909–1946*, Loftus, NSW, Australian Military History Publications, 2005

Preston, Lt-Col R.M.P., *The Desert Mounted Corps: An Account of the Cavalry Operations in Palestine and Syria 1917–1918*, London, Constable & Company, 1921

Rimington, Maj-Gen M.F., *Our Cavalry*, London, Macmillan & Co., 1912

Ross, Jane, *The Myth of the Digger: The Australian Soldier in Two World Wars*, Sydney, Hale & Iremonger, 1985

Scott, Ernest, *The Official History of Australia in the War of 1914–1918*, vol. 11, *Australia During the War*, Sydney, Angus & Robertson, 1971 (7th edn); first published 1936

Sheffy, Yigal, *British Military Intelligence in the Palestine Campaign 1914–1918*, London, Frank Cass, 1998

Smith, F., *A Veterinary History of the War in South Africa 1899–1902*, London, H. & W. Brown, 1919; originally published as Anon., *A Veterinary History of the War in South Africa 1899–1902*, London, publisher unknown, 1910

Smith, Lt-Col. Neil C., *The Third Australian Light Horse Regiment 1914–1918: A Short History and Listing of Those Who Served*, Gardenvale, Vic., Mostly Unsung Military History Research and Publications, 1993

Smith, W.H.B. & Smith, Joseph E., *Small Arms of the World: A Basic Manual of Military Small Arms*, Harrisburg, Stackpole Company, 7th edn, 1962

Spence, Iain G., '"To shoot and ride": Mobility and firepower in mounted warfare', P. Dennis & J. Grey (eds), *The Boer War: Army, Nation and Empire: The*

1999 Chief of Army/Australian War Memorial Military History Conference, Canberra, Army History Unit, 2000

Stanley, Peter, *The Remote Garrison: The British Army in Australia 1788–1870*, Kenthurst, NSW, Kangaroo Press, 1986

Starr, Joan & Sweeney Christopher, *Forward: The History of the 2nd/14th Light Horse (Queensland Mounted Infantry)*, Brisbane, University of Queensland Press, 1989

Stevenson, David, *1914–1918: The History of the First World War*, London, Penguin Books, 2005

Stone, Jay & Schmidl, Erwin A., *The Boer War and Military Reforms*, New York, University Press of America, 1988

Strachan, Hew, *From Waterloo to Balaclava: Tactics, Technology and the British Army, 1815–1854*, Cambridge, Cambridge University Press, 1985

Templeton, Col J.M., *The Consolidation of the British Empire: The Growth of Citizen Soldiership and the Establishment of the Australian Commonwealth*, Melbourne, Sands McDougall, 1901

Tulloch, Maj-Gen Sir Alexander Bruce, *Recollections of Forty Years' Service*, London, William Blackwood & Sons, 1903

Twining, Andrew & Sandra, *South Australian Military Volunteers for 1855*, Kogarah, NSW, the authors, 1992

Tylden, Maj G., *The Armed Forces of South Africa*, Johannesburg, City of Johannesburg Africana Museum, 1954

Vane, Amoury, *North Australia Observer Unit: The History of a Surveillance Regiment*, Loftus, NSW, Australian Military History Publications, 2000

Vazenry, G.R., *Military Forces of Victoria 1854–1967*, Melbourne, Central Army Records Office, 1970

Vernon, P.V. (ed.), *The Royal New South Wales Lancers 1885–1985: Incorporating a Narrative of the 1st Light Horse Regiment AIF 1914–1919*, Parramatta, Royal New South Wales Lancers Centenary Committee, 1986

Vincent, Phoebe, *My Darling Mick: The Life of Granville Ryrie 1865–1937*, Canberra, National Library of Australia, 1997

von Bernhardi, Lt-Gen Frederick, *Cavalry in Future Wars*, trans. Charles Sydney, Goldsmith, London, John Murray, 1906

—— *Cavalry in War and Peace*, trans. Maj G.T.M. Bridges, London, Hugh Rees, 1910

Wallace, R.L., *The Australians at the Boer War*, Canberra, Australian War Memorial & AGPS, 1976

Wavell, Archibald, *The Palestine Campaigns*, London, Constable, 1928

Weick, George F., *The Volunteer Movement in Western Australia 1861–1903*, Perth, Patterson Brokensha, 1966

Wilcox, Craig, *For Hearths and Homes: Citizen Soldiering in Australia 1854–1945*, Sydney, Allen & Unwin, 1998

—— 'Defending Australia 1914–1918: The Other Australian Army', P. Dennis & J. Grey (eds), *The Boer War: Army, Nation and Empire: The 1999 Chief of Army/Australian War Memorial Military History Conference*, Canberra, Army History Unit, 2000

——— *Australia's Boer War: The War in South Africa 1899–1903*, Melbourne, Oxford University Press with Australian War Memorial, 2002

Wilkinson, Frank, *Australian Cavalry: The NSW Lancer Regiment and the First Australian Horse*, Sydney, Angus & Robertson, 1901

——— 'Australian army reorganisation', in C. Kinloch Cooke (ed.), *The Empire Review*, vol. 4, London, Macmillan & Co., 1903

Wilson, Brig-Gen L.C., *Narrative of Operations of Third Light Horse Brigade, AIF, from 27 October to 4 March 1919*, Cairo, Oriental Advertising Company, 1919

Wingfield, Maj. W.J.R., *Lectures to Cavalry Subalterns of the New Armies*, London, Forster Groom & Co., 1915

Wood, Gen. Sir Evelyn, *Achievements of Cavalry with a Chapter on Mounted Infantry*, London, George Bell & Sons, 1897

Woodward, David R., *Hell in the Holy Land: World War I in the Middle East*, Lexington, University Press of Kentucky, 2006.

Wyatt, Maj D.M., *With the Volunteers: A Historical Diary of the Volunteer Military Forces of the North-West and West Coasts of Tasmania, 1886–1986*, Tasmania, the author, 1987

——— *A Lion in the Colony: An Historical Outline of the Tasmanian Colonial Volunteer Military Forces 1859–1901*, Hobart, 6th Military District Museum, 1990

——— *Tasmanian Light Horse 1844–1943*, self-published, 2007

Young, P.J., *Boot and Saddle*, Cape Town, Masken Millar, 1955

INTERNET RESOURCES

Thomas, Robert, 'The history of the emu plume and the Australian Light Horse', www.anzacday.org.au/educational/tff/slouch.html

Index

1st Australian Horse, 34, 65, 75, 78, 85, 102, 122, 125, 135, 136, 180, 262
  in Boer War, 40, 44, 49, 54
2nd AIF units
  1st Independent Light Horse Squadron, 252
  1st Independent Light Horse Troop, 252
  6th Division Cavalry Regiment. 252
  North Australia Observer Unit, 252

A&NZ Mounted Division, 154, 157, 158, 160, 162, 163, 164, 165, 173, 178, 185, 191, 193, 195, 197, 200, 260
  formation of, 150
  and swords, 192
  views on mounted attack, 182, 184
Aborigines and frontier warfare, 14
African horse sickness, 51
AIF 140, 232
AIF units
  See also light horse (AIF)
  XXI Corps Mounted Regiment, 143, 150–2
  Australian Corps, 151
  Australian Flying Corps, 194
  1st Division, 141, 150
  Australian Mounted Division, *See* Australian Mounted Division
  Australian and New Zealand Mounted Division, *See* A&NZ Mounted Division
  Imperial Mounted Division, *See* Imperial Mounted Division

1st Light Horse Brigade, 141, 143, 145, 148, 150, 155, 156, 173, 182, 185, 187, 191, 201, 208
2nd Light Horse Brigade, 143, 145, 146, 150, 156, 187, 195
3rd Light Horse Brigade, 143, 145, 146, 150, 155, 163, 173, 178, 182, 195, 198
4th Light Horse Brigade, 145, 150, 163, 173, 179, 182, 187, 188
5th Light Horse Brigade, 198
1st Light Horse Regiment, 146, 182, 207
2nd Light Horse Regiment, 179, 208
4th Light Horse Regiment, 152, 163, 173, 177, 201, 241
5th Light Horse Regiment, 145, 146, 178, 182, 208, 211, 215
6th Light Horse Regiment, 155, 211
7th Light Horse Regiment, 190, 200, 207
8th Light Horse Regiment, 146
9th Light Horse Regiment, 154
10th Light Horse Regiment, 146, 179, 196, 209, 249
11th Light Horse Regiment, 150, 152, 163, 173, 181, 194, 210
12th Light Horse Regiment, 150, 152, 163, 173, 180, 181, 194, 216, 223
13th Light Horse Regiment, 150–1, 211
14th Light Horse Regiment, 189
15th Light Horse Regiment, 189, 198
Bourchier's Force, 210

350

INDEX

Composite Australian Light Horse Regiment, 148
light horse training regiments, 149
New Zealand and Australian Division, *See* New Zealand and Australian Division
remount units, 144
territorial origins of, 141
aircraft, 171
Aleppo, 197
Allenby, Field Marshal Edmund, 1st Viscount Allenby, 165, 171, 183, 186, 195
 Egyptian uprising, 201
 plan for Megiddo, 193
 Surafend, 200
American Civil War, 5, 23, 27, 31, 37, 96
Amman operation, 185, 223
Anderson, Brig-Gen Robert, 164
Anglo-Boer War, *See* Boer War
Anglo-Japanese Alliance, 92
Antill, Maj-Gen John, 50, 54, 59, 146, 156
ANZAC, *See* Australian and New Zealand Army Corps
Anzac Cove, 145, 146
Anzac Mounted Division, *See* A&NZ Mounted Division
Arabs, 201
 Arab revolt, 185, 186, 195, 196
 Bedouin 200
  See also light horsemen (AIF) views of Arabs
 Egyptian uprising, *See* Egyptian uprising
 views of by light horsemen, *See* light horseman (AIF), views of Arabs
arme blanche, 7, 10, 47, 65, 69, 70, 98, 190, 202, 233, 250, 257
 definition of, 6
armoured cars, 239–41
Army Council, 11, 87
artillery, 99, 105, 150, 171, 181, 182
 13-pounders 173, 187
 18-pounders, 159, 173
 at First Gaza, 160
 at Second Gaza, 162
 at Megiddo, 194

Australian and New Zealand Army Corps, 145
Australian and New Zealand Mounted Division, *See* A&NZ Mounted Division
Australian Army
 See also: light horse units and formations (militia); AIF units
 1st/15th Royal New South Wales Lancers, 263
 2nd/14th Light Horse Regiment, 262, 263
 3rd/9th Light Horse (South Australian Mounted Rifles), 263
 4th/19th Prince of Wales's Light Horse, 263
 10th Light Horse Regiment, 263
 12th/16th Hunter River Lancers, 263
 Administrative and Instructional Staff, 141, 230
 Army Headquarters, 240
 Australian Instructional Corps, 230
 Australian Military Forces, 227, 247
 Australian Regular Army, 262
 Australian Staff Corps, 230
 Central Training Depot, 230
 Citizen Military Forces, 262
 Commonwealth Military Forces, 65, 91
 Field Force, 61, 73, 81, 86, 97, 99, 113, 258
 Garrison Force, 61, 71, 77
 Permanent Force, 61
 Royal Australian Armoured Corps, 262
Australian Comforts Fund, 218
Australian Commonwealth Horse, 58, 339
Australian Imperial Force, *See* AIF
Australian Mounted Division, 182, 187, 191, 193, 194, 197, 199, 229, 260
 formation of, 165
 reorganisation of, 1918, 188
Australian Regiment, 44

Barada Gorge, 196
barbed wire, 175

Barton, Sir Edmund, 60, 63, 80
bayonets, 84, 93, 97
  Australian Mounted Division's mounted training with, 184
  at Beersheba, 180
  mounted training leading to sword training, 192
  used as lance, 178
Bedouin, See Arabs, Bedouin
Beersheba, 171, 180, 184, 250, 260
  battle of, 172–6, 222, 223
Beersheba charge photo, 278–9
Berrie, Lt George, 211, 215, 223, 225
Bir el Abd, 156, 178
Birdwood, Field Marshal William, 1st Baron Birdwood, 153, 164
Black, Donald, See Gray, John
Black Week, 41, 44, 46, 48
Bloemfontein, 42, 44, 46, 47
Boer War, first, 22, 27, 31, 37, 46
Boer War, second, 9, 21, 36, 132, 232
  Australian Commonwealth Horse, See Australian Commonwealth Horse
  Australian contingents to, 42
  British request for troops, 40
  Bushmen contingents, 41
  draft contingents, 42
  Imperial Bushmen contingents, 42
  influence of, 96, 126
  logistic failures, 48, 49
  value of Australians in, 55
  veterans of in post-Federation forces, 81, 82
Boers, 55, 108
  characteristics of and commando system, 44–5
  example of, 22, 31, 132, 137, 138
  shooting standards, 45
Bourchier, Brig-Gen Sir Murray, 175, 209, 210, 241
Brassey, Lord, 32, 63, 135
  imperial service proposal, 32–3
Bridges, Maj-Gen William, 141
British Army, 22, 97, 132, 138, 240, 244
  XX Corps, 172, 176, 177, 185
  XXI Corps, 171, 172, 193, 194
  4th Cavalry Division, 188, 193, 194, 197
  5th Cavalry Division, 188, 193, 194, 196, 197
  52nd Division, 156, 181
  53rd Division, 160, 163
  60th Division, 181, 185, 187
  5th Mounted Brigade, 163, 165, 181, 187
  6th Mounted Brigade, 163
  7th Mounted Brigade, 165
  22nd Mounted Brigade, 163
  British Expeditionary Force, See British Expeditionary Force
  Cape Mounted Rifles, 7, 18, 23, 138
  Cavalry Division (Boer War), 44, 46
  cavalry in Second World War, 251
  Desert Column, See Desert Column
  Desert Mounted Corps, See Desert Mounted Corps
  Eastern Force, 158, 160, 165
  Egyptian Expeditionary Force, See Egyptian Expeditionary Force
  horse artillery batteries attached to light horse, 150
  Imperial Yeomanry, 56
  Mounted Infantry Brigade (Boer War), 44, 60
  Western Frontier Force, 148
British Expeditionary Force, 9, 168, 186, 251
Bruce, William, government of, 229
Bruche, Maj-Gen Julius, 240
Burns, Col James, 34, 78, 79, 91, 120
bushman-soldier legend, See horse soldier mythology

Camden, 34, 117
Cameron, Lt-Col Donald, 180
Casino, 125
cavalry, 184
  in Australia, 30, 31, 33, 35, 79
  in Boer War, 47
  conversion of light horse to, 190–2, 228
  debates about, 78
  popular view of, 4, 9
  reform of, 5–12, 46, 48
  in Second World War, 251–4
  tactics, See tactics

cavalry charges 98, 153–4, 158–60, 167, 177–9
  See also tactics
  Beersheba, 173–6
  Bir el Abd, 178
  in Boer War, 48
  during advance to Damascus, 198
  El Mughar, 181
  form of in 1918, 184
  Huj, 181
  Katia, 178
  Kaukab, 196
  Magdhaba, 179
  rediscovered utility of 1917–18, 178–9
  Semakh, 195
  Tel el Sheria, 181
  thinking about in EEF in 1917, 177–8
  use of pistol in, 69
Cavalry Journal, 85
Cavalry School of Instruction at Zeitoun, 183
cavalry schools of instruction, *See* schools of instruction
cavalry spirit, 10
Cavalry Wing, *See* Australian Army, Central Training Depot
Chasseurs d'Afrique, 190
Chauvel, Lt-Gen Sir Harry, 4, 19, 44, 56, 96, 121, 123, 146, 148, 167, 193, 207, 209, 228, 232, 233
  agrees to request for sword, 191
  and Es Salt raid, 186
  at Beersheba, 173
  at Magdhaba and Rafah, 158
  at Megiddo, 194
  at Romani, 156
  attempts at mechanisation, 239
  command of 1st Light Horse Brigade, 143
  command of A&NZ Mounted Division, 149
  command of Desert Column, 165
  involvement in sending AIF to Egypt, 143
Chaytor, Maj-Gen Sir Edward, 155, 163, 185, 187, 193
  command of A&NZ Mounted Division, 164

Chaytor's Force, 193, 195
Chetwode, Field Marshal Philip, 1st Baron Chetwode, viii, 158, 160, 164, 165, 167, 173, 176, 177, 186
  and Gaza, 1917, 171
Chief of the General Staff, 232, 240
Childers, Erskine, 10
citizen mounted troops
  attractiveness of over infantry, 118
  and industrial disputes, 130–2, 215
citizen mounted troops (social), 118
  costs of being a member of, 119–20
  difficulties of service, 126–7
  failures of early units, 16–19
  industrial unrest, 125
  leisure in units, 128
  offers for service and acceptance, 117
  officers, 120–3
  popular view of, 17, 125–6
  retention and personnel discharges, 129
  social interaction, 123–5
citizen soldiers, 96, 107
Colonial Defence Committee, 24, 32, 36, 63
colonial defence thinking, 19, 22
colonial mounted units, 116
colonial mounted units, New South Wales
  1st Australian Horse, *See* 1st Australian Horse
  Border Scouts, 66
  Corps of Permanent Mounted Infantry, 21
  Governor's Body Guard, 13
  Mounted Brigade, 27
  Mounted Infantry Regiment, *See* New South Wales Mounted Rifles
  Mounted Regiment, 27
  New South Wales Cavalry, 27
  New South Wales Cavalry Brigade Reserves, 21, 117
  New South Wales Mounted Brigade, 138
  Permanent Cavalry, 66
  Sydney Light Horse Volunteers, 20, 117, 120
  Ulmarra Light Horse, 118, 121

colonial mounted units (*cont.*)
   Upper Clarence Light Horse, 118, 121
   West Camden Light Horse, 122
colonial mounted units, Queensland
   Queensland Light Horse, 16, 70
   Queensland Mounted Infantry, *See* Queensland Mounted Infantry
   Queensland Mounted Rifles, 16
colonial mounted units, South Australia
   Adelaide Mounted Rifles, 14, 19, 122, 129
   Duke of Edinburgh's Light Dragoons, 16
   Reedbeds Cavalry, 16
   Regiment of South Australian Volunteer Cavalry, 16
   South Australian Mounted Rifles, *See* South Australian Mounted Rifles
   South Australian Volunteer Cavalry, 14
   South Australian Volunteer Mounted Rifles, 19
colonial mounted units, Tasmania
   First Light Cavalry Corps, 15
   Tasmanian Mounted Infantry, *See* Tasmanian Mounted Infantry
   Tasmanian Volunteer Light Horse, 15
colonial mounted units, Victoria
   Melbourne Cavalry, *See* Melbourne Cavalry
   Prince of Wales's Light Horse Hussars, 70
   Royal Victorian Cavalry Regiment, 15
   Sandhurst Troop, 17
   Victorian Cavalry, 19
   Victorian Mounted Rifles, *See* Victorian Mounted Rifles
   Victorian Yeomanry Corps, 15
   Yeomanry Cavalry Corps, 15
colonial mounted units, Western Australia
   Pinjarrah Mounted Volunteers, 16, 18, 138
   Union Troop of Western Australian Mounted Volunteers, 16, 18
   Western Australian Mounted Infantry, *See* Western Australian Mounted Infantry
Cooma, 75, 116
Cootamundra, 125
Cox, Maj-Gen Charles, 39, 91, 155, 192, 208, 304
Crimean War. *See* war scares

Damascus, 193, 195, 197, 198, 210, 220
   first troops into, 196
Deakin, Alfred, government of, 92
Defence Act, 63, 132, 140
Delpratt, Lt Bert, 208, 211, 213, 214, 215, 219, 221
Dengate, Tpr Edward, 211, 212, 216, 218, 225
Denison, George, 6, 23, 27, 30, 86, 256
Department of Defence, 33, 106, 109
Deraa, 186, 195
Desert Column, 159, 160, 163, 165
   formation of, 158
Desert Mounted Corps, 44, 171, 180, 182, 187, 188, 191, 260
   at Beersheba, 173
   formation of, 166
   post-Beersheba operations, 177
   role for at Megiddo, 193
   views on mounted attack, 183
divisional structure, for militia, *See* light horse (militia) – divisional structure
Dobell, Lt-Gen Sir Charles, 160
Drake, James, 75
drinking, 128, 218, 219
Duntroon, 96, 179, 209, 249

Edwards, Maj-Gen Sir J. Bevan, 23, 63, 92, 99
Egyptian Expeditionary Force, 156, 160, 162, 170, 171, 186, 188, 192, 196, 210, 216, 217, 260
Egyptian uprising, 202, 222
El Arish, 154, 158, 162
El Mughar, *See* cavalry charges
Elands River, battle of, 44, 46
Elgin Commission, 47, 55, 57
emu plumes, 215, 231, 262
Es Salt raid, 185, 186–8, 191, 225

Finn, Maj-Gen Henry, 64, 75, 78
Fisher, Andrew
  government of, 98
Forrest, Sir John, 68, 80
fortresses, 22, 31
Franco-Prussian War, 5, 6, 23
fraud, 113
French, Field Marshal John, 1st Earl of Ypres, 9, 10, 43, 46, 54
French, Maj-Gen George, 31–2, 33, 125, 138
frontier warfare, *See* Aborigines and frontier warfare

G in Gap, 193–4
Gallipoli, 178
  See also light horse (AIF) – at Gallipoli, 107, 144, 145
Gammage, Bill, 205
gas, 162
Gaza, 171
Gaza, first battle of, 161–2
Gaza, second battle of, 162, 167
German spring offensive, 151, 185
Germans, 6, 92, 148, 151, 171, 176, 185, 186, 191, 194, 196, 211, 222, 223, 259
Glen Innes, 119
Godley, Gen Sir Alexander, 145, 151, 177
Grant, Brig-Gen William, 173, 182, 187, 208
Gray, John, 214, 219
Great Depression, 235, 244
guidons, 231
Gullett, Sir Henry, 3, 199, 204, 207, 211

Haig, Field Marshal Douglas, 1st Earl Haig, 9, 10, 54, 186
Hamilton, Gen Sir Ian, 57, 108, 247
  report on Australian forces, 107
Hatten's Ringers, 135
helmets, steel, 187, 225
Hill, Alec, 164
Hoad, Maj-Gen Sir John, 44, 92, 93, 96, 98
Hodgson, Maj-Gen Sir Henry, 163, 197, 260
  advocacy of sword, 184, 190
  at Es Salt, 187
  mounted attack orders before Beersheba, 180
  observations on light horseman, 219
home training, 88, 95, 103, 105, 112, 230
Hopkins, Maj-Gen R.N.L, 209
horse allowance, 101, 105, 123, 127, 245
horse soldier mythology, 1–4, 55–8, 107, 132–8
horsemastership 52, 53, 143
horses, 82, 117, 127, 155
  Australian in Boer War, 48–55
  breeding standards in Australia, 238
  compensation for loss of, 127
  costs of owning, 75
  disposal of, 200
  in First World War, 144
  light horseman's view of, 216
  number of Australia during First World War, 238
  quality of, 236–9
  remounts in Second World War, 251
Hotchkiss guns, 168, 184, 192, 207, 216, 225, 228, 230, 234
  issue of, 167
Hughes, Col Frederick, 146, 147
Hughes, William, Nationalist government of, 229
Huj, *See* cavalry charges – Huj
Hutton, Maj-Gen Sir Edward, 6, 33, 74, 78, 80, 85, 87, 90, 92, 94, 95, 97, 99, 105, 107, 113, 127, 133, 137, 138, 140, 153, 229, 231, 237, 256
  in Boer War, 44, 47
  appointment as GOC Commonwealth Military Forces, 60
  early career of, 26
  efforts to keep costs of service down, 122
  imperial service plan, 63
  and Melbourne Cavalry, 65, 77
  Minute Upon the Defence of Australia, 60
  and problems with Victorian Mounted Rifles, 79

Hutton, Maj-Gen Sir Edward (*cont.*)
  reforms of NSW forces, 26–31
  views on cavalry, 68
  views on lancers after Federation, 69

Idriess, Tpr Ion, 212, 214, 221, 223, 225, 274
Illawarra, 118
Imperial Camel Brigade, See Imperial Camel Corps
Imperial Camel Corps, 152–3, 158, 165, 166, 258
  break-up of 1918, 190
  conversion of Australians to light horse, 188
Imperial Mounted Division, 162, 163, 165
Indian cavalry, 188, 191, 216
Inspector-General, xiii, 18, 53, 92, 103, 112, 232, 247, 296, 299

Jackson, Tpr Pelham, 210, 212, 214, 219, 225
Jaffa, 177, 185, 192, 193, 219
Jamieson Raid, 133
Japan, 92, 108, 115
Jericho, 185
Jerusalem, 144, 171, 177, 185, 219
Jews, 221
Jifjaffa, 154
Jones, Ian, 4, 278–9
Jordan River, 185, 186, 192
Jordan Valley, 185, 188, 189, 191, 193, 197, 225

Katia, 156, 178, 179
Kaukab, 196, 198
Kia Ora Coo-ee, 199, 204, 218
King Edward's Horse, 142
Kirkpatrick, Maj-Gen George, 103, 104
Kitchener, Field Marshal Horatio, 1st Earl Kitchener, 43, 106
  Australian inspection and report. 99
Kyneton, 130

Laffin, John, 205
Laing's Nek, battle of, 22
lance, 78, 98, 191, 229
  abolition of, 9, 69
  Australian experimentation with 1916, 178
Lassetter, Col Henry, 21, 138
Lawrence, T.E., 196
Lee, Col George, 54, 97, 107
  and Victorian Mounted Rifles, 79
Lewis guns, 161, 166
light cars, 251–2
  inter-war adoption of, 241–2
light horse
  conversion from colonial units, 73–80
  convert to cavalry, See cavalry
  creation of, 68–71
  depictions of, 1–3, 4, 107
    See also horse soldier mythology
  disbandment of, 252–4
  equipment of, 85, 92, 103
  established as mounted rifles, 68–70, 97
  historiography of, 4
  last regiment, 254
  limitations of in battle, 160, 173
  naming of, 70
  not mounted infantry, 73
  perpetuation of titles and traditions after 1945, 262–3
  place in defence forces, 99
  and Second World War, 251–2
light horse (AIF)
  See also AIF units
  at Gallipoli, 145–7
  on Western Front, 152, 222
  organisation of, 144, 150, 162, 165, 188
  strengths and establishments, 141, 148
  training of, 142, 149, 167, 168, 171, 178, 207
light horse (militia)
  converted to 2nd AIF, 252
  divisional structure planning 1912–18, 110
  and First World War, 109, 113
  equipment of, 251
  expansion of 1914–17, 109
  mechanisation of, See mechanisation; armoured cars; light cars; machine-gun regiments
  organisation of, 99, 103, 106, 110, 229, 233, 239, 244

post-war planning for, 227–8
reductions in 1929–30, 235–6
reductions in early 1920s, 229–30
renumbering, 102, 110, 231
strengths and establishments, 88, 106, 110, 114, 228, 229, 235, 244, 250
training of, 72, 81, 93–4, 95, 105, 112–13, 126, 128, 230, 233, 244, 246, 247
light horse legend, *See* horse soldier mythology
light horse reenactment groups, 3
light horse schools of instruction, *See* schools of instruction
light horse tactics, *See* tactics
light horse units and formations (AIF), *See* AIF units
light horse units and formations (militia)
   1st Cavalry Division, 229
   2nd Cavalry Division, 229, 240, 241
   1st Cavalry Brigade, 241
   6th Cavalry Brigade, 236
   1st Light Horse Brigade, 93, 94, 95, 102
   2nd Light Horse Brigade, 83, 93, 109
   3rd Light Horse Brigade, 102
   8th Light Horse Brigade, 103
   1st Armoured Car Regiment, 240
   2nd Armoured Car Regiment, 241
   1st Light Horse (MG) Regiment, 246
   1st Light Horse Regiment, 82, 85, 102, 110, 232
   1st/21st Light Horse Regiment, 243
   2nd Light Horse Regiment, 82, 94, 102, 123, 128, 235, 236
   2nd/14th Light Horse Regiment, 241, 252
   3rd Light Horse Regiment, 82, 85, 94, 102, 123, 235, 236, 244
   5th Light Horse Regiment, 88
   6th Light Horse Regiment, 118, 129, 232
   7th Light Horse Regiment, 102, 103
   9th Light Horse Regiment, 102, 236
   11th Light Horse Regiment, 90, 102, 128
   12th Light Horse Regiment, 88, 125, 128, 241
   13th Light Horse Regiment, 129
   16th Light Horse Regiment, 90
   17th Light Horse Regiment, 90, 235
   18th Light Horse Regiment, 94, 235, 236
   19th Light Horse Regiment, 103, 235, 240
   22nd Light Horse Regiment, 103, 251
   23rd Light Horse Regiment, 103, 236
   26th Light Horse Regiment, 112, 129
light horseman (AIF), the, and his experience
   bonds within the organisation, 215–16
   casualties among, 222–5
   commissioning of, 209
   compared to Western Front, 205, 223
   creation of by training, 207
   depictions of, 204–5
   experience of fighting, 223–6
   four-man section, sketch of, 214
   and horses, 216
   labours of, 211, 216
   leave, 218
   mythologising of, *See* horse soldier mythology
   origins of, 208
   physical environment of, 217
   and pre-war militia service, 208–9
   relations between ranks, 210–13
   relationships within the ranks, 213–15
   relaxation, 217–20
   views of Arabs, 200, 220–2
Lismore, 116, 118, 125
Liverpool, 117, 130
Lloyd George, David, 171
Lynden-Bell, Maj-Gen Sir Arthur, 164, 219
Lyster, Col John, 55

Macarthur-Onslow, Brig Gen George, 190
Macdonald, Col Malcolm, 21, 27, 138
machine-gun regiments, conversion of light horse to, 242–4
machine-gun squadrons, creation of, 166
machine-guns, 166, 173, 179, 182, 191, 195, 198, 201, 233, 244, 247
See also Hotchkiss guns; Vickers guns; Maxim guns
Mackay, Col James, 65, 102, 122, 123, 237
imperial service proposal, 34
The Yellow Wave, 135
Magdhaba, battle of, 158, 173, 179, 249
Majuba Hill, battle of, 22, 37, 132
malaria, 197
manuals
Bushman's Military Guide, 135, 137, 205
Cavalry Drill, 136
Cavalry Training, 11, 91, 92, 98, 242
Field Service Regulations, 100, 183
Light Horse Manual 1907, 91, 97
Light Horse Manual 1910, 98, 99
Manual of Drill and Field Service for Mounted Rifles, 25
Manual of Drill for the Mounted Troops of Australia, 30
Mounted Service Manual for Australian Light Horse and Mounted Infantry, 73
Mounted Service Manual for Mounted Troops of the Australian Commonwealth, 72, 88, 90
Regulations and Field Service Manual for Mounted Infantry, 25
Yeomanry and Mounted Rifle Training, 99, 183, 191, 229, 233
Maxim guns, 10, 81, 92, 141, 142, 166
Maxwell, Gen Sir Archibald, 145
McCay, James, 93
mechanisation, 239–44, 249
during Second World War, 252
Megiddo, battle of, 195
Melbourne Cavalry, 65, 67, 76
Meldrum, Brig-Gen William, 192

Military Board, 88, 89, 102, 105, 109, 110, 112, 227, 233, 235, 239, 241, 242
debate about light horse during 1940, 247–50
and horses, 238
military districts, 101, 229
Moe, 123
Monash, John, 2
Monash Valley, 146
mounted attacks, *See* cavalry charges
mounted infantry, 73, 117
in Boer War, 47
definition of, 8, 28
discussions about in 1940, 249
Imperial Camel Corps, 153
and light horse not, 70, 159
Queensland conception of, 25
in Queensland Shearers' Strike, 131
Mounted Infantry Schools, 11, 26
Mounted Police, 14, 36
mounted rifles, 100, 132, 192, 193
confusion with mounted infantry, 8
definition of, 7, 28
evolution in Boer War, 47
and light horse, 68–9, 97
small distinction with cavalry 1917, 184
mounted troops in early colonial Australia, 13–14
Murray, Gen Sir Archibald, 156, 162, 163, 164, 165, 170, 171, 273
mutiny, 212

Neild, Senator J.C, 74, 91
Nek, the, 146
New Guinea campaign
light horse in, 252
New South Wales
and Boer War, 40
defence spending, 67
forces in, 18, 19, 20, 26, 34, 65, 77, 83, 90, 116, 117, 121, 125, 130, 135
light horse in, 88, 94, 101, 108, 229, 235, 251
See also colonial mounted units; New South Wales
New South Wales Lancers, 13, 28, 33, 65, 92, 103, 120, 126, 262

in Boer War, 43, 44, 49, 54
imperial service proposal, 34
and the lance, 69, 77, 78
objections to becoming light horse, 77
offer of service in South Africa, 39
training contingent in England, 38
New South Wales Mounted Rifles, 27, 126, 128, 262
in Boer War, 40, 45, 47, 49, 50
problems after Boer War, 65
New Zealand and Australian Division, 145
New Zealand Division, 146
New Zealand Mounted Rifles, 144, 150, 259
at Amman September 1918, 195
at Beersheba (Tel el Saba), 173
at Gallipoli, 145
at Rafah, 158
at Romani, 155
views on sword, 192
New Zealand Mounted Rifles Brigade, See New Zealand Mounted Rifles
Nimmo, Lt-Gen Robert, 209
non-commissioned officers, 232

officers
ex-AIF in militia, 232–3
in AIF, 142, 144, 147, 168, 208–10
in Boer War, 56
in citizen mounted units, 120–3
militia, 72, 82, 95–7, 104, 105, 111, 112
permanent, 96
preference for war experience of in inter-war years, 232
Orange Free State, 42, 44
O'Sullivan, Edward, 31, 37, 126, 132, 138, 205
Ottoman army, 225
defeat at Amman, 195
destruction of at Megiddo, 195
at Es Salt, 187
on eve of Megiddo, 192–3
final offensive in Palestine, 191
at First Gaza, 160
at Magdhaba and Rafa, 158
at Romani, 156
at Second Gaza, 162
in Sinai, 154

in southern Palestine, 171
surrender of, 197
withdrawal in Palestine and Syria, 195

Parramatta, 117, 121, 126
pay, 16, 66, 75, 101, 105, 113, 123, 127, 245
Pearce, Sen George, 215
Peterloo, 131
pistols, 69, 84
Price, Col Tom, 20, 23, 30, 79, 126, 138
in maritime strike, 131

Queen's Diamond Jubilee, 32, 34
Queensland
and Boer War, 39
forces in, 16, 17, 19, 21, 25, 64, 83, 90, 117, 130
horses in after Russo-Japanese War, 237
light horse in, 94, 101, 228, 229, 235, 263
See also: colonial mounted units, Queensland
Queensland Imperial Bushmen, 54, 58
Queensland Mounted Infantry, 21, 25, 64, 130, 136, 262
and Boer War, 41, 43
Quinn's Post, 146

Rafah, battle of, 158, 173
recruiting, 89, 94, 101, 105, 109, 111, 116, 118, 129, 231, 251
for AIF, 141, 207, 223
for Imperial Camel Corps, 152
Red Hill, 225
reenactment groups, See light horse reenactment groups
Reid, George, 34, 36
remount trade, 49, 237
renumbering, See light horse (militia) – renumbering
Rhodesian Field Force, 44
Ricardo, Col Percy, 25, 41, 46, 54
riding test, 168
Roberts, Field Marshal Frederick, 1st Earl Roberts, 9, 42, 55, 69, 91
Robertson, Lt-Gen Sir Horace, 179, 209, 249

Romani, battle of, 157, 225, 260
Royal Air Force, 194
Royal Military College, Duntroon, *See* Duntroon
Royal New South Wales Lancers, 243
Russo-Japanese War, 92, 237
Ryrie, Maj-Gen Sir Granville, 51, 56, 57, 75, 146, 148, 155, 164, 192, 208, 209, 213, 231

saddles, 82, 84, 93, 120, 127
Salonika, 163, 171, 197
schools of instruction, 72, 95, 104, 232
Scullin, James, government of, 235
Second World War
   and light horse, 250
Semakh, 194, 198
Senussi, 148, 153, 164
sexually transmitted disease, *See* venereal disease
Shearers' Strike. *See* colonial mounted troops – and industrial disputes, 130
Shunet Nimrin, 186
Singapore Strategy, 229
Smith, Maj-Gen Sir Charles, 31, 133, 138
society (and the light horse), *See* citizen mounted troops (social); horse soldier mythology; light horseman (AIF)
South African Republic, 42
South Australia
   forces in, 18, 19, 21, 24, 64, 83, 90, 119, 122
   light horse in, 88, 90, 103, 229, 235, 236
   See also colonial mounted units, South Australia
South Australian Mounted Rifles, 21, 33, 64, 103, 124, 126
Spahis, 190
sport, 125, 217
Squires, Lt-Gen Ernest, 247
staff rides, 72, 96
Sturdee, Lt-Gen Sir Vernon, 249, 252
Suez Canal, 150, 154, 157
Sullivan, Tpr Henry, 211
Sunnyside, battle of, 44
Surafend, 200, 221

Swinburne, George, committee chaired by, 227
swords, 35, 97, 98, 136, 195, 260
   1908 cavalry sword, 191
   and Australian Mounted Division, 190–2
   during Second World War, 249, 250
   and militia light horse regiments, 228
   training difficulties for militia in 1920s, 233
   view in favour of after Megiddo, 197–9
   views on after Beersheba, 182
   yeomanry equipped with in 1914, 183
Syrian Campaign, 1940, light horse in, 251, 252

tactical exercises without troops, 233
tactics, 182–3, 184–5, 197–8
   See also cavalry charges
tanks, 162
Tasmania
   defence spending, 67
   difficulties recruiting in, 89
   forces in, 19, 21, 64, 83
   light horse in, 88, 129, 228, 229, 231, 251
   See also colonial mounted units, Tasmania
Tasmanian Mounted Infantry, 64, 118
Tel el Saba, *See* Beersheba – battle of
Tel el Sheria, battle of, 181
TEWT, *See* tactical exercises without troops
trans-Jordan operation, first, *See* Amman operation
trans-Jordan operation, second, *See* Es Salt raid
Transvaal, *See* South African Republic
trooper, rank of, 142, 231

uniforms, 3, 14, 16, 18, 20, 21, 27, 64, 76, 77, 78, 81, 83, 85, 112, 120, 122, 123, 127, 138, 226, 231, 243
universal training, 105, 108, 111, 113, 230, 258
   introduction of, 98

and light horse, 101–2, 235–6
reintroduction of in 1940, 250

veld, 45, 49, 136
venereal disease, 220
veterinary officers, 52
Vickers guns, 166, 184, 207, 243
Victoria
   and Boer War, 39
   defence spending, 67
   forces in, 16, 19, 24, 33, 64, 74, 83, 121, 135
   light horse in, 90, 94, 229, 235
   See also colonial mounted units, Victoria
Victorian Mounted Rifles, 19, 20, 23, 33, 64, 67, 123, 125, 127, 129, 262
   and Boer War, 41
   and conversion to light horse, 79
   in maritime strike, 131
Victorian Rangers, conversion to light horse, 74
volunteers, 119
   burdens on, 16–17
   post-Federation scheme for, 61

walers, *See* horses
wallaby fur pugaree, 215
'war babies', 210, 211
War Office, 10, 56, 58, 59, 135, 143, 150, 165, 189, 190, 332
war scares, 14–15, 19, 24, 63
Washington Naval Conference, 229
Western Australia
   forces in, 19, 21, 63
   light horse in, 94, 103, 228, 229, 254
   See also colonial mounted units, Western Australia
Western Australian Mounted Infantry, 64
Western Front, 146, 188, 203, 205, 217, 229, 260
   comparison of Palestine to, 222
Wilson, Brig-Gen Lachlan, 148, 182, 208, 209, 211, 212, 213, 222
Wilson's Lookout, 147

yeomanry, 138, 163, 183, 188, 259
Young Men's Christian Association, 218